Comparing Husserl's Phenomenology and Chinese Yogācāra in a Multicultural World

Also available from Bloomsbury

Cross-Cultural Existentialism, by Leah Kalmanson
Chinese and Buddhist Philosophy in Early Twentieth-Century German Thought,
by Eric S. Nelson
Husserl's Phenomenology of Natural Language, by Horst Ruthrof
Interpreting Chinese Philosophy, by Jana S. Rošker

Comparing Husserl's Phenomenology and Chinese Yogācāra in a Multicultural World

A Journey beyond Orientalism

Jingjing Li

BLOOMSBURY ACADEMIC
LONDON • NEW YORK • OXFORD • NEW DELHI • SYDNEY

BLOOMSBURY ACADEMIC
Bloomsbury Publishing Plc
50 Bedford Square, London, WC1B 3DP, UK
1385 Broadway, New York, NY 10018, USA
29 Earlsfort Terrace, Dublin 2, Ireland

BLOOMSBURY, BLOOMSBURY ACADEMIC and the Diana logo are trademarks of
Bloomsbury Publishing Plc

First published in Great Britain 2022
This paperback edition published 2023

Copyright © Jingjing Li, 2022

Jingjing Li has asserted her right under the Copyright, Designs and Patents Act, 1988, to be identified as Author of this work.

For legal purposes the Acknowledgments on pp. vii-viii constitute an extension of this copyright page.

Cover image: Yukon, Canada © Chinaface / iStock

All rights reserved. No part of this publication may be reproduced or transmitted in any form or by any means, electronic or mechanical, including photocopying, recording, or any information storage or retrieval system, without prior permission in writing from the publishers.

Bloomsbury Publishing Plc does not have any control over, or responsibility for, any third-party websites referred to or in this book. All internet addresses given in this book were correct at the time of going to press. The author and publisher regret any inconvenience caused if addresses have changed or sites have ceased to exist, but can accept no responsibility for any such changes.

A catalogue record for this book is available from the British Library.

Library of Congress Control Number: 2022932380

ISBN:	HB:	978-1-3502-5690-3
	PB:	978-1-3502-5694-1
	ePDF:	978-1-3502-5691-0
	eBook:	978-1-3502-5692-7

Typeset by RefineCatch Limited, Bungay, Suffolk

To find out more about our authors and books visit www.bloomsbury.com and sign up for our newsletters.

Contents

List of Tables	vi
Acknowledgments	vii
Abbreviations	ix
Note on Usage and Convention	x
Prologue	1

Part One The Journey

1	Overcoming Orientalism with Multiculturalism	11
2	Contextualizing Chinese Yogācāra	23
3	Contextualizing Husserl's Phenomenology	35

Part Two The Road

4	Intentionality in Husserl's Phenomenology	51
5	Intentionality in Chinese Yogācāra	67
6	Intentionality and Non-conceptualism	85

Part Three The Tracks

7	Essence in Husserl's Phenomenology	103
8	Essence in Chinese Yogācāra	119
9	Essence in Comparative Philosophy	135

Part Four The Destination

10	The Gate of Practice	155
11	The Path Towards Awakening	169
12	Revisiting the Process of Awakening	183

Epilogue	195
Notes	199
Bibliography	225
Index	251

Tables

1	The contrast between early Yogācāra and later Yogācāra	129
2	The early Buddhist theory of twelve links	156
3	Xuanzang's reformulation of the twelve links	158
4	The Yogācāra view of dependent-evolution	166

Acknowledgments

This book was completed during the Covid-19 pandemic. Like many of you who have opened this book and are reading this paragraph for the time, I too struggled to get accustomed to the "new normal" of living and working in a global pandemic. I used to separate work from the rest of my life. When I wanted to work, I went to my office, whereas my time at home was for my loved ones. Suddenly, the pandemic forced me to change a way of life that had become all but second nature. Nevertheless, the unexpected shift had one small silver lining, as it let me perceive my work from a different angle. Most of the thinkers that you will meet in this book endured lives of hardship, yet these hardships never prevented them from moving forward. Rather, they mustered up the necessary courage and carried on. Eventually, their ideas blossomed like flowers on a rock. It is perseverance, resilience, and optimism like this that make us humans extraordinary, regardless of the fact that we are and continue to be historically conditioned sentient beings. Thus, when I was revising the manuscript for this book, these past minds became a major source of personal inspiration and empowerment. This is why I wish to thank the protagonists of this book—especially Xuanzang, Kuiji, and Edmund Husserl—for their quiet yet powerful support, which makes writing not so much a solitary exercise but rather a solidary experience.

One's sense of solidarity arises when one finds a shared space of meaning. I found mine with the help of many dear friends and colleagues. I began my academic journey under the guidance of my mentors at McGill University: Victor Hori and Garth Green. They are both my teachers and my role models, individuals who had complete confidence in me even when I had none. It was Hori sensei who introduced me to the academic study of Buddhism and reminded me of the importance of making philosophy more socially engaged. I owe him a huge debt of gratitude because I learned from Hori sensei that the philosophy of non-duality is both a theory and a way of life. Garth Green, for his part, encouraged me to develop my competence in the philosophy of religion. Under their supervision, I began to think about how my work could facilitate human flourishing in a multicultural world, which led me to the field—or perhaps, the battlefield—of comparative philosophy.

During my time at McGill, Don Beith, Jason Blakeburn, Chris Byrne, Ruifeng Chen, Daniel Heide, Matthew Nini, Naznin Patel, Amanda Rosini, Ying Ruo Show, Nanying Tao, Kevin Walker, and Qinglong Wang gave me substantial and actionable suggestions on the earlier version of my draft when it was still in the dissertation stage. Afterward, when I began to rewrite the draft from the beginning and rework it into a book manuscript, I was grateful to be able to exchange views and ideas with friends: Susan Andrews, Barbra Clayton, Melissa Curley, Jing Hu, Miriam Levering, Fan Lin, Jessica Main, Erin Reid, Vanessa Sasson, and Jessica Zu. I owe a deep debt of gratitude to Jiang Tao and Arvind Sharma, both of whom offered valuable critiques and constructive comments on this project. I cherished the help I received from Jennifer Guyver, Alexander Nachaj, and Shaun Retallick, who read through the entire manuscript and offered their insightful feedback.

The academic community that surrounds me and which I value also extends beyond McGill. I would like to thank David Wong for inviting me to be a visiting fellow at Duke University's Center for Comparative Philosophy (CCP). I was inspired by the conversations I had with colleagues at CCP, especially Bobby Bingle, Songyao Ren, and Sungwoo Um. I am grateful to Katherine Young for establishing the Katherine Young Travel Award that allowed me to be a research fellow at the University of Victoria's Centre for Studies in Religion and Society (CSRS). My special thanks go to Paul Bramadat and Rachel Brown for welcoming me to the CSRS community. Outside North America, I was able to advance my knowledge of Chinese philosophy and phenomenology with the help of numerous teachers, not the least of whom include Ruiquan Gao and Sophie Loidolt.

My thanks must also go to Leiden University's Institute for Philosophy for providing me with primary sources for bringing this project to fruition. Several colleagues at Leiden have provided me with tremendous help and plenty of critical feedback: Douglas Berger, Frank Chouraqui, Hilde de Weerdt, Johan de Jong, and Stephen Harris. I equally benefited from the questions and comments made by students in my course "Consciousness in Buddhism." I am honored to have received funding at different stages of my research, from several organizations including the *Les Fonds de recherche du Québec – Nature et Technologies* (FRQNT), the Chung-Hwa Institute of Buddhist Studies (CHIBS), and the Van Haersolte Fund.

This project would have not been possible without the generous support of Colleen Coalter, acquisition editor at Bloomsbury Academic for philosophy. I am grateful for the assistance of the editorial and production team at Bloomsbury. I have published a preliminary discussion of the problem of essence in "Buddhist Phenomenology and the Problem of Essence" in *Comparative Philosophy 2016 Vol. 1*. Besides this, I have used the elements from two articles, "From Self-Attaching to Self-Emptying: An Investigation of Xuanzang's Account of Self-Consciousness" in *Open Theology 2017, Vol. 1* and "Through the Mirror: The Account of Other Minds in Chinese Yogācāra Buddhism" in *Dao: A Journal of Comparative Philosophy, 18(3)* (with permission granted by Springer Nature). After collecting new data, I was able to further expound upon the findings in these articles and refine my viewpoints for the current book.

Finally, I would like to thank my family—my parents Ying Shi and De Li, my husband Zhicong Liao, and my cats—who continually motivate me to become a better version of myself. The Chinese Yogācāra master Xuanzang once compared the non-dualist self–other relationship to the way in which the lamps light up the dark. Each lamp does not lose its irreducible identity but shines together with one another brightly and warmly. My family and my friends are the lamps that light up my world and warm up my heart. I hope this book can also bring some of this warmth to you, my readers, in the same vein that I have been inspired by the many protagonists of this project. Let us not lose hope.

Abbreviations

DDJ	*Dao De Jing*
DM	*Discourse on the Method*
Hua	*Husserliana*
KrV	*Critique of Pure Reason*
MZ	*Mengzi*
T	*Taishō Tripiṭaka*
ZJZ	*Laozi Daode Zhenjing Zhu*
ZS	Zen Sand

Note on Usage and Convention

All terms from non-English languages—including Chinese, French, German, Japanese, Latin, and Sanskrit—are italicized. These non-English terms are followed by the words in the original languages, for instance, essence (*Wesen*). Concerning characters from the Chinese language, this book uses the *pinyin* system. These characters are paired with transliterations in *pinyin* along with English translations. If a Chinese character has a corresponding Sanskrit term, then this Sanskrit term with diacritical marks is also provided, such as, concentration (*ding* 定, *samādhi*). There are several cases where the Wade-Giles system is used, for instance, in personal names and in previously published texts. A note on the transliteration of names of persons is also needed. This book follows how scholars normally write their names or how the names normally appear on their publications. If a scholar's name has been transliterated differently, the book uses brackets to include all the translations that have appeared. Buddhist clerics are referred to by their dharma names, for instance, Xuanzang (玄奘 *c.* 602–664). Moreover, this book follows the standard way of citing Buddhist texts and Husserl's work. All the Buddhist texts used in this book come from the *Taishō Tripiṭaka* edited by Takakusu Junjirō, Watanabe Kaigyoku, and Ono Genmyo (1924–32). When citing these texts, this book puts the volume number, sequence number, page number, column number, and line number of these texts, the same way they are originally listed. For instance, the definition of consciousness can be found in line 29 and column 2 on page 1 of the text under sequence number 1585 in volume 31 of the *Taishō Tripiṭaka*. That is why this definition is cited as "T31N1585, P1a29" inside the book. All the writings of Edmund Husserl come from the *Husserliana* and, therefore, are cited in accordance with the volume number in the collection. For example, Husserl discusses the interplay between the active and passive genesis on page 113 of *Cartesian Meditations*, which is the first monograph in the *Husserliana*. That is why this interplay is cited as "Hua 1/113" inside the book.

Prologue

One of the early encounters between phenomenology and Buddhism took place in the 1920s. At that time, Edmund Husserl (1859–1938), the founder of modern phenomenology, acquired a copy of Karl Eugen Neumann's *The Sayings of Gautama Buddha* (*Die Reden Gotamo Buddhos*), a translation of early Buddhist texts from the Pali canon. Fascinated by this intellectual tradition, Husserl elevated Buddhism as one "with the highest forms of the philosophical and religious spirits (*mit den höchsten Gestaltungen des philosophischen und religiösen Geistes*)," paralleling it to its European counterpart (Hua 27/126).[1] For Husserl, Buddhism was a transcendental philosophy that turned inward to pursue the absolute truth with its distinctive "religio-ethical methodology (*religiös-ethische Methodik*)" (Hua 27/125). This impression led Husserl to entertain the possibility that a Buddhist version of transcendental philosophy—not just as a way of seeing the world but also as a way of living an ethical life—could expand the horizon for European philosophers, enable them to overcome existential crises, and eventually facilitate the renewal (*Erneuerung*) of European culture (Hua 27/126).

This encounter marks the beginning of the philosophical exchanges between phenomenology and Buddhism. For Husserl, one enters the field of phenomenology whenever one initiates an investigation of the salient feature of consciousness *qua* intentionality (Hua 3/156). Consciousness is intentional because it is always the consciousness *of* something (Hua 3/181). Therefore, this notion of intentionality is deployed to describe how a mental act is directed towards and targeted at a particular phenomenon. Many contemporary scholars acknowledge that Husserl's phenomenology shows great potential for comparative studies, insofar as it provides an approach to examining theories of the mind as presented in Buddhist philosophical traditions, including a particular school of Buddhism known as Yogācāra.[2]

Commonly referred to as the School of Mind-only or Consciousness-only (*weishi*唯識, *vijñaptimātra*), Yogācāra is one of the major Mahāyāna Buddhist schools, dating back to the early fourth century CE. Within the Yogācāra tradition, this book focuses on its development in the Chinese language context, especially the theories articulated by Xuanzang (玄奘 *c.* 602–64) and his disciples Kuiji (窺基 632–82), Huizhao (慧沼 648–714), and Zhizhou (智周 668–723). Therefore, the term "Chinese Yogācāra" is utilized to paraphrase the notion of *hanchuan weishi* (漢傳唯識) that refers to the Yogācāra doctrine of consciousness-only transmitted in the Chinese language.[3] In their doctrine of consciousness-only, Xuanzang and his disciples characterize consciousness through its intentional feature of causing mental acts to know and discern objective phenomena (T31N1585, P1a29). This characterization of consciousness allows for the possibility of performing a comparative study between Chinese Yogācāra and Husserlian phenomenology. Since Husserl mainly relied on Neumann's translation of early Buddhist texts, he was likely unfamiliar with Mahāyāna philosophy, let alone Chinese Yogācāra. Nevertheless, considering how these Yogācārins investigate the intentional feature of consciousness, contemporary scholars have proposed reading their philosophy as a version of phenomenology in the Buddhist sense, or in short, as Buddhist phenomenology.[4]

Nevertheless, the surface similarity has the capacity to obscure a perceived incompatibility at the core. Such incompatibility revolves around the notion of essence—a notion that defines what a thing really is and supports the theory of intentionality. To be more specific, Husserl acknowledges the existence of essence (*Wesen*) and articulates phenomenology as the science of essence (*Wesenwissenschaft*) (Hua 3/4–10), whilst Xuanzang and his disciples (along with Mahāyāna Buddhists in general) refute the concept of essence altogether in their critique of *svabhāva* (T31N1585, P1a23–24). If phenomenologists and Yogācārins derive incompatible positions regarding the nature of reality from their respective views of essence, is it still possible to claim that Chinese Yogācāra belongs under the same umbrella as Husserl's phenomenology?

As this question remains unanswered by most scholars in the field of comparative philosophy,[5] researchers in Buddhist studies have expressed their concern over the fusion of Buddhist philosophy and various types of essentialism ever since the 1990s.[6] Hence, the purpose of this book is to examine these seemingly incompatible standpoints in order to secure a common ground from which a comparative study of Husserl's phenomenology and Chinese Yogācāra can be undertaken. That is to say, in order to resolve a problem, we need to first recognize the existence of a problem. In the study of philosophy, a problem comes into existence if and only if we accept a specific set of philosophical presuppositions when thinking about a subject matter. As such, a problem can be resolved if those philosophical presuppositions are removed. For our comparative project, it then requires us to shed light on basic concepts such as intentionality, which are used to inform their respective theories of essence. Despite the disagreements surrounding this notion, essence is central to both Husserl's phenomenology and Chinese Yogācāra.

Essence is a crucial and complex notion. It encapsulates Husserl's continuing development of intentionality after departing from Franz Brentano's psychology in the initiation of his transcendental philosophy. The meaning of this notion is rendered even more complicated by the attempts of English translators to conflate several different terms used by Husserl—*Wesen*, *eidos*, *Essenz*—as simply *essence*. In understanding how Husserl's concept of essence undergoes a number of changes and transformations, it is helpful to trace the different phases of his philosophical thinking process. Husserl first defines intentionality as the feature of directedness in his early work. That is to say, each mental act has two inseparable constituents: the quality that directs itself towards and the matter being directed upon (Hua 19/412). The concept of essence (*Wesen*) is formulated by Husserl to describe the ideal union of quality and matter, which is distinct from any actually existent contingent realities (Hua 19/417–18). After his transcendental turn, Husserl reformulates intentionality as the *noesis-noema* correlation. The pure essence *qua eidos* becomes the ideal union of *noesis* and *noema* (Hua 3/184–90). Finally, when Husserl expands his phenomenological investigation from the individual mind to a plurality of minds, he accentuates the genetic nature of mental acts and articulates intentionality as the tripartite structure of the underlying flows of consciousness, the intending acts, and the intended phenomena (Hua 6/187–9). Accordingly, the essence (*Wesen*) for each individual is not a static entity (Hua 1/101), but rather the *a priori* of its being in the world and being with others (Hua 6/255–6). As such, the preliminary presentation of essence serves multiple purposes. It bespeaks the rich meaning of essence in Husserl's writings and reveals the correlation between intentionality and essence. More importantly, it suggests how and why it is a challenge to determine what Husserl exactly means by essence.

The concept of essence is equally significant in Chinese Yogācāra. The English term "essence" has been frequently employed to translate the Sanskrit word *svabhāva*. The literal meaning of *svabhāva* is "coming into being on its own." Considering how *svabhāva* captures the self-determined, *sui generis*, intrinsic nature of sentient and non-sentient beings, it has been commonly translated as "essence" in the English language scholarship of Buddhist studies.

Svabhāva becomes a central notion in Buddhist philosophy largely through the efforts of Mahāyāna clerics. However, differing from Mahāyāna philosophy, most early Buddhist teachings contend that the self of sentient beings does not exist as a *svabhāva*, although non-sentient dharmas do have *svabhāvic* existence (T45N1861, P249a19).[7] Mahāyāna philosophers then expand the narrative of no-self by arguing that everything—be it sentient being or non-sentient dharma—is interdependent with one another and, therefore, does not have *svabhāvic* existence. As followers of the Mahāyāna tradition, Yogācārins put forward their doctrine of consciousness-only to support the refutation of *svabhāva*. In their refutation, they turn to consciousness to describe how the mind of a sentient being serves as the necessary condition for the possibility of these objects to appear as phenomena in this sentient being's experience. As such, if the perceiver *qua* a sentient being has no *svabhāvic* existence, neither does the perceived dharma. The concept of emptiness is therefore formulated to describe how everything in the cosmos is empty of *svabhāva* (T31N1585, P1b9). When Yogācāra begins to flourish in the Chinese language context, Buddhist clerics like Xuanzang and his disciples propose their respective objections to *svabhāva*, further developing their innovative articulations of emptiness through translating and interpreting Sanskrit Buddhist texts.

For various reasons, the concept of essence presents a challenge for a comparative study of Husserl's phenomenology and Chinese Yogācāra. The crux is that Husserl appears to affirm the existence of essence in consciousness, whilst Xuanzang and his disciples refute this concept in their defense of emptiness. Does the Husserlian essence amount to *svabhāva* and entail the sense of "coming into being on its own"? The question at stake is further compounded by the multilingual context. Both Husserl and Chinese Yogācārins have imported terms from other languages (Greek/Sanskrit) to explain their philosophical viewpoints and translated these terms into their native tongues (German/Chinese). These various terms of disparate origins continue to be translated into English as the singular concept of "essence." In order to reach a common ground from which a comparative project can actually begin, this complex term along with its Chinese, Sanskrit, German, Greek homeomorphic equivalents must be scrutinized within the perspectives of their own traditions. From such a wide range of challenges, there arises what I call the "problem of essence" in comparative studies of phenomenology and Yogācāra.[8]

In a multicultural world, resolving the problem of essence serves a deeper purpose, not simply because this resolution secures the foundation of a comparative study of phenomenology and Buddhism, but also because it epitomizes how we can tackle disputes between two traditions across a cultural, historical, and linguistic divide. When one English concept has been evoked to translate a wide range of ideas from non-English languages—a common practice in academic research and everyday life— we often encounter scenarios in which we endorse incompatible understandings of the concept. How then shall we manage these tensions if we wish to participate in and appreciate a coherent multicultural life? As such, we must examine and scrutinize the nuances of the concept in question for the purpose of abating misunderstanding and advancing mutual understanding. The problem of essence, therefore, serves as an exemplar of incompatibility as well as the potential to overcome said incompatibility.

Instead of making overarching claims, I argue that what Husserl means by essence differs from what Xuanzang and his disciples mean by *svabhāva*. While some phenomenologists might have a more absolutist understanding of essence that is irreconcilable with the Buddhist critique of *svabhāva*, the problem of essence is not a problem for the protagonists of this book. In the history of European philosophy, Husserl refashions an understanding of essence that is not tantamount to an absolute in itself and thus does not yield any self-determined, immutable existence. Gradually, Husserl breaks with scientific naturalism and brings his insight to the European philosophical tradition that can be dated back to antiquity. In doing so, he begins laying the foundations of the modern phenomenological movement. Emerging from an entirely different context, Xuanzang and his disciples evoke philosophical binaries to present their critique of *svabhāva*. They continue to demarcate emptiness from nothingness and distance themselves from nihilism, which marks the beginning of a distinct development of Yogācāra philosophy in the Chinese language context. As such, Husserl and these Chinese Yogācārins do not have a real dispute over essence.

Though it is not an obstacle, the problem is hardly irrelevant. Our investigation of the problem of essence calls attention to important implications when considering a comparative study of philosophy in a multicultural and multilingual world. Primarily, we problematize the overgeneralized East–West dichotomy that presents the East and the West as mutually exclusive. It is this overgeneralization that undergirds common stereotypes such as the Western self has an essential core *qua* individuality whereas the Eastern self has no essence at all in a collectivist worldview (Wong 2004). When we are accustomed to overgeneralizing the linguistic, historical, and cultural nuances of philosophical ideas, we internalize this way of thinking as the philosophical presupposition that renders us incapable of recognizing and resolving the problem of essence as articulated in the current book. This problem can be tackled once this overgeneralization is cleared. Positioning ideas in their historical context and linguistic system, we can make an effort to avoid such overgeneralization and misrepresentation, which becomes the first step to overcoming Orientalism.

Upon recognizing and resolving the problem of essence, we do not go back to the starting point to cancel this problem for good. Rather, we deepen our understanding of both Husserl and Chinese Yogācārins, especially how they perceive the nature of reality as interrelated and interconnected. To be more specific, they delineate the way in which the mind of a sentient being serves as the necessary condition for the possibility of phenomena in experience and reaches out to other minds to constitute an intersubjectively accessible and empirically real world. Such a correlation of transcendental ideality and empirical reality further secures the non-duality of binaries, exemplified by the mutual constitution of the subject and the object, the interdependence of self-mind and other minds, and the transformation of ignorance and awakening. Therefore, this form of transcendental idealism can be considered as a version of correlative non-dualism, which encourages our protagonists to outline the fluid translation of knowledge into action. On this front, Xuanzang and his disciples march further than Husserl in putting forward a detailed plan for personal rehabitualization, moral action, and social construction. Thereby, their articulation of Yogācāra philosophy is more than a Buddhist version of Husserlian phenomenology. Nevertheless, Husserl's preliminary accounts of ethics and social ontology continue to inspire later scholars such as Edith Stein (1891–1942), Hannah Arendt (1906–75), Alfred Schutz (1899–1959), and Frantz Fanon (1925–61), whose writings form the next phases of the modern phenomenological movement. As such, the resolution of the problem of essence is, in fact, a rejection of the East–West dichotomy at the heart of Orientalism and a promotion of correlative non-dualism as the way of living a multicultural life. In this process, comparative philosophy furnishes us with access to a plurality of lived realities, continuously shedding light on possible incompatibilities between cultures and securing a middle ground where we can expand the shared horizon as a way of thriving together in a multicultural world. That is why the title of this book is *Comparing Husserl's Phenomenology and Chinese Yogācāra in a Multicultural World: A Journey Beyond Orientalism*.

Here, I would like to borrow the following verse from the Zen capping phrases to illustrate the difference between and the interdependence of the views of Husserl and Chinese Yogācārins: "the road is the same but we travel in different wheel tracks (同途不同轍)" (ZS 210). The four-part "journey–road–track–destination" analogy provides the organizing principle of the book itself. In this analogy, the "journey" represents our approach to comparative study. The "road" symbolizes the descriptive level at which Husserl and Chinese Yogācārins describe the intentional feature of consciousness and depict our knowledge of (no-)self and other minds. The different "tracks" suggest how these two schools of thought, based on their respective theories of intentionality, come to elucidate the nature of reality and exhibit seemingly opposite appraisals of essence. Finally, the "destination" epitomizes the last prescriptive level where they outline the translation of knowledge into action and prescribe rules for the universal awakening of all sentient beings.[9] For Husserl and Chinese Yogācārins, their roads are the same in that they both center their research on consciousness and its intentional feature, yet they leave different tracks in their stances towards essence. Placing Husserl in the history of European philosophy, we come to see that he does not follow in the footsteps of numerous other modern thinkers in making the essence of a person completely interior.[10] While the transcendental turn guides Husserl in shifting his focus from the exterior world to the interior mind, the investigation of other minds and lifeworlds prompts Husserl to open the interior mind to the intersubjective communal life. Husserl continues to sketch philosophical principles for ethics and social ontology, yet he has not completed the mechanics. Turning back to Xuanzang and his disciples who lived in premodern China, we notice how they likewise move from the exterior world to the interior mind in their articulation of consciousness-only and eventually return to the exterior communal life in detailing the pursuit of the Bodhisattvas' path. For these Buddhist philosophers, a return to the exterior *is* the superior goal of becoming a Bodhisattva—the one who realizes initial awakening but dwells back to the realm of *saṃsāra* to help other sentient beings. Therefore, these Yogācārins have detailed the mechanics of ethics and community building as integral parts of the Bodhisattvas' path. This is how Husserl and Chinese Yogācārins eventually arrive at their own respective, but not altogether divergent, destinations.

As such, I would like to invite readers to undertake a journey with me as we travel alongside Husserl and these Chinese Yogācārins, taking the same road but being mindful of their respective tracks and destinations. It is a four-part trip. In Part One, we focus on the meaning of the "journey" to address general methodological questions. Hence, we inquire into how comparative studies of philosophy can promote the exchange of views in a multicultural and multilingual world. Chapter 1 begins by scrutinizing how comparative philosophy was once imbued with different versions of Orientalism and its associated cultural imperialism. Afterward, this chapter puts forward the "both–and" approach to the comparative study of Husserl's phenomenology and Chinese Yogācāra. It is referred to as the "both–and" approach in that it *both* maintains the distinctiveness of each tradition in its own context for exploring their middle ground *and* manifests their interconnectedness on a broader horizon for conversations and collaborations. Employing the "both–and" approach, Chapters 2 and 3 offer a historical overview of the development of Yogācāra and Husserl's phenomenology consecutively. The structure of a treatise composed by Xuanzang on consciousness provides a paradigm for studying Chinese Yogācāra that can also be inferred from and adapted to Husserl's phenomenology. It is from this paradigm that we derive the three-level (descriptive–explicative–prescriptive) framework, which constitutes the middle ground of these two traditions.

In Part Two, we move on to the "road," where we explore the descriptive level of Husserl's phenomenology and Chinese Yogācāra. After elaborating on the meaning of "descriptive," we fix our scope to the salient feature of consciousness, known as intentionality. To unpack the rich concept of intentionality proposed by Husserl, Chapter 4 pinpoints four phases in his philosophical thinking process through which he defines intentionality: first as directedness; next as the *noesis–noema* correlate; subsequently as the *ego–cogito–cogitatum* schema; and finally, as the tripartite structure of the act of intending, the intended phenomena, and the plurality of minds of the *we*. In this process, Husserl gradually divorces himself from psychologism and naturalism to promote transcendental phenomenology, further expanding his scope from the individual mind to the plurality of minds in a community. Husserl's view of intentionality can be related to that in Yogācāra Buddhism. Chapter 5 explores how Xuanzang and his disciples express their view of intentionality first in their translation of *vijñāna* and *vijñapti*, and then in their depiction of the fourfold structure of mental acts. In light of their definition of consciousness, these Chinese Yogācārins continue to outline our knowledge of (no-)self and other minds. While Husserl's notion of intentionality can be related to that in Yogācāra Buddhism, the two are not completely identical. Through analyzing how their viewpoints are compatible and non-identical, we reflect upon the overgeneralized East–West dichotomy at the center of several versions of Orientalism. Our analysis further inspires us to investigate the possible input of these two traditions to the ongoing discussion of epistemic non-conceptualism in Chapter 6.

In Part Three, we examine the "tracks." After delineating the meaning of "explicative," we analyze how Husserl and Chinese Yogācārins clarify the ultimate nature of reality at the explicative level of their systems of thought, based on their theories of intentionality. In their explication of what and how things actually are, Husserl affirms the existence of essence and articulates phenomenology as the science of essence (Hua 3/4–10). In contrast, Xuanzang and his disciples argue that everything in the cosmos is empty of essence (*svabhāva*) (T31N1585, P1a23–4). At least on the surface, Husserl and these Chinese Yogācārins endorse different—even disparate—stances towards essence. This is where their paths diverge, leaving dissimilar wheel tracks. Chapter 7 investigates whether or not Husserl's conception of essence is the same as that of *svabhāva*. As suggested in this chapter, since Husserl continues to enrich and expand the notion of essence in various phases of his philosophical thinking process, his conception of essence is not *svabhāvic*. Chapter 8 examines whether the Yogācāra articulation of three natures is compatible with Husserl's transcendental idealism. As to be argued in this chapter, it is compatible insofar as the negation of *svabhāva* does not yield nihilism but rather points to the correlative non-duality of philosophical binaries that underpins a distinctive form of transcendental idealism. Since Husserl's definition of essence is different from what Xuanzang and his disciples mean by *svabhāva*, the problem of essence can be resolved and will not undermine the current comparative project. However, this does not mean that the problem is irrelevant. By investigating the problem of essence, we call attention to numerous important implications for a comparative study, which in turn deepens our understanding of Husserl's contribution to European philosophy and Chinese Yogācārins' input in East Asian philosophy. These implications are examined in Chapter 9, where we explore how the resolution of the problem of essence will enable philosophers to move towards a broader horizon beyond Orientalism.

In Part Four, we arrive at the "destination" and elaborate on the prescriptive level of Husserl's phenomenology and Chinese Yogācāra in which they translate their philosophical insights into actions. Upon elucidating the meaning of "prescriptive," we keep track of how, on their respective journeys, Husserl arrests his study at transcendental idealism and thus leaves a rather nascent account of the prescriptive level of phenomenology, whereas Xuanzang and his disciples put forward an elaborative systematic theory of religious practice, known as the Bodhisattvas' path towards the wisdom of emptiness and compassion. Since most scholars tend to perceive Chinese Yogācāra through the lens of Husserlian phenomenology, the prescriptive level constantly escapes scholarly attention. The last part of our trip, thus, analyzes Xuanzang and his disciples' answers to questions of agency, moral actions, and community building. Chapter 10 addresses the possibility of agency. These Chinese Yogācārins propose a distinct way of interpreting causality that affirms the existence of agency without violating the universal influence of *karma*. Chapter 11 tries to comprehend Xuanzang and his disciples' promotion of the five-*gotra* theory as their way of accentuating Bodhisattvas' compassion and criticizing incorrect aspirations in the pursuit of awakening. Chapter 12 compares the theory of awakening in Husserl's phenomenology and that in Chinese Yogācāra. As discussed at the beginning of this Prologue, Husserl does consider an awakening to authentic humanity crucial to what he refers to as the renewal of European culture. Nonetheless, the mechanics of such a renewal envisioned by Husserl remain underdeveloped. It is probably for this reason that Husserl has expressed his genuine admiration of Buddhist philosophy. The translation of knowledge into action, then, entails a framework through which the insight of correlative non-dualism becomes enacted and embodied as a collaborative effort of all sentient beings to realize universal awakening.

Indeed, the theory of awakening at the prescriptive level eventually makes Chinese Yogācāra much more than a Buddhist version of Husserlian phenomenology. Instead of assimilating Yogācāra philosophy into Husserl's phenomenology or treating the two as mutually exclusive systems of thought, we explore how they can draw inspiration from one another, beyond the specter of Orientalism. Our journey in this book, thus, showcases that, through doing comparative philosophy, we can *both* preserve the distinctiveness of each tradition for finding a middle ground *and* expand their horizon for conversations on shared philosophical questions. This result gives us hope that it is indeed possible to envision and establish a multicultural world as one in which people from different backgrounds are thriving together.

Part One

The Journey

The Buddhist philosopher Nāgārjuna (*c.* 150–250) once referred to his opponent as the one who rides on horseback but forgets about the horse (T30N1564, P33a26–7). The horse here is a metaphor for methodology. Reminding his interlocutors how their mistakes can be found in the premise of their argumentation, Nāgārjuna likewise reveals to us the danger of overlooking the underlying implications in our approach to the philosophical study of ideas. Bearing in mind this warning, we will not jump directly into a comparative study of Husserl's phenomenology and Chinese Yogācāra in our project. Rather, we must first ask what is involved when a comparison is made across a cultural, historical, and linguistic divide as major as this one. As such, by examining our own approach to comparative studies and explicating our methodologies, we can remain mindful of the horse we are on when we begin our journey.

After decades of development, comparative philosophy has faced several critiques and challenges, in no small part owing to the field's tangled history with Orientalism. As a discourse popularized since the time of colonization, Orientalism epitomizes a way of thinking that overgeneralizes the world into the East and the West. If comparative philosophy can furnish people with a method to go beyond the Orientalist bifurcation, it then retains the potential to showcase the ways in which we engage in intercultural dialogues in the era of globalization. And so, against this backdrop, we hope to foreground three questions. First, how can comparative philosophy promote multiculturalism without perpetuating Orientalism and its related cultural imperialism? Second, why are we continuing to adopt the comparative approach in this book given the recent developments in the field? And lastly, what do we mean when we refer to our project as "comparative philosophy"?

To remind us of the horse we are riding for our journey, the first part of this book is dedicated to examining our methodologies. After scrutinizing how the approaches employed by comparative philosophers were once imbued with different versions of Orientalism, I propose the "both–and" approach that refuses to treat intellectual traditions as being mutually exclusive and realizes the correlative non-duality of these traditions. To be more specific, this approach will *both* maintain the distinctiveness of each tradition in its own context for exploring their middle ground *and* manifest their interconnectedness in the broader shared space of meaning for conversations and collaborations. The purpose of this approach is threefold: first, to avoid assimilating traditions into a third entity; second, to refrain from treating these traditions as polar opposites; and third, to expand their shared horizon. Sources of inspiration for the term "both–and" come from the phenomenological as well as the Buddhist traditions. Hans-Georg Gadamer envisions the expansion of the shared horizon through the traveler analogy, in which a traveler with the capacity of entering different lived realities remains *"both here and there"* (Gadamer 1989: 458). In Buddhist terms, "both–and" encapsulates the idea of the middle path in its stress on the irreducibility and interdependence of binaries (T30N1564, P33b11–12). We will further the discussion of methodology in Chapter 1.

In Chapters 2 and 3, we position Husserl's phenomenology and Chinese Yogācāra in their respective contexts. For intercultural dialogues, contextuality is important in that ideas are cultivated—though not always produced—by the greater sociopolitical climate in which they came to be. In contextualizing phenomenology and Yogācāra, we distance ourselves from synthetization and juxtaposition to enter a plurality of lived realities different from our own. Traveling between these realities, we will secure a middle ground for our journey. This middle ground transpires when we introduce the framework for comparison. It is a three-level framework—the three levels being the descriptive, the explicative, and the prescriptive—which can be inferred from and therefore applied to both Husserl's phenomenology and the Yogācāra philosophy articulated by Xuanzang and his disciples. Far from being mutually exclusive to one another, these two traditions can be brought into constructive conversations on multiple levels. It is therefore possible for people coming from these traditions to collaborate with one another in a multicultural world.

1

Overcoming Orientalism with Multiculturalism

In 2016, an editorial entitled "If Philosophy Won't Diversify, Let's Call It What It Really Is" sparked a heated debate on the position of world philosophies inside academia.[1] The authors of this editorial, Jay Garfield and Bryan van Norden (2016), expressed a deep concern about the fact that most philosophy departments in Europe and North America constrain their scope to—and only to—Euro-American traditions. As a follow-up, Van Norden published the monograph *Taking Back Philosophy: A Multicultural Manifesto* to expound on how the absence of world philosophies bespeaks a lack of recognition and representation of intellectual traditions outside Europe and North America (Van Norden 2017). Thus, what has been pinpointed by Garfield and Van Norden is the importance of recognizing and representing the diversity of philosophical traditions inside and outside the public domain, which matters not only for academic studies of philosophy but also for cross-cultural exchange in general.[2]

Most scholars come to engage with world philosophy first by means of comparative studies. Throughout the history of comparative studies between European and Buddhist philosophies, two approaches have been proposed, which I refer to as the "synthetic" and the "juxtapositional." Scholars in favor of the synthetic approach perceive different philosophical traditions as manifestations of one underlying universal system, whereas those endorsing the juxtapositional approach treat philosophical traditions as polar opposites. These two approaches illustrate and encapsulate two different versions of Orientalism. Borrowing the terminology utilized by Canadian philosopher Charles Taylor (1992),[3] I trace how the synthetic approach involves an *extreme* form of the politics of universalism whilst the juxtapositional approach indicates an *extreme* form of the politics of difference. After scrutinizing both modes of politics, I explore how comparative philosophers can rethink recognition as that of the equal, irreducible value and worth of philosophical traditions. Drawing upon this notion of recognition, comparative philosophy can facilitate the redistribution of discursive resources and the representation of diverse voices inside the field,[4] which promotes multiculturalism as an endeavor to eschew both Orientalism and cultural imperialism. Hence, I put forward the "both–and" approach that moves away from synthetization and juxtaposition, with a capacity of appreciating and celebrating the difference between and the interdependence of cultures and their philosophies.

Synthetization and Juxtaposition[5]

Few comparative philosophers are satisfied with a list of similarities and dissimilarities. Some turn instead to the synthetic approach and propose to synthesize various traditions into a new architectonic of knowledge, in the hope of closing the divide among said traditions. Such a new architectonic inevitably yields a third, culture-neutral entity.

In the comparative studies of European and Buddhist philosophy, the synthetic approach could be traced back to the second half of the nineteenth century. At that time, Max Müller (1823–1900) promoted the synthetic approach in his comparative study of the philosophy of religion. Müller found it pressing to renew methodologies for the field because he was deeply disappointed by how comparative studies were conducted in his time (Müller 1870: 92). He largely deemed these studies to be superficial because they only enumerated similarities between traditions (Müller 1870: 92). To bring about a non-superficial study of comparative philosophy, he initiated the project of "universal religion" (Müller 1870: 92). In this project, he aimed to reveal the universal truth foundational to all philosophies of religion by comparing similar accounts of morality, faith, and ritual practices (Müller 1870: 92). For Müller, all doctrinal philosophies, despite having developed across time and place, derived from the same broad foundation of the ultimate truth of reality (Müller 1872: 46). Articulated in this manner, these philosophies were depicted as manifestations of the third culture-neutral entity *qua* the universal foundational truth in his project of universal religion (Müller 1872: 51). During the Parliament of Religions in Chicago in 1893, Müller repeated the need for a universal religion that could resolve what he discerned as the "disturbing and distressing" situation of treating different intellectual traditions as divided (Müller 1893: 350). As envisaged by Müller, "above and beneath and behind all religions there is one eternal, one universal religion, a religion to which every man, whether black, or white, or yellow, or red, belongs or may belong" (Müller 1893: 350). Müller was confident that such a universal religion, which was by no means superficial, could enable humans to bridge the cultural gap and bring harmony to the world.

In Müller's idealized presentation of the project of universal religion, it seems that he is impartial to all philosophies, be they Asian or European. Nevertheless, closer scrutiny exposes why and how his project is problematic. First, Müller acknowledges only eight philosophies of religion, which he refers to as Brahmanism, Buddhism, Christianity, Mosaism, Zoroastrianism, Mohammedanism, Confucianism, and Daoism (Müller 1872: 32). More importantly, these traditions are construed as manifesting the foundational truth in varying degrees, some being more rational and thus revealing a higher level of truth whilst others being less rational and therefore conveying a lower level of truth (Müller 1872: 44). Subsequently, a spectrum is opened with Christianity on one end as the most rational tradition and all the remaining less advanced traditions on the other end (Müller 1872: 44). Contrary to Christianity that is "to become more and more exalted the more we appreciate the treasures of truth" (Müller 1872: 22), Buddhism draws humans far away from the truth (Müller 1872: 113). Chinese Buddhism is deemed to be even less desirable in that it consists of the Chinese corruptions of earlier Buddhist teaching (Müller 1872: 37). At this point, it is clear that the issues related to the project of universal religion stem not only from the ways in which Müller overgeneralizes philosophies of religions as manifestations of a third universal entity, but also from how Müller formulates this universal entity in Christian terms with a Eurocentric undertone. As remarked by Victor Hori, Müller's project of universal religion, in its pursuit of proving the superiority of Christianity, comes to define all the other intellectual traditions in terms of a Christian prototype (Hori 2016: 46). If a comparative study of the philosophy of religion that aims to list similarities is dangerous because it is superficial, the project of universal religion is even more precarious due to its teleology of assimilating all other traditions into a Christian philosophical framework.

Instead of trying to uncover a universal foundation, some scholars turn to the juxtapositional approach that opposes Buddhist philosophy with its European counterparts. Here, they affirm the East–West contrast but argue for the superiority of Buddhism. Suzuki Daisetsu Teitaro (鈴木大拙貞太郎 1870–1966), commonly known as D. T. Suzuki, can be considered as an exponent of this approach. Almost fifty years after Müller's proposal of universal religion, Suzuki rearticulated Zen teachings, contrasting Buddhist philosophy with European philosophy to justify the superiority of Zen. Similar to Müller, Suzuki identified rationality as the salient feature of European philosophy. Yet, different from Müller, Suzuki continued to reveal the limits of rationality.[6] For Suzuki, it was rationality that entrapped Europeans in dualistic thinking as well as the related crisis of meaning (Suzuki 1927: 6). By the force of dualistic thinking, a rift appeared between the self and the other, between the subject and the object. As scrutinized by Suzuki, knowledge was produced only when a subject was able to represent and objectify things to the mind, but dualistic thinking was far from being able to provide perfect knowledge (Suzuki 1927: 17). He delineated how philosophers like Aristotle and Hegel consistently constructed their edifices of knowledge, only to be demolished and remodeled by their successors (Suzuki 1927: 18). In Suzuki's description, the intellectual pursuit never ended, which cultivated a false hope in reason and aggravated the egocentric worldview. Eventually, when selfhood transformed into an "ego-shell" and was closed from the outside, a person would find it hard to meaningfully relate to the world and to others (Suzuki 1927: 16). For Suzuki, this was how European philosophy ultimately put Europeans in the grip of an existential crisis.[7]

Suzuki argued that, unlike European philosophy, the salient feature of Buddhism, and particularly Zen, was non-rationality (Suzuki 1927: 8). Indeed, Zen went beyond dualistic thinking and presented sentient beings with the immediate wisdom (Suzuki 1927: 24). Suzuki was certain that Zen was not only able to offer this wisdom as perfected knowledge devoid of all differentiations but also capable of remedying issues caused by duality (Suzuki 1970: 73). In Suzuki's proposal, Buddhist philosophy became the antidote to egocentrism and the modern existential crisis in Europe by closing the subject–object rift. Following Suzuki's line of reasoning, any attempt to assimilate or reduce Zen into European philosophy was futile in that non-rationality did not make Buddhist philosophy undesirable. Rather, Europeans would yearn for the wisdom of Zen to cure their crisis of meaning. Rediscovering the value of Zen for the modern world, Suzuki concluded that the non-dual wisdom justified the superiority of Buddhist philosophy to its European counterparts.

When we are first presented with Müller's synthetic approach and Suzuki's juxtapositional approach, we are probably left with the impression that they sharply contrast with each other. Müller suggests that non-rational Buddhist philosophy is undesirable and needs to be assimilated into a universal religion, whilst Suzuki strives to reassess Buddhist philosophy by demonstrating how the non-dual wisdom of Buddhism is superior to European rationality due to the former's capacity to overcome the limitation of the latter. Interestingly, underneath the stark contrast is a shared consensus on the mutually exclusive dichotomy between the East and the West. That is to say, both Müller and Suzuki essentialize Eastern philosophy as the non-rational way of thinking in contrast to Western rationality. As such, their portrayals of the East and the West conform to what Edward Said refers to as Orientalism.

Orientalism, as coined by Said, underlines how the West projects its own image on the East and presents the East as the non-rational, backward Other (Said 1978: 38). In the nineteenth century, Orientalism became a hallmark of the colonial discourse. Euro-American colonizers glorified their invasion of Asian countries as their way of helping these "backward" nations rationalize and modernize. Under this guise, colonizers exported their ideologies to Asia in an attempt to assimilate and subsume Asian cultures into their own. Gradually, Westernization became synonymous with social progress, technological advancement, and modernization itself. It was through this process that Orientalism was coupled with cultural imperialism.

According to Iris Young, cultural imperialism involves a process whereby a dominant group universalizes its experience and value system, becoming the standard model for the entire society (Young 1988: 285). As for those from marginalized groups, they often feel displaced and dismissed, insofar as the discourse outlined by the dominant group in mainstream culture does not match their lived experiences. As such, they have no sense of belonging to mainstream culture and, more importantly, have no vocabularies at their disposal to articulate their lived realities. That is why Young describes this impossible situation for marginalized group members as a paradox: these members are both highlighted as the Other and dismissed to the point of invisibility by the dominant group (Young 1988: 286). The ways in which the dominant group silences the marginalized groups can be read as insidious ways of consolidating power and claiming control in a society.

And so, by combining cultural imperialism with Orientalism, Euro-American colonizers universalized their culture as the standard model of modernity, which singled out people from non-Western cultures, devalued their traditions as non-rational and backward, deprived them of alternative ways of expressing themselves, and left them with no option but to adopt the way of living dictated by the colonizers. The injustice of such an Orientalist discourse together with the related cultural imperialism derives from the way in which the East–West dichotomy eventually facilitates the subordination of people outside the Euro-American culture to the predominant Euro-American group.

Max Müller's project of universal religion, in allusion to the perceived superiority of Christianity and its pursuit of assimilating different philosophies into a universal doctrine, is hardly immune to the critique of cultural imperialism. Although D. T. Suzuki does not endorse assimilation and synthetization, his approach likewise internalizes the stereotype of the West as rational and the East as non-rational. Different from Müller and other Orientalists, Suzuki appropriates this binary to argue for the superiority of non-rationality. In doing so, he champions a new development of Orientalism in which philosophers reflect the colonial discourse. As explained by Victor Hori, "reflecting" is a technical term that describes how intellectuals re-project and appropriate the West's misrepresentations (Hori 2016: 63). Aside from Hori, scholars have also depicted this new development as "secondary Orientalism" (Faure 1993: 53), "reverse Orientalism" (Faure 1993: 92), "inverted Orientalism" (Borup 2004: 452), and "Occidentalism" (Borup 2004: 452). In both versions of Orientalism, intellectuals perpetuate the oversimplified, mutually exclusive dichotomy between the rational West and the non-rational East.

Over the years, Suzuki has come to be respected as the Zen master who introduced Eastern wisdom to the West (Ge 1986). Recently, scholars represented by Robert Sharf (1993) and Brian Victoria (1997) have discerned how this reverse Orientalism in Suzuki's writings contributed to Japan's cultural nationalism during the 1930s. As detailed by Suzuki, Buddhism shaped the effortless and desireless lifestyle associated with Japanese culture (Suzuki 1934: 319). Due to the advantage of Buddhist thinking over Euro-American philosophy, Buddhism did not so much contradict but rather complemented the nation-building of a modern Japan (Suzuki 1938: 13). Upon witnessing how rationality triggered the existential crisis in Europe and North America, Japan needed to find an alternative to the Western model of modernization through rediscovering its own treasure *qua* the Buddhist wisdom of non-duality (Suzuki 1938: 14). More importantly, such an alternative could only be derived from the Japanese culture because Buddhism had degenerated in other Asian countries to the point where the Buddhist wisdom was no longer available outside of Japan (Suzuki 1938: 14). In this narrative of reassessing the East, Japanese culture was portrayed as unique and superior not only to that of the West but also to that of its Asian neighbors (Li 2020: 91). When Japan became militarily powerful and quickly transformed itself into a new colonial power in East Asia proceeding the Meiji restoration in the Meiji Era (1868–1912), the aforementioned reverse Orientalism became an integral part of Japanese Imperialism during the 1930s (Li 2020: 92). Subsequently, Japan glorified its invasion of other Asian countries as an effort to unite the East against the expansion of the West.[8] As such, reverse Orientalism facilitated the rise of Japanese Imperialism, in parallel to how the earlier version of Orientalism fueled Euro-American colonialism.

The Politics of Recognition in Multiculturalism

Since the second half of the 1900s, comparative scholars have been deliberating over how to initiate a project that can accomplish a twofold goal: first, completing more than a list of similarities; and second, correcting the previous mistakes of assimilation and juxtaposition. Still, this begs the question: if comparative philosophy as a field has a rather troubled history, why don't we simply replace it with a better model? To answer this, we must delve deeper into the politics—namely, a set of beliefs and principles—that underpin the synthetic and juxtapositional approaches. Borrowing terms coined by Canadian philosopher Charles Taylor (1992), we come to see how the synthetic approach involves an *extreme* form of the politics of universalism. Under the guise of promoting equal respect, people must treat a wide range of traditions in a difference-blind manner in order to explore a third universal entity to which all traditions shall be assimilated and homogenized. In contrast, the juxtapositional approach exemplifies an altogether different but still *extreme* form of the politics of difference. Rejecting assimilation, people in favor of the juxtapositional approach highlight the exclusive identity of each philosophical tradition to prioritize particularity as the first step of justifying the superiority of one particular tradition over others. These two types of politics inevitably come into conflict, as explained by Taylor, because the former considers the latter to be violating the universal principle of nondiscrimination whilst the latter criticizes the former for enforcing homogenization (Taylor 1992: 43).

Although these two types of politics have their own distinctive values in different contexts, once they undertake an extreme form, they can be summoned by people to perpetuate injustice as well. In our previous analysis, we have elucidated how the synthetic and juxtapositional approaches seem to contradict one another, yet they thrive on the same basis of the oversimplified East–West dichotomy. Such a mutually exclusive dichotomy between the East and the West risks misrepresenting traditions and consolidating the self–other confrontation. In this narrative of confrontation, people would embrace the East–West dichotomy, ignore self–other interdependence, and subsequently depreciate the value and worth of their significant other(s). This is how the lack of proper recognition takes place once people downplay the significance of sociopolitical contexts. When ideas are disengaged from history and are designated to be above spatiotemporality, the value and worth of cultures can be manipulated to fulfill non-philosophical purposes. Inevitably, we arrive at Orientalism and cultural imperialism, two interrelated discourses of misrepresentation and misrecognition that enable the dominant cultural group to silence and subordinate others.

Living in a multicultural world demands that we depart from these extreme, radical forms of universal sameness and difference to find a middle path. This demand, therefore, leads us to the politics of recognition as a recognition of equal, irreducible value and worth of cultures that motivates us to perceive traditions as they actually are and not to project or impose fantasized images on them. In Taylor's terms, "we all recognize the equal value of different cultures; that we not only let them survive, but acknowledge their worth" (Taylor 1992: 64). That is to say, we surpass a difference-blind homogeneity and an ethnocentric particularity by recognizing the irreducible value and worth of different cultures. As a result, we acknowledge the existence of a plurality of lived realities. The goal of recognition is not to cultivate homogeneity (as in Müller's project) or perpetuate superiority (as in Suzuki's model). Rather, we call for recognition because we cherish the hope that all cultures in our world can not only survive separately but also thrive together. Building a multicultural society requires that people in these cultures "move in a broader horizon within which … the background to valuation can be situated as one possibility alongside the different background of the formerly unfamiliar culture" (Taylor 1992: 67). In this kind of multicultural society, we can commute between a plurality of lived realities, communicate about cultural differences, and learn to appreciate dissimilar viewpoints, even when we are unable to convince one another of adopting our own values.

In an endeavor to help us move in a broader horizon, scholars have put forward their proposals for redefining the field of comparative philosophy. Bo Mou highlights how comparative philosophy can enable a constructive engagement of philosophical traditions (Mou 2003: iv). Also stressing the importance of engaging and dialoguing with one another, Tao Jiang reminds comparative philosophers of the importance of contextuality (Jiang 2006: 6). As specified by Jiang, to enjoy an intercultural dialogue, scholars need to appreciate the original context of each tradition and attempt to forge a new context as the backdrop for conversation (Jiang 2006: 6). Recently, scholars championed by Mark Siderits (2003; 2016) have proposed replacing comparativism with fusion or confluence philosophy, which becomes another debate altogether. Exponents of confluence philosophy expose the limitations of comparativism that treat various schools of thought as separate entities for the purpose of listing similarities and dissimilarities (Siderits 2016: 129). In contrast, confluence philosophy furnishes intellectuals with a method of breaking the cultural boundaries and bringing philosophical traditions together for resolving one specific problem (Siderits 2003: 1). Nonetheless, critics such as Michael Levine are worried about whether confluence philosophers will essentialize intellectual traditions—and, thus, obscure their differences—when extracting ideas from the cultural-philosophical context (Levine 2016). At the first glance, confluence philosophy seems to beget a return to the type of universalism envisioned by Max Müller when Siderits argues for the possibility of lifting theories out of their cultural contexts (Siderits 2014: 79). What triggers the controversy of confluence philosophy has to do with the understanding of Siderits's claim that philosophical traditions can be lifted out of their original cultural contexts. How shall we make sense of this claim? One way to interpret Siderits's notion of "lifting-out" is as a method that enables people in one culture to go beyond their own lived reality, to recognize their stereotypes, and to secure a middle ground for dialogue with people from another culture. Following this interpretation, confluence philosophy does not resume the synthetic approach proposed by Max Müller. Rather, it opens up a new perspective for comparative scholars, which further allows for the possibility of moving towards a broader horizon. If this is the case, confluence philosophy, instead of becoming *the* only future of comparative philosophy, remains one of the many possible models of conducting comparative studies in a multicultural world.

Therefore, I find it reasonable to maintain the name of comparative philosophy while expanding the possible connotations of this term for the field. I consider comparative philosophy as an exercise that not only brings philosophical traditions into dialogue, but also recognizes the distinctive value of cultures, respects their irreducible worth, and constitutes a middle ground as the shared space of meaning for these traditions. Such a version of comparative philosophy also goes beyond comparativism. By nature, it is intercultural, or to be more precise, multicultural. Comparative philosophy, due to its role in cross-cultural exchange, positions itself in and proposes a way of contributing to a multilingual and multicultural world. As envisioned by Taylor (1992), multiculturalism serves as a model for guiding people in one cultural tradition to recognize, respect, and appreciate different traditions. It also means that a multicultural world imposes challenges on various types of hierarchies and inequalities that were once normalized (Taylor 2012: 415–16). As such, a multicultural world will not empower people to prioritize one culture and isolate themselves from others, in the way that first-class citizens would demarcate themselves from second-class ones (Taylor 1992: 37). Nor will it foster a homogenous culture, for which the distinctiveness of each culture is to be dismissed and assimilated into the identity of the dominant group (Taylor 1992: 38). Although the tendency of homogenizing cultures arises as a reflection on social hierarchy, being difference-blind is just as biased as being close-minded, insofar as the homogenous narrative refuses to appreciate the diversity of values and, thus, resolves to assimilate other cultures (Taylor 1992: 42). On the contrary, a multicultural world is where people can preserve the distinctiveness of each culture and provide a broader horizon for mutual understanding without losing the universal value of equal respect (Taylor 1992: 67). The salient feature of this type of multiculturalism is indeed the recognition of the equal value and worth of cultures, which prepares people for traveling between a plurality of lived realities.

Throughout history, comparative philosophers have been among the forerunners of cross-cultural exchanges. Our research likewise embodies and epitomizes how people from a wide range of cultural backgrounds initiate conversations to examine perceived incompatibilities and enhance mutual understanding. Comparative philosophers do not believe that each intellectual tradition exists as a closed system unable to communicate with one another, and therefore we do not shun possible tensions. Nor do we close our eyes to incommensurability between cultures in an effort to assimilate all philosophical traditions into a third culture-neutral sphere. Respecting diversity, comparative philosophers draw upon the politics of recognizing the equal value and worth of cultures, in the pursuit of securing a middle ground between philosophical traditions. As such, people from a wide range of cultures can discover and tackle potential incompatibilities. As Tao Jiang specifies, such a middle ground enables people to first engage with theories in their original contexts and then bring them into a new context that facilitates dialogues (Jiang 2006: 6). Historical contextuality plays a crucial role here because it reminds us how philosophical ideas are integral parts of the worldviews shared by people in various communities in order to make sense of their lived realities. Positioning ideas in their own proper historical context and linguistic system, we can trace the kinds of vocabulary people in a community would use to formulate their lived experiences. As such, our recognition of the equal value and worth of philosophical traditions will facilitate the redistribution of discursive resources and the representation of diverse voices inside the field, with a particular focus on giving a voice back to people outside the mainstream culture and placing their lived realities on an equal footing. In doing so, our job as philosophers no longer entails a process of composing monologues in an armchair. Rather, our job is part of the ongoing battle against Orientalism and cultural imperialism with the aim of promoting conversations and collaborations in a multicultural world.

The "Both–And" Approach

Keeping this mission in mind, we must embark on an adventurous journey eschewing the synthetic and juxtapositional approaches. Our ultimate purpose on this journey is to enable philosophers from different traditions to move into a broader horizon and communicate in a shared space of meaning without losing their respective identities acquired from their affiliated cultures. Different from the synthetization and juxtaposition that either forges homogeneity or foregrounds particularity, this new approach draws upon Jiang's proposal of taking into account significant context and Siderits's focus on making comparative philosophy about problem solving. By means of this approach, we can recognize the value and worth of the parties being compared so as to initiate what Mou (2010) refers to as a constructive engagement. I call this new approach the "both–and" approach, considering that it enables us to *both* preserve the unique identity of each tradition in its own context for locating a middle ground *and* promote their interconnectedness in the broader shared space of meaning for conversations and collaborations on solving philosophical problems.

The "both–and" approach is inspired by writings preserved in the phenomenological and Buddhist traditions. Phenomenologist Hans-Georg Gadamer expresses this idea of "both–and" in his analogy of the traveler in which those who are proficient in multiple languages and can move through different worlds of sense, are "*both here and there*" (Gadamer 1989: 458). The free movement of being at once *both here and there* epitomizes the way in which comparative philosophy maintains the distinctiveness, makes explicit the middle ground, and manifests the interconnectedness, of traditions. Buddhists speak of this free movement as that of the middle way. As unpacked by Candrakīrti, a wise person has learned to move beyond polarities (Siderits & Katsura 2013: 160). Indeed, wise people do not stand in the middle as they do not treat extremes as unrelated; nor do they assume a third neutral position over these extremes. Rather, they demonstrate wisdom by acquiring the capacity of moving freely along the middle path by being *both here and there*, further recognizing the interdependence of binaries.

More importantly, being *both here and there* suggests that a traveler *qua* a comparative philosopher not only affirms the existence of a plurality of lived realities to which intellectual traditions belong, but also acknowledges the ways in which these lived realities have not always stood on equal footing. Indeed, as pinpointed by María Lugones, if travelers come from the dominant cultural group, they will find it easier to exercise their mobility and extend their lived reality to those of the marginalized groups (Lugones 2003: 17). Conversely, those from underrepresented and disadvantageous groups are usually forced to leave their own world and become unwillingly assimilated into the lived reality of the mainstream culture (Lugones 2003: 17).[9] That is to say, a traveler's experience is grounded in the existing power dynamics and sociopolitical discourse. Earlier, we observed how the privilege of Euro-American colonizers provided them with willing experiences for expanding their lived reality, whereas the colonized in Asia suffered from having the unwilling experiences of traveling away from their original cultures. Being mindful of the importance of the power dynamics as well as the related sociopolitical discourse, we need to redistribute the discursive resources to place intellectual traditions on an equal footing with one another in our comparative study. That is why we strive to find the language together with the vocabularies employed by philosophers in each tradition to represent their lived experience and make sense of their lived reality. As such, traveling is not a one-way conversation on how to universalize the dominant culture as well as its philosophy and lived reality; neither is it a practice of extracting one intellectual tradition out of its own context for assimilating this tradition into the lived reality of the dominant cultural group. Rather, as indicated by the phrase "*being both here and there*," traveling is a reciprocal process in which travelers make a joint effort to explore a middle ground and expand their shared horizon.

Hence, we enact the "both–and" approach in our comparative study of Husserl's phenomenology and Chinese Yogācāra. It demands us to *both* maintain their distinctiveness by positioning these traditions in their concrete contexts for exploring their middle ground *and* manifest their interconnectedness on a broader horizon for conversations about shared philosophical questions (such as the problem of essence). As a matter of fact, many renowned scholars who have helped lay the foundations for the field have discerned a tension between the Buddhist critique of *svabhāva* and Husserl's affirmation of essence. Iso Kern fully acknowledges that he puts aside key elements of Xuanzang's philosophy, especially those that concern metaphysics and soteriology (Kern 1992: 268). Inspired by Kern's work, Liangkang Ni (2009) has furthered the comparative study of Husserl and Xuanzang, notably remarking that Chinese Yogācārins have gone one step further than Husserl in their assertion of everything being empty and inexistent, including consciousness (Ni 2010: 85–6). Instead of tackling the problem of essence, Ni explains how he centers his work on the analysis of the intentional structure of consciousness (Ni 2010: 86). Similarly, Dan Lusthaus argues for reading Xuanzang's Yogācāra philosophy of consciousness-only as a Buddhist theory of knowledge (Lusthaus 2002: 6). It follows that the critique of *svabhāva* is by nature epistemic, not ontological (Lusthaus 2002: 462). However, the ways in which these scholars restrain from discussions on the nature of reality point to the limitation of their methodologies. Indeed, when interpreting Yogācāra ideas in the phenomenological framework and when translating Yogācāra philosophy in phenomenological terms, scholars have shown a tendency to leave Yogācāra concepts, especially those that seem to be incommensurable with phenomenology such as the Buddhist refutation of *svabhāva* (essence), outside of their projects.

With the help of the "both–and" approach, we can draw upon and develop previous research to overcome its limitation. While eschewing a return to the nineteenth-century style of synthetization, we must also refrain from the juxtapositional approach and therefore refuse to treat philosophical traditions as mutually exclusive. As such, we continue to deepen the philosophical understanding of the ultimate nature of consciousness, the mind–world relationship, and the self–other interconnectedness in the broader shared space of meaning. In our free movement of being *both here and there*, we pay particular attention to a plethora of languages that have been employed by Husserl, Xuanzang and his disciples, and their English translators. Subsequently, we can extend the shared space of meaning that is embedded in languages to the interlocutors of Husserl and Chinese Yogācārins throughout the intellectual history of the traditions they belong to.

This is how we come to see that Husserl embarked on his investigation of consciousness within the history of European philosophy. Under the influence of ancient Greek philosophers, medieval theologians borrowed Greek vocabularies to expand the Latin lexicon when shifting their focus from the exterior material world to the interior immaterial soul for the purpose of achieving the superior God. In the advent of the Enlightenment movement, European scholars stressed the interior mind to prioritize this-worldly life over any other-worldly existence. Accordingly, the essence of a person was no longer defined by existence but rather by the mind and consciousness. This turn towards the subject soon made the essence of a person into an absolute in itself, which brought in new problems exemplified by solipsism. Notably, if a person was defined by what stayed inside the mind, could this person go beyond the mind to meaningfully access the world and other minds? Living through the First World War, Husserl followed in the footsteps of his contemporaries in his reflection on Enlightenment philosophy. Even though he continued to employ notions such as intentionality and essence, he invested new meaning in these concepts to highlight the mutual constitution of the subject and the object, of the self and the other, and eventually of the mind and the world. As a reflection on solipsism, Husserl's phenomenology reopened the interior ego to the intersubjective lifeworld, further marking Husserl's breakthrough in modern European philosophy.

Similar to how Husserl constantly initiated conversations with the most eminent thinkers of the European philosophical tradition through reintroducing Latin and Greek terms to German and redefining these key philosophical notions in the early 1900s, Xuanzang and his disciples communicated with Buddhist patriarchs in South Asia and their fellow literati in East Asia in the 600s. In translating Sanskrit terms into Chinese, these Yogācārins profited from the widely used philosophical binaries to unpack the idea of emptiness and elaborate upon the non-duality of opposites. That was how emptiness in their writings became defined as the fluidity and transformability of philosophical binaries. Through their effort, Chinese Yogācāra was no longer a passive reception of Sanskrit concepts in the Chinese language but rather an innovative development of ideas in the local cultural, intellectual, and linguistic context.

Coming from this context, Xuanzang and his disciples shifted their focus from the exterior world to the interior mind and finally to the exterior community in their study of consciousnesses. They developed a different trajectory than Husserl due to their respective stances towards the notion of essence. They eventually arrived at their respective destinations in that these Yogācārins perceived the final return to exteriority as the superior goal of undertaking the Bodhisattvas' path. In contrast, Husserl did not explicitly depict the intersubjective communal life as superior and religious. And so, after revisiting the philosophical trajectories of Husserl and Chinese Yogācārins, we remark that their road is the same, but their wheels travel in different tracks.

2

Contextualizing Chinese Yogācāra

In this chapter, we outline the intellectual history of Yogācāra philosophy with a particular focus on the rich diversity of this term in the Chinese language context. As a tradition known for its investigation of consciousness, Yogācāra can hardly be spoken of in the singular, given the plurality of doctrinal viewpoints and canonical languages preserved inside this tradition. Therefore, our first task is to elaborate on the nuances of this umbrella term *qua* "Chinese Yogācāra." As previously mentioned in the Prologue, the concept of Chinese Yogācāra is evoked to paraphrase the term "*hanchuan weishi* (漢傳唯識)" that literally means the Yogācāra doctrine of consciousness-only transmitted in the Chinese language.[1] Mindful of how the boundaries of "Chinese" and "Yogācāra" are negotiated and renegotiated throughout history, we explore how Chinese Yogācārins consistently strive to develop their tradition from the originated Sanskrit language context. That is to say, we consider Chinese Yogācāra as an intellectual fruit of cross-cultural exchange between South Asia and East Asia, rather than a passive continuation of the earlier tradition.

Indeed, our main protagonist Xuanzang (玄奘 *c.* 602–64) grew up in a time when such cross-cultural exchange facilitated the transmission of Yogācāra inside the Chinese Buddhist community. Doctrinal debates over major Buddhist concepts convinced this young adept that he should search for the authentic Yogācāra teaching in India. Upon his return to the capital city of the Tang Empire (618–907), Xuanzang translated numerous Sanskrit texts into the Chinese language and composed *The Treatise on the Perfection of Consciousness-only* (*Cheng weishi lun* 成唯識論, henceforth referred to as *CWSL*). This treatise, together with its commentaries written by Xuanzang's disciples Kuiji (窺基 632–82), Huizhao (慧沼 648–714), and Zhizhou (智周 668–723) become foundational to Chinese Yogācāra. In understanding the importance of their seminal work, it is helpful to investigate how Xuanzang and his disciples' presentation of Yogācāra should not be viewed as a passive reception of ideas from a different language but rather an innovative development of the tradition to the local context. Towards the end of this investigation, we explain how and why we can outline Chinese Yogācāra as a study of consciousness on three levels, namely: the descriptive, the explicative, and the prescriptive.

Yogācāra before Xuanzang

Xuanzang was born in 602, the second year of the Renshou era during the regime of Emperor Wen of the Sui dynasty. Emperor Wen (541–604) united the Chinese Empire in 590, ending over three hundred years of social turmoil that followed the collapse of the Han dynasty (202 BCE–220CE). Born and raised in a literati family, Xuanzang was drawn to Buddhism at a very young age. He was particularly attracted to the Yogācāra doctrine of consciousness-only (*weishi* 唯識, *vijñaptimātra*).

As documented in the Buddhist scriptures, together with Madhyamaka, Yogācāra is one of the major Mahāyāna schools in South Asia. Yogācārins famously use their study of consciousness to argue how and why everything is empty of *svabhāva*.[2] It is said that Yogācāra was founded by the bodhisattva Maitreya and developed by the brothers Asaṅga and Vasubandhu at the end of the fourth century. While Asaṅga began his training as a Mahāyāna monk, Vasubandhu worked on Abhidharma doctrines in a non-Mahāyāna Buddhist community (T51N2087, P896b29). Vasubandhu soon made a name for himself by composing the *Verses on the Treasury of Abhidharma* (*Abhidharmakośakārikā*) (T29N1558, P1a5). Worried about how his brother was marching on the wrong path, Asaṅga asked his disciples to chant *Daśabhūmikasūtra*—a Yogācāra text on the ten phases of the Bodhisattvas' practice—in front of Vasubandhu (T51N2087, P896c25). Upon hearing this *sūtra*, Vasubandhu attained initial awakening and turned to the Greater Vehicle of Mahāyāna (T51N2087, P896c26). To repent for negative *karma* accumulated in his pre-Mahāyāna years, Vasubandhu wrote a large number of treatises in Sanskrit, including the *Thirty Verses of Consciousness-only* (*Triṃśikāvijñaptimātratā*) and the *Twenty Verses of Consciousness-only* (*Viṃśatikāvijñaptimātratā*) (T51N2087, P897a4–6). With the joint effort of Asaṅga and Vasubandhu, Yogācāra rose to prominence in South Asia.

From the story of Vasubandhu, we can infer that Yogācārins take Abhidharma clerics—a camp of Buddhists outside the Mahāyāna circle—as their main interlocutors. Indeed, Abhidharma philosophy, especially that of the Sarvāstivāda and the Sautrāntika schools, remains a source of inspiration for Yogācārins. In defense of the stance that sentient beings have no substantial, *sui generis*, and immutable self-existence but non-sentient dharmas do have *svabhāvic* existence, Sarvāstivādins enact an epistemic approach to argue for the mind-independent real existence of non-sentient dharmas. They describe the acquisition of knowledge in a causal process: dharmas or objects serve as stimuli that affect the mind which reflect and represent external objects (T43N1830, P236c1–2). As such, if the mind is able to perceive, the cause of such representation *qua* external dharma must have a mind-independent real existence in every phase of cosmic time (T43N1830, P236b28–9). Contemporary philosophers characterize the viewpoint articulated by Sarvāstivādins as direct realism, which can be contrasted with the indirect realism espoused by another group of Abhidharma philosophers known as the Sautrāntikas.[3]

In his critique of Sarvāstivādins and Sautrāntikas, Vasubandhu follows in the footsteps of previous Mahāyāna philosophers. Indeed, if non-sentient dharmas exist in a causal chain together with the mind of a sentient being, these dharmas can hardly be considered to have self-determined *svabhāvic* existence. Furthermore, Vasubandhu highlights how the mind does not passively receive given data from external stimuli but rather actively serves as the condition for the possibility of experience. The mind is a system of eight different types of consciousness. The underlying eighth consciousness constantly functions and subsequently gives rise to the seventh consciousness as the subjective aspect of experience and to the other six consciousnesses as the objective aspect (T31N1586, P60b–c). Sentient beings are prone to misperceive the subjective aspect and objective aspect as a *svabhāvic* self and a *svabhāvic* dharma, a misperception that animates various affective mental states *qua* mental factors (*caitasikas/caittas*) to entrap sentient beings in suffering (T31N1586, P61a1–a12). Ultimately, anything that sentient beings are inclined to perceive as *svabhāva* is only a mental construction (T31N1586, P61a13). Therefore, the concept of consciousness-only (*vijñaptimātra*) is introduced to encapsulate how everything arises because of consciousness (T31N1586, P60a27). To further summarize why and how consciousness-only entails emptiness, Vasubandhu puts forward the account of three natures: the imagined nature explains how the *svabhāvic* views of the self and the dharma are wrong; the dependent nature elucidates how the function of consciousness gives rise to misperception; and the ultimate nature expounds on how consciousness in its incessant function is also empty of *svabhāvic* existence (T31N1586, P61a14–a27).

When Yogācāra garnered popularity in South Asia, its followers began to transmit the doctrine of consciousness-only to East Asia. At that time, Chinese history entered the Northern and Southern dynasties period (*c.* 386–589). The continent was divided by a number of kingdoms that waged constant war on one another. Since 386, partial unification was accomplished with one dynasty presiding in the North and another in the South. Living in this sociopolitical climate, clerics were not able to access all existing Yogācāra teachings. Hence, they worked with what was available to them at that time. Two groups took the lead in translating the Yogācāra teaching of consciousness-only into the Chinese language: the Dilun group (*dilun pai*地論派) and the Shelun group (*shelun pai*攝論派). While the Dilun group centered their study on the *Shidijing lun* (十地經論, *Daśabhūmikasūtraśāstra*), the Shelun group prioritized the *She dacheng lun* (攝大乘論, *Mahāyānasaṃgraha*). These two groups were therefore named after their primary scriptures. Moreover, they were referred to as groups (*pai*派) or teachings (*shishuo* 師說), and not as schools (*zong* 宗), primarily because Dilun and Shelun did not possess a temple complex as their monastic base and nor did they form their own dharma lineage. Such a situation was almost inevitable in the wake of the North–South division because the institutionalization of Buddhist teachings typically required tremendous financial and political support from the ruling class.[4] During times of social turmoil and political chaos, clerics could only harness limited resources for institutionalization. Nevertheless, Yogācārins were mindful of the importance of patronage. The initiator of the Dilun group, Bodhiruci (菩提流支), arrived in East Asia in 508 and soon won the royal family of the North dynasty over as benefactors. Meanwhile, the founder of the Shelun group, Paramārtha (真諦 499–569), received the support of the emperor of the South dynasty.

In their translation and transmission of Yogācāra treatises, Dilun and Shelun masters highlight how misperception is underpinned by subject–object duality. These Yogācārins contend that the subject–object duality is illusory and therefore empty of *svabhāvic* existence. What gives rise to this duality is consciousness (T31N1587, P61c7). Among all eight types of consciousness, the eighth consciousness serves as the origin that gives rise to the seventh consciousness *qua* the subjective aspect of experience, and the other six consciousnesses *qua* the objective aspect (T31N1587, P62a–b). As long as consciousness is working, sentient beings enact dualistic thinking to differentiate the subject from the object, which further keeps them captive of illusions and away from the truth of non-duality *qua* emptiness (T31N1587, P62b20–1). To realize emptiness, sentient beings must terminate the movement of consciousness and recuperate the non-dual state of mind (T31N1587, P62b22–4).

Regardless of their shared views on illusions, clerics in the Dilun and Shelun groups also developed their respective understanding of consciousness. In particular, they characterized the eighth consciousness differently. In the writings of Dilun philosophers, the eighth consciousness consists of two aspects, the polluted aspect as the origin of duality and the purified aspect as the non-dual state of mind *qua* emptiness (T26N1522, P180a). Shelun clerics, however, disapprove of this delineation of the eighth consciousness as both pure and impure. They speak of it as the origin of duality and illusion (T31N1587, P62c19). Sentient beings can make an effort to remove duality and recuperate the non-dual state of mind. This purified luminous mind evolves into the ninth consciousness *amalavijñāna* that is further equated with emptiness (T31N1616, P864a26–8). As such, Shelun clerics follow their master Paramārtha to incorporate more explicitly the thought of *tathāgatagarbha* (*rulaizang*如來藏, Buddha Matrix) in their interpretation.[5] *Tathāgatagarbha* is defined as the Buddha nature inherent to all sentient beings, which suggests how the mind is originally pure and non-dual, only temporally polluted by illusion due to the activity of consciousness (T30N1584, P1018c). Once the illusions are removed, the inherent Buddha nature will reveal, and awakening will be realized.

Through translation and interpretation, Yogācārins in the Dilun and Shelun groups began to enrich the doctrine of consciousness-only in the local Chinese context. Nevertheless, the task they embarked upon was not easy. Aside from the social turmoil, the lack of textual resources, and the discrepancy between available translations, the challenges they faced were compounded by another factor: the Yogācāra tradition continued to develop in South Asia. In the 500s, Dignāga (*c.* 480–540) introduced logic and epistemology to systematize the Yogācāra formulation of consciousness, further marking the rise of later Yogācāra in South Asian Buddhism. Additionally, there were ten great commentators on Yogācāra philosophy, represented by Sthiramati, Nanda, and Dharmapāla, throughout the sixth century. Sthiramati and Nanda concentrated on early Yogācāra texts penned by Vasubandhu, whilst Dharmapāla studied with Dignāga to elaborate on doctrinal ideas. In Sanskrit, Sthiramati and Nanda were considered to be the representatives of *nirākāravijñānavāda* (non-image consciousness-only) in contrast to *sākāravijñānavāda* (consciousness-only with images) promoted by Dignāga and his disciples.[6] These newly emerged thoughts were also brought to East Asia by translators.[7]

Confronted with these challenges, Dilun and Shelun followers during the Northern and Southern dynasties never ceased in their effort to disseminate Yogācāra ideas. It was due to their agency that Yogācāra philosophy began to thrive outside South Asia, which set the stage for Xuanzang's journey to India. When Emperor Wen defeated the ruler of the South dynasty and eventually unified the country in 590, Buddhism prevailed in the newly established Sui dynasty (581–619). Due to his interest in Yogācāra, Xuanzang visited most clerics in the Dilun and Shelun groups, only to realize that it was impossible to reconcile their apprehensions.[8] He ascribed their disputes to the fact that they did not have full access to the complete teaching of consciousness-only. After much deliberation, Xuanzang decided to travel to South Asia, not only for his pursuit of the true Yogācāra wisdom but also in the hope of using this wisdom to liberate all sentient beings from suffering (T51N2087, P868b7-9). In 629, Xuanzang embarked on his journey (T50N2053, P222c4-5). But by then, the Sui dynasty was replaced by the Tang dynasty (618-907).

From Sanskrit *Vijñaptimātra* to Chinese *Weishi*[9]

It was an arduous journey. Xuanzang marched through the Gobi Desert and crossed the Pamir Mountains. Since his journey was not permitted by Emperor Taizong (598-649) of Tang, the emperor ordered local authorities throughout the Silk Road to arrest him. In response, Xuanzang took a detour through Central Asia to avoid capture and arrived at the Nālandā Temple. There, he became a protégé of Śīlabhadra (戒賢 c. 529-645), a direct dharmic heir of Dharmapāla (T51N2087, P914c7). Under the guidance of Śīlabhadra (T50N2052, P216c), Xuanzang familiarized himself with the systems of thought of Abhidharma, Madhyamaka, and Yogācāra (T50N2053, P237a). Further profiting from his language skills, Xuanzang consulted collections archived at the Nālandā Temple, including Buddhist scriptures as well as Brahmanical classics like the *Vedas* (T50N2053, P237b). Aside from his stay at Nālandā, Xuanzang traveled throughout South Asia to perfect his knowledge of local intellectual traditions. Mindful of the previously mentioned debates between the *nirākāravijñānavādins* and *sākāravijñānavādins* inside the Yogācāra community, Xuanzang visited the *nirākāravijñānavāda* master Jayasena to advance his comprehension of Sthiramati's thoughts (T50N2053, P244a10). Fully aware of the importance of *hetuvidyā* logic in Dignāga's argumentation, Xuanzang improved his study of the theory of *pramāṇa* with the help of a prominent Brahmin priest (T50N2053, P241b11). Prior to Xuanzang's return to the Tang Empire, he acquired all the qualifications of a dharma master and became a star student of Śīlabhadra (T50N2053, P244c). Under Śīlabhadra's instruction, Xuanzang lectured on the Yogācāra doctrine of consciousness-only in Sanskrit to scholar-monks at Nālandā (T50N2053, P244b27).

Traveling back to the capital city of Tang in 645, Xuanzang was warmly welcomed by Emperor Taizong. Although the emperor declined Xuanzang's initial travel request in 629, he decided to patronize Xuanzang's project of translating Sanskrit Buddhist texts into Chinese upon learning about Xuanzang's fame outside his empire (T51N2087, P868b16). Under imperial orders, several developments occurred: new temples were constructed as venues for translation and monks were ordained; language experts were invited to be Xuanzang's assistants; and high-level statespersons and distinguished literati became Xuanzang's lay students. Such all-inclusive support entailed a rather subtle way for Emperor Taizong to exert comprehensive control over Xuanzang and his work (Yoshimura 1995; Liu 2009). Aware of the importance of imperial patronage, Xuanzang strove to maintain the ruler's favoritism, frequently sending in reports to express his gratitude (T52N2119, P821). There began an interesting exchange between the ruler and the master. Similar to how Emperor Taizong could never convince Xuanzang to disrobe and serve as a statesperson in the royal court yet still supplied Xuanzang with almost everything he would want for his translation project (T50N2053, P253c), Xuanzang never converted Emperor Taizong to Buddhism yet continued to declare complete loyalty to the ruler all the while befriending most of Emperor Taizong's confidants (T50N2053, P256a). As such, imperial patronage accelerated the thriving of Yogācāra. Emperor Taizong prefaced Xuanzang's translations, which indicated his acknowledgment of Xuanzang's leadership in the monastic community (T50N2053, P256a27–b29).

When Xuanzang translated Buddhist scriptures from Sanskrit to Chinese, he and his team faced at least four obstacles: first, there were huge grammatical differences between the Chinese and Sanskrit languages; second, there were indigenous intellectual traditions in the Tang dynasty that remained distinct from those in South Asia; third, Yogācāra ideas had been partially transmitted in the Chinese language through the effort of the Dilun and Shelun groups; fourth, previous translators were not fully aware of doctrinal differences inside the Yogācāra community in South Asia. These obstacles compounded upon one another. Eventually, clerics like Xuanzang who were proficient in both languages and familiar with both intellectual contexts, found a method of traveling between these systems of thought and making sense of these different lived realities. Such a method was encapsulated in their translation of Buddhist texts, which involved more than the passive reception of ideas written in a foreign language. Indeed, they exercised their agency, harnessing all the intellectual, philosophical, and philological resources in order to incorporate their own understanding of Buddhist teaching in their Chinese translations. Consequently, these translations came to represent an active comprehension of concepts in the local context, through which Xuanzang and his disciples were able to initiate meaningful dialogues with their interlocutors throughout Asia.

Though under the auspices of the ruler, Xuanzang's new translations provoked major controversy inside the Buddhist community. Dilun and Shelun clerics deemed these new translations to be disrespectful to previous masters like Bodhiruci and Paramārtha (T50N2060, P459c7). What added another layer of complexity to the old–new debate on translation, amounted to their different understandings of Yogācāra philosophy. As documented in *The Expanded Biographies of Great Masters* (*xu gaoseng zhuan*續高僧傳), supporters of the old translation stressed how everything was ultimately empty, whilst Xuanzang and his disciples highlighted how emptiness was manifested through illusory phenomena, in their new translation (T50N2060, P459a).[10] Moreover, defenders of Paramārtha advocated for an interpretation of consciousness-only that was harmonized with the notion of *tathāgatagarbha*, an interpretation that Xuanzang's disciples found implausible.[11] Due to a plethora of factors, the debate over translation was both philological and philosophical (T50N2060, P458c27). To defend his master, Kuiji composed extensive commentaries on Xuanzang's texts and founded the Dharma-Image School of Consciousness-only (*faxiang weishi zong*法相唯識宗).[12] This school possessed its own dharma lineage, revered texts, and location in the Ci'en Temple, which marked the official institutionalization of later Yogācāra in the Tang dynasty.

The doctrine of *weishi* (唯識, consciousness-only) articulated by Xuanzang and his disciples constitutes a crucial moment in the history of Chinese philosophy. This doctrine is the fruit of a decade-long exchange between intellectuals in Asia. Consequently, the lineage of early and later Yogācāra expands the aforementioned *nirākāravijñānavāda* and *sākāravijñānavāda* differentiation.[13] Among the early Yogācārins, we can count Asaṅga, Vasubandhu, Nanda, and Sthiramati in South Asia, and Bodhiruci, Paramārtha, and Woncheuk (613–96) in East Asia. The representatives of later Yogācāra are Dignāga, Dharmapāla, and Śīlabhadra in South Asia, together with Xuanzang, Kuiji, Huizhao, and Zhizhou in East Asia.

The early–later distinction entails two different interpretations of the doctrine of consciousness-only and therefore epitomizes the diversity of viewpoints inside Yogācāra.[14] As such, it yields more than a temporal difference. In certain historical periods, early and later Yogācārins were even contemporaries, like Jayasena and Śīlabhadra in South Asia, or Woncheuk and Kuiji in East Asia. In our comparative study, we focus on the later Yogācāra philosophy articulated by Xuanzang and his disciples in the Tang dynasty to detail how logic and epistemology have shaped the outlook of the philosophy of *weishi*. As to be further elucidated in the rest of this book, the difference between early and later Yogācāra arises from their respective delineations of the functionality of consciousness, which continues to shape their dissimilar viewpoints on the nature of reality and their theories of awakening.

Decline and Revival of *Weishi*

Xuanzang's friendship with the imperial ruler eventually backfired on his translation project. Emperor Taizong passed the throne to his son who was later coronated as Emperor Gaozong (628–83). After the death of his father, the new emperor started to consolidate imperial power. That is why Emperor Gaozong pushed back against the old clique of officials previously appointed by his father and removed most of them from the court. Given that several members of the old clique were lay Buddhists who studied with Xuanzang, this young ruler did not appreciate Xuanzang's work as much as his father (T50N2053, P266b). To protect his tradition from factional politics inside the imperial court, Xuanzang stayed in the Ci'en Temple to focus on translating Buddhist texts (T50N2053, P260a18). His friendship with the previous emperor and the old clique, which once facilitated his promotion of Yogācāra teaching, ended up devastating this enterprise during the regime of Emperor Gaozong (Liu 2009). Although Kuiji fought to defend his master, he was not favored by the new ruler either. Eventually, this resulted in Kuiji leaving the capital city.

The decline of the study of *weishi* was accelerated by the Great Persecution (840–6) of non-indigenous traditions during the regime of Emperor Wuzong (814–46) of the Tang dynasty. While Xuanzang was teaching Yogācāra philosophy in the Tang capital, numerous monks from Korea and Japan came to study with him. They managed to transmit and promote the philosophy of consciousness-only outside the Tang Empire and back to their respective homelands (Moro 2017). In Japan, *weishi* philosophy became foundational to the Hossō school, one of the key players of Buddhism during the Nara (710–94) and Heian (794–1185) periods. At the advent of the Kamakura period (1185–1333), the emperors lost control of the country at the expense of the rising warrior class. No longer having its main patronage from the royal family, Hossō clerics faced a notable challenge. Living in this critical time, these Japanese Yogācārins felt obliged to restore the previous glory of their tradition. Among them, the most eminent master was Jōkei (貞慶 1155–1213).[15] To compete with the newly established schools of Zen and Pure Land, Hossō monks like Jōkei attempted to reformulate the Yogācāra doctrine of consciousness-only as an effort to recover the authentic version of Yogācāra thinking. Differing from masters in Heian Japan who opted for classical Chinese as the standard canonical language, Hossō monks in the Kamakura period composed their treatises in Japanese. In reorganizing Yogācāra thoughts, they prioritized the theory of three natures. As remarked by many intellectual historians,[16] three factors indicate how Yogācāra became Japanese Hossō: first, by elevating the theory of three natures to the center of Yogācāra doctrine; second, by making Yogācāra philosophy more accessible both conceptually and linguistically; and third, by stressing the importance of religious practice.

Returning to the Chinese context, although Yogācāra philosophy continued to be studied and examined by scholar-monks in the following dynasties, they never managed to restore its past prestige. The philosophy of *weishi* did, however, resurge towards the end of Ming (1368–1644), which led to an exchange between Chinese and Japanese Yogācārins.[17] Shortly afterward, Manchu warriors took over, replacing the Ming dynasty with the Qing dynasty (1616–1912). In the mid-1800s when the Taiping Rebellion (1851–64) broke out, numerous Buddhist temples were destroyed. Most Yogācāra texts were lost and did not find their way back to China until the early Republican period. In collaboration with Nanjō Bunyū (南條文雄 1849–1927), a lay Buddhist named Yang Wenhui (楊文會 1837–1911) established the Jinling Sūtra Publishing House (*jinling kejingchu* 金陵刻經處) in the city of Nanjing in 1866 to print lost Buddhist scriptures and promote Yogācāra studies.[18] Constant regional flows of ideas and knowledge ushered in the full revival of Yogācāra.[19] Expanding the publishing house, Ouyang Jingwu (歐陽竟無 1871–1943) founded the Chinese Academy of Inner Learning (*zhina neixueyuan* 支那內學院) in 1922 with his protégé Lü Cheng (呂澂 1896–1989).[20] In the newly established academy, scholars presented Buddhist studies as a scientific discipline and provided students with resources to study Buddhism outside monasteries. At almost the same time, the Wuchang Buddhist Academy (*wuchang foxueyuan* 武昌佛學院) under the direction of master Taixu (太虛 1890–1947) recruited scholar-monks and nuns as well as Buddhist scholars.[21] In the history of Buddhist modernization, these two academies served as the hubs of Buddhist studies and trained numerous scholars. Most of them found the Yogācāra study of consciousness to be as profound as Euro-American science and philosophy. Hence, they borrowed Yogācāra concepts to rearticulate Buddhist thoughts and translate Euro-American philosophical ideas. Aside from Buddhist scholars, the first generation of modern Confucians, notably Xiong Shili (熊十力 1885–1968) and Liang Shuming (梁漱溟 1893–1988), advanced their knowledge of Buddhism at the Chinese Academy of Inner Learning. Although many modern Confucians were indebted to Yogācāra, they turned to promote Confucianism insofar as they could not locate a systematic theory of ethics and social construction in the philosophy of *weishi*. As a result, the Yogācāra revival set the stage for scholars to modernize Buddhism and Confucianism in the early Republican period.[22]

Three Levels in Chinese *Weishi*

In the wake of this revival, the philosophy of *weishi* articulated by Xuanzang and his disciples continues to garner scholarly attention.[23] Dan Lusthaus proposes to interpret Xuanzang's philosophy of consciousness-only as an epistemic inquiry of the human mind, an interpretation that shall be demarcated from any metaphysical reading of Yogācāra as a version of idealism (Lusthaus 2002: 6). Scrutinizing Lusthaus's approach, Alexander Mayer discerns how Lusthaus does not fully distance his interpretation from metaphysical examination of the ultimate nature of reality (Mayer 2009: 192–6). Similarly, Lawrence Y.K. Lau identifies the limitation of the epistemic approach (Lau 2007b: 249). For Lau, epistemic inquiries are secondary to the goal of resolving the existential crisis facing all sentient beings (Lau 2007b: 252). He maintains that Yogācāra Buddhism should be understood as a two-pronged project: the epistemological investigation of the cause of ignorance and the existential-ontological explanation of the cure for suffering (Lau 2007b: 254). Recently, more scholars have come to recognize that the philosophical doctrines articulated by Buddhists are inherently preceptive. Considering the crucial roles of meditative practices and moral actions, Lai Shen-Chon proposes his project of Buddhist hermeneutics (*fojiao quanshixue* 佛教詮釋學), which conceives of Buddhist thought as a system of epistemology (*zhishilun* 知識論), ontology (*cunyoulun* 存有論), and practice (*shijianlun* 實踐論) (Lai 2009).

In determining how the philosophy of *weishi* developed by Xuanzang and his disciples should be interpreted, it is helpful to consider the structure of its foundational text, namely, the previously mentioned *The Treatise on the Perfection of Consciousness-only* (*Cheng weishi lun* 成唯識論). Up until the 1920s, scholars assumed that the *CWSL* was first composed by Dharmapāla and then translated by Xuanzang.[24] This interpretation was based, in part, on the *Taishō Tripiṭaka*'s version of the *CWSL*, which began with the statement "Xuanzang received the imperial decree to translate [the text] (*Xuanzang fengzhao yi*, 玄奘奉詔譯)" (T31N1585, P1a6). This statement, in expressing Xuanzang's loyalty to Emperor Taizong, is probably a formality. As explained by Kuiji, when Xuanzang decided to compose a treatise on the philosophy of *weishi*, he foregrounded Dharmapāla's interpretation of Vasubandhu's *Thirty Verses of Consciousness-only* against the backdrop of doctrinal debates between Yogācārins and their interlocutors (T43N1830, P229b17). As such, Kuiji suggests that Xuanzang is indeed the author of this treatise. More importantly, Kuiji perceives this treatise as Xuanzang's effort of systematizing a diversity of thoughts inside the Yogācāra school and providing a coherent introduction of these ideas in the Chinese language. If this is the case, then Xuanzang has already furnished us with a framework of understanding Yogācāra philosophy in his *CWSL*.

This important treatise consists of two halves. The first half preserves the Yogācāra critique of their rivals inside and outside the Buddhist community. Then, Xuanzang moves on to detail the theories of consciousness put forward by Yogācārins. The second half that presents the articulations of the doctrine of consciousness-only further consists of three parts. In the first part, Xuanzang describes the intentional feature and epistemic function of eight different types of consciousness together with their mental factors (T31N1585, P7b26). This is where Xuanzang contrasts later Yogācāra with early Yogācāra, detailing how later Yogācārins incorporate Abhidharma epistemology to enrich the characterization of consciousness. It is therefore crucial for Xuanzang to determine the name for all eight consciousnesses and deny the surmised existence of the ninth consciousness. On the basis of this description, in the second part, Xuanzang centers his analysis on the theory of three natures (*sanxing* 三性). He expounds on the meaning of consciousness-only and emptiness in order to elucidate the ultimate nature of reality (T31N1585, P39a2–4). To do so, he clarifies how the Yogācāra account of three natures complements the Madhyamaka twofold truth and how later Yogācārins refine their critique of *svabhāva* differently than early Yogācārins. These philosophical insights translate into actions in the last part of this treatise. Xuanzang prescribes rules and precepts to Yogācāra followers, encouraging them to gradually enter consciousness-only (*jianci wuru weishi* 漸次悟入唯識) (T31N1585, P48b10–11), which becomes the Yogācāra articulation of the Bodhisattvas' path towards awakening.

Modeled on the structure of the *CWSL*, a framework can be proposed to study the philosophy of *weishi* put forward by Xuanzang and his disciples. In defining the three levels, we eschew terms such as epistemological, ontological/metaphysical, and ethical, partly because these terms from Euro-American philosophy have their distinct nuances that do not always match that in the writings of Xuanzang and his disciples,[25] and partly also because philosophers are still debating how to demarcate one category from another. To redistribute the discursive resources and represent the position of Yogācārins based on their own writings, we replace the "epistemic–metaphysic–ethic" trio with the "descriptive–explicative–prescriptive" tripartite in the following chapters. Positioning Chinese Yogācāra in the "descriptive–explicative–prescriptive" framework, we come to understand it as a three-level study of consciousness. At the descriptive level, Xuanzang and his disciples define the meaning of consciousness, describe the functionalities of consciousness, and depict correct and incorrect knowledge of no-self and other minds. It is at this level that these Yogācārins provide substantial resources for modern studies of epistemology, especially for the debate over non-conceptualism.

Descriptions of consciousness and knowledge prepare these Yogācārins for the second explicative level. It is referred to as explicative because it is where Xuanzang and his disciples explain the ultimate nature of reality and expound on the truth of emptiness. Most of their ontological and metaphysical analyses are preserved at this level, which enables these Yogācārins to guide their readers in entering the gate of practice. At the last prescriptive level, Xuanzang and his disciples prescribe rules for action. Given that everything is empty of *svabhāvic* existence and is interdependent with others, they encourage their readers to embark on the Bodhisattvas' path to correct misperceptions through contemplation, to conduct moral actions, and to collaborate with one another in building an ideal society in the human realm. Although the last prescriptive level has not been fully explored since the modern revival of Yogācāra, it lays out the principle and mechanics for the realization of awakening, which suggests the crucial place of ethics and social construction in the Yogācāra philosophical framework. It shall be mentioned that these three levels are neither mutually exclusive nor jointly exhaustive. Nevertheless, they serve as the skillful means through which we can access the Yogācāra doctrine of consciousness-only.

3

Contextualizing Husserl's Phenomenology

Thus far, we have reviewed how Xuanzang and his disciples developed and injected innovation into the Yogācāra doctrine of consciousness-only in the Chinese context. We have also made a case for the three-level framework as one that can be derived from a foundational Yogācāra text authored by Xuanzang. In the current chapter, we will outline how Husserl began formulating his philosophical inquiries at the end of the 1880s within the greater sociopolitical climate of Germany. As such, we inquire into whether the three-level framework can also be inferred from Husserl's work and applied to the study of Husserlian phenomenology. Notably, in 1935, Husserl delivered the lecture "Die Philosophie in der Krisis der europäischen Menschheit (The Philosophy in the Crisis of European Humankind)" before the Vienna Cultural Society (Hua 6/314). Upon voicing his concern for a general crisis of meaning in Europe, Husserl explained how transcendental phenomenology could serve as the tool for liberating Europeans from this crisis (Hua 6/315). By then, it had been over fifty years since Husserl completed his doctorate at the University of Vienna in 1883.

The Influence of Franz Brentano

Born in Prossnitz, which was a city in the Austrian Empire at that time, Husserl was an assiduous student who dedicated his youth to the exploration of knowledge. After studying physics and philosophy in Leipzig and Berlin, Husserl moved to Vienna and received his doctorate in mathematics from the University of Vienna. He then stayed in Berlin to work as the assistant for Karl Weierstrass (1815–97) before returning to Vienna to study with Franz Brentano (1838–1917). Brentano's work on empirical psychology opened Husserl's eyes to a new method of studying the human mind. It is said that Brentano was a rather charismatic lecturer (Huemer 2019). He attracted a number of philosophers including Anton Marty (1847–1914), Carl Stumpf (1848–1936), Alexius Meinong (1853–1920), and Edmund Husserl, to name a few. Contemporary scholars contend that these students advanced Brentano's theories of the mind in their own directions and led to the rise of the Brentano school in modern philosophy (Dewalque 2017; Kriegel 2017).

Brentano was born and raised in a devout Catholic family (Binder 2017: 15). In his youth, he received classical training and achieved competence in scholastic philosophy. Afterward, he deepened his knowledge of ancient Greek philosophy—especially

Aristotle's system of thought—under the guidance of top Aristotelian experts Friedrich Trendelenburg (1802–72) in Berlin and Franz Clemens (1815–62) in Münster (Binder 2017: 15). As documented by Thomas Binder, Brentano gradually distanced himself from Catholicism (Binder 2017: 16). What catalyzed this change was Brentano's revised understanding of philosophy. Inspired by British empiricism and French positivism that rose to prominence in the second half of the 1800s, Brentano initiated a scientific study of the mind that would later become systematized into empirical psychology (Binder 2017: 16). Brentano's turn to science from theology epitomized the zeitgeist at that time in the wake of the Enlightenment. Most intellectuals believed that reason would furnish humans with the capacity to think and science would open the door to truth. In this disenchanted worldview, humans no longer needed to depend on any superior beings to derive a meaningful life—they could do so of their own determination.

Indeed, we can still observe Brentano's conviction in science and reason in the foreword to the first edition of his monumental *Psychologie vom empirischen Standpunkt* (*Psychology from an Empirical Standpoint*) published in 1874. As clarified by Brentano, the title of this book characterizes both the subject matter *qua* mental activities in one's experience and the method that is based on observation. In Brentano's terms, "My psychological standpoint is empirical; experience alone is my teacher" (Brentano 1995: xxvi). He speaks of psychology as the scientific study of the soul and defines the soul as the substantial bearer of various mental activities. In his analysis of mental activities, Brentano begins with the crucial distinction between inner and outer perception, which is also translated as that between internal and external perception. While inner perception furnishes one with mental phenomena, outer perception provides one with physical phenomena (Brentano 1995: 91). Among the two types of phenomena, only mental phenomena in one's inner perception have "intentional inexistence (*intentionale Inexistenz*)" because physical phenomena need the mediation of inner perception to become part of one's self-consciousness (Brentano 1995: 85–91). In formulating intentional inexistence as the salient feature of mental phenomena, Brentano introduces the concept of intentionality, a notion he borrows from scholastic philosophy to pinpoint how every mental act is directed towards an object. Drawing upon this definition of intentionality, Brentano specifies that a presentation is the presentation of something; a judgment is an affirmation or a denial of something; a love is the love of something; and a desire is the desire of something, etc. (Brentano 1995: 68).

Through inner perception, a person becomes conscious of an object and is reflexively aware of this perception. This is why Brentano characterizes each mental act as that of the twofold intentionality which enables the act to direct towards an object and revert towards itself. Tim Crane refers to this twofoldness as the primary and secondary intentionality articulated by Brentano (Crane 2017: 45). As such, Brentano *ipso facto* delineates inner perception as a mental act that is able to mediate, synthesize, and conceptualize outer perception. Therefore, inner perception can be understood as that which enables one to introspectively appraise and assess phenomena. The rules of synthesizing and conceptualizing become psychological laws that will ensure the evidence and incorrigibility of inner perception (Brentano 1995: 91).

Husserl's early study of consciousness is notably indebted to Brentano's psychology. A similar view of intentionality can be found in one of Husserl's early works, *Philosophie der Arithmetik* (*Philosophy of Arithmetic*), which was published in 1891 when Husserl was working at the University of Halle. In this book, Husserl also characterizes a mental act—or what he refers to as a "psychical act (*psychisches Akt*)"—as an act directing itself upon a phenomenon (Hua 12/69). Following Brentano, Husserl pinpoints directedness as the defining feature of a mental act. That is to say, the acts of representation, judgment, and feeling are directed upon a diversity of contents (Hua 12/69). Husserl also shares Brentano's aspiration that it is necessary to develop a rigorous science of the mind to furnish people with the indisputable truth. Phenomenology, as envisioned by Husserl, is indeed a descriptive study of experience.

Nonetheless, Husserl soon became critical of Brentano's empirical approach. What he found problematic was not so much how the scientific study of the mind should be descriptive, but rather that he grew concerned by the assumption of the existence of external objects held by Brentano in his articulation of psychology. Husserl discerns an epistemological realism in Brentano's psychology in that psychology hints at understanding the acquisition of knowledge as a causal process. Since perception begins with outer perception through which an external object is presented as a physical phenomenon, then the cause of this perception *qua* an external object must have real existence independent of the mind. Husserl points to a number of objects that can be perceived but have only fictional, imaginary existence, which demonstrates how psychology falls short in accounting for the perception of these fictionally existed objects.

Husserl detailed his critique of Brentano's psychology in the two-volume *Logische Untersuchungen* (*Logical Investigations*) released between 1900 and 1901, right before he relocated to the University of Göttingen. Towards the end of this monograph, Husserl deliberates upon whether it is possible to find an alternative approach to empirical studies of the human mind, an approach that stresses the ideal nature of consciousness. Husserl speaks of this approach as that in which "all this does not depend on the empirical contingencies of the course of consciousness" (Hua 19/704). This deliberation signals Husserl's departure from Brentanian psychology and his subsequent shift towards transcendental philosophy that explores the necessary condition for the possibility of knowledge.

Phenomenology as Transcendental Philosophy

Husserl's transcendental turn was marked by the release of *Ideen zu einer reinen Phänomenologie und phänomenologischen Philosophie. Erstes Buch* (*Ideas Pertaining to a Pure Phenomenology and to a Phenomenological Philosophy. First Book*, henceforth, *Ideas I*) in 1913. In *Ideas I*, Husserl characterizes phenomenology in the transcendental sense as the "descriptive eidetic doctrine of pure experiences (*descriptive Wesenslehre der reinen Erlebnisse*)" (Hua 3/139). Articulated in this manner, phenomenology is descriptive, since it observes phenomena in pure consciousness and examines the necessary condition for the possibility of various phenomena to appear. It is also explicative because phenomenology refutes the view of explaining the world as being pre-given to and independent of the mind.

To divorce his position from Brentano's psychology, Husserl updates most of his terminology. He introduces numerous Greek philosophical concepts into his writings and invests new meaning into these notions. For instance, Husserl replaces directedness with the *noesis–noema* correlate to define intentionality (Hua 3/189). Similarly, he evokes the Greek term *eidos* to describe essence in the phenomenological sense (Hua 3/10). *Eidos* captures the ideal nature of mental acts, which is contrasted with the abstract factuality (Hua 3/10). He continues to specify that phenomenology is not merely a scientific descriptive study of experience. By nature, phenomenology is an eidetic examination of intentional mental acts (Hua 3/57). Subsequently, the method of *epoché* is proposed by Husserl (Hua 3/57). Enacting this method, a person will first suspend the previous metaphysical assumptions along with related judgments of things, and then observe eidetically the function of mental acts (Hua 3/60). Therefore, *epoché* bespeaks a change of the way of living and perceiving, namely, a change from the natural attitude to the phenomenological attitude. Altogether, these new concepts have enriched Husserl's articulation of phenomenology.

Presenting transcendental phenomenology as the "secret nostalgia of all modern philosophy (*die geheime Sehnsucht der ganzen neuzeitlichen Philosophie*)," Husserl brings to the fore how his project is an integral part of the philosophical tradition that can be dated back to Descartes, Locke, Hume, and Kant (Hua 3/119). Husserlian scholar Iso Kern once concluded that there are three ways of enacting the phenomenological approaches: first, one can begin with the Cartesian method of doubt and depart from Cartesian dualism to enter the path of phenomenology; second, one can begin with intentional psychology and move beyond Brentano's psychologism to become a phenomenologist; and third, one can commence the study by following Kant's transcendental idealism (Kern 1962: 304).[1] In this manner, framing phenomenology as transcendental philosophy, Husserl engages in a dialogue with Immanuel Kant (1724–1804).[2] In *Ideas I*, Husserl speaks highly of Kant's transcendental philosophy, especially how Kant initiates the Copernican Revolution to place the subject in the center of knowledge for exploring the necessary condition for the possibility of appearance. Husserl particularly underscores the first edition of the *Kritik der reinen Vernunft* (*Critique of Pure Reason*) (Hua 3/119). In the first edition, Kant details how the manifold of sense data is first received in intuition, subsequently represented to the mind, then reproduced in a synthesis, and finally recognized as an objective unity in a concept (KrV A99–105). Different from this deduction, Kant prioritizes the function of understanding in the second edition where he details the way in which understanding mediates the manifolds given in intuition and combines them into a unity (KrV B130–1). Therefore, one of the major differences between these two editions comes from Kant's approach to intuition. Indeed, Kant acknowledges the roles of both intuition and understanding in the production of knowledge in the first edition, something which Husserl applauds and admires. However, what Husserl renders problematic seems to be the unmentioned second edition in which Kant fails to reserve a place for intuition in explicit knowledge but implies that anything presented to the mind is already conceptual. To this end, Husserl becomes critical of Kant's strong conceptualism in the second edition in which Kant suggests that one cannot have an experience of something unless this person can express it by means of a concept (Hua 3/119).

Husserl first raises his objection to such strong conceptualism towards the end of *Logical Investigations* (Hua 19/722). According to Husserl, when Kant derives the laws of the universal validity of knowledge from conceptual thinking, Kant miscomprehends the laws of knowledge (Hua 19/711). That is why Husserl concludes in *Ideas I* that Kant was "on the phenomenological ground (*auf phänomenologischen Boden*)" in the first edition of the transcendental deduction but eventually deviated from this realm when Kant endorsed a version of psychologism (Hua 3/119). Throughout his phenomenological analysis, Husserl mirrors Kant to shift the focus back to the subject and make the perception of various things conform to the mind. Subsequently, he departs from Kant to determine the crucial role of intuition that serves as the foundation for abstract conceptual thinking and provides meaningful content for concepts.

In investigating the constitutive nature of intuition, Husserl expands his critique from psychologism to naturalism. As a salient feature of scientific studies of the mind *qua* psychology and the world *qua* physics, naturalism entails a reductionist worldview that generalizes the world into a factual reality pre-given to the mind (Hua 3/53). As such, naturalists depict the world as a mechanical system operating on natural, physical laws. While the world is disenchanted into a mechanical universe, the mind is disembodied from lived experiences and is further treated as the unity of factually real psychological activities (Hua 3/40). Adopting the naturalist worldview, people perceive the mind and the world as separate and mutually exclusive, which propels them to miss the meaning of life (Hua 19/706). For Husserl, phenomenology is a science of essence through which people can move beyond the natural attitude. It reveals to people how abstract thinking in science requires lived experiences to be meaningful. By virtue of phenomenology, people can revert to intuition to examine how the mind and the world come to interact in the first place in experience.

Reflection on the Crisis of European Science

In *Ideas I*, Husserl problematizes naturalism owing to its limitations when producing meaningful knowledge. He gradually extends his investigation from epistemological questions to existential issues in Europe when he discerns how, armed with naturalism, science separates human consciousness from the rest of the world, further stripping away meaning from human life and reducing the world into a mechanic system. Husserl later formulates transcendental phenomenology as the remedy for the prevailing crisis of meaning in Europe (Hua 6/318).

Husserl's reflections on naturalism allude to the larger sociopolitical climate of Germany, which acted as the lived reality for Husserl and his contemporaries. Although the previous generation of intellectuals, among whom we can count Franz Brentano, placed unshakeable faith in the natural science developed in modern times (Carson 2013: 180), the next generations at the advent of the twentieth century found the predominate scientific rationalism filled with disillusionment (Gordon 2003: 29). These emotions cumulated after the First World War (Gordon 2003: 30). In postwar Weimar Germany, intellectuals sensed a pervasive crisis of meaning (Bambach 2013: 134). Driven by the doubts concerning scientific rationalism, many among the younger generation felt the need to scrutinize previously dominant systems of thought, be it positivism or neo-Kantianism (Gordon 2003: 31). As recounted by those in the East Asian intelligentsia who once looked upon Europe for modernization, the victory of science and technology did not bring humans harmony and happiness but rather reinforced egoism and egocentrism that eventually put Europe in the grip of war. For intellectuals who lived in the Weimar era, they started to experiment with their own methods to reconsider the formerly unquestioned foundation of scientific rationalism, which led to the flourish of a diversity of schools of thought across several disciplines (Gordon & McCormick 2013: 4–5). Cathryn Carson describes this inverse attitude towards science in the Weimar era as a change from the rhetoric of triumph to the narrative of crisis (Carson 2013: 183), considering how the narrative of crisis allowed for new possibilities of reimagining the scientific enterprise in modern society as well as modernity in general.

Lived through the First World War, Husserl lost one of his sons and several eminent students to the battlefield (De Warren & Vongehr 2018: 6).[3] After the Great War, he particularly expressed his concern about the crisis of meaning triggered by natural science, especially how science brought in a reductionist worldview that made meaningful life impossible (Hua 6/3–5). Once a student of natural science himself, Husserl embarked on diagnosing the crisis of European science in the hope of remedying such a crisis and renewing European culture with his transcendental phenomenology. He continued to teach and research on phenomenology at the University of Freiburg where he became an emeritus professor in 1929 (Spiegelberg 1982: 154). In his later work, Husserl extended his investigation to the genesis of intentional acts. As depicted by Husserl in *Cartesianische Meditationen* (*Cartesian Meditations*, henceforth, *Meditations*), each ego actively exercises the faculty of reason to conduct intentional mental acts (Hua 1/111). This active genesis of intentionality always presupposes a passive, primordial constitution of both subjective acts and objective phenomena upon which reason is required to act (Hua 1/112). As such, while the active genesis of intentionality elevates the ego to the center of knowledge and experience, the passive genesis pinpoints the limitation of reason (Hua 1/113). More importantly, the passive genesis pronounces the mutual constitution of the ego, the intending act, and the intended phenomena in sensation and intuition (Hua 1/113). In his stress of mutual constitution, Husserl elaborates on how the ego as one origin of intentional mental acts is not a closed system but rather collaborates with other egos to constitute a shared lived reality as a meaningful lifeworld.

Since natural science thrives on the premise of disengaging a person from the rest of the world, it construes the essence of a person as an absolute in itself—namely, as a self-determined and self-sufficient entity (Hua 17/356). It follows that a person would not need others to enjoy a meaningful life. Being cut off from the rest of the world, this person is thus the captive of solipsism, which makes a crisis of meaning inevitable. Contrariwise, phenomenology opens up the possibility for this person to perceive essence as mutually constituted with others in a lifeworld. As such, Husserl accentuates that the essence of each person is a twofold *a priori* of being in the world and being with others, in his *Die Krisis der Europäischen Wissenschaften und die Transzendentale Phänomenologie* (*The Crisis of European Science and the Transcendental Phenomenology,* henceforth, *Crisis*) (Hua 6/255-6). While Husserl attributes the loss of a meaningful life to scientific naturalism, he proposes to renew science by means of phenomenology rather than renounce it for good (Hua 6/508). Similarly, he seeks to pinpoint how reason finds its ground in intuition and how science should have its footing in the intersubjective lifeworld, but he never resolves to cancel reason permanently (Hua 6/509). Nevertheless, Husserl's reflection on scientific naturalism inspired the next generation of intellectuals who drew upon phenomenology to transform German philosophy from transcendental idealism to existential ontology (Gordon 2003: 5).[4] As such, Husserl's philosophy, especially his later work, showcases what Peter Gordon and John McCormick refer to as the continuity and crisis of Weimar thought (Gordon & McCormick 2013: 7).

The *Crisis* was expanded from the lectures Husserl delivered in front of the Vienna Cultural Society in 1935. At that time, Husserl became increasingly isolated inside academia due to his Jewish descent (Beyer 2020). As detailed by Dermot Moran, although Husserl considered himself a dedicated citizen of Germany, he was stripped of his teaching license as well as his German citizenship after the Nazi seizure of power (Moran 2005: 39-40). In 1938, Husserl passed away in Freiburg, right before the outbreak of the Second World War.

Throughout his philosophical thinking process, Husserl turns from the external world to the internal mind and eventually back to the intersubjective communal life. He calls upon community members to make a collaborative effort to resolve the crisis of meaning, a project he refers to as the phenomenological renewal (Hua 27/31). Nevertheless, Husserl does not make his diagnosis of the crisis the opening point of existential ontology or phenomenological theology. Nor does he come to analyze social reality and criticize the power dynamics in a plurality of lifeworlds by means of his phenomenological approach, although his work remains a crucial source of inspiration for the burgeoning field known as critical phenomenology. Indeed, Husserl provides the principles for moral action and community building, but he has not yet detailed the mechanics of this intended communal and cultural renewal.[5]

Two Levels in Husserl's Phenomenology

Acknowledging how Husserl has shifted his focus from epistemology to existential issues, contemporary scholars put forward their own frameworks to capture these different phases in Husserl's philosophical thinking process. Paul Ricoeur depicts Husserl's trajectory as the progress first from descriptive phenomenology to transcendental phenomenology and then from transcendental idealism to genetic phenomenology (Ricoeur 1967). That is to say, Husserl begins by describing how each mental act *qua cogito* is intentionally targeted at a phenomenon *qua cogitatum,* prior to elaborating on the metaphysical and ontological status of this phenomenon (Ricoeur

1967: 9–11). Steadily, Husserl expands his project of transcendental phenomenology so that the elaboration of the ontological status is not confined to static phenomena but expanded to the genesis of intentionality (Ricoeur 1967: 11). According to Ricoeur, Husserl's move from transcendental idealism to genetic phenomenology proves to be revolutionary in its input to French existential philosophy (Ricoeur 1967: 12). Similar to Ricoeur, Dermot Moran characterizes the systematization of Husserl's thinking as that from epistemological inquiries in his early work where Husserl criticizes and problematizes psychologism, to metaphysical and ontological discussions on the being-and-sense of what appears in consciousness (Moran 2005: 4). David Woodruff Smith regards these two consecutive moments in Husserl's phenomenology as the study of themes in logic including meaning and intentionality, and the inquiries of concepts in ontology such as essence and mind–body relations (Smith 2007: 3). Liangkang Ni presents the development of thoughts in Husserl's writings as that from the analysis of intentionality, to the investigation of subjective ideality (Ni 2010: 102). Many Husserlians continue to accentuate the importance of what Ricoeur refers to as the revolution inside transcendental phenomenology. As such, Don Welton proposes to read Husserl's phenomenology as both static and genetic (Welton 2003: 3). Anthony Steinbock argues for understanding transcendental phenomenology as both descriptive and generative (Steinbock 1995: 268). In his study of transcendental philosophy, David Carr differentiates that which is empirical from that which is transcendental in Husserl's writings to pinpoint the paradox of subjectivity, a paradox that posits each person as both the transcendental subject for the world and the empirical object in the world (Carr 1999: 134). Each of these frameworks acknowledges the ways in which Husserl, after the transcendental turn, gradually places more weight upon metaphysical and ontological inquiries than descriptive and epistemological questions.

Drawing on and developing these frameworks, I propose to borrow the terms "*beschreibende*" and "*erklärende*" from the Vienna lectures to define Husserl's phenomenological project. As remarked by Husserl later in *Crisis*, the purpose of phenomenology is to renew the schema of the "descriptive and explanatory (*beschreibende und erklärende*)" in natural science (Hua 6/224). To highlight the contrast with natural science, I translate this schema envisaged by Husserl as that of the descriptive and explicative. That is to say, the descriptive-explicative schema in phenomenology is to be demarcated from that in natural science, insofar as explication does not entail any general abstraction of the descriptions but rather finds its basis in them (Hua 6/226–7). For Husserl, phenomenology is first and foremost a descriptive science that examines and observes the essential structure of intentionality in pure consciousness (Hua 3/156). Phenomenology as a descriptive doctrine of consciousness emerges as the major theme in Husserl's early work and continues to be an integral part of his later writings. Husserl's transcendental turn is marked by the shift in focus from how objects are given to the mind to how the mind serves as the necessary condition for the possibility of the appearance of phenomena. In his articulation of phenomenology, Husserl enacts this transcendental turn as a move to the explicative level and inquires into the ultimate nature of phenomena in the domain of pure consciousness (Hua 6/229). He considers pure phenomenology as a version of transcendental idealism because it explains how there is no mind-independent reality in one's experience.

The two-level reading can be related to that in Yogācāra Buddhism, insofar as both Husserl and Chinese Yogācārins have pinpointed the intentional feature of consciousness to describe our knowledge of the (no-)self and of other minds, subsequently using this description to explain how reality is not mind-independent. Although the Yogācāra view of the mind can be related to that in Husserl, they are not completely identical. At the descriptive level, Chinese Yogācārins like Xuanzang and his disciples extend their study to extreme mental states (such as pre-death experiences) and associate mental acts with their moral consequences. Furthermore, at the explicative level, these Chinese Yogācārins and Husserl put forward dissimilar positions as to the concept of essence. As such, it is possible to explore how, on the one hand, their related yet different views of knowledge can advance the current discussion on non-conceptualism, and how, on the other hand, the problem of essence can be tackled.

Having identified the descriptive and explicative levels in both Yogācāra Buddhism and Husserl's phenomenology, we continue to deliberate upon whether Husserl has formulated the prescriptive level of consciousness in his phenomenology. Hanne Jacobs once addressed the question in a similar fashion, regarding how the phenomenological study of lived experience can inform everyday action (Jacobs 2013: 363). As mentioned in the previous chapter, the term "prescriptive" is used to capture normative values for actions that lead to the transformative process of awakening in Yogācāra Buddhism. Defining "prescriptive" in this manner, I maintain, as noted earlier, that the prescriptive level remains rather nascent in Husserl's phenomenology. Although Husserl alludes to a need for becoming awake to genuine humanity in his proposal of renewing European culture, he only outlines the basic principles for moral action and community building (Hua 27/51). Nor does he prescribe the mechanics of such a phenomenological renewal of life and culture. Therefore, phenomenology in the Husserlian sense is teleological (Hua 6/509), likely even soteriological, but hardly prescriptive in any explicit manner. And so, differing from the nascent account of awakening in Husserl's phenomenology, Chinese Yogācārins like Xuanzang and his disciples, who also endorse a worldview that can be interpreted as transcendental idealism, articulate concrete mechanics for individual contemplative rituals, community building, and the construction of an ideal society. For these Yogācārins, awakening is not an individual achievement but a universal realization through the collaborative effort of all sentient beings.

Given this difference at the prescriptive level, we refuse to reduce Chinese Yogācāra into a mere Buddhist version of Husserlian phenomenology. More importantly, the prescriptive level entails what happens after one reverts from the internal mind to the external world. For Husserl, the reversion back to exteriority reminds one of the importance of conducting moral actions and community building in an intersubjective lifeworld where each individual can lead a meaningful life. In particular, Husserl tries to locate a middle path between the naturalistic practice of this-worldly science and the religious pursuit of other-worldly transcendence (Hua 6/508). That is why he underlies how transcendental phenomenology enables a person to realize and renew a meaningful life on the historical horizon of a lifeworld (Hua 6/510–11). In this manner, living a phenomenological life requires a person to constantly reflect upon and be critical of any given viewpoints, norms, and values, through which the selfhood of this person is always in the making together with other persons (Hua 6/513). Husserl delineates such a process of the composition (*Dichtung*) of selfhood, from any naïve way of living undergirded by both scientific naturalism (that takes scientific reason *per se* as the absolute and unshakable) and religious faith (that perceives the divinely revealed truth as the unconditional and unquestionable) (Hua 6/508–9). Following Husserl's suggestion of philosophizing on the historical horizon of a lifeworld (Hua 6/510), we can perceive his deliberations upon the realization and renewal of a meaningful life as an integral part of the development of what Charles Taylor refers to as the Enlightenment secularism in Europe (Taylor 2007: 559).

As Husserl remarks in his reading notes, Buddhism presents a transcendental, rather than transcendent, philosophy that turns inward to pursue the absolute truth (Hua 27/125). Indeed, Yogācāra Buddhists like Xuanzang and his disciples enact a turn towards the mind to argue for emptiness and then a return to the external communal life. Nevertheless, for Xuanzang and his disciples, the return to exteriority is an affirmation of superiority in that it marks the beginning of the Bodhisattvas' path through which people can purify their minds through contemplation, help others remove their misperception, and finally collaborate with one another in constituting an ideal society for their fellow sentient beings. Hence, a universal awakening in the Yogācāra sense also does not entail an achievement of any other-worldly transcendence or a break-away from this-worldly life. It is realized through a collaborative effort of all sentient beings, which bespeaks the highest goal of Buddhist practice.

The nascent account of awakening in Husserl's philosophical thinking has been acknowledged by several scholars who consider Husserl's work foundational to the contemporary phenomenological movement. Indeed, drawing on Husserl's writings, phenomenologists championed by Edith Stein (1891–1942) have put forward more systematic forms of phenomenological theology.[6] More recently, scholars championed by Alia Al-Saji and Lisa Guenther have employed the phenomenological approach to address critical issues related to race, gender, class, and social justice, which facilitates the development of critical phenomenology.[7] To this day, phenomenology in its widest sense has become a distinct discipline in contemporary philosophy that furnishes scholars with an approach to the structure of consciousness as well as people's lived experience. Phenomenology continues to flourish and has been incorporated into religious studies, psychology, cognitive science, and critical studies.

Thus far, we have made a case for the three-level framework through demonstrating how it is modeled on seminal works in Husserl's phenomenology and Chinese Yogācāra philosophy articulated by Xuanzang and his disciples. Such a framework epitomizes the "both–and" approach, which aims at *both* maintaining the distinctiveness of each tradition in its own context for exploring their middle ground *and* manifesting their interconnectedness in the broader space of meaning for tackling shared philosophical questions. Placing these two intellectual traditions on an equal footing with one another, we have compared these three levels to the road, the tracks, and the destination. More importantly, we present how and why the East–West dichotomy at the center of

Orientalism overgeneralizes philosophical traditions in terms of the simplified opposition between non-rationality and rationality. Now that we have elucidated our methodologies and found an approach to properly recognize and represent these traditions, we can continue our journey and examine the road traveled by Husserl and Chinese Yogācārins, beyond Orientalism.

Part Two

The Road

Employing the "both-and" approach, we can set out on our journey with Husserl and the Chinese Yogācārins, together exploring the ways in which they follow the same road but leave different tracks. In the second part of this book, we will be focusing on the "road," namely, the descriptive levels of phenomenology and Yogācāra philosophy. Our examination centers on the articulations of the intentionality of consciousness and the descriptions of knowledge as presented and preserved in these two traditions. To commence our examination, I would like to ask the following question: how does one come to perceive the things one experiences? In our daily lives, we tend to take the functionality of consciousness for granted. As I wake up in the morning, I am immediately aware of my surroundings: I hear the rain pattering against the window; I see the leaves rustling on the tree in front of my house; I feel my cat licking my hand, and so forth. Even while I am asleep, my mind experiences a plethora of objects: some real, such as the cold breeze from my open window; others imagined, such as the unicorn flying over my head in my dreams. Though we rarely stop to consider how all of this takes place, many of the great minds throughout history have been intrigued by the functionality of consciousness, including the protagonists of this book: Edmund Husserl and the Chinese Yogācārins such as Xuanzang and his disciples.

We refer to our examination of mental activities as "descriptive" insofar as they represent the ways in which mental acts (such as the acts of perceiving, intuiting, imagining, or judging) are directed towards an object. That is to say, the mental act of perception is always a perceiving *of* something—be it the rain, the tree, the cat, and so forth. Equally so, the mental act of dreaming is always a dreaming *of* something, such as the unicorn. Therefore, every mental act is characterized by the salient feature of directedness that opens the mind to the world. In virtue of these mental acts, we come to perceive and subsequently acquire knowledge of that which enters into our experience.

We utilize the term "descriptive" to replace the more widely used notion of "epistemological," partly because the term "descriptive" is more in line with the terminology used by Husserl to define his phenomenological approach, and partly also because the Euro-American notion of knowledge cannot be directly imposed upon Yogācāra Buddhism. Husserl defines phenomenology as the descriptive study of consciousness (Hua 3/139). He argues that being *descriptive* is required in order to observe the ways in which we perceive the world and deduce what lies beyond our empirical perception. In this way, being "descriptive" characterizes a science not only on par with but also more rigorous than any other empirical sciences, which in turn gives Husserl's phenomenological approach legitimacy (Hua 3/139). In the meantime, the term "epistemology" prioritizes how we arrive at the knowledge of an object, further subordinating the question of how our mind perceives to the question of knowledge acquisition itself. If that is the case, then the term "epistemological" leads us too far ahead of where Yogācārins insist that we begin, that is, understanding the functionality of consciousness for realizing emptiness. Thus, for these Yogācārins, achieving a descriptive understanding of consciousness comes before—and further secures—an epistemic account of the mind's cognitive faculty.

To further elaborate on the notion of "descriptive"—a notion that serves as the hallmark of this part of our discussion—we summarize the goals of a descriptive study of consciousness in the following manner:

1. A descriptive study of consciousness depicts how mental acts are always intentional in one's experience.
2. Intentionality allows for examining mental acts from three perspectives: the first-person perspective (subjective), the second-person perspective (intersubjective), and the third-person perspective (objective).
3. Intentionality provides one with the tools to conduct a rigorous examination of mental acts at all levels, including the conceptual and non-conceptual acts, as well as the active and passive acts.
4. Such a rigorous examination enables one to describe the connections of mental acts, especially how a compounded act can be built upon and therefore become dependent on the simplest acts of presenting.
5. The connections of mental acts depict how one comes to acquire and justify knowledge, especially that of (no-)self and that of other minds.
6. A study of consciousness at the descriptive level lays the methodological foundation for elucidating the ultimate nature of reality at the explicative level.

As such, both Husserl and Chinese Yogācārins conduct a comprehensive examination of the intentionality of mental acts at the descriptive level through which they are able to depict the production of knowledge. As I will argue, their characterizations of consciousness are compatible, though hardly identical, insofar as Xuanzang and his disciples extend their investigations to extreme mental states (such as the pre-death experience) and these Chinese Yogācārins bind mental acts with their moral consequences. Given that they both employ their respective descriptions of consciousness when investigating the origin of knowledge, it is possible to draw inspiration from their writings to mark the limits of conceptuality and make a case for non-conceptualism.

In Chapter 4, we will survey Husserl's notion of intentionality. There, I demonstrate how Husserl enriches the formulation of intentionality in four phases of his philosophical thinking process. Throughout these phases, we can see that he gradually departs from Brentanian psychologism to develop his transcendental phenomenology and expands his phenomenological investigation from that of the individual mind to that of a *plurality* of minds. As a result, intentionality characterizes how consciousness is not only directed towards objects but also points back to the underlying flow. To put it differently, consciousness is always the consciousness *of* and the consciousness *for*. Husserl's notion of intentionality can therefore be related to that in Yogācāra Buddhism, as Chinese Yogācārins also define consciousness through the intentional relation of intending acts, the intended objects, and the underlying flow of consciousness. Thus, in Chapter 5, we will investigate the Yogācāra view of consciousness and its mental factors in order to examine how Xuanzang and his disciples depict the knowledge of no-self and other minds.

Although the Yogācāra conception of intentionality can be related to that of Husserl, the two are not identical. Their similar but non-identical view of intentionality prompts us to investigate the underlying assumptions held by the conceptualist view of experience and knowledge, which shall become the focus of Chapter 6. In particular, our investigation will enable us to problematize the ways in which the Orientalists construe Eastern thinking as non-rational and Western thoughts as rational as if rationality and non-rationality were mutually exclusive. Therefore, upon scrutinizing what it is meant to be conceptual and what counts as the content of a mental act, we explore whether and how these two intellectual traditions can furnish us with the necessary resources for rethinking the meaning of (non-)conceptuality. In this part of our journey, we follow the "both–and" approach in *both* placing these two intellectual traditions in their respective cultural and linguistic context for exploring their middle ground *and* enabling them to move into a broader horizon for conversations on non-conceptualism.

4

Intentionality in Husserl's Phenomenology

In contemporary philosophy, intentionality is commonly understood as the feature of directedness or aboutness.[1] That is to say, intentionality describes how a mental act is always *directed* towards an object and is therefore *about* an object. As clarified by Elizabeth Anscombe, "like many concepts marked by intentionality, though unlike intention itself, these are expressed by verbs commonly taking direct objects" (Anscombe 1965: 159). Intentionality is important in contemporary philosophy of mind because it indicates how every mental act has a structure. To be more specific, in every mental act, there are two inseparable and interdependent constituents—namely, the act of perceiving, imagining, judging, feeling, etc., and the targeted object to be perceived, imagined, judged, felt, etc.

The concept of intentionality is fundamental to phenomenology because Husserl uses this concept to lay the grounds for his investigation of knowledge.[2] In his own terms, intentionality stands "at the beginning of phenomenology (*zu Anfang der Phänomenologie*)" (Hua 3/172). Throughout his life, Husserl continues to develop and enrich the concept of intentionality.[3] To facilitate our understanding of this expansive concept, as well as its function in Husserl's phenomenological project, I differentiate four phases in Husserl's philosophical thinking process:

1. In the first phase, intentionality entails the feature of directedness (Hua 19/379). The concept of intentionality helps Husserl outline the pure principles of knowledge, which are integral parts of his critique of psychologism.
2. After his transcendental turn, intentionality is rearticulated in terms of the *noesis–noema* correlate (Hua 3/169).[4] In the second phase, this concept performs the function of demarcating transcendental phenomenology from naturalism and thus undergirding Husserl's view of knowledge.
3. In the third phase, intentionality is described as the *ego–cogito–cogitatum* schema (Hua 1/87). The expanded notion of intentionality is central to a phenomenological theory of temporality and selfhood in Husserl's later writings.
4. In the last phase when Husserl tackles the issue of solipsism, intentionality is formulated as the tripartite structure of the *we*, the acts of intending, and the intended phenomena (Hua 6/187–9). Such an account of intentionality demonstrates how phenomenology at its descriptive level is an analysis of experience from the first-person, second-person, and third-person perspectives, which enables Husserl to unravel a general crisis of meaning triggered by naturalism in modern Europe.

Our examination in the current chapter is admittedly far from exhaustive, yet it nevertheless demonstrates how Husserl departs from Brentanian psychologism to initiate his transcendental phenomenology, and gradually expands his phenomenological investigation from that of an individual mind to that of a plurality of individual minds *qua* the consciousness of the *we*. Through tracing the trajectory of Husserl's theory of intentionality, I contend that intentionality describes how mental acts allow objects to appear as phenomena for individuals. Consciousness is intentional because it is always the consciousness of something.

Phase 1: Intentionality as Directedness

Husserl introduces the concept of intentionality in his early writings when he speaks of intentionality as directedness. In his reformulation of directedness, Husserl specifies how directedness encapsulates a two-place relation between that which directs itself towards and that which can be directed upon. As he further unpacks in *Logical Investigations*, this two-place relation involves the quality (*Qualität*) and the matter (*Materie*) of a mental act. That is to say, quality refers to the general character of a mental act and defines a mental act as such, to be contrasted with the matter that amounts to the content of the act and captures what the act is about (Hua 19/412). Together, quality and matter are two heterogeneous, yet inseparable, constituents of an intentional mental act (Hua 19/411). For instance, Cindy's recollection of her cat sleeping by the window is different from her perception of the cat sleeping by the window. Such a difference is contingent upon the quality of the mental act: while the matters of these two mental acts remain the same—namely, the cat sleeping by the window—the quality of these two acts (recollecting versus perceiving) bespeaks their respective distinctness. Likewise, two acts of the same quality can possess dissimilar matter. That is why Cindy's recollection of her cat sleeping by the window is not the same as her recollection of her cat sleeping on the sofa.

Husserl's conception of intentionality prepares him for his investigation of knowledge. For Husserl, knowledge of an object is acquired and justified when various intentional mental acts present such an object as it is (Hua 19/572). To this end, Husserl puts forward several principles of knowledge that are derived from his notions of founding, fulfillment, and identification (Hua 19/572). Through the concept of founding, Husserl explains how intentional mental acts build on one another. Husserl begins his explanation with a discussion of sensuous perception as an act of perceiving in which the content appears as the perceived object (Hua 19/508). For instance, when Cindy perceives the Christmas tree in the foyer of McGill University's Birks Building, she sees it in a straightforward manner, as right in front of her eyes. Husserl refers to this way of seeing an object as the narrow and popular meaning of seeing, and this way of perceiving as the narrow and popular meaning of perceiving (Hua 19/646). However, the Christmas tree is not all that Cindy perceives; when she perceives the Christmas tree, she also perceives it as part of the entire foyer. Although the content of her perception of the Christmas tree in the foyer is still presented in a straightforward manner, Husserl identifies something new about this act of perceiving. The act aims at the overall state of affairs *qua* "the Christmas tree is in the foyer," in which "the Christmas tree" and "the foyer" are both sensed objects presented through individual acts of perceiving whereas the prepositional term "in" corresponds not to any particular object but to the relation between the Christmas tree and the foyer (Hua 19/652).

At this point, Husserl expands the meaning of seeing and perceiving to capture this straightforward presentation of a state of affairs, a state that encapsulates a situation or a set of circumstances, such as "the Christmas tree is in the foyer." He coins the term "categorial intuition (*kategoriale Anschauung*)" to describe any mental act that is directed towards a state of affairs (*Sachverhalt*) (Hua 19/653). To further delineate how the act of perceiving an entire state of affairs is built on several simple acts of perceiving each specific object, Husserl introduces the concept of founding (*fundierende*) (Hua 19/403). It is therefore through founding that a plurality of simple acts become integral parts of one unified, singular act that has its own intentional directedness (Hua 19/403). Seeing the state of affairs in categorial intuition does not mean seeing with one's eyes but rather it entails grasping the state of affairs "in one stroke (*in einem Schlage*)" (Hua 19/646). As such, categorial intuition becomes an intuitive act in a supersensuous sense that is founded on a wide range of sensuous intuitions (Hua 19/654).

The process of founding does not stop at categorial intuition. Husserl moves on to the idea of universal intuition, which describes how higher levels of abstraction can continue to compound one another. Husserl portrays this higher level of abstraction as synthesizing a number of mental acts of intuitions (Hua 19/669). The object of universal intuition *qua* an "idea (*Idee*)" can be seen in the sense that an idea can be grasped in a straightforward manner (Hua 19/670). There also arise even more abstract acts of conceptual thinking—such as symbolizing, signifying, and expressing—each one further founded on the act of universal intuition. The concept of founding, therefore, explains how simple acts of presenting can be combined and compounded to give rise to more complex, higher-level acts.

While founding is mainly concerned with the formation of mental acts, fulfillment and identification are largely about the meaningfulness of such acts (Hua 19/634–5). A founded act is indeed more abstract regarding its quality, yet such an act does not yield knowledge unless its content is fulfilled by certain matter. For instance, Cindy can think about the Christmas tree in the foyer of McGill University's Birks Building, but it does not mean she has knowledge about that tree. The thought—or in Husserl's terms, the meaning-intention (*Bedeutungsintention*)—is empty unless its content is fulfilled by perpetual matter. When Cindy walks into the Birks Building and sees the Christmas tree, her perception of this tree confirms her abstract thought, and the thought generates knowledge in the sense that the content of the thought is fulfilled by the matter in perception. Yet, if Cindy does not see a tree but instead sees a bookshelf in its place, her abstract thought of the tree remains empty and meaningless so that it offers no valid knowledge about the Christmas tree in the Birks Building. This example illustrates that knowledge of the Christmas tree can only be acquired when the content of a mental act is fulfilled—in other words, when what is meant meets what is presented.

As it stands, Husserl formulates the concept of fulfillment (*Erfüllung*) to explain how knowledge arises in synthesis as a coherent combination of the quality and the matter of a mental act through which an object itself is presented to consciousness (Hua 19/572). The abstract act of thinking can obtain its meaning when the content of a thought, or a meaning-intention, is fulfilled by intuition (Hua 19/624). Categorial intuition can be seen and grasped in one stroke when its content is fulfilled by ideally structured sensuous intuitions, and sensuous intuition can be perceived when its content is presented (Hua 19/625). While founding allows a person to exercise the power of reason to engage in abstract thinking, fulfilling brings reason back to the starting point of intuition in which an object itself is presented (Hua 19/690). Once what is meant becomes identical with what is presented, knowledge becomes true. The notion of identification (*Identifizierung*) is hereby used when a person attests to whether the knowledge is true or not (Hua 19/630).[5]

Husserl is confident that these principles allow for a more nuanced view of knowledge than what is possible under Brentanian psychologism.[6] As detailed by Husserl in the "Appendix (*Beilage*)" to the Sixth Investigation, upon formulating intentionality as directedness to external objects—namely, as directedness to objects that transcend consciousness—Brentano presupposes the real existence of these objects (Hua 19/745). Subsequently, Brentano espouses subjectivism upon construing knowledge as the product of psychological laws, laws that are deduced through how inner perceptions represent the external objects directly given through outer perceptions (Hua 19/746). Scrutinizing Brentano's viewpoint, Husserl finds this subjectivism inherent in Brentano's psychology as well as the dogmatic metaphysical assumption of the existence of objects problematic (Hua 19/744). Husserl renders the distinction between the inner and the outer ineffective, since both physical and psychical objects need to be transformed into the ideal content of a mental act (Hua 19/744).

In light of his analysis of intentionality, Husserl contends that knowledge goes beyond the realm of factual reality—be it physical matters or psychological activities—by virtue of intentionality. If that is the case, anything whose nature is psycho-physical cannot provide the universal and necessary conditions for the possibility of knowledge and science in general (Hua 19/744). As such, knowledge is not secured by psychological laws through which a person can examine, scrutinize, and reflect on what is presented to the mind (Hua 18/240). Nor is knowledge attested to by laws that govern physically real objects (*Gegenstände*) (Hua 19/744). Quite to the contrary: the *a priori* laws of knowledge pertain to the realm of ideality and consist in the principles based on the notions of founding, fulfilling, and identifying (Hua 19/698).[7] In Husserl's presentation, phenomenology differs from Brentano's psychology in that phenomenology explores these *a priori* laws through a thorough investigation of the phenomena (Hua 19/744). The manifested phenomenon—as all experiences in an ego's experiential unity—is pure, not only because it is more than factuality, but also because it demonstrates the mutual constitution of that which intends and that which is intended. As to be seen shortly, Husserl's pronouncement that pure phenomenology "does not build on the ground" and "it makes no empirical assertions, it propounds no judgments that relate to objects transcending consciousness," heralds his discussion of *epoché* (Hua 19/744). His definition of matter as ideal, not factually real, entails his promotion of transcendental idealism. Indeed, through the inquiry into the *a priori* laws of knowledge, Husserl comes to establish phenomenology as the theory of essence (*Wesenslehre*) in *Ideas I*.

Phase 2: *Noesis–Noema* Correlate

Aspiring to replace psychologism with a more plausible alternative, Husserl begins to revise his articulation of intentionality to ensure that mental acts are not limited to those about factually existent objects. For Husserl, this alternative presents consciousness as that which goes beyond the realm of factual reality (Hua 19/705). In *Logical Investigations*, Husserl does not explicitly delineate this alternative, although he continually accentuates the contrast between the ideal and the real. It is only at the beginning of the second phase of his philosophical thinking process that he brings this alternative to the fore, which he refers to as transcendental phenomenology. Differing from psychology and other natural sciences, phenomenology is a science of essence (*eidos*), not one of matters of fact (Hua 3/4–10). Furthermore, as a transcendental philosophy, phenomenology shifts the focus from how real objects are given to the mind, to how the mind serves as the necessary condition for the possibility of the appearance of these objects. In light of this shift, Husserl renews his terminology. He redefines intentionality as the *noesis–noema* correlate or the *noetic–noematic* structure in *Ideas I* (Hua 3/189–93). For Husserl, the *noesis–noema* correlate is the name of "all-inclusive phenomenological structures (*durchgehender phänomenologischer Strukturen*)" of consciousness (Hua 3/169).

The *noetic–noematic* structure is encapsulated in Husserl's widely known formula, consciousness is "the consciousness *of* something (*Bewusstsein von etwas*)" (Hua 3/177–82). In this formula, the italicized "*of*" can be considered as Husserl's accentuation of the twofold relationship between the act of consciousness that makes people "conscious of," and the phenomenon for people to be "conscious of." It follows that *noesis* describes which kind of act has been emitted by consciousness to seize upon a phenomenon (Hua 3/176), and *noema* reveals the phenomenon as the object appears in the mind (Hua 3/182). To understand how the *noetic–noematic* structure becomes Husserl's new expression of intentionality in the second phase of his philosophical thinking process, it is helpful to explore the function of this structure in Husserl's transcendental phenomenology, that is, how the *noetic–noematic* structure underpins transcendental phenomenology and how it undergirds Husserl's view of knowledge.

Noesis and *noema* are integral parts of Husserl's transcendental phenomenology. What demarcates a transcendental, pure phenomenology from any natural scientific studies of matters of fact is the distinct *attitude* adopted by phenomenologists. Husserl uses the term "attitude (*Einstellung*)" to capture "a habitually fixed style of willing life (*einen habituell festen Stil des Willensleben*)" (Hua 6/326). Hence, different attitudes bespeak dissimilar habitual styles of perceiving and living. The phenomenological attitude describes the habitual lifestyle and worldview of phenomenologists, whilst the natural attitude is embraced by the main antagonists of phenomenology *qua* naturalists.

According to Husserl, naturalists have internalized the natural attitude and are conditioned to perpetuate assumptions about the factually existent actuality

(*Wirklichkeit*) of various objects in the world (Hua 3/53). That is why naturalists are prone to reduce the objects around them to factually existent realities independent of their consciousness. To be more specific, they take it as a given that these objects exist prior to the perception of them. Husserl speaks of followers of the Brentanian psychologism as representatives of naturalism, for they maintain that objects are given directly to the mind through perception. As the first cause of knowledge, these objects must have pre-existed on their own. That is why naturalists do not doubt the independent existence of things in the factual world (Hua 3/53). When naturalists put aside these assumptions and proceed through a radical alteration, they come to adopt the phenomenological attitude that is pure and devoid of any assumptions. In a phenomenological attitude, these individuals regain access to the domain of pure consciousness to start their phenomenological inquiry of mental activities (Hua 3/53).

Husserl refers to the radical alteration from a natural attitude to a phenomenological attitude as "ἐποχή (*epoché*)" (Hua 3/56). He borrows this term from ancient Greek philosophy whose original meaning is to suspend judgment, for highlighting how this change of attitude requires a person to put aside all assumptions about the material, factual existence of objects (Hua 3/60). For Husserl, *epoché* is a two-step process of phenomenological reduction *qua* bracketing and transcendental reduction *qua* seeing the essence (Hua 3/60). That is to say, upon enacting *epoché*, a person first performs phenomenological reduction to suspend all the assumptions and the related judgments of factually existent actuality (Hua 3/57). Afterward, this person is able to revert to the domain of pure consciousness (Hua 3/60). In virtue of transcendental reduction, this person comes to grasp the essential condition that allows for the possibility of objects to appear as phenomena and manifest themselves through intentionality (Hua 3/60). Through *epoché*, this person opens the eyes to how an object is not passively given to the mind but rather relies on the activities of the mind to appear as a phenomenon. As such, in this person's pure consciousness, those that can appear as phenomena are not limited to factually real objects but are inclusive of the ideal ones. Accordingly, seeing the essence implies figuratively how this person grasps in one stroke an object, a state of affairs, a universally idealized object, and the *a priori* self-evident laws of knowledge.

To illustrate the notion of *epoché*, Husserl puts forward the example of perceiving a blossoming apple tree (Hua 3/182–3). That is to say, for a real person like Cindy, if she is in her natural attitude, the tree exists as a matter of fact outside of and therefore transcendent to her mind. From naturalist-Cindy's perspective, her perception of this tree and her liking of this tree are nothing but contingent, real psychical states of a real person like Cindy. Upon enacting *epoché*, Cindy is supposed to put aside all her convictions about the tree and human psyches. As described by Husserl, Cindy shall suspend her generally held presumptions on the existence of things in the physical and psychological realms (Hua 3/182). Such a suspension opens the door to the transcendental realm of pure consciousness. Now, naturalist-Cindy transforms into phenomenologist-Cindy who shifts her focus to the universal and necessary condition for the possibility of the appearance of an object. Phenomenologist-Cindy comes to see things as they actually are, that is, both the perceiving and the perceived, both the liking and the liked, are given as essentially correlated on the ground of phenomenologically pure mental acts in the transcendental stream of a mental process (Hua 3/183). As

Husserl likes to say, an apple tree of factuality out there can be burnt into ashes or cut into pieces in front of naturalist-Cindy, but the apple tree as a *noema* can never be burnt up or chopped down, in the pure consciousness of phenomenologist-Cindy (Hua 3/183). A *noema* retains all the nuance of the features and attributes of the corresponding object, due to the essential *noesis–noema* structure that correlates the mental act with its phenomenon (Hua 3/184).

That is why Husserl depicts the "fundamental correlation between *noesis* and *noema* (*fundamentalen Korrelation zwischen Noesis und Noema*)" as the universal, all-inclusive structure of mental acts in pure consciousness (Hua 3/189). He employs this structure to explain the widest sphere of intentionality (Hua 3/189). In this structure, the concept of correlation stresses how mental acts are not directed to any factually real objects exterior to the mind, but rather correlated with ideal phenomena in pure consciousness. By nature, the *noesis–noema* correlate is transcendentally ideal, not factually real. Husserl continues to express this ideality as a "halo of undetermined determinability (*Hof von unbestimmter Bestimmbarkeit*)" (Hua 3/130). What is given at a specific time and place is undetermined, insofar as this *noesis–noema* correlation of several mental acts remains a possibility. Nevertheless, what is given at each time is also determinable, insofar as nothing can be experienced without the *noetic–noematic* structure. As such, Husserl highlights how the mind does not passively receive a given object but rather actively serves as the condition for the possibility, or, for the undetermined determinability, of a phenomenon.

Aside from supporting Husserl's articulation of transcendental phenomenology, the *noetic–noematic* structure likewise facilitates Husserl's exploration of the origin of knowledge and the connection of intentional mental acts at all levels. As expressed by Husserl, the universal *noetic–noematic* structure of pure consciousness characterizes the acts from the simple act of presenting to the more abstract acts of liking and judging. When the *noesis* is founded on one another, the correlated *noema* arises accordingly (Hua 3/193). Returning to the previous example of perceiving an apple tree, upon feeling happy and liking after seeing the blossoming apple tree, phenomenologist-Cindy can continue to make a judgment that this apple tree is auspicious. In any phenomenological inquiry, as Husserl contends, phenomenologist-Cindy comes to see the correlation of judgment-*noesis* and judgment-*noema* (Hua 3/195). The *noesis* of this judgment of the tree is founded on previous *noetic* acts of perceiving and liking, further defining the act of judging as such. Understood in a *noetic* sense, judging is just "as any judging whatever, with an eidetic universality determined purely by the form" (Hua 3/197). The correlated *noema* of this specific judgment becomes the state of affairs about the blossoming apple tree (Hua 3/195). All these acts can further give rise to abstract thinking. Phenomenologist-Cindy can talk about this apple tree even when she does not have it in front of her eyes. As Husserl remarks, "everything is connected by eidetic relations, thus especially *noesis* and *noema*" (Hua 3/194). Considering the way in which more abstract acts of thinking can be founded and constituted, curious readers might immediately question the objectivity of *noema*. Husserl is positive that there pertains to every *noema* an objective core (*Gegenstandskerne*) (Hua 3/273). Nevertheless, how and why can the object always appear as the same *noema* first after *epoché* and then after continuous founding? The issue of objectivity continues to transpire, which Husserl finds necessary to tackle in order to make phenomenology the remedy of subjectivism.

Phase 3: *Ego–Cogito–Cogitatum*

In tandem with his elaboration on the *noesis–noema* correlate, Husserl is confronted with another question. If consciousness is always the consciousness-of, then how do these intentional mental acts arise and perish in a unified stream of consciousness? When using the *noetic–noematic* structure to trace the connection of intentional acts at all levels, Husserl continues to inquire into the question of the unity of conscious activities of a person (Hua 3/168). This question of unity leads Husserl to investigate temporality. Since temporality cannot be reduced to what Brentano refers to as the linear process of the succession and association of inner perceptions, Husserl proposes to initiate a phenomenological account pertaining to how intentional mental acts of the past, present, and future coalesce with one another to form a unified stream of consciousness. In his proposal, the schema of *ego–cogito–cogitatum* gradually comes to be Husserl's new definition of intentionality. As an expansion of the *noesis–noema* binary, the *ego–cogito–cogitatum* schema fulfills the function of providing a phenomenological theory of temporality and selfhood.

In his phenomenological investigation of temporality, Husserl first conducts *epoché* and shifts to the phenomenological attitude. As such, he is able to suspend any convictions about the natural time that can be measured through watches, clocks, calendars, or any other chronometers (Hua 10/4). Husserl continues to examine a distinct set of mental acts that make the entire temporal experience coalesce into what he calls the "inner time (*immanente Zeit*)" (Hua 10/5). To avoid any possible interference of spatiality, Husserl selects melody as the exemplar of temporal objects that do not occupy any material space (Hua 10/6). He then details how inner time unfolds as a "two-dimensional infinite series (*zweidimensionale unendliche Reihe*)" (Hua 10/10).[8] To understand this two-dimensional infinite series, let us turn to Husserl's example of our perception of melody.

Take a melody, for instance, which consists of a series of tones such as tone 1, tone 2, tone 3, etc. When we are listening to a melody, our impression of the first tone as T1 passes away and gives its place to the impression of tone 2 in the current now-moment. Instead of vanishing, the past T1 is preserved in its absence from the present moment of tone 2 (T2) and becomes sedimented together with T2. Husserl defines this act of preserving the immediately passed impression as "retention (*Retention*)," which brings in a unique kind of temporal intentionality (Hua 10/31). As detailed by Husserl, the *noetic* act of retention is founded on the simple presenting of tone 1. The *noematic* content of this retention, then, remains the same as that in the primal impression of the previous moment. That is to say, the content of retention is that which appears as tone 1. Retention of tone 1 as T1' co-exists with our primal impression of tone 2 (T2) in the current now-moment. Likewise, we have another unique intentionality that captures the immediate future of tone 3 (T3), which Husserl refers to as protention (*Protention*) of tone 3 as T3" (Hua 10/53). The intentional act of protention explains our spontaneous feeling of being startled when we are enjoying Beethoven's symphony and the music suddenly changes to one of Taylor Swift's pop songs. As such, for every single moment when it becomes the now-moment where the current impression takes place, its immediate past is sedimented through retention and its near future is foreseen through protention. If impression co-exists with retention and protention in the current moment of experience (Hua 10/29), a temporal horizon soon opens up as a horizon in the up-and-down direction between T3", T2, and T1', which brings the immediate past and the upcoming future together in this very now-moment (Hua 10/44). Eventually, founded on the acts of retention, impression, and protention, there arises the act of perceiving the whole *qua* T3"-T2-T1' that synthesizes the past tone 1, the present tone 2, and the upcoming tone 3. Those which are absent in this current now-moment like the immediate past and the near future, do not vanish. Rather, they persist as the backdrop for the present now-perception on the temporal horizon. It is in virtue of this horizon that we do not hear any individual tone as a tone-in-itself, when listening to a melody. On the contrary, each singular tone is heard upon this horizon as an integrated part of the melody as-a-whole. Such a horizon as that of T3"-T2-T1' in every single moment points to the up–down dimension—as the first infinite dimension—of inner time consciousness.

Similarly, our experience of the distant past and future unfolds throughout our lives on a continuous horizon. Husserl depicts this horizon as the left–right dimension in the continuum of consciousness of all the moments between T1, T2, and T3 etc. Such a horizon as that of T1-T2-T3 stretches in the left-and-right direction, which becomes the second infinite dimension of inner time consciousness. When one perception flows away into the past, its retention–impression–protention in the related moment becomes afloat in our stream of consciousness (Hua 10/85). By flowing (*fließend*), Husserl is bearing in mind the aforementioned character of undetermined determinability, in comparison to the determined retention–impression–protention in our perception of the current now-moment *qua* the perception of T3"-T2-T1' right here right now (Hua 10/85). The undetermined yet determinable previous retention–impression–protention will not be determined again until it is reproduced in our recollection. Sometimes, it is easy to determine this possibility and reproduce previous retention–impression–protentions when we summon our earlier perceptions from time to time. Yet, it is also commonplace that memories can escape us if, say, we attempt to recollect the face of a childhood friend and the face just does not come to mind right away. The same can be said for anticipation. We can anticipate what will happen in the future after being conditioned by our previous experience, even though we will never actually know what the future will be until it takes place. For instance, we have come to expect that our cat will jump onto our bed at five o'clock in the morning, but this anticipation remains empty until it becomes determined every day at 5 a.m. The new model of recollection–perception–anticipation, thus, extends its arms to our entire temporal experience and ensures experiential coalescence.

As such, a temporal horizon is two-dimensional. It unrolls not only in the up–down dimension in virtue of retention–impression–protention, but also through recollection–perception–anticipation in the left–right dimension. The former is inherent to the consciousness of each moment at the current point (T3"-T2-T1'), whereas the latter is represented in the continuum of consciousness of all moments (T1-T2-T3), throughout every phase of the experience. Our experience of inner time unfolds through these two dimensions, which cannot be reduced to a linear process. This description helps Husserl answer the question of why we never hear one single tone after another when listening to a song, but a consistent melody instead.

If what happens in the past does not vanish but becomes sedimented, these past experiences require a place to reside. Husserl thus discerns the flow of consciousness as the absolute subjectivity that serves as the temporal ground for the flowing-away past and the forthcoming future (Hua 10/75). As such, consciousness flows as a two-dimensional continuum that brings the present to coalesce with its past and future. The pure ego of each individual is unraveled through this time-constituting flow (Hua 10/75). Moment by moment, there arises a *noetic* act from this flow, which is targeted upon and constitutes its *noematic* content (Hua 10/73). The interaction of the absolute flow of consciousness, the constituting acts, and the constituted phenomena continues to be refined by Husserl as the *ego–cogito–cogitatum* schema in *Meditations* (Hua 1/ 87). Paul Ricoeur specifies that constitution is not the same as construction and fabrication, but rather suggests the way in which the intentionality of consciousness unfolds (Ricoeur 1967: 9). In light of the schema, consciousness is both the consciousness *of* something, and the consciousness *for* someone. Through expanding the *noesis–noema* structure into the *ego–cogito–cogitatum* schema, Husserl proposes a non-linear delineation of time, in contrast to the linear view in psychologism. To be more precise, Brentano construes temporality as the one-dimensional linearity of the succession and association of inner perceptions, whilst Husserl conceives of temporality as a two-dimensional infinite series that makes the entire experience coalesce.

It seems that Husserl espouses solipsism when introducing the idea of a pure ego as the origin of all intentional acts in his phenomenological theory of temporality. However, Husserl's view of the emergence of—or in his terms, the genesis of— intentional acts is much more complicated and does not yield a solipsist account of selfhood. As elucidated by Husserl, the ego is the underlying flow of consciousness as the absolute subjectivity, inseparable from the constituting act and the constituted phenomenon. Since an ego mutually constitutes itself with the subjective act of *cogito* and the objective phenomenon *qua cogitatum*, it never transforms into a closed system or an outstanding pole. To understand Husserl's notion of mutual constitution—especially how it reveals the way in which intentionality arises—it is important to introduce Husserl's distinction between two types of the genesis of intentional mental acts: the active and the passive. As to be seen shortly, active and passive geneses summarize two different ways for intentional acts to arise, found, and fulfill themselves.

Activity is the salient feature of reason that is able to operatively conduct intentional acts from categorial intuition to conceptual thinking (Hua 1/111). In Husserl's terms, "in active genesis, the I functions as productively constitutive, by means of subjective processes that are especially the acts of the I" (Hua 1/111). As, indeed, each I (*Ich*) is able to operatively constitute the act of perceiving by combining simple presentations of the manifold (Hua 1/111). Further founded on perception, this ego effectively constitutes the act of categorial intuition and universal intuition (Hua 1/111). Thus, founded on universal intuition, the ego actively constitutes the act of conceptualizing, naming, and expressing (Hua 1/111).

Nonetheless, the continuously founded mental act would remain meaningless and empty, if this mental act did not have its content fulfilled by a corresponding phenomenon (Hua 1/113). Such a phenomenon is presented through the synthesis of a passive experience (Hua 1/113). Passivity characterizes the experience of a wide range of sensations and intuitions in which the subjective act and the objective phenomenon are constituted primordially in each phase of the experience (Hua 1/112).[9] Therefore, when an ego actively conducts the intentional act of perceiving in the current moment, this active act of perceiving has already presupposed the primordial constitution of a horizon in virtue of a passive genesis. In the previous analysis of inner time consciousness, passivity penetrates the constitution of impression, retention, and protention on the same horizon. Through sensuous impression, an object is passively constituted. On the basis of the previous impression, retention is founded as a mental act, whose content remains the previously constituted object. Further built upon retention, impression, and protention, a horizon opens up in the current moment. Such a constitution of a horizon is passive in that none of us can use our reason to forge a change of temporality in inner time consciousness. We cannot hide our spontaneous feeling of being startled when we are enjoying Beethoven's symphony, but the music suddenly switches to one of Taylor Swift's pop songs. There are also times when we push ourselves to recollect the past, yet the memory does not come back to us immediately. Similarly, just because these constitutions are passive, the moment they are damaged by traumatic experiences, it is extremely hard to reverse the damage.[10] Or even, once they have been internalized as integral parts of our worldview, it requires substantial effort to reform such an internalized perspective.[11]

While activity attributes a privileged position to the ego and elevates the ego to the center of one's experience, passivity pinpoints the limits of reason, insofar as the active exercise of reason presupposes a primordial constitution of worldly objects in one's experience. The primordial act of constituting these worldly objects amounts to an intentional act of perceiving the entire world throughout every phase of time. It, thus, becomes a perception in a holistic sense. Husserl revises the definition of apperception in *Meditations* to describe such a holistic perception that passively generates (Hua 1/113).[12] For Husserl, apperception—the forming of perpetually new syntheses—is passively constituted prior to any perception actively conducted by the pure ego. This holistic perception primordially constitutes the lived experience for the ego, although the ego might not always have access to the passively constituted objects in apperception.

Our previous examples of recollection and anticipation illustrate this limit of reason. As stated, we can try to recollect certain memories and yet they continue to elude us. Since we do not lose the memory, there is always the possibility that it will come back to us in the future. The undetermined determinability of intentional acts, like recollection, hence, alludes to the interplay between passive and active geneses of experience. In the wake of the idea of genesis, intending alludes to constituting in that constituting (*konstituierende*) entails the unfolding of the intentionality of consciousness. In such a case, the threefold *ego–cogito–cogitatum* schema does not present the underlying ego as a passive receiver of given objects; nor is the ego transformed into an absolute that actively produces experience. This new schema portrays how intending acts, intended phenomena, and the underlying flow of consciousness mutually constitute the identity of one another. Eventually in *Crisis*, Husserl substitutes "ego" with "I-subject (*Ichsubjekt*)" to distance himself from a Cartesian understanding of selfhood.

Phase 4: Intentionality of the *We*[13]

Towards the end of his investigation of the individual mind, Husserl clarifies the mutual constitution of the subject and the object, further highlighting the foundational role of the underlying flow of consciousness. In doing so, he finds himself cornered by the problem of other minds: if the pure ego is an absolute flow of consciousness, can it perceive or be perceived by other minds? To further the discussion on how the ego of one person is not a closed system in itself, Husserl elaborates on his notion of apperception and expands intentionality from that of the *I* to that of the plurality of the *I* as the *we*. As a result, intentionality goes beyond the *ego–cogito–cogitatum* schema. It brings together the *we*, the act of intending, and the intended lifeworld. The intentionality of the *we*—or in short, the collective intentionality—performs a twofold function: first, it demonstrates how transcendental phenomenology entails no solipsism; second, it also reveals how phenomenology is an analysis of experience from the first-person, second-person, and third-person perspectives at the descriptive level.

Husserl addresses the problem of other minds at the beginning of the Fifth Meditation (Hua 1/121). Indeed, transcendental philosophers propose a turn from how things exist *out there* to how the mind serves as the necessary condition for the possibility of appearance. While such a turn towards the subject places the ego in the center of knowledge and experience, it also brings out the issue of solipsism. In Husserl's terms, "when I, the meditating I, reduce myself to my absolute transcendental ego by phenomenological *epoché*, do I not become *solus ipse*?" (Hua 1/121). If a person indeed becomes a *solus ipse*, then they would perceive everything (including other minds) as a mental fabrication, which confronts them with the problem of other minds. That is to say, if other minds are perceived as phenomena in the experience of a transcendental ego, then the alterity of other minds is canceled, and they are no longer the others (Hua 1/122). Yet, if other minds retain their alterity, can they still be perceived and intended?

Psychologists championed by Brentano respond to this question by asserting that we cannot directly perceive other minds and therefore have no direct knowledge of the consciousness of others. Otherwise put, if we want to know other minds without negating their alterity, we can only infer them indirectly and analogically. According to Brentano, others express themselves to us, either verbally in "mutually intelligible communication (*gegenseitiger verständliche Mittheilung*)," or non-verbally through "behavior and voluntary action (*die Handlungen und das willkürlichen Thun*)" (Brentano 1995: 28–9). As such, we infer what others have in mind through how their internal ideas are externalized.[14] For Husserl, the way in which psychologists, like Brentano, presume others to be pre-given and foreign to us is problematic, for it is a presumption that contradicts the idealism intrinsic to Husserl's transcendental phenomenology. If everything depends on the mind to appear as a phenomenon, why cannot we have direct knowledge of other minds without negating their alterity? This question prompts Husserl to inquire into alternative means of resolving the problem of other minds.

Husserl approaches this problem by drawing a parallel between the bodily experience of a transcendental *I* and the lived experience of the "transcendental *we* (*transzendentale Wir*)" (Hua 1/137). Both experiences are characterized by the part–whole relation, and both allude to the role of apperception generated from passive synthesis (Hua 1/139). To provide an example of this, let us turn to our bodily experiences. Suppose that I am standing in front of the Notre-Dame Basilica in Old Montreal. I conduct *epoché* and withdraw from the natural attitude. Therefore, I no longer reduce space to square meters but rather envisage space as a phenomenon that appears in my consciousness. My body always occupies a locus that limits what can appear in my perception. For instance, when I stand "here" facing the forefront of the Basilica, its backside remains invisible. As a mobile being, I can move my body, changing my position from the "here" *qua* facing-the-front to the "there" *qua* facing-the-back, to make the invisible "there" visible in my perception. As such, my body, similar to the now-moment in time, opens up a horizon on which the visible "here" co-appears with the invisible "there." Even though the Basilica cannot present all its aspects to me from one given locus—or in Husserl's terms, the Basilica cannot fully appresent itself to me—I can move my body consecutively from one side to another to perceive the Basilica as-a-whole (Hua 1/138). Thereby, my active perception of each aspect of the Basilica presupposes a primordially passive constitution of the Basilica as-a-whole in my experience. Such a passive constitution entails the "primal instituting (*Urstiftung*)," which is referred to as apperception in the Fifth Meditation (Hua 1/141).

Indeed, Husserl underscores how apperception in this sense is not a thinking act of inferring and thus cannot be defined as conceptual thinking in an abstract manner (Hua 1/141). Rather, it suggests a primordial constitution of experience (Hua 1/141). As previously mentioned, those that are currently absent reappear in a specific way for us, together with those that are present. The appresentation of an object as-a-whole alludes to the primordial constitution of the object in apperception, which exists in the direct, immediate perception in the holistic sense, as that of the entire horizon—be it present or absent. Every perception that has been enacted and therefore determined by us the subjects in one specific moment and locus presupposes the role of apperception to which we might not always have access. Articulated in this manner, apperception for Husserl is marked by its indeterminacy and passivity, which serves as the ground for any active, determined perception.

In the same manner that the invisible sides of the Basilica serve as parts of my perceptual background, so too are other egos with whom we share the same perceptual field. Other minds are constituted primordially in the experience of the transcendental *we*, the same way the invisible parts of the Basilica are constituted in the experience of a pure I-subject. In the meantime, in parallel to how each part of the Basilica is irreducible and irreplaceable, each individual member in the collective *we* likewise has an irreducible and irreplaceable identity, which makes the *we* a collection of concrete

I-subjects (Hua 6/258–9). Husserl continues to coin the concept of lifeworld (*Lebenswelt*) to describe this primordially constituted world in which all the I-subjects live together. As Husserl describes, "the constitution of the world essentially involves a harmony of the monads (I-subjects)" (Hua 1/138), and "each of us has a lifeworld, meant as the world for all" (Hua 6/257). Other I-subjects manifest themselves in my apperception of the lifeworld and become constituted in an appresentative manner in my consciousness (Hua 1/143). To put it differently, I can perceive others as the *you* with whom I collaborate to constitute our shared primordial lifeworld. Without them, I would never be able to have an experience of the world and of myself.

As Husserl details in the Vienna lectures, a lifeworld is mutually constituted by those in a community throughout history, through which culture comes into being (Hua 6/314–15). The life of a person as an individual *I* is always contextualized in the lifeworld on a collective horizon of the *we*. It is the horizon of empathy (*Einfühlung*) that becomes a shared space for the genesis of a meaningful life for an *I* among the *we*, consequently becoming foundational to the life of each individual in a community (Hua 1/137). As such, a shared horizon known as *Gemeinschaftshorizont* (communal horizon) is the ground for the realm of language, much broader than that which can be put in speeches, expressions, or voluntary actions. Abstract symbolic signs used in verbal or non-verbal communications need concrete experience to fulfill their meanings. When we can communicate and understand others, we have already presupposed the background experience, or to be more precise, the collective consciousness of the *we*. It is the *we* in the transcendental sense since the transcendental *we* serves as the necessary condition for the possibility of various phenomena in the shared experience.

Drawing on his discussion of appresentation and apperception, Husserl expands the articulation of intentionality from that which characterizes the consciousness of a transcendental *I* to that which defines the consciousness of the transcendental *we* (Hua 6/258). In the *Kaizo* articles written in the 1920s, Husserl describes communal life as that which is collaboratively constituted by a community full of individuals, namely, by the transcendental *we* (Hua 27/44). Upon extending the scope from individual life to the life shared by a plurality of individuals, Husserl subsequently expands the schema of *ego–cogito–cogitatum* into the tripartition of the *we*, the acts of intending, and the intended phenomena.

Aside from demonstrating that phenomenology is an idealist philosophy devoid of solipsism, the conception of collective intentionality also enables phenomenologists to examine experiences from different perspectives. Husserl employs the term "*Einfühlung*" (Hua 4/169), commonly translated in English as empathy, to encapsulate our experience of other minds (Hua 6/259). Husserl's notion of empathy indicates the mutual non-exclusivity and inseparability of the self and the others. As such, the essence of a person becomes a twofold *a priori*—"consciousness of oneself as being in the world (*Bewusstsein seiner selbst als in der Welt Seiend*)" and "self-consciousness and consciousness of others are inseparable (*Selbstbewusstsein und Fremdbewusstsein untrennbar ist*)" (Hua 6/255–6). Contemporary Husserlians interpret empathy as a perception of other minds from the second-person perspective (Zahavi 2005; Crowell 2016).

Over the years, phenomenology has been characterized as a study of experience from the first-person perspective. Aside from the first-person standpoint, Husserl also describes the third-person perspective of experience. To understand this, let us revisit the previous example of our perception of the body. When I turn myself from the front to the back of the Basilica, I treat myself and my body as one—*I* am my body. Such an articulation demonstrates the first-person experience of the body. Then, after walking to the backside of the Basilica, I begin to recollect my previous experience when I stood at the front. Upon recollection, my body reveals itself as a foreign object, which allows me to experience my body through the third-person perspective as an *it*. The way in which I can objectify my own body further indicates that alterity is a crucial dimension of my own experience. That is to say, it is common to acquire a sense of the alter-ego as the ego perceived from the third-person perspective (Hua 1/142).

Unlike the first-person standpoint which indicates a lived experience as that of *me* and the third-person perspective that objectifies the perceived phenomenon as a foreign *it*, the second-person standpoint appears in a collective setting, which differs from that of *me* but is not fully objectified to be an *it*. The second-person standpoint encapsulates intersubjectivity and points to the I–You relationship, which characterizes a lot of collaborative acts such as dancing the tango or singing in a chorus (Gomez 1996; Reddy 1996; Gallagher 2001). One exemplar of this I–You relationship is friendship: our friends, though different from ourselves, are still one of *us*, not one of *them*. The interaction between friends can be as harmonious as performing a symphony as part of an orchestra. Sometimes, our friends understand us even when we are unable to consistently express our feelings and emotions. The ways in which friendship unfolds point to how we have a shared horizon with our friends. And so, the second-person standpoint has been articulated as irreducible to that of the first-person and third-person, which allows Husserlian scholars represented by Dan Zahavi (2005; 2010a) and Steven Crowell (2016) to argue for interpreting Husserl's way of describing empathy as a second-person phenomenology of the mind.

Even though the *Kaizo* articles are one of the few places in which Husserl addresses questions related to ethics, he has not outlined a phenomenological theory of ethics based on the account of the perception of other egos or empathy. In Steven Crowell's terms, Husserl does not directly connect his study of other minds and transcendental intersubjectivity with ethics or moral philosophy (Crowell 2016: 71). Nevertheless, later phenomenologists, as represented by Edith Stein, Hannah Arendt, and Frantz Fanon, continue to develop the normative level of Husserl's transcendental phenomenology and propose their own articulation of phenomenological ethics. In addition, relevant to but also quite different from Husserl's phenomenology, the Yogācāra account of other minds serves to justify their ethical theory, which we will explore in the next chapter.

5

Intentionality in Chinese Yogācāra

Thus far, it is clear that Husserl puts forward a rich notion of intentionality at the descriptive level throughout the four different phases of his investigation of consciousness. The current chapter proceeds to explore how the Husserlian concept of intentionality can be related to Yogācāra Buddhism. Yogācārins are known for their doctrine of *vijñaptimātra*, commonly translated in English as that of "Mind-only" or "Consciousness-only." Due to the historical development of the Yogācāra school across time and place, it is impossible to speak of the Yogācāra descriptions of consciousness in the singular. There are clear differences between the early and later Yogācārins' interpretations of the mind, as well as differences between Yogācāra in East Asia and that in South Asia. The interpretation explored in this chapter is that of the later Chinese Yogācārins, which has been preserved in the texts composed by Xuanzang (玄奘 c. 602–664), Kuiji (窺基 632–682), and their disciples.

In our interpretation, the first question to be addressed is the following: since Xuanzang and his disciples have not directly utilized the concept of intentionality, how shall we understand their conception of consciousness? Here, I find it helpful to examine their translation of Sanskrit terms. Through paraphrasing both *vijñāna* and *vijñapti* as the Chinese word consciousness (*shi* 識), Xuanzang and his disciples insert their understanding of the intentional feature of consciousness into their translations, which becomes more explicitly expressed through their presentation of the fourfold intentional structure of mental acts. In this manner, these Yogācārins define consciousness through its salient feature that captures how an intending act is always mutually constituted with an intended phenomenon in the underlying stream of consciousness. In their stress of the interdependence of the stream, the act, and the phenomenon, these Yogācārins pinpoint the intentional feature of consciousness that is compatible with Husserl's formulation of intentionality. Furthermore, they are able to portray the knowledge of (no-)self and of other minds, a portrait that can likewise be related to that in Husserl. While the Husserlian account of intentionality can advance our understanding of Yogācāra Buddhism, the two are not completely identical. That is to say, Xuanzang and his disciples are interested in several extreme mental states, such as the pre-death mental state or the mental state at the beginning of each rebirth, which do not figure into Husserl's discussions. Moreover, these Yogācārins associate all mental acts with their moral consequences. As such, the analysis in this chapter allows me to argue that Chinese Yogācārins like Xuanzang and his disciples have characterized consciousness through its intentional feature at the descriptive level, which can be related to, but remains non-identical with, and therefore should not be assimilated into Husserl's phenomenology.

In what follows, I begin with the Yogācāra definition of consciousness and examine how Xuanzang and his disciples express a view of intentionality implicitly in their translation of Sanskrit terms and explicitly in the presentation of the fourfold structure of mental acts. Afterward, I analyze how the Yogācāra systemization of intentional consciousnesses lays the ground for their epistemic theories of no-self and other minds. To end this chapter, I introduce the Yogācāra theory of mental factors. Our analysis in the current chapter prepares us for exploring the explicative level of Yogācāra philosophy that elaborates on the ultimate nature of reality encapsulated in the notions of *svabhāva* (essence) and *śūnyatā* (emptiness) later in Chapter 8.

Intentionality in Translation and Elaboration

In his articulation of consciousness, Husserl enters into a discourse with a long philosophical tradition that stretches back to the ancient Greeks. His choice of terminology, including terms such as *epoché*, *eidos*, transcendental, *a priori*, essence, conditions, etc., is reflective of the tradition that he draws from. Likewise, Xuanzang and his disciples adopt a set of vocabularies that reflects their own intellectual background.

In order to comprehend these Chinese Yogācārins' description of consciousness, it is therefore important to understand the intellectual context that informs their specific terminology. Chinese clerics speak of consciousness as *shi* (識), a character that is utilized to translate two different yet related Sanskrit terms "*vijñāna*" and "*vijñapti*." Both Sanskrit terms derive from the root √*jñā*, which means "to know." The prefix *vi-* is used to indicate "apart," "separate," or "divided." The literal meaning of *vijñāna* is "knowing distinctly." This is the Sanskrit term Buddhists use to coin all types of consciousness. For instance, eye-consciousness is referred to as *cakṣuvijñāna*. From the root *vi*+√*jñā*, one can make a causative verb *vijñapayati* (to make/cause to know distinctly) of which the past passive participle becomes *vijñapti*. When Xuanzang and his disciples refer to their doctrine as that of consciousness-only (*vijñaptimātra*), they have in mind the term "*vijñapti*" (T43N1831, P608c24). Ultimately, the meaning of *vijñāna* and *vijñapti* can be understood as follows:

Vijñāna (one-place knowing)—knowing distinctly
Vijñapti (two-place knowing)—causing A to know P distinctly

I propose to describe *vijñāna* as a one-place knowing in that this notion indicates a sense of knowing in which the mental act does not have to direct itself towards something specific but that it just "knows" in general.[1] In contrast, I characterize *vijñapti* as a two-place knowing, considering how the literal meaning of this term— causing A (act) to know P (phenomenon) distinctly—entails an interplay between a subjective act of knowing and an objective phenomenon to be known, an interplay that bespeaks a sense of aboutness or directedness. In addition, etymologically, *vijñapti* denotes the salient feature of mental acts and shares an affinity with the definition of intentionality in Husserl's early work.

Though they derive from the same root, the meanings of the two terms are evidently different. Due to this difference, scholars represented by Alan Sponberg have struggled to understand why these Yogācārins reserve the Chinese term "*shi* (識, consciousness)" for both *vijñāna* and *vijñapti* (Sponberg 1979: 50). Recently, Buddhologists championed by Zhou Guihua (2004; 2007) have argued that it is inaccurate for Xuanzang to render *vijñapti* as consciousness.² Upon comparing Xuanzang's Chinese translation of Yogācāra literature with the original Sanskrit texts and versions in the Tibetan language, Zhou finds it more cogent to paraphrase *vijñapti* as "distinct representation (*biaobie* 表別)" (Zhou 2004: 60).³ According to Zhou, the term "distinct representation" can better demonstrate the two-place relation (between a subjective act of knowing and the objective phenomenon) encapsulated in the concept of *vijñapti* (Zhou 2004). While critics have provided counterarguments (Wu 2006; Cheng 2013, 2014; Cao 2014), the focus of their debate remains on whether Xuanzang's translation is accurate, that is, whether his translation properly reveals the original meaning of these terms in Sanskrit. Therefore, regardless of their disputes, both the Buddhologists and their critics share the assumption that there is only one appropriate understanding of the text, and its translation should be conducted in conformity with this understanding.

There are two limitations to this claim. First, it does not take into account how grammatical differences between the Chinese and Sanskrit languages can condition the translation of terms from one linguistic system to the other. Second, it ignores other intellectual traditions that have informed the thinking of Xuanzang and his disciples and privileges the Buddhist tradition in South Asia over indigenous Chinese philosophical traditions. For these reasons, discrepancies between Sanskrit and Chinese Buddhist texts should deserve more scholarly attention, not because they reflect defects of translation, but because they indicate unique understandings specific to individual language systems. Different from Sanskrit, the Chinese language does not conjugate verbs and nouns. Philosophical thinking by means of the Chinese language is also not contingent on assembling and analyzing compounds. Clerics, like Xuanzang and Kuiji, who have mastered both Sanskrit and Chinese, have a clear idea of the meaning of the term in its original and translated languages. Their translation is not a passive reception of ideas from foreign languages; rather, their translation, like all translations, is self-reflexive and brings forward the active comprehension of concepts in the local context. Upon translating both *vijñāna* and *vijñapti* as consciousness, Xuanzang and his disciples manage to introduce the Chinese philosophical binary of *ti* (體) and *yong* (用)⁴ to unpack the dialectical relation of these two Sanskrit terms, further proposing an indigenous articulation of what we know today as intentionality, in the Chinese language context. As such, what looks like a simplified, and even inaccurate, translation is in fact the first step towards a complicated and innovative account of consciousness.

We can track down this creative understanding of consciousness first through the different terms Xuanzang and his disciples utilize to characterize *vijñāna* and *vijñapti*. Aside from translating them both as *shi* (識, consciousness), these Yogācārins also refer to *vijñāna* as *liao* (了, knowing) (T43N1830, P238c29), and *vijñapti* as *liaobie* (了別,

causing one to know distinctly) (T43N1831, P608c23–609b2).⁵ Xuanzang's protégé Kuiji continues to evoke the classic *ti-yong* (體用) binary to elaborate on the dialectical relationship between *vijñāna* and *vijñapti*.⁶

As described by Kuiji in his commentaries, consciousness (*shi* 識) is defined as *vijñapti* (*liaobie*) because it is the function (*yong* 用) of consciousnesses to cause [an act] to know an object distinctly (T43N1831, P609b2–3). Considering how there are different ways of causing an act to know, Yogācārins delineate different types of *vijñāna* (*liao*) and designate dissimilar names to them (T43N1834, P981b11). Altogether, there are eight types of *vijñāna*. Kuiji follows his mentor Xuanzang to group them as *Xin* (心, i.e. the eighth consciousness *qua ālayavijñāna*), *Yi* (意, i.e. the seventh consciousness *qua manas*), and *Shi* (識, i.e. the first six consciousnesses) (T43N1834, P981b24–c2). As such, *vijñapti* as the function (*yong* 用) of causing to know an object distinctly not only demarcates one *vijñāna* from the other but also unveils (*xian* 顯) the *ti* (體) of consciousness (T43N1834, P981c7–18). From this elaboration on the meaning of consciousness, Kuiji suggests that *vijñāna* and *vijñapti* can be paraphrased as *shi* (識, consciousness) for the purpose of highlighting their complementarity. That is to say, *vijñāna* is the *ti* of consciousness that gives rise to *vijñapti* as the function or the *yong* of causing to know distinctly, whilst the function *qua yong* unveils the underlying *ti* and further demarcates one type of consciousness from another.

Chinese intellectuals have formulated the *ti-yong* binary to epitomize what is currently known as dialectical logic and did so even prior to the flourishing of Buddhism in East Asia. In this dialectic, *ti* serves as the ground and origin that gives rise to the function *qua yong*, whilst the function manifests the underlying origin *qua ti*. Although *ti* and *yong* seem to be separate on the surface, they complement each other at their core, in that they define the identity of one another and are able to transform from each other. As to be further unpacked in Chapter 9, the *ti-yong* binary has been widely evoked in Daoist philosophy to describe the fluid transformation between the *ti* of Dao that is shapeless and nameless and the *yong* of Dao that is always shaped and named. That is to say, the Dao itself as the invisible *ti* gives rise to its function (*yong*) of nourishing a myriad of things and the function, in turn, manifests the underlying invisible *ti* of Dao. When Kuiji evokes the *ti-yong* binary to explain the definition of consciousness, he likewise indicates the complementarity between *vijñāna* and *vijñapti*.

If this interpretation is tenable, then it will help us answer at least one question regarding how causality in the Yogācāra framework can be related to intentionality in the Husserlian sense. As previously mentioned, *vijñapti* is derived from the past passive participle of the causative verb *vijñapayati* (to make/cause to know distinctly). In Sanskrit, every causative verb naturally alludes to two doers. For instance, in *vijñapti* (causing to know distinctly), there are two doers: a doer that causes and a doer that knows. In our previous analysis of *vijñapti* as a two-place relation, we have explained that the mental act is the second doer *qua* the subjective act of knowing. If that is the case, what serves as the first doer that causes this subjective act? Following our interpretation of *vijñāna* as *ti* and *vijñapti* as *yong*, it can be inferred that Chinese Yogācārins attribute the cause of *vijñapti* to *vijñāna*.

Thus, when Xuanzang and his disciples decided to translate *vijñāna* and *vijñapti* as *shi* (識, consciousness), they have inserted their innovative understanding in the translation. On the one hand, *vijñāna* as the *ti* (體) of consciousness continually manifests itself through *vijñapti* that is the function (*yong* 用) of causing a subjective act to know an objective phenomenon moment by moment; and on the other hand, this manifestation finds its grounding in the underlying flow of consciousness. Formulated in this manner, *shi* (識) or consciousness encapsulates the dynamic fluidity of the underlying flow that gives rise to the acts of knowing and the phenomena to be known. To put it in the Husserlian language, consciousness unfolds through the interaction of its three constituents: the underlying process of knowing, the act of knowing, and the phenomenon to be known. If we follow Husserl's work where he later defines intentionality as a mutual constitution of the underlying flow, the intending act, and the intended phenomenon,[7] it is fair to characterize the Yogācāra view of consciousness as their expression of what we currently call intentionality.

The idea of intentionality is more explicitly expressed by Xuanzang and his disciples in their articulation of the structure of consciousness.[8] In the *CWSL*, Xuanzang introduces the threefold structure articulated by Dignāga to depict the intentional feature of consciousness. In this threefold structure (*sanfen* 三分), the underlying flow is referred to as self-awareness (*zizheng* 自證, *svasaṃvitti*),[9] the act as the seeing part (*jianfen* 見分, *darśanabhāga*), and the phenomenon as the image part (*xiangfen* 相分, *nimittabhāga*) (T31N1585, P10b6–7).[10] This formulation of the threefold structure encapsulates the complementary relationship between *vijñāna* (as the *ti* enclosed in the conception of underlying self-awareness) and *vijñapti* (as the *yong* expressed by the seeing–image interaction).

Xuanzang follows previous Yogācāra masters in using the concept of transformation (*bian* 變, *pariṇāma*) to expound upon the fluidity and transformability of the *ti* and *yong* of consciousness (T31N1585, P7b25). Nevertheless, Xuanzang addresses a question posed by Dharmapāla, the eminent disciple of Dignāga. This question asks whether the underlying self-awareness is reflexively aware of its own functionality (T31N1585, P10b18). Dharmapāla argues for the existence of this reflexive awareness, which becomes the fourth part of consciousness known as the awareness of self-awareness (*zheng zizheng* 證自證) (T31N1585, P10b18–22). This fourfold structure (*sifen* 四分) of consciousness—the awareness of self-awareness, self-awareness, the seeing part, and the image part—is that which Xuanzang and his disciples promote. That is to say, the fourfold structure represents Xuanzang and his disciples' understanding of intentionality. For these Chinese Yogācārins, consciousness is not only the *vijñapti* through which a mental act *qua* the seeing part is caused to arise and is directed towards its targeted phenomenon *qua* the image part, but also points back to the underlying *vijñāna* through the reflexive self-awareness. As such, intentionality in later Chinese Yogācāra describes how consciousness is always directed towards a phenomenon as the consciousness *of*, and simultaneously points back to the underlying flow as the consciousness *for*, a description that can be related to and compatible with that in Husserl.

More importantly, in their presentation of the fourfold structure, Xuanzang and his disciples object to the structure of consciousness formulated by their rivals, especially early Yogācārins and non-Mahāyāna Buddhists. Early Yogācārins center their study of consciousness on either *vijñāna* as the one-place knowing or *vijñapti* as the two-place relation between the image part and the seeing part. Hence, they depict intentionality as the one-place relation or the two-place relation (T43N1831, P609b4). For these early Yogācārins, as long as consciousness is in function, it generates a subject–object duality that further animates various types of illusions to entrap sentient beings in endless suffering. As such, illusions result from the functionality of consciousness *per se*, which is sharply contrasted with the view of Xuanzang and his disciples.

Meanwhile, most Buddhists outside the Mahāyāna community formulate their respective threefold intentional structure of consciousness as that between an intending act, the intended image, and the external object (T31N1585, P10b2–4).[11] Drawing on this structure, these non-Mahāyāna Buddhists suggest that knowledge is acquired through the representation of external objects. As the cause of knowledge, external objects must have an existence on their own, independent of consciousness and other factors. That is how these non-Mahāyāna Buddhists make a case for "the mind-independent existence of objects in one's perception (有離識所緣境)" (T31N1585, P10b2). Later Yogācārins like Xuanzang and his disciples demarcate their position from these non-Mahāyāna clerics. As indicated by the fourfold structure, nothing in one's mind can be viewed as *sui generis*, self-determining, and *svabhāvic*, due to the interplay between the underlying self-awareness, the seeing part, and the image part.

For Xuanzang and his disciples, the mind of each sentient being is a system of eight types of consciousness. Considering how each consciousness has its unique function of knowing, Xuanzang sorts them into three groups: *xin* (心, *citta*, namely, the eighth consciousness), *yi* (意, *manas*, namely, the seventh consciousness), and *shi* (識, namely, the first six consciousnesses).[12] These eight consciousnesses not only represent eight different types of cognitive faculties but also associate themselves with affective mental states known as the mental factors, which we will visit in the last section of this chapter. Among the eight consciousnesses, the function of the first six is the most explicit and easy to observe in everyday life. The first five consciousnesses (*yanshi* 眼識, *ershi* 耳識, *bishi* 鼻識, *sheshi* 舌識, *shenshi* 身識) correspond to the five senses of seeing, hearing, smelling, tasting, and touching. According to the *CWSL*, these consciousnesses are defined by their respective functions of sensing (T31N1585, P37a25). To process and synthesize the manifold sensations provided by these five consciousnesses, one needs the sixth consciousness (*yishi* 意識, *manovijñāna*). Even the sixth consciousness is not continuously present nor in function because the flow of this consciousness can be terminated in extreme circumstances. For instance, when someone becomes extremely exhausted and falls into a deep sleep, that person loses consciousness entirely (T31N1585, P38a23). Likewise, one has no explicit consciousness in their comatose state or in deep meditation (T31N1585, P38a28).

Unlike the first six consciousnesses that are easily observed in everyday experience, the seventh consciousness known as *mona* (末那, *manas*) and the eighth consciousness called *alaiyeshi* (阿賴耶識, *ālayavijñāna*) exist in a more profound (*shen* 深) and subtle (*xi* 細) way (T31N1585, P14c5). Since their functionalities are too profound to be discerned in everyday life, Xuanzang provides proof for their existence. It should be noted that each proof consists of arguments that point to the necessary condition for the possibility of a phenomenon, allowing us to interpret his arguments as transcendental arguments.

In his proof of the existence of *mona*, Xuanzang contends that this seventh consciousness serves as the necessary condition for the possibility of five phenomena. To put it differently, without *mona*, these five phenomena would be impossible: ignorance could not sustain from one life to another (T31N1585, P25a1); the sixth consciousness could not arise continuously after interruptions (T31N1585, P25b4-6); one could not have a continuous flow of consciousness from the past to the present and to the future in this life (T31N1585, P25b16); one could not purify ignorance in two types of meditation (T31N1585, P25b23-8); and lastly, the attachments to the self could not arise in the first place (T31N1585, P25c10).

In his proof of the existence of *alaiyeshi*—in short, *laiye*—Xuanzang argues for conceiving of this eighth consciousness as the necessary condition for the possibility of ten phenomena. That is to say, without *laiye*, these ten phenomena would not be possible: the acts of all consciousnesses would not be able to influence the future states of the mind or be influenced by the previous mental states (T31N1585, P15b19-20); consciousness would not be able to shape one's karmic action (T31N1585, P16a16-17); the endless circle of death and rebirth would not be sustainable (T31N1585, P16b3-4); sentient beings could not maintain their current bodily form (T31N1585, P16b20-1); sentient beings could not hold vitality and heat in their current bodily form (T31N1585, P16c6-7); consciousness could not exist in the moments prior to death or right after rebirth (T31N1585, P16c23-4); it would be impossible to explain dependent arising (T31N1585, P17a23-4); the regeneration of life forms would not be possible (T31N1585, P17b11-12); consciousness would not continue to flow for those who live in deep meditation (T31N1585, P17c25-8); and lastly, consciousness would not be polluted by or purified from mental defilement (T31N1585, P18c24-5).

Each of these consciousnesses—be it the obvious one or the subtle one—are intentional. Therefore, they can transform (*bian* 變, *pariṇāma*) in order to give rise to the moment-by-moment fourfold structure of the seeing part, the image part, the underlying self-awareness, and the awareness of the self-awareness. To understand the concept of transformation, it will be of help to borrow the Husserlian notion of genesis. In his study of the origin of mental acts, Husserl introduces two types of genesis, namely, the passive and the active. While the active genesis demonstrates the power of reason that enables a pure ego to build a more abstract intentional act upon simple acts of presenting, the passive genesis exposes the limit of reason insofar as the active use of reason presupposes a primordial constitution of worldly objects in one's experience. Referring to Husserl's distinction between passivity and activity, I contend that the transformation of the subtle consciousnesses—namely, of the seventh and the eighth consciousnesses—is characterized by passivity, in contrast to the actively functioned first six consciousnesses. Thereby, the question for the subtle consciousnesses is not *whether* they can intend or not, but rather *how* they intend differently than the others.

Given that the seventh and eighth consciousnesses passively transform themselves, sentient beings do not always have full access to—and therefore are not always mindful of—their constitution of the primordial self and the primordial world. In Yogācāra terms, they are extremely subtle and profound in the sense that any active function of the first sixth consciousnesses presupposes such a primordial constitution of the world and the unified self-identity. Considering its salient feature of being subtle and profound, contemporary scholars refer to the eighth consciousness as the subliminal consciousness (Jiang 2006: 48), the ultimate unconsciousness (Ni 2010: 90), or the unconscious mental flow (Waldron 2003: xi), each of which cannot be perceived intuitively but can only be known through deduction. Though inspired by their insight and indebted to their research, I believe that the notion of subliminal or unconscious requires further clarification. The functionality of the eighth consciousness appears to be subliminal, or unconscious, but it bespeaks passivity, rather than the non-existence of its transformation. As to be seen shortly, the way in which the eighth consciousness primordially constitutes these objects amounts to an intentional act of perceiving the entire cosmos throughout every phase of *saṃsāra*, a primal instituting to which a person may not even have access. The passivity of the eighth consciousness, therefore, differs from that of the seventh consciousness. To help shape our understanding of such a distinction, we will investigate how the passive transformation of the eighth consciousness gives rise to the passive and active conceptions of selfhood.

Intentionality, No-self, and Self-attachments

The Yogācāra notion of no-self has garnered a growing level of scholarly attention due to its input to the contemporary discussion of epistemology.[13] In the framework of eight types of consciousness, Xuanzang and his disciples account for our experience of no-self and how this experience propels us to develop misperceptions of—and attachments to—the self. To begin, let us delve deeper into the function of eight types of consciousness.

As previously mentioned, the transformation of the eighth consciousness *ālayavijñāna* (*alaiyeshi* 阿賴耶識)—abbreviatedly referred to as *laiye*—is characterized by passivity. Xuanzang refers to the functionality of *laiye* as obscure (*bukezhi* 不可知), which can be understood as the Yogācāra expression of passivity (T31N1585, P10a11). In this sense, the way in which *laiye* perceives is close to the Husserlian notion of apperceiving as the perceiving that yields a sense of constituting (T31N1585, P10a12). That which is passively, primordially, and obscurely constituted consists of the three image parts of the material cosmos, the corporeal body, and seeds (T31N1585, P10a13-14). That is to say, when *laiye* functions, it gives rise to the act of apperceiving that, in turn, primordially constitutes the phenomena of the material cosmos and the corporeal body in every phase of *saṃsāra*. Such a primordial constitution is presupposed by any active perception of objects in one's experience.

Aside from the phenomena of the material cosmos and the corporeal body, the eighth consciousness also gives rise to seeds. Yogācārins utilize the term "seed (*zhongzi* 種子, *bīja*)" in a figurative way to express the notion of tendency.[14] To be more specific, the concept of seed describes how the transformation of *laiye*—though passive and sometimes inaccessible to the first six consciousnesses—paves the way for the functionality of other consciousnesses. In the figurative depiction proposed by Xuanzang, when *laiye* transforms, it constitutes seeds and conceals tendencies for the operation of the other seven consciousnesses throughout endless time so that consciousness can motivate and invite actions. In turn, actions can cultivate seeds and condition the transformation of consciousnesses. Given that seeds are cultivated in different ways, the eighth consciousness stores the tendencies of perpetuating and purifying ignorance.

When *laiye* passively apperceives and constitutes the material cosmos, corporeal bodies, and seeds, its act of apperceiving becomes misperceived as a *svabhāvic* self by the seventh consciousness *qua mona* (末那, *manas*) (T31N1585, P19b8). This is how the seventh consciousness passively constitutes the *svabhāvic* sense of selfhood. As described by Xuanzang, *mona* takes *laiye*'s act of apperceiving as its "intended object (*suoyuan* 所緣)" (T31N1585, P22a8). Through its transformation, *mona* passively constitutes the primordial self as a habitual sense of selfhood prior to a full-fledged category of ego or self (*wo* 我, *ātman*). The constitution of this habitual selfhood elevates the ego to the center as if it were an absolute self-in-itself (*zineiwo* 自內我) in one's experience throughout beginningless time (T31N1585, P22a10). In light of this distinct transformation, Xuanzang demarcates *mona*'s act of intending as conceptualizing (*siliang* 思量) in a generatively passive sense (T31N1585, P19b9). It is passive since *mona* constitutes selfhood in a habitual way through which sentient beings are conditioned to internalize the idea of an absolute self-in-itself. Yet, it remains conceptual since this seventh consciousness nourishes a *svabhāvic* concept of the self as a self-in-itself independent of and irrelevant to others. Due to its passivity, it becomes time-consuming for sentient beings to rehabitualize themselves and to remove *mona*'s misperception. Further based on the passive transformation of the eighth and seventh consciousnesses, the first six consciousnesses can operatively and actively transform themselves to give rise to a wide range of intentional acts (T31N1585, P26b4–6).

One example that can be used to unpack the interplay of these eight types of consciousness is the knowledge of no-self. As such, let's direct our attention to the experience of our own body. In the Yogācāra framework provided by Xuanzang and his disciples, the passive transformation of the eighth consciousness, *laiye*, furnishes us with what we refer to as the subjective sense of the body. The subjective body consists in the apperceiving act of *laiye* that primordially constitutes the image part *qua* the corporeal body. The ways in which we can use our bodies spontaneously and effortlessly in actions such as biking or swimming alludes to the apperceiving of the eighth consciousness, *laiye*, especially how it passively constitutes the corporeal body without the mediation of conceptual thinking.

Only the sixth and seventh consciousnesses are capable of conceptual thinking. When the eighth consciousness apperceives, *mona* takes *laiye*'s act of apperceiving as the target. As such, *mona* derives a habitual sense of a self-in-itself from the subjective body (T31N1585, P22a13). Otherwise put, *mona* passively constitutes the first type of a *sui generis*, immutable self-identify. Based on this habitual misperception, sentient beings like us are conditioned to internalize the egocentric view of life, which continues to be internalized as our innate self-attachments (*jusheng wozhi* 俱生我執, *sahajātmagrāha*) (T31N1585, P2a10).

In comparison, the transformations of the other six consciousnesses presuppose the image parts of *laiye*—be it the image of the material cosmos or the image of the corporeal body. As such, the sixth consciousness operatively constitutes the objective sense of body. For instance, we can talk about how much we enjoy biking, and we can describe our swimming techniques to our friends. In these conversations, we speak of our body as an object. Indeed, based on the image of the corporeal body passively transformed from the eighth consciousness *qua laiye*, the sixth consciousness processes the data delivered by the five senses to formulate an objective representation of this corporeal body and is inclined to consider this objective body again as the manifestation of a *sui generis*, immutable self (T31N1585, P2a14). This habitual misconception is gradually internalized as an innate attachment to the self in the objective sense, parallel to that in the subjective sense derived from the seventh consciousness (T31N1585, P2a15).

On the basis of these types of innate self-attachments, the sixth consciousness further enables us to put forward categories to differentiate our "self" from others. We can identify ourselves as good bikers or strong swimmers in contrast to those who do not know how to bike or swim. These differentiations lead to our discriminative self-attachments (*fenbie wozhi* 分別我執, *vikalpitātmagrāha*) (T31N1585, P2a21). These two types of self-attachment, as the innate and the discriminative, conspire to strengthen the conviction that our self-identity is *sui generis* and unchangeable, which renders us unable to recognize our interdependence with others in our life story.

From this analysis, we can infer that not all consciousnesses can generate misperception and attachment. To be more precise, what triggers self-attachment is not the functionality of consciousness but a false manner of intending and perceiving in virtue of the seventh and the sixth consciousnesses. It is only by force of their misconceptions that we come to internalize the view of our self-identity as an accomplished *svabhāvic* entity at the habitual and the conceptual levels. Thus, we ignore the fact that, throughout our entire life, our consciousness is an ongoing process of functioning through the joint effort of subject–object interaction. For these Yogācārins, self-attachment is not only an epistemic issue but also an existential one. The moment we become ignorant of who we really are, the egocentric worldview holds us captive and propels us to maintain our current state of life. Any effort of maintaining such a state ends up being futile, as we eventually find ourselves in the grip of frustration and suffering.

Intentionality, Other Minds, and Dharma-attachments[15]

In their account of no-self, Xuanzang and his disciples detail how the so-called *svabhāvic* self is nothing but a misperception of the functionality of consciousness. Admittedly, the eighth consciousness *laiye* is too passive and profound to generate a self. Nonetheless, if everything in one's experience is primordially constituted by *laiye* and generatively intended by all the other consciousnesses, does the mind of each sentient being become another closed-in-itself *svabhāva*? Similar to Husserl, Yogācārins are confronted with the insidious possibility of solipsism in their depiction of consciousness. Therefore, they strive to demonstrate that they do not conceive of consciousness-only as "one-consciousness-only (*weiyishi* 唯一識)" (T31N1585, P39c18). Upon accounting for the notion of no-self, Yogācārins come to tackle the problem of other minds. Yet, different from Husserl, the concern for other minds in the

Yogācāra context is closely related to the Buddhist notion of compassion, which is also the salient feature of the Bodhisattvas—the compassionate beings who postpone their own awakening to help others. Through resolving the problem of other minds, Xuanzang and his disciples provide a theory that reveals how the minds of sentient beings are interconnected. As such, they prove that their doctrine of consciousness-only does not yield solipsism nor any reaffirmation of the *svabhāvic* view of the self. Furthermore, their study of consciousness likewise exhausts all three perspectives of experience from that of the first-person, to the second-person, and finally to the third-person.

In the *CWSL*, Xuanzang comes to tackle the problem of other minds after explaining how things that are external to the mind do not have *svabhāvic* existence (T31N1585, P39c9). Indeed, to criticize their non-Mahāyāna interlocutors, Xuanzang and his fellow Yogācārins contend that everything depends on the mind to appear in one's experience. With this turn towards the subject, nothing is mind-independent. However, the perception of other minds soon becomes a new challenge for these Yogācārins (T31N1585, P39c10). As detailed by Xuanzang, external objects are not *svabhāva* because they depend on the mind to be perceived (T31N1585, P39c9). Yet, other minds should exist in the same manner as one's own mind (T31N1585, P39c10). It begs the question as to whether one can perceive them or not (T31N1585, P39c10). Kuiji further unpacks this question in the following manner: if a sentient being can perceive other minds, then, other minds will be like external objects and lose their alterity in this sentient being's experience (T43N1834, P1006b23–4). If other minds retain their real existence in this sentient being's perception, then other minds transform into the mind-independent *svabhāva* (T43N1834, P1006b18–19). If other minds cannot be perceived, then, the overarching argument of consciousness-only is not sustainable (T43N1834, P1006b14–15). From these dilemmas, there arises the problem of other minds. To resolve this problem, Yogācārins need to find a solution that affirms the knowability of other minds without canceling their alterity.

In his analysis of this problem, Kuiji continues to present two resolutions, one from early Yogācāra and the other from later Yogācāra. Early Yogācārins propose to resolve the problem of other minds by merging the other with the self. That is to say, early Yogācārins attribute the self–other dichotomy to dualistic thinking (T43N1834, P1007b13). When consciousness begins to function, it gives rise to dualistic thinking, which propels sentient beings to treat the self and the other as polar opposites (T43N1834, P1007b12). Therefore, sentient beings should terminate the function of consciousness, eradicate dualistic thinking, and imagine themselves to become others to experience other minds (T43N1834, P1007b13). However, what does it mean to merge the self with the other through imagination and emulation? If it means that sentient beings need to imagine themselves to become others and go through what others are going through, then what these sentient beings are experiencing is no longer other minds but what others *have* in mind. As such, it seems that early Yogācārins confuse other minds with what others *have* in mind. On top of that, they also cancel the alterity of other minds when they argue for merging the other with the self. That is why Kuiji remarks that "other minds *per se*, we do not really perceive them (他本質心，實不緣著)" (T43N1834, P1007b14). As to be seen shortly, later Yogācārins represented by

Xuanzang and Kuiji propose a new approach to the perception of other minds insofar as they go beyond the first-person perspective and bring to light what is currently known as the intersubjective experience.

In the later Yogācāra proposal, Xuanzang affirms the possibility of experiencing other minds and analyzes the distinctive ways in which such an experience is enacted. He specifies that sentient beings can directly perceive other minds, although other minds are not cognized as *qin suoyuan* (親所緣, *intimate ālambana*) (T31N1585, P39c11–14).[16] The concept of *suoyuan* or *ālambana* has been used by Yogācārins to describe the perceived phenomenon. From a Yogācāra standpoint, everything depends on consciousness to appear in the experience, which counters the argument that external objects are directly given to the mind. Indeed, what has been perceived by consciousness amounts to *ālambana*, rather than external objects. There are further two types of *ālambana*: the intimate (*qin* 親) and the remote (*shu* 疏) (T31N1585, P40c16).[17] An intimate *ālambana* fulfills three requirements: it is perceived by a consciousness; it is not separate from this consciousness; and it derives from this consciousness (T31N1585, P40c17). Therefore, for each consciousness, its image part is its intimate *ālambana*. In parallel, remote *ālambana* also holds three qualifications: it is perceived by a consciousness; it is separate from this consciousness; and it stems from another archetype (*zhi* 質) (T31N1585, P40c18). Kuiji clarifies that these archetypes are either transformed by other minds or by other consciousnesses in the mind of one's own (T43N1830, P501a15–17). For instance, when the eye-consciousness perceives blue, it does not perceive blue as an external object but rather as a phenomenon. Moreover, as underscored by Louis de la Valleé Poussin, blue-the-phenomenon is contextualized in the material cosmos constituted by the eighth consciousness (La Vallée Poussin 1928: 446). While blue-the-phenomenon becomes the intimate *ālambana* for this eye-consciousness, this consciousness takes the image of the material cosmos as that which stems from an archetype, to be the remote *ālambana*.[18] As such, similar to how blue is an integral part of the entire cosmos, one's mind is a crucial unit among the minds of all sentient beings. Other minds collaborate with one's own mind to constitute the shared horizon in *saṃsāra*, which, in turn, cultivates the shared seeds in one's own mind (T31N1585, P11a). As such, sentient beings do not perceive other minds by emulating others. Rather, they perceive other minds as the remote *ālambana* through collaborative acts.

Borrowing phenomenological terminology, I interpret this perception of other minds as an experience from the second-person perspective that entails the ways in which we collaborate with others to mutually constitute a shared space of meaning. Different from the first-person perspective in which we remain the subject of experience and the third-person perspective that objectifies things in our experience, the second-person perspective characterizes the I–You relationship in an intersubjective collaboration. For instance, when we tango with our partners, dancing in a smooth and harmonious manner, we do not need to imagine ourselves being our partners in order to work with them. Nor do we infer their next move from their verbal or non-verbal actions. Instead, a harmonious partnership functions like a habit that remains with our partners and us intuitively. And that is how sentient beings in the cosmos collaborate to constitute a shared horizon.

The following metaphor in the *CWSL* can be used to illustrate this second-person perspective of experience: "when all the lamps are turned on, they illuminate each other as if they were a larger whole (如眾燈明，各遍似一)" (T31N1585, P10c15–16).[19] The minds of all sentient beings are like the lamps that shine harmoniously with one another to light up the dark. In this process, each illuminating lamp as each individual mind maintains its irreducible identity while mutually reflecting other minds as if they became a larger whole. As such, Xuanzang proposes a resolution that affirms the knowability of other minds without canceling their alterity.

Our second-person experience of other minds soon yields an open possibility. If we are able to see other minds as they actually are, we realize that alterity is indispensable for ourselves. Nonetheless, incorrect ways of perceiving can propel us to perpetuate self–other polarity. In our previous analysis of self-attachments, we have established how we have innate self-attachments when the seventh consciousness *mona* and the sixth consciousness misconceive the eighth consciousness *laiye* as the *sui generis*, immutable ego. The sixth consciousness further produces categories to differentiate others and nourishes the discriminative self-attachments. Aside from these attachments to the self, misconceptions also give rise to a wide range of attachments to the dharmas. These dharma-attachments include that to other minds.

When the eighth consciousness *laiye* perceives other minds as remote *ālambana*, *mona* habitually misperceives *laiye*'s seeing part as an unchanging self-identity. This habitual misperception nourishes our innate self-attachments (T31N1585, P2a10). Simultaneously, it cultivates our habit of treating those outside our own minds (including other minds) as irrelevant and inaccessible to us, namely, as other *svabhāvic* entities. Internalizing such a view of other minds, we steadily develop innate dharma-attachments (*jusheng fazhi* 俱生法執, *sahajadharmagrāha*) (T31N1585, P6c27). Meanwhile, the sixth consciousness synthesizes the data produced by the five senses and objectifies the image parts (i.e., the image of the body and the image of the material cosmos) transformed by the eighth consciousness *laiye*. That is how we begin to obtain the third-person perspective of experience. When forming an objective representation of a phenomenon, the sixth consciousness is prone to cultivate innate self-attachments in the objective sense and equally treat various things in the material cosmos, including other minds, as *sui generis* and immutable entities. Such an attitude is thus internalized as an innate attachment to a specific type of dharma *qua* other minds.

Supported by these innate dharma-attachments, the sixth consciousness is capable of formulating abstract names and concepts to consolidate the self–other divide. In this process, our rudimentary attitude to demarcate the self from the other matures into discriminative self-attachments (*fenbie wozhi* 分別我執, *vikalpitātmagrāha*) (T31N1585, P2a21), and the discriminative dharma-attachments (*fenbie fazhi* 分別法執, *vikalpitadharmagrāha*) (T31N1585, P7a06). These attachments to the self and dharmas exacerbate the ignorance of sentient beings both at the habitual and conceptual levels.

Combining the analysis of the knowledge of no-self and other minds, we come to see how the transformation of consciousness is neutral by nature, which therefore furnishes sentient beings like us with an open possibility. That is to say, the mind serves as the necessary condition for the possibility of phenomena in experience and reaches out to other minds to constitute a meaningful intersubjective world. As sentient beings, we can navigate this world in two manners. First, with an ignorant mindset, the function of consciousness is perceived in such a way that we falsely view our "self" and other things in the cosmos (including other minds) as *svabhāvic* entities. Following misperception, the rift between the self and the other comes into existence, which further fuels various forms of egocentrism. Second, and contrariwise, the awakened ones realize the pure state of mind and embrace self–other interdependence. Such realization arouses compassion in these awakened ones, which motivates them to return to *saṃsāra* as Bodhisattvas. Eventually, we are the ones who determine this open possibility as well as the evolution from ignorance to awakening. In this sense, we are not only the subject who can acquire knowledge, but also the agent who can act to become one with such knowledge. By then, knowledge evolves into wisdom. Although Xuanzang and his disciples negate the *svabhāvic* notion of self and dharma, they do not reject subjectivity and agency. If we want to fully awaken from suffering, we need to change our manner of perceiving, both habitually and conceptually, by pursuing the Bodhisattvas' path.

The Intentionality of Mental Factors

Different from the eight types of consciousness that are capable of discerning and knowing objects distinctly, the mental factors are affective mental states that accompany the function of consciousness, such as feeling, attending, willing, and numerous kinds of mental affliction. In the Yogācāra context, there are fifty-one mental factors in total. For our purpose here, I will give a brief description of mental factors and their functionality, which allows for an exploration of how the Yogācāra portrait of consciousnesses is compatible with, yet remains distinct from, and thus cannot be assimilated into that of Husserl's.

In the *CWSL*, Xuanzang delineates three salient features of mental factors: first, they perpetually depend on consciousness to arise; second, they always accompany consciousnesses; and third, they likewise have a fourfold intentional structure (T31N1585, P26c15–16). As Xuanzang documents, mental factors are supposed to facilitate the function of consciousnesses (T31N1585, P26c17). To illustrate this interplay, Kuiji compares the mental factors to the servants of the king *qua* the consciousness (T43N1830, P320c16). The king–servant metaphor alludes to the way in which mental factors find their basis in consciousness. Borrowing the Husserlian terminology, we can conceive of these mental factors as the compound acts that are not only founded upon the acts of perceiving, but also targeted at the same object.

This insightful depiction of mental factors demonstrates how emotions and feelings are hardly unorganized manifold mental states related to sensory pleasure. Differing from thinkers such as Plato and Descartes, who downplay the importance of sensory pleasure in their admiration of reason, Chinese Yogācārins like Xuanzang and his disciples recognize the epistemic character of these affective mental states. We can take the emotion of regret as an example. In the Yogācāra framework, regret (*hui* 悔, *kaukṛtya*) is one of the mental factors that only accompanies the function of the sixth consciousness. When the sixth consciousness begins to work, it gives rise to the mental factor of mindfulness (*nian* 念, *smṛti*) to allow for recollecting previous misconducts (T31N1585, P28b18–25). Thereafter, regret arises on the basis of this act of recollecting (T31N1585, P35c11). That is to say, once a sentient being experiences regret, such an experience presupposes the cognitive work of the sixth consciousness and therefore entails an understanding of what is morally right and what is morally wrong. The emotion of regret sometimes co-exists with another mental factor *qua* feeling (*shou* 受, *vedanā*) (T31N1585, P36b14). Feeling is one of the omnipresent mental factors associated with all eight types of consciousness. When it arises on the basis of the eighth or the seventh consciousness, it always begins as a neutral feeling (*sheshou* 捨受, *upekṣāvedanā*) (T31N1585, P23c2). Nevertheless, the feeling can become more diverse as it accompanies the first six consciousnesses. By then, feelings can become full of joy (*le* 樂, *sukha*), pleasure (*xi* 喜, *saumanasya*), suffering (*ku* 苦, *duḥkha*) and worry (*you* 憂, *daurmanasya*) (T31N1585, P27a26). For instance, together with regret, the feeling of worry arises, which thus accompanies the sixth consciousness. As such, sentient beings experience a wide range of feelings when they possess a coherent understanding of the situation in which they find themselves and have moral judgments about their actions, such as in the case of regret. Meanwhile, it is also commonplace that feelings can consume sentient beings when they have merely a pre-reflective sense of the surroundings.

Thus far, we have detailed how the Yogācāra conception of the mind as a system of eight types of consciousness accompanied by their mental factors, can be related to that in Husserl. Not only do they both pinpoint the salient feature of intentionality as the mutual constitution between the underlying flow of consciousness, the intending act, and the intended phenomenon in their respective manners, but they also depict how the function of consciousness is animated by both the passive and active geneses. Furthermore, Chinese Yogācārins and Husserl employ their formulation of intentionality to detail how the underlying flow of consciousness is not a *svabhāva*, not a self-closed system, but rather interdependent with other objects, including other minds.

Although the Yogācāra view of consciousness can be related to that of Husserl's, the two are not completely identical for at least four primary reasons. First and above all, Chinese Yogācārins like Xuanzang and his disciples use the fourfold structure to describe the intentional feature of consciousness, which is a structure of the seeing part, the image part, the underlying self-awareness, and the reflexive awareness of the self-awareness. In contrast, Husserl does not differentiate the two layers of self-awareness in his investigation of consciousness, although he might also agree that the underlying self-awareness reflexively knows itself due to the functionality of the passive genesis. For these Yogācārins, these two layers of self-awareness, together with the eighth consciousness, lay the ground for the possibility of removing misperception and realizing awakening at the prescriptive level, which will be detailed in the next chapter.

Second, these Chinese Yogācārins do not find it necessary to superimpose the name "ego" on the continuous flowing consciousnesses in their affirmation of subjectivity. For these Yogācārins, it suffices to simply settle on the notion of consciousness to sketch the wide range of mental acts. In his investigation of temporality, Husserl describes the underlying flow of consciousness as the "absolute subjectivity (*absolute Subjektivität*)" (Hua 10/74). He evokes the term "I-subject" in place of "ego" to highlight such an absolute subjectivity. The language of "ego" and "egos" appears more frequently in *Meditations* when Husserl details how to engage in phenomenology by departing from René Descartes.[20]

In the third place, Yogācārins expand their study to several extreme mental states—such as pre-death experience, dreamless sleep, and unconsciousness—that Husserl does not fully tackle, despite expressing his intention to do so in *Crisis* (Hua 6/192). In the context of the *CWSL*, we have inquired into these extreme states when exploring the ways in which the first six consciousnesses can cease functioning from time to time. According to these Yogācārins, even when we faint due to heat exhaustion, consciousness does not sever itself from our minds (T31N1585, P38a26). In virtue of the seventh consciousness *mona* and the eighth consciousness *laiye*, we are able to maintain our memories after waking up from a coma. Likewise, Chinese Yogācārins argue that we do not lose our consciousness during a pre-death experience, insofar as the eighth consciousness functions throughout endless time and preserves the previously cultivated seeds for the future. This continuity of consciousness makes it possible for the chain of *karma* to influence every stage of existence from this round of life to that of the next. Thus, the Yogācārins utilize the continuous flow of consciousness to explain their cosmological view of death and rebirth, a view enclosed in the notion of *saṃsāra*.

In the fourth place, Yogācārins like Xuanzang and his disciples provide a detailed description of the way in which each consciousness is paired with its respective set of mental factors. In contrast, Husserl does not articulate a fixed association of affective mental states with cognitive faculties. As documented in the *CWSL*, five omnipresent mental factors assist the function of all eight types of consciousness: contacting (*chu* 觸, *sparśa*), attending (*zuoyi* 作意, *manaskāra*), feeling (*shou* 受), thinking (*xiang* 想, *saṃjñā*), and purposing (*si* 思, *cetanā*). These factors indicate how we direct our attention to an object, discern it from others, generate feelings towards it, designate a title to refer to it, and eventually, purposefully carry out verbal or non-verbal actions relating to it. To illustrate the interplay between consciousness and its mental factors, Xuanzang provides an analogy of a painter. As the subject and the agent, each one of us is the painter of our own worldview. In the process of painting, the eight types of consciousness enable us to outline our mental images on the basis of which various mental factors finalize these images with colors (T31N1585, P26c18). Thus, it is in virtue of both consciousness and its mental factors that we experience a rich and colorful life, sometimes with suffering and attachment, and sometimes with awakening and compassion.

To highlight this distinction, Yogācārins ascribe moral qualities to consciousness and their mental factors. Such an association of mental acts with moral consequences alludes to how mental factors can motivate moral actions, further facilitating a transition from the descriptive account of consciousness to the prescriptive account. In all, there are four types of moral qualities: good (*shan* 善), evil (*e* 惡), neutral with ignorance/pollution (*youfuwuji* 有覆無記), and neutral without ignorance/pollution (*wufuwuji* 無覆無記) (T31N1585, P12a20). The moral quality of the eighth consciousness is neutral without pollution (T31N1585, P12a27–9). As such, *laiye*, which passively constitutes one's experience throughout endless time, is destined to be neither good nor evil, neither polluted by nor purified from misperception. *Mona*, the seventh consciousness, is neutral with pollution when it misperceives *laiye* as the *sui generis*, immutable self-identity (T31N1585, P23c7). As opposed to the latter two, the first six consciousnesses have all four types of qualities (T31N1585, P26b11). As to be elaborated in the last part of our book, the moral qualities of consciousness and its mental factors are crucial to the Buddhist cosmology of *saṃsāra* and moral actions. While ethics remain rudimentary in Husserl's articulation of phenomenology, the Yogācārins perceive ethics as an integral part of the Bodhisattvas' path, as a path towards the realization of emptiness and compassion at the prescriptive level of their doctrine of consciousness-only, which indicates their different destinations.

Considering how the Yogācāra articulation of consciousness can be related to but also demarcated from that in Husserl, we continue to reflect upon the limitation of a popular approach that translates Xuanzang's doctrine of consciousness-only as a Husserlian phenomenology in the Buddhist sense. Although this approach makes crucial contributions to engaging Yogācāra in contemporary discussions of the mind, it also raises questions. Notably, what should we do with concepts and ideas that do not appear to have matching counterparts in Husserl's phenomenology, such as the notion of rebirth and the concept of essence? Ultimately, this is why we refrain from taking a purely phenomenological standpoint to perceive Chinese Yogācāra, viewing it as a Buddhist version of Husserlian phenomenology. Adopting the "both–and" approach, we put these two traditions in their respective intellectual and linguistic contexts in order to locate their middle ground at the descriptive level of their theories. And now that we have found this middle ground in the articulations of intentionality, we can bring them into a conversation on the possibility of non-conceptualism, for expanding their shared horizon at the descriptive level.

6

Intentionality and Non-conceptualism

For both Husserl and Chinese Yogācārins like Xuanzang and his disciples, consciousness is intentional because it is always directed towards a phenomenon as the consciousness *of*, and simultaneously points back to the underlying flow as the consciousness *for*. With the help of intentionality, Husserl and these Chinese Yogācārins are able to examine mental acts from the simplest act of presenting to the more compounded act of conceptualizing. In this process, both expand the scope from the first-person perspective to that of the second-person and third-person. Both highlight how an abstract thought—or a meaning-intention (*Bedeutungsintention*), in Husserl's terms—produced by conceptual thinking not only presupposes the passive function of intuition, but also needs to return to non-conceptual intuition in order to fulfill the meaning. Equally so, both pinpoint the limits of reason and conceptual thinking. More importantly, both are confident that their respective approaches to consciousness allow for the possibility of seeing things as they present themselves in the experience. Indeed, it is Husserl's pronouncement that "we must go back to things themselves" by virtue of phenomenology to perceive them as they are (Hua 19/6). For Xuanzang and his disciples, it is imperative to correct misperceptions in order to realize the wisdom of emptiness and suchness, which further manifests things as they really are (T43N1830, P546a8). Now that both Husserl and Chinese Yogācārins prioritize the role of non-conceptual intuition over conceptual thinking, we can explore how to draw on their writings to make a case for non-conceptualism.

In its very literal sense, non-conceptualism entails a doctrine that argues for the existence and significance of the non-conceptual content of mental acts in someone's experience.[1] Currently, the debate over non-conceptualism concerns itself not merely with philosophical studies of knowledge; rather, it is also related to the general understanding of experience. For the study of knowledge, non-conceptualism highlights how intuition and sensation provide a zone where the mind and the world come into contact and interact with one another—an interaction that has largely been glossed over in conceptualism. For the general understanding of experience, non-conceptualism contests the popular view among philosophers that people cannot experience something unless they can form a concept to capture it, represent it, and express it. As such, if experience is sustained by non-conceptual faculties like intuition, then sentient beings such as infants and animals who do not have a full-fledged capacity of reasoning and conceptualizing can still have a coherent experience. By acknowledging the cognitive faculty of other sentient beings, non-conceptualism motivates philosophers to reflect on an anthropocentric view of experience and knowledge. Therefore, the on-going discussion on non-conceptualism in the field of philosophy sets the stage for our investigation of Husserl and Chinese Yogācārins in the current chapter.

More importantly, for comparative studies of philosophy and religion, non-conceptualism is closely related to the question of unmediated experience—a pure experience in which people transcend conceptual thinking and mundane cognition to immediately realize ultimate reality (Komarovski 2012: 88). Considering how several philosophical and religious traditions across time and place have affirmed and acknowledged the existence of such unmediated experience, non-conceptualism holds a special allure for comparative scholars (Gunther 2003: 2). Throughout the history of comparative philosophy, previous thinkers represented by D. T. Suzuki have commonly identified non-conceptualism as the salient feature of the worldview of the East in contrast to that of the West characterized by conceptualism. In this Orientalist narrative, conceptuality entails dualist thinking that differentiates the subject from the object through representation and objectification, which further defines rationality at the heart of the Western worldview; accordingly, non-conceptuality is said to be devoid of any differentiation whatsoever, which bespeaks non-rationality that delineates the worldview of the East. As previously discussed in Chapter 1, the mutually exclusive dichotomy between the East and the West, in its contribution to the Orientalist discourse, involves a substantial amount of overgeneralization and, therefore, misrepresents traditions on both ends.

To debunk this exclusive dichotomy and denounce the Orientalist discourse, we must then revisit how previous thinkers demarcated conceptualism from non-conceptualism. As such, we will first clarify what it means to be a "concept" and what counts as the "content" of a mental act. Through this examination, we can scrutinize the myriad of presumptions that have been inserted in these notions. After broadening the meaning of content and narrowing the meaning of concept, we explore whether it is possible to entertain the content of a mental act that is both non-conceptual and intentional. Subsequently, we will delve deeper into Husserl's phenomenology and Chinese Yogācāra to inquire into the possibility of drawing resources from their work in making a case for non-conceptualism.

What is (Non-)conceptualism?

When philosophers debate over non-conceptualism, they are in fact investigating whether non-conceptual content such as intuition and sensation exists in one's experience and can serve as a source of justification for knowledge. Depending on their respective answers to these questions, philosophers either join the camp of non-conceptualism or that of conceptualism. Non-conceptualists affirm the existence and the justificatory role of non-conceptual content, with conceptualists acting as their rivals. This debate in modern epistemology can be traced back to Immanuel Kant (1724–1804).[2] In his *Critique of Pure Reason*, Kant initiates an investigation of the principles for knowing an object, upon acknowledging both intuitions and concepts as the stems of knowledge (KrV A51/B75). To understand the debate, it is important to elucidate what philosophers mean when they utilize the notions of content and concept.

From our previous discussion on Husserl's notion of intentionality, we can track down at least two different meanings of this term "content." In his early writings, Husserl defines the content of an intentional mental act as the "interpretative, objective sense (*Sinn der gegenständliche Auffassung*)"—namely, as the sense of objective reference (*gegenständliche Beziehung*) (Hua 19/415–16). After his transcendental turn, Husserl revises the definition as he realizes how content cannot be reduced to interpretative sense. He then speaks of the content of a mental act as the *noema*, namely, the idealized presentation of an intended object (Hua 3/186). Therefore, from Husserl's vantage point, content can mean either the interpretative sense or the ideal presentation of an object.

In contemporary studies of philosophy, it remains popular to equate the content of a mental act with the interpretative sense of objective reference. Differing only slightly from early Husserl, Christopher Peacocke defines content as the *that*-clause, which refers to various objects in the world (Peacocke 1983: 1). For instance, the content of Cindy's perception or her feeling is expressed through the proposition: Cindy perceives *that* a Christmas tree is in the foyer; Cindy feels *that* she is happy to see the blossoming apple tree. Aside from understanding content as interpretative sense, Brentano perceives it as the mental representation of an object (Brentano 1995: 62). Such a definition continues to be espoused by numerous scholars today (Dennett 1987; Cussins 1991; Crane 1992; Bermúdez 2007).

The view that each mental act has its proper content can also be traced back to Kant when he proclaims that "thoughts without content are empty; intuitions without concepts are blind" (KrV A51/B75). Nevertheless, Kant does not define what he means by content; nor has he given a clear definition of concepts either. We can, however, determine that Kant uses the notion of concept in at least three ways:

1. Concepts are abstract ideas. This is the definition of "concept" in the pure sense, namely, a concept as the form of understanding (KrV A50/B74).
2. Concepts are synonymous with representations that contribute to the content of consciousness in general, including understanding. According to Kant, a concept is "one consciousness that unifies the manifold that has been successfully intuited, and then reproduced, into one representation" (KrV A103).
3. Concepts entail the spontaneous mental faculty of understanding, or what we today call the capacity of conceptualizing. Kant pinpoints two stems of knowledge, one as the faculty of intuition *qua* the "receptivity of impressions" and the other as the faculty of understanding *qua* the "spontaneity of concepts" (KrV A50/B74).

It is not difficult to see how these three senses conveyed by Kant set the paradigm for contemporary discussion of concepts. Among the three, the second definition of concepts—concepts as representations—has become prevalent in contemporary studies of philosophy (Harman 1987; Carruthers 2000; Fodor 2003; Margolis &

Laurence 2014). In this regard, Michael Tye specifies that a concept is a mental representation in a thought, which shall be demarcated from the linguistic term we use in our everyday language, namely, not as concept in the first sense listed above (Tye 2005: 222). As further detailed by Tye, since concepts are representations that unify the sense data given through intuition, concepts function to mediate between the subject and the object, further enabling a person to relate to a represented object (Tye 2000: 17). Considering how concepts possess references that allow someone to relate to an object, concepts can be used to determine semantic value. That is to say, someone cannot have knowledge of something unless this person can formulate a concept to express it. Aside from understanding concepts as mental representations, several philosophers also endorse the last sense of concepts as the mental faculty of conceptualizing (Dummett 1993; Bennett & Hacker 2008; Millikan 2000; Kenny 2010). According to these philosophers, concepts entail the cognitive faculty of forming a representation, making reference to an object, and providing principles for justifying knowledge of this object, a faculty that cannot be reduced to representations *per se*.

In our examination of the meaning of content and concept, we have elucidated three definitions of content (as an interpretative sense, an ideal presentation, and a mental representation), and three senses of concept (as an abstract idea, a mental representation, and the capacity of conceptualizing). A clear overlap transpires, as most philosophers define both content and concept as representation. However, if a concept is the same as its content, then it is not only tautological to talk about conceptual content—since the concept *is* the content—but also futile to entertain any possible existence of non-conceptual content. For this reason, we need to revise this definition. Here I draw upon Husserl's definition of content as that which is associated with an intentional act. As such, content can be either abstractly interpretive or concretely phenomenal. *Mutatis mutandis*, I narrow the meaning of concept. By concept, I do not mean mental representation in general, but rather the capacity of producing abstract categories, which Husserl refers to as meaning-intentions. As such, if content entails what an intentional act is about and concept suggests the capacity of producing abstract categories, it becomes possible for us to entertain and examine non-conceptual content. We then speak of non-conceptual content as that which does not involve abstract names and categories but immediately presents an object. And meanwhile, we conceive of conceptual content as that which is not only abstract and categorial, but also inferentially and intermediately related to an object.

The ways in which we acknowledge the existence of non-conceptual content guide us in rethinking what non-conceptuality actually entails. Over the years, philosophers have considered non-conceptual content as that which goes beyond any subject–object differentiation whatsoever. Since there is no such differentiation, non-conceptual content is not *about* an object but becomes one with the object. As such, by saying that non-conceptual content is unmediated, scholars generally mean that this type of content is not representational nor intentional. Under this assumption, two stances towards non-conceptuality have been proposed. One group of philosophers contend that we cannot consciously be aware of any non-conceptual content because it is not part of our explicit experience (Sellars 1968; Katz 1978). As described by Gareth Evans, non-conceptual content remains to be subconscious, which is not part of the explicit perceptual experiences but can become a state of a conscious subject through serving as the input of a thought (Evans 1982: 157–8). In this manner, non-conceptuality exists as an attribute of subconsciousness. Others argue that non-conceptual content can still be part of our explicit experience, insofar as it pertains to a unique type of experience *qua* a mystical and ineffable experience, an experience that yields knowledge through a direct realization of ultimate reality (Forman 1990; Griffiths 1990; Rothberg 1990). As such, non-conceptuality becomes a salient feature of mysticism.

The reason why philosophers are propelled to choose between subconsciousness and mysticism is that they assume non-conceptuality to be devoid of any types of differentiation and further equate the non-conceptual with the non-intentional. It is not hard to discern how this assumption internalizes the conceptualist view of experience. That is to say, such an assumption perpetuates the idea that people cannot experience something unless they form a concept to objectify it, represent it, and express it. In line with this viewpoint, if the content of a mental act is unmediated, non-conceptual, and thus non-representational, this mental act has no intentionality, cannot bring about knowledge through objectification, and cannot become part of our explicit experience, unless it is ineffable and mystical.

Indeed, when we perceive intentionality as a static form of what is directing and what is directed—or of what is representing and what is represented—intentionality entails a polarity between the subject and the object. However, if intentionality characterizes a dynamic process of mutual constitution brought about by a joint effort of the subject and the object, then it alludes to correlative non-duality, rather than pure polarity. That is to say, the subject and the object are not mutually exclusive but mutually constituted. As pinpointed by Victor Hori, "Katz and his opponents both agree in dividing the spectrum of consciousness into those with cognitive content and those without, into those that are mediated (not pure) and those that are unmediated (pure)" yet they never consider possibilities outside the polarities (Hori 2000: 282).

Then, is it possible to entertain non-conceptuality as that which remains different from conceptual thinking, but not devoid of intentionality? Turning back to Husserl and Chinese Yogācārins like Xuanzang and his disciples, we come to see that we can indeed explore this possibility. In particular, we want to pay attention to that which stands outside various sets of exclusive dichotomies. Borrowing Hori's expression, we hope to "destroy the habit of thinking in terms of mutually exclusive dichotomies like pure and impure in the first place" (Hori 2000: 283). That is why we make a shift in focus from a static to a dynamic description of intentionality. Through the phenomenological discussion of genesis and the Yogācāra articulation of transformation (*bian* 變, *pariṇāma*), Husserl and Xuanzang stress how the non-conceptual act of intending (such as intuition and sensation) is neither polarized from nor merged with the intended phenomenon. If the act of intuiting were polarized with its content *qua* the intuited phenomenon, then this act would become representational and transform into conceptual thinking. Likewise, if the act of intuiting were merged with its content, then the content would be assimilated into the act as in a mystical experience. Quite to the contrary, the non-conceptual act of intending and its content *qua* the intended phenomenon mutually constitute each other with the underlying flow of consciousness. Such mutual constitution bespeaks collaboration and interconnection, rather than polarity or unity, of the act and its phenomenon. To stress such interdependence, Husserl eventually characterizes intentionality as mutual constitution, rather than directedness. Similarly, Xuanzang and his disciples foreground the interdependence of the intending act *qua* the seeing part, the intended phenomenon *qua* the image part, the underlying self-awareness, and the reflexive awareness of such self-awareness in their articulation of the fourfold intentional structure of consciousness. The dynamic fluidity between these four parts entails how non-conceptual content as that of the eighth consciousness can be immediate and intentional, although intentionality does not necessarily yield subject–object polarity. In virtue of their conceptions of intentionality, we *ipso facto* broaden the meaning of non-conceptual content as that which does not involve a production of abstract names and categories but can still present an object immediately as the intended phenomenon.

Therefore, non-conceptual content can be immediate and intentional. Here, with the intending act, the intended phenomenon, and the underlying flow of consciousness, their distinctness is not canceled, nor do they merge into a higher unity. Rather, through a dynamic process of mutual constitution, things present themselves as they actually are to us. Such presented phenomena in non-conceptual content further lay the ground for the active use of reason in conceptual thinking. To fulfill their meaning, concepts need to go back to their non-conceptual content. Knowledge, thus, is produced when what is meant becomes what is presented. As such, the non-conceptual content of a mental act furnishes us with a primordial, habitual understanding of the world even prior to the exercise of reason, which is possessed not only by humans but also by all sentient beings. Our expanded view of non-conceptual content indicates a revised version of non-conceptualism—we cannot have knowledge of something unless we can habitually, intuitively experience the thing itself in worldly life together with other sentient beings. Now that we have redefined the notions of content, concept, and conceptual content, we can continue to explore whether and how we can substantialize this revised version of non-conceptualism by drawing upon the writings of Husserl and Chinese Yogācārins like Xuanzang and his disciples.

Husserl's Contribution to Non-conceptualism[3]

Husserl acknowledges the existence of non-conceptual content in experience first and foremost through expanding the meaning of intuition. He attributes intentionality to all mental acts so that even sensation and intuition have intended phenomena as their content. He further puts forward the ideas of categorial intuition and universal intuition for the purpose of affirming the constitutive function of intuition. To further explore how Husserl credits the non-conceptual type of content as the source of justification, I find it helpful to revisit the principles for knowing, based on the notions of founding, fulfilling, and identifying.

Let us first examine the notion of founding. According to Husserl, our abstract thinking is founded on a set of simple presentational acts. As such, abstract thinking originates from and fulfills its meaning in intuition (Hua 19/6). Husserl later evokes the analogy of the ladder to account for the way in which we can formulate more abstract concepts on the basis of intuition (Hua 19/691). Indeed, through the active use of reason, we are able to proceed from the basic mental act of perception to the more abstract act of synthesizing, analyzing, and judging. Such a process can be compared to that of climbing up a ladder. That is why Husserl remarks that "[logical concepts] must arise out of an ideational intuition founded on certain experiences" (Hua 19/6). In light of the analogy of the ladder, Husserl shows that non-conceptual mental acts, such as presenting and categorial intuiting, serve as the ground and foundation for all upper-level mental acts. Recall the previous examples of the Christmas tree in the foyer seen by Cindy. When Cindy is looking at the tree, its color, shape, texture, and smell are presented to her directly through sensation. Founded on these simple acts of presenting, the act of perceiving arises as the integral perception of the tree as-a-whole. Further founded on the perception of the tree and the foyer, the act of perceiving the state of affairs presents directly the entire situation of the tree's being in the foyer to Cindy. Such an act of perceiving, also known as categorial intuition in Husserl's early work, expands the notion of intuition from a sensuous perception to a supersensuous perception. Categorial intuition remains intuitive and non-conceptual insofar as its content is directly, immediately given, in one stroke. Nonetheless, it is a supersensuous, categorial type of intuition considering how it enables Cindy to perceive not only an object like a tree, but also a state of affairs *qua* the tree's being in the foyer. Therefore, on the basis of various acts of perceiving, Cindy is able to formulate abstract concepts.

The above example indicates how more complex acts, such as conceptualizing or categorizing, can continue to constitute themselves consecutively on the simple acts of presenting in sensation. Through several rounds of founding, it seems that a ladder gradually takes shape from the simple act of presenting to the compound act of judging. To perceive an object, we need to begin with intuitions, not concepts. As such, we go back to things themselves and see them as they actually are. Furthermore, the ladder allows us to walk both ways—on the one hand, more abstract and complex acts can rise one after another on the foundations, and, on the other hand, these upper-level mental acts need to return to non-conceptual content to fulfill their meaning. In figurative terms, "fulfillment is carried out in a chain of acts which take us down a whole ladder of 'foundations'" (Hua 19/691). That which determines fulfillment likewise comes from non-conceptual content, which alludes to a deeper meaning of Husserl's statement on how concepts find their origins in intuition (Hua 19/5).

In our introduction to Husserl's investigation of inner time consciousness, we encountered a special case where when we try to recollect the past, the previous memory cannot be retrieved right away. This incapacity to recall does not indicate our inability to carry out the act of recollecting but implies how the *noematic* content of this act remains missing. For even higher-level acts, such as naming, they likewise need to have their content fulfilled. Otherwise, the meaning of these acts becomes empty. For instance, we can formulate the concept of an iPhone 50. Yet, the concept will remain empty until the content of this naming is furnished, and its meaning is fulfilled, such as when this product appears on the market. We can therefore have various mental acts, although not all of them contain meaning. What determines the meaningfulness of these acts is their non-conceptual content. That is why Husserl stresses that "meanings inspired only by remote, confused, inauthentic intuitions—if by any intuitions at all—

are not enough: we must go back to things themselves" (Hua 19/6). For Husserl, we only have knowledge of an object when the content of an intentional mental act is fulfilled, that is, when what is meant meets what is presented.

While several founded acts come to take shape, the issue of justification arises. There are times when Cindy believes that she runs into her friend Jen. Yet, upon closer inspection, she realizes that this person is a stranger. As such, perception can make mistakes and reasoning can become fallacious. In Husserl's account of intentionality, he proposes a way of justifying through identification. As previously mentioned, the concept of identification shows that what is meant becomes identical with what is presented. By then, knowledge of one object can be justified. In understanding Husserl's view, it will be helpful to return to the issue of fallacy. Husserl documents a similar example in which he mistook a waxwork figure for a real person (Hua19/443). In this experience of being deceived and making a fallacious judgment, Husserl pinpoints two mental acts that are at play: perceiving and believing (Hua 19/443). He first saw a waxwork figure that had color and shape. This perception constituted a ground, on the basis of which the act of believing arose and propelled him to assume that he saw a real person (Hua 19/443). More often than not, upon closer inspection, he would realize he had made a mistake and recognize that it was a wax figure all along. Through examination, Husserl notes that he was not able to confirm his belief because the *noematic* content of perceiving *qua* the wax figure is in conflict with the *noematic* content of believing *qua* a person. Husserl describes this conflict as a contradiction in which the content of the act of perceiving fails to be identical with the content of the act of believing (Hua 19/444). From the issue of deception, I infer that for Husserl, what determines our justification is, again, the non-conceptual content given through sensation and intuition. Through non-conceptual content, we are able to go back to things themselves, which furnishes us with the source of justification.

In the first two phases of his study of consciousness, Husserl does not foreground the question of genesis regarding how various intentional acts arise and emerge. In the next two phases, however, genesis becomes central in Husserl's phenomenology. As previously mentioned, Husserl differentiates between two types of geneses: the active and the passive. The active use of reason always presupposes the passively generated synthesis of non-conceptual content in intuition, sensation, and impression. As such, while it is true that we can only communicate with one another through concept and language, the possibility of communication presupposes a primordial lifeworld shared and constituted by a plurality of individuals. At this point, Husserl directs our focus to the lifeworld in which individuals act, interact, and collaborate with one another. Accordingly, knowledge is not confined to the cognitions inside the mind but extends its arms to bodily performances in an intersubjective setting. That is to say, sentient beings have developed a primordial comprehension of the intersubjective lifeworld that presents things as they are directly and prepares sentient beings for the exercise of reason. It is on the horizon of a mutually constituted lifeworld that each individual can actively exercise reason to conceptualize and communicate.

Following this Husserlian interpretation of intentionality, we can appreciate the ways in which sentient beings without a full-fledged capacity of reason still possess knowledge of the world and have a coherent experience of it. Infants cannot express themselves in words, but they can endure anxiety after being separated from their loved ones. Similarly, animals get stressed easily once they are exposed to change, for instance, some cats quickly find a place to hide when a new person is in the house. Emotional stress indicates how infants and animals have a preliminary understanding of their surroundings, even though they cannot use language to describe it to us. Compared with them, humans can indeed conceptualize their experience and come up with a consistent life story. However, when humans overlook the constitutive role of non-conceptual content in the production and justification of knowledge, they embrace the natural attitude and reduce life into factuality, which makes them unable to meaningfully connect to their life. Confronted with the prevalence of naturalism together with the related crisis of meaning, Husserl puts forward his pronouncement of "going back to things themselves (*auf die Sachen selbst zurückgehen*)" (Hua 19/6). The examination of consciousness at the descriptive level, therefore, provides a methodological approach for Husserl to inquire into the ultimate nature of reality. Thus far, we have explained how Husserl can contribute to non-conceptualism. Not only does he argue for the role of non-conceptual content furnished by intuition as the origin of knowledge and as the source of justification, but he also discovers how conceptuality always presupposes and needs the existence of non-conceptual content.

Chinese Yogācārins' Contribution to Non-conceptualism

Similar to Husserl, Yogācārins expand the meaning of non-conceptuality.[4] The move is signaled by Xuanzang and his disciples when they impose the fourfold intentional structure on all consciousnesses and their mental factors, and equally when they highlight the existence of the eighth consciousness that passively functions to serve as the ground for conceptual thinking. To further explore their stance on non-conceptuality, we can turn to their doctrine of measuring (*liang* 量, *pramāṇa*). This doctrine constitutes an integral part of Buddhist logic (*yinming* 因明, *hetuvidyā*), which brings to light the "straight principles [that] denote things as they actually are (正理者，諸法本真之體義)" (T44N1840, P91c25). Upon seeing things as they actually are, sentient beings will be able to realize the wisdom of emptiness (T43N1830, P546a8).

The literal meaning of this Chinese term *liang* (量) or *pramāṇa* in Sanskrit is measuring. According to Kuiji, whenever tailors use a tape to measure something, they need three things: first, a tool capable of measuring, (e.g., the tape); second, the object to be measured (such as a piece of silk); and third, the result of measurement (e.g., the length of that silk-piece) (T44N1840, P140b12–13). Measuring is thus analogous to our way of knowing: in the fourfold structure of consciousness, the seeing part undertakes the role of knowing, parallel to the tool of measuring; the image part is the object being measured, similar to the piece of silk; the underlying self-awareness can be compared to the result of a measurement; and the underlying self-awareness can also measure itself, the result of which is the reflexive awareness of self-awareness.

In order to elucidate the sources of knowledge, Yogācārins further outline three types of measuring through which knowledge is produced. These are: direct perception (*xianliang* 現量, *pratyakṣapramāṇa*), inference (*biliang* 比量, *anumānapramāṇa*), and erroneous knowledge (*feiliang* 非量, *apramāṇa*). The first type is referred to as *xianliang*, which entails a direct perception of what appears right here right now. By definition, a direct perception "does not entail any nominal differentiation (離此名言分別)" (T44N1840, P139a26). Modern Yogācāra scholar Lü Cheng (呂澂 1896–1989) interprets the nominal (*minyan* 名言) as the conceptual (*gainian* 概念) (Lü 2007: 254). Therefore, the salient feature of this direct perception is how it is devoid of conceptual dichotomization. Among all types of consciousness, there are several that can directly measure their objects, among them, the first five senses, the sixth consciousness (T44N1840, P139b13), and the eighth consciousness *laiye* (賴耶, *ālayavijñāna*) (T43N1830, P320b16).[5] Besides, in the fourfold structure of each consciousness, the underlying self-awareness and the reflexive awareness are also characterized by direct perception (T68N2270, P420).

It has been introduced earlier that Chinese Yogācārins like Xuanzang and his disciples characterize consciousness with its fourfold intentional structure. Now, it has also been clarified that a direct perception shall be apart from differentiations. If this is the case, can a direct perception be compatible with the fourfold structure in which the seeing part *qua* the subjective act is demarcated from the image part *qua* the objective phenomenon? To put it differently, can a direct perception be intentional? From the commentaries penned by these Chinese Yogācārins, we can infer that they are confronted with a similar set of questions, especially due to the fact that Buddhists from other schools do consider direct perception to be detached from any differentiation whatsoever and, therefore, be devoid of an intentional structure. That is why Kuiji's disciple, Huizhao, finds it necessary to elaborate on the meaning of being "apart (*li* 離)" from differentiation (T44N1840, P139a24–b12).[6] As specified by Huizhao, direct perception is apart from and devoid of differentiations associated with abstract names, categories, and fictitious postulations, which does not mean direct perception cannot be constituted by several different parts (T44N1840, P139b11). In other words, direct perception does not reject the intentional correlation of the seeing part and the image part. Those that are vacant in direct perception include abstract names, categories, and fictitious postulations, which reflects the very last sense of concepts listed in section 1, namely, concepts *qua* the mental faculty of producing abstract categories. As such, direct perception is intentional and immediate.

This is how Xuanzang and his disciples implicitly provide an account of non-conceptual content as that which presents an objective image directly to the mind without any mediation or inference by abstract concepts. If direct perception does not involve conceptual thinking, it furnishes us with non-conceptual content. It is the direct knowledge of that which appears in front of us. The first five senses generate sensations of various aspects of a phenomenon on the basis of which the sixth consciousness processes these sensations to give rise to a coherent image. The perception of the sixth consciousness, in this case, resembles what Husserl refers to as a categorial intuition, which founds itself on simple acts of presenting in sensations. The eighth consciousness *laiye* passively transforms to constitute the images of the material cosmos and the corporeal body as-a-whole, in parallel to what Husserl calls apperception. Then, whenever consciousnesses and mental factors begin their function, they are self-aware of such functionality. This self-awareness in the fourfold intentional structure can also perceive directly. Since direct perception defines the cognitive capacity of the first five consciousnesses and *laiye,* we can infer that Xuanzang and his disciples acknowledge the existence of non-conceptual content in the experience.

Surely, the sixth consciousness can function without the five senses. By then, it is exercising its capacity of producing a general idea (*gongxiang* 共相, *sāmānyalakṣaṇa*) of various distinct phenomena. Knowledge of general ideas gives rise to *biliang* (比量) or inference. For instance, *biliang* is always exercised during our study of analytic geometry, in the case of which we can analyze spatial relations through the Cartesian coordinate system. Inferring is premised on reasoning, which allows for knowledge acquisition first through comparing direct perceptions and then through abstracting a general image from these perceptions. Among eight types of consciousness, the sixth consciousness is capable of both directly perceiving and indirectly reasoning. For instance, whenever we see smoke, we know there is fire. This is because "we have learned from our previous experiences that when there is smoke, there is fire (憶本先知，所有煙處，必定有火)" (T44N1840, P140a9). The way in which we infer fire from smoke entails the pure function of inferring. In this case, the inference is grounded in perception. Nonetheless, it is also quite often the case that inferring can set its premise on previous inferences. Kuiji illustrates this type of inference through the way in which we comprehend impermanence from the transformation of consciousness (T44N1840, P140a5). As detailed by Kuiji, we can never directly perceive the quality of impermanence but can only "infer impermanence from how various events arise and perish [through the course of our lived experience] (了無常等，從所作等，比量因生)" (T44N1840, P140a8). Articulated in this way, inference suggests the existence of conceptual content in our knowledge.

Aside from direct perception and indirect inference, Yogācārins discern a third type of knowing *qua* erroneous knowledge. Hence, this type of knowing is tantamount to fallacies that can stem from both inference and perception. When it comes to fallacious inference, Kuiji turns to the scenario in which someone sees smoke and infers fire, yet this inference ends up being wrong because smoke turns out to be a mist rising over a waterfall (T44N1840, P141b21–2). Erroneous perception, on the other hand, is quite different from fallacious inference. For instance, the function of the seventh consciousness *mona* (末那, *manas*) shows the erroneous type of perception. It is because this seventh consciousness conflates direct perception with the habitual concept of a self-in-itself. Indeed, *mona* passively constitutes the primordial sense of selfhood, further misperceiving the seeing part of the eighth consciousness *laiye* as a permanent self-in-itself. The conflation of direct perceptions with abstract categories yields the erroneous type of perception. As elucidated by Lü Cheng, we can only infer the general idea of red from a tangible red object, whilst it is never possible for us to directly perceive the concept of red (Lü 2007: 258).

Having clarified the three modes of knowing, we can inquire into the ground for knowledge. As we have deduced earlier, the eighth consciousness *laiye* transforms itself to give rise to the overall images of the material cosmos, the corporeal body, and seeds. The seventh consciousness *mona* takes the eighth consciousness *laiye*'s act of (ap) perceiving and misconceives it as a *svabhāvic* self, whereas the first five consciousnesses perceive the image of an object in the context of the images constituted by the eighth consciousness. On the basis of these five senses, the sixth consciousness arises to integrate data from these senses and further produces general concepts by comparing one objective image with another. Considering the way in which the sixth consciousness exercises its capacity of inferring on the basis of direct perception, we can argue that direct perception serves as the ground for indirect inference.

It follows *a fortiori* that we always need to go back to direct perception at a specific moment to eliminate fallacy from our cognition and to justify our knowledge. Kuiji details this justification through his rope–snake analogy (T45N1861, P259a15–16). This analogy describes how someone walking in the dark mistakes a rope on the road for a snake. Misperception can further elicit unpleasant feelings of discomfort, fear, and worry. One might even scream out loud or faint upon believing that a poisonous snake appeared. In the Yogācāra framework, fallacies emerge when the sixth consciousness, in the process of inferring, commits errors of false inference, which further provokes the mental factors of fear and anxiety that make a person suffer. Articulated in this manner, a fallacy is not only an epistemic issue, but also an existential one.

For Xuanzang and his disciples, three conditions make it possible to awake from misperception: first, various types of consciousness are self-aware of their functionality; second, previous perceptions can be recollected in virtue of the incessant transformation of the eighth consciousness; and third—which will be unpacked in Chapter 11—even an ignorant mindset is interconnected with another mind that is not only awake but also willing to guide this ignorant sentient being back to the right path. Therefore, by contrasting the perceived phenomenon *qua* the rope with the phenomenon in the belief *qua* the snake, this person who was once petrified comes to recognize the fallacy. Furthermore, through recollecting, this person will understand how the incessant transformation of the eighth consciousness gives rise to the open possibility of either seeing the rope as it really is or misperceiving the rope as a snake. As such, Kuiji remarks that both the misperception of the snake and the perception of the rope arise in the same manner, *viz.* through the transformation of consciousness. The ground for justification is constituted by the direct perception of the eighth consciousness and the reflexive self-awareness of the sixth consciousness, both being characterized by non-conceptuality. Once knowledge is justified and misperception is removed, the direct and correct cognition evolves into truth and encourages sentient beings to become one with such true knowledge. Indeed, it means that any readers of the rope–snake analogy will take a step back and come to realize that the person described in this analogy is not anyone else but themselves. The rope and the snake are equally metaphorical ways of describing things as they are and misperceptions. Just like how the person in this analogy suffers from mistaking the rope for a snake, sentient beings who are reading about this analogy also suffer from misperceiving things as *svabhāva*. As such, readers of this analogy will be motivated to go beyond a conceptual understanding of the analogy to enact and embody truth in their everyday experience. By then, wisdom (*zhi* 智, *jñana*) is realized as the embodied truth (T45N1861, P259a29).

As Xuanzang and his disciples unpack these concepts, direct perception serves as the origin of knowledge and as the source of justification. This is how we can draw upon the writings of these Chinese Yogācārins to make a case for non-conceptualism.

Subsequently, as demonstrated by Kuiji, this descriptive account of consciousness paves the way for inquiries of the ultimate nature of reality at the explicative level of the Yogācāra philosophical system. Returning to the rope–snake analogy, after seeing the rope as it is, a sentient being will continue to learn that a phenomenon, either as a rope-phenomenon or as a snake-phenomenon, appears in their mind by the virtue of the transformation of consciousness. Thus, things in the cosmos depend on consciousness to arise and perish in sentient beings' experience. Instead of being *sui generis*, self-determining, and immutable, things are interdependent with one another and, therefore, empty of *svabhāva*. After being introduced to the teaching of emptiness, sentient beings will make an effort to correct conceptual and habitual misperceptions, for removing the discriminative and innate attachments. They will engage in systematic training to renounce misperception, remove attachments, and realize the non-dual wisdom of seeing things as they are. This line of reasoning explains how Yogācārins subordinate epistemological inquiries to the description of consciousness, which makes a case for our use of the term "descriptive" in place of "epistemological." Moreover, according to these Yogācārins, the description of consciousness is the first step to explicate the realization of emptiness and compassion.

It is worth noticing that Xuanzang and his disciples do not interpret the ultimate non-dual wisdom (*wufenbie zhi* 無分別智, *nirvikalpakajñāna*) as a mystical experience. Xuanzang describes this wisdom as that which "has the seeing part but does not have the image part (*jianyou xiangwu* 見有相無)" (T31N1585, P49c28). To be more precise, this wisdom has no image part because it allows sentient beings to "see the image as mutually arising and self-interdependent (*dairuxiang qibuli* 帶如相起不離)," rather than misperceive this image as *svabhāvic* (T31N1585, P50a1). From Xuanzang's description, it can be inferred that awakening in the Yogācāra sense is not a mystic experience that dissolves all differentiations. Rather, the ultimate non-dual wisdom is realized universally through the way in which each subject acts to collaborate with one another to become one with the transformation of consciousness.

In our analysis, we have drawn upon the work of Husserl and Chinese Yogācārins to make a case for non-conceptualism. More specifically, we have explored how they advance the meaning of non-conceptuality. As examined above, both Husserl and Chinese Yogācārins define intentionality in a dynamic manner as the mutual constitution of the subjective act and the objective phenomenon, which reveals that non-conceptual content can be both immediate and intentional. As such, when they affirm the existence of non-conceptual content, and acknowledge this type of content as the source of knowledge and justification, they also explore the complementary fluidity of the subject and the object, of rationality and non-rationality, and of conceptuality and non-conceptuality. As such, these binaries are not mutually exclusive but mutually constituted. From their shared insight on non-conceptuality, we can infer how and why the overgeneralized dichotomy between the rational West and the non-rational East at the center of the Orientalist discourse falls short. On the one hand, Husserl problematizes the conceptualist understanding of experience and proves the epistemic importance of non-conceptual content in his examination of intentionality, which debunks the portrayal of the West as overly rational against non-rationality. On the other hand, Xuanzang and his disciples incorporate the discussion of logic in their doctrine of consciousness-only and refine the definition of non-dual wisdom, further raising a question to the framing of the East as sheerly non-rational and antagonistic against rationality. Indeed, there are numerous thinkers like our protagonists whose systems of thought pose a serious challenge to the dichotomy between the rational West and the non-rational East. More importantly, their theories allow us to defy the type of thinking in terms of mutually exclusive dichotomies. Overgeneralizing philosophical traditions and downplaying the diversity of viewpoints on both ends, the Orientalist discourse is far from cogent. Our analysis has touched upon how the shared insight of non-conceptuality reveals the middle ground between our protagonists' explanations of the ultimate nature of reality. Now, we can move forward to the explicative level in the following part of our journey.

Part Three

The Tracks

The previous part of this book examined the intentional character of consciousness as described by Husserl and Chinese Yogācārins like Xuanzang and his disciples. Through their descriptions, both parties have depicted how intentional consciousness is always the consciousness *of*, since mental acts are directed towards a phenomenon, and also the consciousness *for*, because mental acts point back to the underlying flow. Employing the notion of intentionality, Husserl and these Chinese Yogācārins continue to investigate the origin of the knowledge of (no-)self and other minds. Both are confident that we can return to things themselves and perceive them as they actually are, in virtue of intentionality. Putting forward transcendental arguments to stress how the mind serves as the necessary condition for the possibility of phenomena in our experience, they express what can be considered as a similar insight on non-conceptuality. This insight brings to the fore the following set of questions: what is the ultimate nature of things as they appear in our experience? Are they mind-independent entities that come into existence on their own or are they nothing but mental productions? If the latter is true, would it make the mind another *sui generis* entity invariant across time and space?

In answering these questions, Husserl and the Chinese Yogācārins move on from the descriptive level to the explicative level of their study of consciousness. As such, prior to our examination, it is a must to clarify the meaning of the notion of "explicative," a notion that remains central to this part of our journey. We have briefly defined this concept in the prologue, observing that what is "explicative" entails an elaboration of the ultimate nature of various things, including consciousness. Here, I evoke the term "explicative" to replace the more widely used notion of "metaphysics," partly because many scholars of Chinese Buddhism have alerted us to the danger of overlooking the distinctive nuances of the concepts of ontology and metaphysics that are not always commensurable with the Buddhist notion of emptiness (Xia 2002; Fu 2002). Moreover, I find the term "explicative" more suitable, given that the concept of metaphysics has a rich history in Euro-American philosophy.[1] Even inside Husserlian scholarship, scholars continue to debate Husserl's stance on metaphysics. Some have argued that phenomenology is not metaphysical but epistemological, considering that Husserl suspends his metaphysical discussions to make phenomenology his rigorous study of knowledge (Carr 1999: 134; Hopp 2011: 3). Others, like Dan Zahavi, appeal to rethinking what Husserl means by metaphysics in the first place. As unpacked by

Zahavi, Husserl proposes metaphysics in a new sense as that which can go beyond the traditional polarity of ideality and reality (Zahavi 2017: 206).

Indeed, Husserl and Chinese Yogācārins like Xuanzang and his disciples strive to problematize the traditional, static view of perceiving binaries as mutually exclusive categories. Coming from different contexts, they each explore how ideality and reality, subjectivity and objectivity, the mind and the world, self-mind and other minds, mutually constitute one another. Upon closing the rift between these polarities, Husserl and these Chinese Yogācārins continue to expound on the correlative non-duality of things through a worldview that can be termed "transcendental idealism." Nevertheless, due to the ambiguities surrounding the term "metaphysics" in both Yogācāra Buddhism and Husserlian phenomenology, I find it necessary to renew our terminology and use the term "explicative" to capture metaphysics in the new sense envisioned by Husserl (Hua 7/188). "Explicative" likewise characterizes the Yogācāra theory of three natures as a theory proposed to explain how things arise and perish but remain ultimately empty. As such, the meaning of "explicative" can be further delineated in the following manner:

1. An explicative study of consciousness is first and foremost a clarification of what and how things actually are; that is, an elucidation of the status of reality.
2. For the purpose of revealing the mutual dependence of things in the world, this elucidation problematizes our current assumptions and presumptions of existence and being.
3. An elaboration of what and how things actually are prepares one for further inquiries on agency in moral action and community building.

In his explication of what and how things actually are, Husserl contends that phenomenology centers on the ideation of a factually existent object, not factuality *per se* (Hua 3/6–10). To describe an object as what it actually is shall be demarcated from describing the object's factual existence. Indeed, it refers to the ideal *a priori*—namely, the essence of the object. Husserl, thus, defines phenomenology as a "science of essence (*Wesenwissenschaft*)" (Hua 3/4), its major theme being the essence of consciousness (Hua 3/60). Conversely, through their investigation of consciousness, Xuanzang and his disciples argue that everything in the cosmos—be it the self of sentient beings or other objects *qua* dharmas—are empty of essence (*svabhāva*) (T31N1585, P1a23-4). At least on the surface, Husserl and these Yogācārins endorse different, or even disparate, stances towards essence. This is where we encounter the differences in the tracks left by their wheels at the explicative level of their investigations of consciousness.[2]

Therefore, the third part of our journey unveils and unravels the problem of essence. The first question that shall be addressed is: what exactly does the term "essence" mean in the writings of Husserl and Chinese Yogācārins? At this stage of our discussion, translation adds another layer of complexity to the question, insofar as both Husserl and Chinese Yogācārins have never directly used the English term "essence," although the concept of essence has been evoked to translate a wide range of terms of different origins in phenomenology and in Chinese philosophy. Due to these factors, a closer examination of the concept of essence and its rich nuances—especially how the term has been translated and applied in cross-cultural and multilingual contexts—is henceforth required. Such an examination will ultimately determine whether it is possible to group phenomenology and Yogācāra under the same umbrella.

Unlike the previous part of our journey that focused on the convergences and compatibilities, the current part targets their perceived divergences and differences. Acknowledging the existence of the problem of essence, the following analysis explores how this problem will not undermine our comparative project. As to be argued, since Husserl and Chinese Yogācārins use the term differently, referring to dissimilar things altogether, they do not contradict one another in their discussion of "essence." To unpack this argument, we begin Chapter 7 by investigating whether or not Husserl's conception of essence entails any *svabhāvic* existence. Considering how Husserl continues to enrich and expand the notion of essence in different phases of his philosophical thinking process, the Husserlian essence is neither static nor *svabhāvic*. Following this, in Chapter 8, we shall examine whether Xuanzang and his disciples' articulation of three natures is compatible with transcendental idealism. I will argue that they are indeed compatible since the negation of *svabhāva* is far from a confirmation of nihilism. Rather, these Yogācārins negate *svabhāva* to accentuate the interdependence of ideality and reality, which can be interpreted as a version of transcendental idealism in parallel to that in Husserl.

Having clarified that what Husserl means by "essence" differs from what Xuanzang and his disciples mean by *svabhāva*, we elucidate how the problem of essence does not undercut the current project—with the caveat being that though the problem of essence is not an obstacle for our study, it is also not irrelevant either. That is to say, after recognizing and resolving this problem, we do not go back to the starting point to cancel this problem for good. Rather, through investigating this problem, we deepen our understanding of the implications of a comparative study in a multicultural and multilingual context. These implications are examined in Chapter 9 where it becomes clear why we need to consider not only the linguistic and cultural heritage of the traditions being compared, but also the language and culture into which these traditions are translated. When one English term is summoned to translate several different notions from non-English languages, the nuance of the English term changes accordingly. Tracing the nuance of "essence," in turn, offers us access to a plurality of lived realities embedded in language and culture, which becomes a crucial step for us to avoid misrepresenting traditions and advance mutual understanding. As such, we continue to adopt the "both–and" approach in this part of our journey to *both* reconsider what "essence" really means in each context *and* expand the shared horizon by resolving the problem of essence and moving beyond Orientalism. As conveyed by the last sense of being "explicative," our investigation in this part invites us to deliberate upon how the philosophical insight of correlative non-dualism can be enacted and embodied in everyday, collaborative actions at the prescriptive level.

7

Essence in Husserl's Phenomenology[1]

In this chapter, we embark on a two-pronged project. Primarily, we intend to answer whether Husserl's definition of the notion of essence—a notion that characterizes an object as it actually is—is tantamount to that of *svabhāva*. Moreover, we shall inquire into how and why essence becomes central to Husserl's phenomenology. Our exploration will guide us in understanding Husserl's reflection upon and refutation of naturalism in different phases of his phenomenological project—especially, as he argues, how naturalism jeopardizes the worldview of modern Europeans.

From Husserl's vantage point, naturalists of his time reduce things in the world as factually existent realities that are pre-given to, and independent from, the mind (Hua 3/53). In the naturalistic framework, not only are the mind and the world being misrepresented as contingent realities (Hua 6/68), but the essence of things is also reduced to an abstraction of factuality (Hua 3/8). Confronted with such naturalist reductionism, Husserl addresses how naturalists ignore the mutual constitution of the mind and its surroundings. Once the naturalist attitude becomes internalized as a personal worldview, that person will lose more than an authentic way of knowing the world (Hua 18/68). They will also find it impossible to navigate life in any meaningful manner (Husserl 6/4). Naturalism, therefore, yields both an epistemic and an existential issue. As an antidote to naturalism, phenomenology explains why the ultimate nature of things is much more than factuality. Husserl envisions phenomenology as a science of essence that guides a person back to things themselves to see how and what they actually are (Hua 19/744; Hua 3/4–10). Essence, as defined in the phenomenological project, cannot be reduced to matters of fact; and nor is it tantamount to a metaphysical enigma (Hua 3/4). Rather, essence is ideation that can be examined upon and inquired about (Hua 6/217).

Through his revised view of essence, Husserl is able to develop a new version of metaphysics. As suggested by Dan Zahavi, phenomenology, when viewed as the rigorous science of essence, alludes to metaphysics in a new sense; that is, it is "new" due to its problematization of the presumed polarity of reality and ideality, of subjectivity and objectivity, and of the empirical and the transcendental for the purpose of revealing their interdependence and interconnectedness (Zahavi 2017: 206).

To unpack the new version of metaphysics as well as explain the role of essence therein, the current chapter follows the outline of Chapter 4 to trace Husserl's conception of essence in four phases, through which it shall become clear why essence is crucial for transcendental phenomenology in every phase of Husserl's philosophical thinking process:

1. In the first phase where he interprets intentionality as directedness, essence (*Wesen*) is the ideal union of the matter and the quality of intentional mental acts. In addition, there are further three types of essence (*Wesen*): the intentional, the semantic, and the epistemic. Essence (*Wesen*) is equally distinct from *essentia* (*Essenz*). In this phase, the notion of essence becomes an integral part of Husserl's deliberation on the authenticity of thinking, which derives itself from his critique of Brentanian psychologism.
2. In the second phase, Husserl reformulates intentionality as the *noesis–noema correlation*. In doing so, he articulates pure essence as *eidos*, which entails an ideal union of *noesis* and *noema* encapsulated in the structure of intentionality. *Eidos* stands in contrast to the naturalistic essence that amounts to a general abstraction of matters of fact. As such, the notion of *eidos* becomes central to transcendental idealism in Husserl's phenomenology, contrary to the transcendental realism intrinsic to naturalism.
3. In the last two phases of Husserl's philosophical thinking process, genetic phenomenology replaces static phenomenology. Accordingly, the pure essence (*eidos*) of each person becomes a twofold *a priori* of being in the world and being with others. Defining essence in this manner, Husserl expands his transcendental idealism as a version of correlative non-dualism, which marks his break with the Cartesian-style modern philosophy. For Husserl, this new version of idealism can remedy the crisis of meaning in modern Europe.

These three stages listed above demonstrate the ways in which Husserl constantly enriches the meaning of essence. As I will argue, Husserl defines essence in the phenomenological project as the ideal union of *noesis* and *noema*, which undergirds the structure of intentionality in pure consciousness. Since essence is not self-determined but rather mutually constituted, this Husserlian notion is not tantamount to *svabhāva*. Our following analysis further suggests how essence transforms from a core concept in epistemology and pure logic to a central notion in the renewed metaphysics referred to as transcendental idealism. In his articulation of transcendental idealism, Husserl suggests that the mind of each individual serves as the necessary condition for the possibility of phenomena in experience and reaches out to other minds to constitute a shared and meaningful lifeworld. As such, transcendental ideality becomes correlated with empirical reality, a correlation that further secures the non-duality of binaries—namely, the mutual constitution of subjectivity and objectivity, the interconnectedness of the self and the other, as well as the possible awakening from the natural attitude to the phenomenological attitude. That is why we refer to the Husserlian doctrine of transcendental idealism as a version of correlative non-dualism.

Essence in Early Husserl

In his pre-transcendental phase, Husserl perceives essence (*Wesen*) as that which defines an object in our experience as what it actually is. In the first phase of Husserl's philosophical thinking process, *Wesen* is the ideal union of the quality and content—or the form and matter—of intentional mental acts, rather than a factually existent reality (Hua 19/417). *Wesen* is encapsulated in, though not equated with, the intentional structure of mental acts. Just as intentionality penetrates mental acts at different levels, essence (*Wesen*) also has many layers. With the help of essence (*Wesen*), Husserl reflects on the approach to consciousness presented in psychologism, explaining how knowledge is not governed by laws that are derived from physical or psychological matters of fact. Rather, it is secured by the ideal principles based on the notions of founding, fulfilling, and identification.

The concept of essence (*Wesen*) enters Husserl's philosophical discussions in *Logical Investigations* when he explains how the content of a mental act is a new type of product that differs from the external object *per se*. Husserl begins his explication with the simple intuitive act of presenting and gradually moves on to the abstract and symbolic act of judging. To illustrate this point, he poses a question much like the following: when perceiving an object, how do Cindy and Sandy know that they are perceiving the same object, given that Cindy and Sandy are different individuals? According to Husserl, psychologists such as Brentano propose that this cognitive identity can be attested through inferring the sameness of the perceived object from "empirical contingencies of the course of consciousness (*empirischen Zufälligkeiten des Bewusstseinsverlaufs*)" (Hua 19/704). Husserl deems this answer untenable insofar as psychologism ignores the distinction between the real and the ideal (Hua 18/68). Indeed, when Cindy and Sandy are perceiving the same object or even when Cindy herself is perceiving the object from different angles, what are factually presented in the intentional acts are never perfectly alike, but share an ideal uniformity based on the interpretative sense of the object (Hua 19/418). The ideation of the real object that is presented through the intentional structure of a mental act is the object's essence (*Wesen*) (Hua 19/418). If a simple act of presenting can give rise to more compounded acts, the essence of these intentional acts shall be further differentiated. That is why Husserl demarcates the intentional essence from the semantic essence.

Intentional essence (*intentionale Wesen*) pertains to mental acts such as intuition whose content is either presented or fulfilled (Hua 19/417). In contrast, semantic essence (*bedeutungsmäßige Wesen*)—which can be abstracted to yield meaning—characterizes the expressive and symbolic acts, such as naming and judging (Hua 19/418), whose content needs to be fulfilled by intuitive matter (Hua 19/518). As such, these two types of essence capture a wide range of mental acts from sensuous intuition, to categorial intuition, and to more abstract meaning-intention.

Indeed, Husserl speaks of intentional essence as the union of the quality and the matter of mental acts (Hua 19/417). For intuitive acts, such as sensuous intuition or categorial intuition, an object is presented in a direct and straightforward manner. Therefore, their intentional essence always entails a fullness of presentation. As put by Husserl himself, "the intuitive, not the signitive member, has the character of being the fulfiller, and so also, in the most authentic sense, the giver of fullness" (Hua 19/583). Further founded on intuitive acts, symbolic and expressive acts such as naming or judging have semantic essence that can be ideally abstracted to produce meaning (Hua 19/418). Different from that of intuitive acts, the meaning of these expressive acts comes to its fullness when these mental acts coincide with the intended objects presented intuitively as such; that is, when the content of these expressive acts is fulfilled by the corresponding intuitive matters (Hua 19/603). Having fulfilled its sense, semantic essence evolves into epistemic essence (*erkenntnismäßige Wesen*) and subsequently generates validly true knowledge, insofar as what is meant meets what is intended. That is why Husserl defines epistemic essence as that which derives from a coherent synthesis of quality, matter, and fullness (Hua 19/604).

As such, intentional, epistemic, and semantic essences encapsulate different modes of mental acts. For instance, when Cindy is perceiving the Christmas tree in the foyer of McGill University's Birks building, her perception has an intentional essence insofar as the content of the mental act of perceiving is directly presented. In Husserl's terms, "the fulfilling sense is interpreted as the intentional essence of the completely and adequately fulfilling act" (Hua 19/603). Afterward, Cindy returns to her office in the basement and talks to her colleague Shaun about the tree she just saw. In the conversation, Cindy refers to the tree through formulating a concept of it. Upon hearing Cindy's description, Shaun is curious about the Christmas tree and starts to think about what it looks like. At this point, Shaun's act of thinking has only a semantic essence insofar as the content of his thought is partially, not fully, fulfilled. As Husserl specifies, purely signitive and expressive acts can be empty if they do not have the component of fullness (Hua 19/604). If Shaun is too busy to go upstairs, then his thinking remains to have only semantic essence, incapable of generating authentic knowledge of the Christmas tree in the foyer. Nonetheless, once Shaun walks upstairs to the foyer, his thoughts of the tree acquire their intentional essence *qua* fulfilling sense when the content is fulfilled by his perception of the tree. By then, what Shaun means coincides with what he intends. That is how Shaun comes to acquire knowledge of the tree and his act of thinking is defined by its epistemic essence. He can also come back to the basement office to talk with Cindy about the tree. Notably, Shaun's perception of the Christmas tree is not exactly the same as that for Cindy. It is possible that Cindy is nearsighted and the appearance of the tree in her perception is less perfect than that in Shaun's. It can also happen that it turns dark outside when Shaun walks upstairs, so he sees the tree in the shade while Cindy saw the tree in the daylight. Despite these phenomenological differences, Cindy and Shaun are perceiving the same tree due to the intentional essence. That is why essence (*Wesen*) does not consist in factuality but rather in ideality.

In addition to intentional, epistemic, and semantic essences, Husserl also borrows the scholastic term *essentia* (*Essenz*) to describe the same matter held by two intuitive acts: "we shall say that two intuitive acts have the same *essentia* (*Essenz*), if their pure intuitions have the same matter" (Hua 19/609). As such, *essentia* becomes the ideation of matter, as that which is already presented in individual intuitions. It should be noted that, while Husserl ascribes *Essenz* particularly to the matter of intuitive acts, *Wesen* is articulated to capture the union of quality and content of all intentional mental acts, including the intuitive and symbolic ones.

Husserl delineates the concept of essence (*Wesen*) in this manner to elucidate the authenticity of thoughts and expound on the ideality of laws of thought and knowledge, which marks a prelude to his transcendental turn. As detailed by Husserl, authentic thought leaves the real essence of intentional acts untouched and untarnished (Hua

19/695). For instance, when Shaun is thinking about the tree in the foyer of the Birks building after his conversation with Cindy, his act of thinking is inauthentic insofar as the intentional essence *qua* fulfilling sense remains partially missing. Only when Shaun observes the tree, does his thought become fully meaningful and his act of thinking become authentic. In *Logical Investigations,* Husserl provides a broader idea of thinking: if a mental act is founded upon others and has synthetic or categorial features, this mental act becomes that of thought. Considering how categorial intuitions are founded on simple acts of sensuous intuiting and enable someone to see a state of affairs, Husserl perceives these categorially intuitive acts to be the intuitive acts of thinking (Hua 19/693). For instance, a categorial intuition allows Cindy to perceive that the cat is sleeping on the sofa. This whole state of affairs can further serve as the contents of her abstract concepts. Due to the way in which a categorial intuition can always fulfill its content with intuitive matters, its intentional essence remains unshaped, which makes categorial intuitions the authentic thoughts. As proclaimed by Husserl, if a categorial intuition does not have its foundation of sense, it is nothing but "a piece of non-sense (*Widersinn*)" (Hua 19/694). Here, "non-sense" serves as a pun because it shows how categorial intuition without its content fulfilled by intuitive matter has no meaning and how categorial intuition without a fulfilling sense is absurd. For Husserl, the act of thinking becomes authentic when its content is fulfilled, and its intentional essence is undistorted (Hua 19/693).

For symbolic and semantic acts that sometimes lack—either fully or partially—an intentional essence *qua* a fulfilling sense, they run the risk of generating inauthentic thoughts (Hua 19/702). If a symbolic act, such as the act of judging, does not have its content fulfilled, then this act has no real intentional essence and thereby yields an inauthentic thought. Indeed, authenticity is no longer just about whether an object is given in a straightforward manner but rather resides in the unshaped intentional essence that appears when the content of intentional acts is fulfilled.

Let us unpack this distinction between authentic and inauthentic thoughts through the example of Cindy perceiving the state of affairs that the cat is on the sofa. Cindy's perception of the cat's being on the sofa is a categorial intuition insofar as it is a perception of a state of affairs founded on several sensuous perceptions of the cat and the sofa. When Cindy sees her cat on the sofa, her eyes fall on the cat. On the periphery of her perception is the fuzzy background *qua* the sofa. In her perception, Cindy can change her focus from the cat to the sofa, but she can never wipe that sofa off her perception for good. Abstracting or categorial forming, thus, is not widely free but delimited by its content. Husserl refers to such a restriction as the "law-governed limits (*gesetzlichen Schranken*)" of categorial formation (Hua 19/695). That is to say, although categorial intuition is creative and operative, it remains constrained by the intentional essence *qua* the ideal union of the quality and the fulfilled content. Symbolic thinking, however, is quite different. When Cindy is entertaining the concept of cat, she can relate to a theory of feline behaviors, easily removing irrelevant representations from her mind—such as the sofa or the window. Symbolic thinking becomes the indirect way of forming, which moves remote to sensory manifolds and is less delimited by sensations. Although this means that symbolic thinking becomes very powerful in formulating linguistic expressions, symbols, and theories, it also risks generating empty concepts that can never fulfill their meaning and never acquire intentional essence, which will jeopardize the objectivity of these concepts (Hua 19/704). For instance, Cindy could formulate a statement, such as "some cats speak the human language" by associating symbols such as "cats" and "human language," although she never encounters any cat who can talk. In this case, Cindy's statement does not have its meaning fulfilled by a corresponding state of affairs, therefore failing to yield any valid knowledge. In other words, Cindy's expressive act only has semantic essence, not epistemic essence. That is why such a statement exemplifies the way in which symbolic thinking lacks intentional essence and becomes an inauthentic thought.

Considering how symbolic thinking requires categorial intuition to fulfill its meaning, Husserl remarks that "the *a priori* laws of authentic thinking and authentic expression become norms for merely opinion-forming, inauthentic thought and expression" (Hua 19/707). The law of authentic thinking lies in the existence of an intentional essence as an ideal union of the quality and the matter of an intentional mental act, which demonstrates how the principles based on the concepts of founding, identifying, and fulfilling work together to produce knowledge. As such, the law of thought is not based on psychological, contingent realities, but rather finds its ground in ideality. Husserl's purpose for differentiating authentic thoughts *qua* categorial intuition from inauthentic thoughts can now be seen as thus: any instance of symbolic thinking finds its footing in and secures its objectivity by intuitive thinking, and not *vice versa*.

This is how objectivity is conveyed in Husserl's early writings—it is characterized by the impossibility of reshaping the intentional essence. In sensory intuition, the content of the act is directly given without any modification, and the intentional essence is always presented. Founded on multiple simple acts of sensation, categorial intuition does not entail any significant reshaping of the intentional essence, although it can rearrange presented matters in the state of affairs (Hua 19/700). Husserl further distances himself from the Brentanian psychologism when he makes objectivity and authenticity of knowledge contingent on the essence of intentional acts, not on matters of fact. Different from psychologism which entails epistemological realism, Husserl highlights the ideality of knowing and thinking. After his transcendental turn, he makes his position explicit through the doctrine of transcendental idealism. Indeed, it is his continual reflection on psychologism that nurtures the mature form of a science of essence known as transcendental phenomenology.

Essence after the Transcendental Turn

Husserl's transcendental turn is marked by the release of *Ideas I* in which he extends his critique from psychologism to naturalism. Here, the term "naturalism" is utilized by Husserl to include both psychologism and physicalism. In this phase of his thinking process, Husserl continues to conceive of essence as that which defines what and how things actually are. The concept of essence that features in *Ideas I* begins with Husserl's slogan of phenomenology as the *Wesenwissenschaft* (science of essence), rather than the study of factually existent matters of fact known as naturalism (Hua 3/4–10).

Opposing phenomenology with naturalism, Husserl puts forwards a series of "contrasting pairs (*Gegensatzpaaren*)": essence versus matters of fact, *a priori* versus contingent occurrence, the irreal versus the real, and the transcendental versus the empirical (Hua 3/4–5). As such, essence is associated with several attributes, such as *a priori*, ideality, and transcendentality. To delineate pure essence from any factuality, Husserl evokes the Greek term "*eidos*" in place of the German term "*Wesen*" (Hua 3/6). Thereby, Husserl renews most of his terminology for transcendental phenomenology.

He defines *eidos* as a "new type of object (*neuartiger Gegenstand*)" that is presented and intended directly in experience (Hua 3/11). Anything that is characterized by and related to *eidos* is therefore eidetic. Phenomenology as a *Wesenwissenschaft* means that phenomenology is also an "eidetic science (*eidetische Wissenschaft*)" (Hua 3/4). Drawing a parallel between sensible intuition and eidetic intuition, Husserl continues to specify how *eidos* as the pure essence is the "*Gegebene der Wesensanschauung*" as that which is given in the eidetic intuition (Hua 3/11). From Husserl's definition, it can be inferred that he attempts to encapsulate what he earlier refers to as the intentional, semantic, and epistemic essences all in the concept of *eidos*. Later when Husserl defines intentionality as the eidetic structure of *noesis–noema*, he *ipso facto* formulates essence (*eidos*) as the ideal union of *noesis* and *noema*.

Although Husserl renews his terminology and replaces essence with *eidos* in *Ideas I*, he retains many elements of the "hierarchy of essences (*Stufenreihe von Wesen*)" that he developed in *Logical Investigations* (Hua 3/26). Earlier he attributed different modes of *Wesen* to sensuous intuition and categorial intuition. Now, in parallel, he identifies different modes of *eidos* for individual intuition, universal intuition, and conceptualization (Hua 3/11–13). Likewise, Husserl maintains that essence (*Wesen*) can be both adequate and inadequate—depending on whether the presented content is perfect and complete—through his paired identification of adequate and inadequate *eidos* (Hua 3/10). The distinction between intentional essence (*Wesen*) and semantic essence (*Wesen*) is also preserved in his conceptualization of the self-sufficient *eidos* whose content is fulfilled, and the non-self-sufficient *eidos* whose content cannot be fulfilled without referring back to intuitions (Hua 3/29). Husserl, further, calls non-self-sufficient essence an *abstractum*, self-sufficient essence a *concretum*, and material essence of the concretum an *individuum* (Hua 3/30). While the distinction between the self-sufficient and non-self-sufficient essence is mainly epistemological in *Ideas I*, such a distinction gradually takes on existential and metaphysical features in the last two phases of Husserl's thinking process.

Furthermore, since each mental act consists of its form and matter, there is also the formal essence concerning the character-quality of an act in contrast to the material essence that defines the content of the act (Hua 3/21). What Husserl means by material essence does appear rather similar to the notion of *essentia* (*Essenz*) in *Logical Investigations*. However, in *Ideas I*, Husserl uses *Essenz* in a different way, for here it acts as the opposite of *Existenz qua* the existence that pertains to the matters of fact in the sense of "individual existence as such (*individuell Daseiendem*)" (Hua 3/12). Stemming from the substitution of *Wesen* with *eidos*, there arises an overall renewal of Husserl's phenomenological vocabularies.

Although it seems that Husserl opposes essence to existence through the contrast of *Essenz* with *Existenz*, this is not always the case. He indicates that notions like essence and existence can be understood from different perspectives depending on whether a person adopts a natural or a phenomenological attitude. To put it otherwise, essence and existence can be perceived either naturalistically or eidetically. Here, I use the term "naturalistic" to describe that which is particularly associated with the natural attitude, in contrast to the notion of eidetic that is the salient feature of the phenomenological attitude. In what follows, we will first examine these two types of essence.

In the eyes of naturalists, essence becomes tantamount to an abstract entity that a person generalizes and extracts from various empirical, physical, or psychological data (Hua 3/42). For naturalists, there is only factual reality and nothing more. This metaphysical presumption is reflected in the language of physicists who speak of an object as an object in itself (Hua 3/13), and psychologists who perceive any knowable object as an individually real actuality in our experience (Hua 3/40). For these reasons, Husserl refers to naturalistic essence as a mental construct that facilitates abstract thinking (Hua 3/42).

In sum, the naturalistic worldview presupposes that the world is pre-given as a factual reality, which Husserl finds rather dangerous (Hua 3/42). This is because such a worldview presumes that reality and even essence itself are factually independent from humans and invariant across time and space. Once we internalize this naturalistic set of presumptions as the inherent perspective of our experience, we lose the capacity of being critical of where our perception of reality comes from. That is why Husserl characterizes those in the natural attitude as naive naturalists (Hua 3/79). Once we become naturalists, we can easily miss "the pure and genuine (*reine und echte*)" meaning of our consciousness and our life (Hua 19/706). What is worse, we take the factual existence of things as a given and reduce the world into a mechanical system running upon and self-determined through natural laws. By then, we close our eyes to the concrete lifeworld in front of us. Life also becomes little more than an accumulation of contingently emerged matters of fact, which is ultimately irrelevant to us (Hua 19/706).

The pure and genuine unveils itself when we conduct *epoché* to acquire the insight of the pure eidetic essence or *eidos* (Hua 3/65). *Eidos* delineates what and how things actually are in pure consciousness, further entailing the ideal union of *noesis* and *noema* that undergirds the eidetic structure of intentionality for each mental act (Hua 3/184–90). As previously mentioned, Husserl describes intentionality as the *noesis-noema* correlation in *Ideas I*. Accordingly, the pure essence of *noesis* underpins the form of an act, such as recollecting or judging or willing (Hua 3/177). In parallel, *noematic* essence is the objective core of the perceived phenomenon presented as such—namely, "the core as the sense in the mode of its fullness (*der Kern als Sinn im Modus seiner Fülle*)" (Hua 3/274). As such, when a person acquires insight into pure essence, this person immediately grasps the ideal correlate of *noesis* and *noema* at all levels of intentional acts from perceiving to judging, which allows for the direct presentation of the intended objects, including but not limited to a single object, a state of affairs, etc. (Hua 3/196). The clarity of these insights can vary, considering how *eidos* stems from the constitution of the eidetic *noetic–noematic* structure, a constitution that is secured by subjectivity (3/130).

Consider our previous example of Cindy perceiving her cat on the sofa. Cindy can walk around the sofa to observe the posture of her cat. Every locus she takes has different sensory manifolds. Wherever she stands, her consciousness will reach out to make her perception intelligible in such a way that the cat can always be foregrounded against the backdrop of her perceptual field. There arises what Husserl refers to as the *eidos*, which emerges from the various appearances of the same cat. Albeit the appearance of the cat varies from one locus to the next, it nevertheless reveals to Cindy the same *noematic* object *qua* the cat—not merely as matters of fact but as the ideal phenomenon—through the same type of *noetic* acts of perceiving. That is why Husserl refers to the *noesis–noema* correlate as the essential property of consciousness that can change into a new correlate while retaining the possibility of guiding people back to things themselves (Hua 1/83).

Indeed, through *epoché*, we revert to our pure consciousness and observe the object that appears as the mental phenomenon (Hua 3/188). At this point, our mind is not a passive receiver of given factual data. Rather, consciousness reaches out to the world to make it a perceptual field, which indicates how the mind actively serves as the necessary condition for the appearance of objective phenomenon. Against the backdrop of this field, we can target one specific object and direct a mental act towards it. As such, the *noesis–noema* correlate of perception transpires to enable our intuitive act of seeing this object. In this process, an object is not independent from the mind; quite to the contrary, this object relies on consciousness to appear in our experience. That is why Husserl conceives objectivity as correlated with subjectivity. In his terms, it is possible to burn up a tree in the natural world, but it is never possible to burn up a tree in pure consciousness (Hua 3/183). When we combine the simple acts of perception into a higher-level act of expressing or judging, the intuitive sense of this objective phenomena fulfills the meaning of concepts and makes meaning-intentions valid.

For every mental act, pure eidetic essence entails an ideal union of *noesis* and *noema* encapsulated in the eidetic structure of intentionality (Hua 3/130). Once this mental act is determined, such essence becomes the intelligible sense of the *noesis–noema* correlate. This refashioned concept of essence allows for the formulation of phenomenology as transcendental idealism at the explicative level.[2] If naturalists and phenomenologists have their respective understandings of what things actually are and define essence in their own manners, how then would they explain the existence of these things?

After clarifying the two kinds of essence envisaged respectively by naturalists and phenomenologists, we can move on to the two types of existence/being presented in Husserl's work. He likewise distinguishes "existence" in the transcendentally phenomenological sense from existence in the naturally real sense. Here, I contend that we shall demarcate the "natural" from the "naturalistic"—that is, what is naturally real is synonymous with what is empirically real, whereas naturalistic is always coupled with the natural attitude. Again, we have to cope with a terminological ambiguity in Husserl's work. Those that are natural, "they are as experienceable physical things" that can serve as a correlate of consciousness (Hua 3/89). Husserl could have simply used the term "empirical," yet he nevertheless chooses to settle with the concept of "natural."

Husserl speaks of empirical/natural existence as the existence in a straightforward (*geradehin*) manner (Husserl 1/61). It is the existence of any experienceable factual material reality in the actual spatial-temporal order, either as physical reality or psychological one. Consider our example of perceiving the cat on the sofa. The natural existence of the cat is material and physical—she is made of flesh and covered in fur—and as a finite being, she will die within an anticipatable period of time. Given that natural existence is attributed to matters of fact, we come to find that in his writings, Husserl refers to what we term natural existence, as the "empirical-factual (*empirisch-faktischen*)" (Hua 1/105). When we enact *epoché*, we no longer take our presumptions of the world as a given and distance ourselves from the natural existence. Thereafter, we suspend any presumption about this empirical existence and subsequently shift the focus back to our pure consciousness in which consciousness serves as the necessary condition for the possibility of phenomena. Through this transcendental reflection, there unveils the phenomenological existence of that which appears in pure consciousness.

Phenomenological existence is characterized by ideality (Hua 3/88). As Husserl mentioned in many places, a tree can be burnt up or chopped down in the natural world but a tree in the pure consciousness cannot be wiped out as such (Hua 6/245). That is why natural existence can vanish—that is, the cat will eventually die and no longer remain part of Cindy's life—but the phenomenological existence of the cat persists in Cindy's recollection of the past and her expectation of the future.

It would be inaccurate to describe phenomenological existence and natural/empirical existence as either irrelevant or identical to one another. As detailed by Husserl, phenomenological existence is inseparable from existence in the natural/empirical sense (Hua 3/8–9). That is to say, the cat prior to *epoché* remains the same as that which Cindy can perceive in her post-*epoché* recollection. The relationship between these two types of existence is encapsulated in the notion of correlate (Hua 3/89). As envisioned by Husserl, phenomenological existence alludes to "the multitude of possible worlds and surrounding worlds (*mannigfaltiger möglicher Welten und Umwelten*)" among which there is one special case *qua* the actual world of natural/empirical existence (Hua 3/89). Accordingly, the essence of these phenomenologically existent objects becomes an ideal one, rather than a real one, insofar as such essence reveals a possibility. That is why Husserl contends that the natural existence always presupposes the transcendental existence in the pure consciousness, which makes natural existence secondary (Hua 1/61–2). Depicting natural existence as the correlate of phenomenological existence, Husserl indicates how one cannot be reduced to or exhausted by the other.

Within a naturalistic worldview, there is always the tendency to reduce phenomenological existence to natural existence, further demoting ideality to reality and degrading essentiality into factuality. When natural existence degenerates into the naturalistic for someone of the natural attitude, this naturalist perceives the essence of these factually existent objects as the pre-given, *sui generis* reality invariant across time and space. It again explains why Husserl utilizes the term "naive" to characterize the natural attitude (Hua 3/131). Contrarily, the phenomenological attitude encourages a person to conduct *epoché* and open the eyes to how things actually are. Through the insight of essence, this phenomenologist comes to understand immediately that, without constitutive subjectivity, phenomenological existence is impossible. Indeed, it is not the case that various objects exist as pre-given reality and become represented to the mind through affection. Rather, the subjective mind actively serves as the necessary condition for various things to appear as phenomena in a person's lived experience. In figurative terms, subjectivity opens the door to "the multitude of possible worlds and surrounding worlds" (Hua 3/89). Furthermore, it is this constitutive subjectivity that eventually determines the undetermined determinability of these possible worlds through the *noesis–noema* structure, moment by moment (Hua 6/279). That is why the phenomenological existence is antecedent and prior to the natural existence, not the other way round (Hua 1/61). Subjectivity, therefore, entails a living transcendental ideality, which is enacted throughout each phase of life.

From this stance on subjectivity, Husserl's notion of transcendental idealism gradually develops. Subjectivity has its limits insofar as it cannot determine or exhaust the natural/empirical existence of a wide range of things in the world. The world exists as such, as that which is *de facto*, empirically real, and intersubjectively accessible. In Husserl's terms, the realm of naturally existent matters of fact becomes the "correlate" of the phenomenological realm (Hua 3/88). That is why Husserl acknowledges an empirical form of realism (Hua 6/190-1). While subjectivity has its limits, it conditions the phenomenological existence of things in our experience. After *epoché*, subjectivity serves as the necessary condition for the possibility of phenomena in one's experience, further determining the undeterminable determinability of the *noetic–noematic* structure. As such, subjectivity alludes to transcendental ideality (Hua 6/189).

Transcendental ideality for Husserl is correlated with and interdependent on empirical reality. Such a correlation secures the mutual constitution of subjectivity and objectivity, further furnishing each subject with the freedom of exercising agency. Either the subject can dwell back on the natural attitude or this subject can enact *epoché* to see things as they really are in a phenomenological attitude. Subjectivity in the first sense becomes envisioned as transcendentally real, which can be epitomized by Brentano's psychologism, according to Husserl. Contrariwise, the latter way of being a subject, in virtue of *epoché*, suggests transcendental ideality. As such, transcendental idealism differs from transcendental realism since the latter deems reality to be mind-independent whereas the former does not. Moreover, Husserl also demarcates transcendental idealism from what he refers to as speculative idealism in which an absolute idea can exhaust worldly reality (Hua 6/271).

To sum up, Husserl distances himself from both transcendental realism and speculative/metaphysical idealism. For him, consciousness is not an absolute idea that can exhaust every single naturally existent object. It is also not the case these objects exist mind-independently. He turns to highlight their non-duality. Transcendental idealism, thus, becomes the doctrine that encapsulates the correlative non-duality of subjectivity and objectivity, of ideality and reality, and of the transcendental and the empirical. It is in this sense that transcendental phenomenology becomes a science of essence—namely, an eidetic science that explores and explicates the ideal union of mutually constituted *noesis* and *noema*.

Essence in Later Husserl

Husserl documents the mature version of transcendental phenomenology in *Ideas I* where he continues to develop his notions of intentionality, transcendental idealism, and eventually, essence. In the last two phases of Husserl's thinking process, essence is not only crucial to pure logic and a pure theory of knowledge but also pivotal for remedying the existential crisis in Europe. While naturalism precipitates the paradox of subjectivity and provokes the crisis of meaning, phenomenology guides each person in renouncing the naive mode of existence so as to become a subject in its true, authentic sense (Hua 6/213). Different from the groundless naturalistic essence, the pure and genuine essence of each person amounts to the *a priori* of being in the world and being with others. What defines a person as such is grounded in the interrelation and interaction with other things in the world and with other people in the community. This refined conception of essence facilitates Husserl's endeavor to formulate phenomenology as a remedy for the general crisis of meaning in then-contemporary Europe.

In *Meditations* and *Crisis*, Husserl continues his inquiry into the genesis of intentionality and conceives of the intentional structure as the *ego–cogito–cogitatum* schema (Hua 1/87), which is further expanded into the *we*, the intending act, and the shared intended phenomena tripartite (Hua 6/189). In our previous study of the *ego–cogito–cogitatum* schema, we explained how the underlying ego does not transform into a closed system nor an outstanding pole, but rather mutually constitutes itself with the subjective act of *cogito* and the objective phenomenon *qua cogitatum*. This is the case, in virtue of two types of geneses: the passive and the active. The study of the genesis of intentional acts heralds Husserl's expression of genetic phenomenology (Hua 14/40). In virtue of passive genesis, each ego interacts with other things in the world and with other egos in a community to mutually constitute the primordial temporal horizon in one's entire life and the lifeworld for the community, even before this ego actively uses the faculty of reason to conduct intentional mental acts. It is interesting to see how Husserl utilizes the concept of I-subject (*Ichsubjekt*) or subject (*Subjekt*) in *Crisis* to replace the language of ego for stressing the interpenetration (*Ineinander*) of different subjects in a community (Hua 6/259). Even though Husserl never explicitly espouses the Buddhist view of no-self, the change of language alludes to Husserl's objection to solipsism, which is on a par with the Yogācāra refutation of the *svabhāvic* self. The primordial constitution entails the "inward being-for-one-another and mutual interpenetration (*innerlichen Ineinander- und füreinanderseins*)" as the fundamental interdependence between each I-subject and its surroundings (Hua 6/346). The eidetic essence of a person becomes a twofold *a priori*—"consciousness of oneself as being in the world (*Bewusstsein seiner selbst als in der Welt Seiend*)" (Hua 6/255), and "self-consciousness and consciousness of others are inseparable (*Selbstbewusstsein und Fremdbewusstsein untrennbar ist*)" (Hua 6/256). As such, the eidetic essence of the transcendental I-subject arises from the horizon of lived experience for this individual person, as well as from the collective horizon in which the person shares with others (Hua 6/259). In this manner, the essence of each person is described by Husserl as the twofold *a priori* of being a subject in the world and being with every other subject.

Naturalism, however, neither acknowledges nor appreciates the twofold essence of the I-subject. Empowered by inauthentic thoughts, naturalism reduces the essence of a person to factual materiality (Hua 1/115), which is coherent with the naturalistic view of essence and existence all along (Hua 6/12). Now that Husserl expands his philosophical project to genetic phenomenology, he extends his critique of naturalism by tracing the forces that secure the predominance of inauthentic thinking. The first force surfaces throughout the development of modern physics, the discipline that is characterized by an abstract mathematical view of the world and can be dated back to the time of Galileo Galilei (1564–1642) (Hua 6/36). This worldview empowers scientists to treat the world as a system of sheerly material realities and then, to summon objective rules through experiments on matters of fact in this system (Hua 6/36). When scientists glorify their testable hypothesis as the objective truth, they equally reduce objectivity to a pre-given actuality as that which is irrelevant to and independent from each individual subject (Hua 6/54). Husserl labels this approach to objectivity as "objectivism (*Objektivismus*)" given how it portrays objectivity as that which is in itself and, thus, unconditionally valid (Hua 6/70).

Such a perception of the world as mind-independent and mind-irrelevant soon places a rift between the mind and the world, a rift that Husserl finds intrinsic to the modern European worldview. From this rift, there arises the second force for the prevalence of inauthentic thought: Cartesian dualism (Hua 6/74). This dualism nurtures the flourishing modern psychologism, which reduces the mind to the sum-total of psychical realities. Similar to physicists, psychologists induce empirical rules from psychological experiments and employ these rules to verify the objective validity of subjective knowledge (Hua 6/71). Their approach, thus, entails "transcendentalism (*Transzendentalismus*) (Hua 6/71). As such, psychologism construes subjectivity as the absolute reality in a higher order, through which objectivity can be determined by the capacity of reasoning such as inducing and deducing.

The joint forces of physical objectivism and psychological transcendentalism conspire to bring about the prevalence of modern naturalism in Europe, the salient feature of which is scientific reductionism (Hua 6/71). While physical objectivism reduces each person to nothing but factually existent matters of fact, psychological transcendentalism elevates subjectivity to the highest place as the absolute reality of the world. How then could a person exist both as the extremely passive matter and as the absolutely active mind at the exact same moment? Such a question points to the paradoxical nature of human subjectivity brought about by the flourishing of naturalism (Hua 6/184). Upon distorting objectivity, naturalism likewise menaces subjectivity. In Husserl's terms, naturalism turns the mind and the world into an inaccessible "enigma" insofar as they cannot be connected to each other (Hua 6/4). Through homogenizing individual differences, naturalism facilitates the disconnection of humans from the world, producing the paradox of subjectivity and provoking a crisis of meaning (Hua 6/5).

Indeed, naturalism overlooks the fact that symbolic, inauthentic thoughts always find their ground in authentic, categorial intuition (Hua 19/707). Reducing the eidetic essence to an abstract factuality, naturalists propose a version of essence that is never as truly self-sufficient as it proclaims to be. Naturalistic essence is groundless and baseless insofar as it ignores the genesis of experience in which the mind and the world mutually constitute the shared lifeworld (Hua 17/356). For Husserl, the essence of the world is not an abstract, pre-given reality invariant across time and space. Nor is objective reality devoid of subjectivity. Rather, the world is where we dwell with other concrete individuals with whom we collaborate to constitute the shared horizon of a community. It is this intersubjectively accessible lifeworld that lays the ground for the possibility of scientific studies of the mind and the world (Hua 6/112), not the other way around (Hua 6/230). Therefore, a lifeworld cannot be reduced to material realities. Likewise, an individual in this world cannot be homogenized through physical and psychological rules into a factually existent reality. In Husserl's terms, the "I (*Ich*)" of each person is not an "empty identity pole (*leer Identitätspol*)," but rather is that which constitutes identity through the abidingly accumulated habitualities (Hua 1/101).

With the help of phenomenology, each person can withdraw from their naive attitude and embrace the true essence both in the world and for the world (Hua 6/187). This is how we come to terms with the existential status of our subjectivity. Being a subject does not necessitate any transcendence of worldly life but entails a unique mode of navigating this life. As such, subjective consciousness becomes the transcendental condition for the possibility of how everyday life will appear, further inseparable from the intersubjectively accessible empirical reality. Likewise, being an object does not allude to any irrelevance or even indifference of each individual subject. Instead, objectivity entails a threefold sense: it is the impossibility of reshaping the coherent content of the phenomena that appeared in consciousness; it is the characteristic of being determined and, therefore, retained by constitutive subjectivity in post-*epoché* consciousness; and it points to the correlation between the subject and the world, between the subject and other subjects, further contributing to a meaningful life. Living in the interdependence and mutual constitution of subjectivity and objectivity, each person no longer finds the nature of subjectivity paradoxical.

As the paradox dissolves itself, we likewise recognize the manner in which Husserl divorces himself from Cartesian dualism to formulate transcendental idealism as a version of correlative non-dualism. As Dermot Moran argues, each person lives a double life (Moran 2012: 239). That is to say, we can enjoy two correlated—or in Husserl's terms, interpenetrated—modes of living our worldly life, since we are individuals in an intersubjectively accessible real world and we can exercise our subjectivity to navigate this world meaningfully (Hua 6/346). Indeed, transcendental genetic phenomenology is absolutely self-sufficient insofar as it secures the ground in the mutual constitution of all three components in intentionality (*I-subject*, *cogito*, *cogitatum*). The fundamental essence (*Grundwesen*) of each person consists in the way in which this subject mutually constitutes its own identity and the shared lifeworld with every other subject (Hua 6/346). While naturalism nourishes the paradox of subjectivity, phenomenology guides each I-subject in returning from the natural attitude to embrace its twofold essence of being in the world and with other subjects.

To conclude, we can derive the meaning of Husserl's conception of pure, eidetic essence—or to be more precise, *eidos*—from our analysis. The *eidos* is mutually constituted by the mind and the world as that which underpins intentionality in an intersubjective lifeworld. As such, essence defines how and what things actually are in pure consciousness. Unlike essence in the natural attitude that becomes separate from lived experience, the pure phenomenological eidetic essence is that which one lives through and perceives to be true. Due to these features, *eidos* is the hallmark of transcendental idealism. The subjective mind serves as the necessary condition for the possibility of phenomena in experience and reaches out to other minds to constitute a shared meaningful lifeworld of a community. As such, transcendental ideality becomes correlated with empirical reality, which further secures the non-duality of binaries in terms of the subject–object mutual constitution, the self–other interpenetration, and the connection between the natural attitude and the phenomenological attitude. That is why transcendental idealism in the Husserlian sense is a version of correlative non-dualism.

8

Essence in Chinese Yogācāra[1]

The English term "essence" is frequently employed by Buddhist scholars when translating the Sanskrit word *svabhāva*. Etymologically, *svabhāva* is derived from *sva-*, which means "self" or "own," and *-bhāva*, the literal meaning of which is "coming into existence." As such, the concept of *svabhāva* captures an existence that comes into being on its own, which further implies an intrinsic, *sui generis* nature. Kuiji further pinpoints three defining features of *svabhāva*: (1) it is immutable (*chang* 常) T43N1830, P244c22), (2) it is self-determined (*zhuzhai* 主宰) (T43N1830, P239c3), and (3) it persists throughout time and space (*bian* 遍) (T43N1830, P244c23).

The concept of *svabhāva* becomes central to the Mahāyāna refutation of rival teachings inside the Buddhist community, such as early Buddhist philosophy and the later developed Abhidharma doctrine (e.g., Sarvāstivāda and Sautrāntika). In their exchange with their interlocutors, Mahāyāna followers, including Mādhyamikas and Yogācārins, evoke the concept of emptiness (*śūnyatā*) to express the idea that everything is empty of essence (*svabhāva*). In tracing the various stances towards essence inside the Buddhist community, it is helpful to draw upon the narrative outlined by Xuanzang and his disciples in their *sūtra* classification system (*panjiao* 判教). As such, we can explore the language utilized by these Yogācārins to unpack the doctrinal debates over essence.

As described by Kenneth Chen, the *sūtra* classification system is initiated by clerics to account for the discrepancy, or even disparateness, in a wide range of Buddhist texts translated and transmitted to East Asia (Chen 1973: 10). Such a system is admittedly multifunctional. Philosophically, it is important since it resolves scriptural discrepancies for providing a coherent understanding of the canon. At the same time, this system serves an ideological purpose for justifying the supremacy of the position of one particular Buddhist school over the others—making Kuiji's formulation of the *sūtra* classification system no exception. As clarified by Kuiji, scriptural discrepancies allude to the pedagogy of the Buddha, a pedagogy also known as the skillful means (*fangbian* 方便, *upāya*), to teach in accordance with the audience (T45N1861, P249a19). Consequently, the Buddha turned the dharma wheel three times, giving rise to the gradual development from early Buddhism, to Madhyamaka, and finally to Yogācāra (T45N1861, P248c6). Although on the surface these three schools appear to contradict and even conflict with one another, at their core, they complement and complete each other. According to Kuiji, the gradual development opens the door to a holistic system of Buddhist philosophy for those on the Bodhisattva's path (T45N1861, P248c7-19).

In Kuiji's depiction, the philosophical notions of emptiness (śūnyatā) and essence (svabhāva) mature to their fullness in three stages consecutively. The first stage of the classification captures the stance toward svabhāva in early Buddhism, especially how these followers of the Buddha's first lecture affirm the svabhāvic existence of non-sentient dharmas. According to Kuiji, the first lecture is preserved in the four āgamas (ajimo 阿笈摩) as the teaching of the four noble truths (T45N1861, P249a11). The four noble truths—the depiction of life as suffering, the explication of the cause of suffering, the solution to suffering, and the path towards such a solution—accentuate how there is no permanent self for each sentient being. Constituted by five aggregates, the so-called self will dissolve throughout time (T45N1861, P249a16). Nevertheless, these non-Mahāyāna Buddhists do not negate the svabhāvic existence of non-sentient dharmas. Such a stance towards essence (svabhāva) is systematized in epistemic terms. As previously mentioned in the analysis of the intentional feature of consciousness, these non-Mahāyāna Buddhists contend that knowledge in one's mind is acquired through direct representation of external objects and, as the causes of knowledge, these external objects must have an existence on their own, independent of consciousness (T31N1585, P10b2–4). This distinct understanding of svabhāva likewise shapes the goal of early Buddhist practice. Followers of the four noble truths cherish the ideal of an arhat, in the hope of negating the existence of the self and becoming liberated from suffering (T45N1861, P249a18). According to Kuiji, the pursuit of arhatship obscures the gist of the Buddha's teaching. That is to say, the Buddha scrutinizes the idea of a svabhāvic self, not because non-sentient dharmas have a permanent existence, but rather because the permanent self proves to be the most challenging viewpoint for sentient beings to negate (T45N1861, P249a19).

In due time, those who realize that sentient beings have no permanent self are ready for the second stage where Mādhyamikas debunk the svabhāvic existence of non-sentient dharma in their formulation of emptiness. Although Mādhyamikas elevate the notion of emptiness to the center of Mahāyāna philosophy, new issues arise in their argumentations. That is why Kuiji proclaims that the Madhyamaka philosophy eventually prepares one for the last stage of the Yogācāra teaching of consciousness-only. As such, this chapter will adopt Kuiji's narrative to examine the ways in which Mādhyamikas prioritize emptiness as the central notion in Buddhist philosophy through the critique of their rivals. Nevertheless, the Madhyamaka refutation of svabhāva brings forward previously untouched issues which continue to be tackled by the Yogācārins. Subsequently, the chapter will explore the distinction between early and later Yogācāra, a distinction that derives from their dissimilar interpretations of consciousness-only (vijñaptimātra), emptiness (śūnyatā), and essence (svabhāva). To conclude the discussion, this chapter will make a case for reading the later Chinese Yogācāra worldview expressed by Xuanzang and his disciples as a version of transcendental idealism synonymous with correlative non-dualism, in parallel to the position espoused by Husserl.

Using Kuiji's sūtra classification system as a roadmap, I adopt the perspective of these Chinese Yogācārins to expound on the Buddhist critique of svabhāva. In doing so, I put forward a twofold argument: first, the development of Yogācāra Buddhism in the Tang dynasty is an innovative interpretation of the doctrine of consciousness-only in the Chinese linguistic and cultural context, which cannot be reduced to a passive reception of ideas from South Asia; and second, Xuanzang and his disciples distance themselves from nihilism in their refutation of essence by proposing a worldview that can be interpreted as a version of transcendental idealism *qua* correlative non-dualism.

The Madhyamaka Refutation of Essence (*Svabhāva*)

It is through the efforts of Madhyamaka philosophers that *svabhāva* and *śūnyatā* become foundational concepts in Mahāyāna philosophy. Expanding the notion of no-self, the Mādhyamikas initiate a paradigm shift in their exploration of the ultimate nature of reality. To be more specific, they change their focus from how things really exist to how these things appear in virtue of consciousness. Through this turn towards the subject, they reveal that if the perceiver has no permanent existence, neither does the perceived, insofar as an object relies on a subject to appear as a phenomenon in one's experience. Following this line of reasoning, Mādhyamikas contend that everything, be it sentient being or non-sentient dharma, dependently arises in experience and nothing has an essential core (*svabhāva*) (T30N1564, P2b18–19). To express the idea that everything is empty of *svabhāva*, Mādhyamikas introduce the notion of emptiness (*śūnyatā*).

The Madhyamaka refutation of *svabhāva* is detailed by Nāgārjuna (*c.* 150?–250?) in his *Mūlamadhyamakakārikā* (*zhonglun* 中論). This treatise epitomizes the aforementioned paradigm shift. In one's experience, the perceiver and the perceived object arise interdependently, and it follows that if the perceiver has no permanent existence, neither does the perceived object. This is how and why nothing is permanent and self-determined.

Nāgārjuna speaks of *svabhāva* as the *sui generis*, self-determined, immutable nature that shall "not be affected by conditionality (*buzai zhongyuan zhong*不在眾緣中)" (T30N1564, P2b20). Adopting this definition, Nāgārjuna scrutinizes the arguments provided by non-Mahāyāna Buddhists. Notably, in their argumentation, these non-Mahāyāna Buddhists championed by the Abhidharma clerics contend that sentient beings have no permanent self and that non-sentient dharmas do have eternal existence. For instance, the Sarvāstivādins perceive non-sentient dharmas as the first cause of knowledge and prescribe mind-independently real existence to these dharmas. However, as detailed by Nāgārjuna, if these dharmas can make an impact on the mind in accordance with the karmic law of causality, their existence is affected by conditionality and is therefore not *svabhāvic* (T30N1564, P19c). For Nāgārjuna, even such karmic causality—as a higher-order reality—is far from being self-determined. To make a case for this viewpoint of karmic causality, Nāgārjuna initiates the turn to the subject, further expanding the theory of no-self to the concept of emptiness. He elucidates that the self has no *svabhāvic* existence, because the self in the subjective sense (as that which enacts various actions) and the self in the objective sense (as that which is generated from the five aggregates) are interdependent in their mutual constitution of sentient beings' full-fledged experience as an "I" (T30N1564, P23c20–4) Moreover, for various dharmas that are perceived by the mind and therefore pertain to "my" individual experience, they likewise depend on the perceiver to arise as phenomena (T30N1564, P23c25-6). Anything that is interdependent with others is affected by conditionality (T30N1564, P23c27-8). By definition, nothing has *svabhāvic* existence. Once the *svabhāvic* views of the self and the dharmas are negated, only emptiness remains. To put it in Nāgārjuna's own terms, "*karma* and *kleśa* (defilement) are not real. They arise due to false conceptualization and they cease in emptiness (業 煩惱非實，入空戲論滅)" (T30N1564, P23c29). The concept of *śūnyatā* (emptiness) is therefore introduced by Nāgārjuna to explain how things arise and perish, and are empty of *svabhāvic* existence (T30N1564, P2b19).[2] In the Chinese translation of Nāgārjuna's *Mūlamadhyamakakārikā*, Buddhists refer to *śūnyatā* as either *kong* (空 emptiness) or *wu* (無 nothingness). As an intellectual fruit of his critique of the Abhidharma notion of *svabhāva*, the concept of *śūnyatā* moves to the center of Buddhist philosophy (Nagao 1991: 213-14). At this point, Nāgārjuna *ipso facto* espouses a position that is rather close to metaphysical anti-realism insofar as for him, reality is not mind-independent or *svabhāvic* (Siderits 1988: 321-4).

To capture the ultimate nature of moment-by-moment arising and perishing of things in sentient beings' experience, Nāgārjuna evokes the notion of the middle way— whereby emptiness and the arising-and-perishing illusions are not mutually exclusive. Instead, emptiness overcomes dualistic views of being and non-being, of arising and perishing (T30N1564, P23a5-6). Once sentient beings realize this non-dual wisdom, they acquire the ultimate truth (*diyiyidi* 第一義諦, *paramārthasatya*) of reality (T30N1564, P32c22). Nevertheless, it is very common that sentient beings do not have access to this ultimate truth but only acquire a conventional truth (*shisudi* 世俗諦, *saṃvṛtisatya*) of arising and perishing illusions (T30N1564, P32c20). Therefore, Nāgārjuna encourages sentient beings to pursue the Bodhisattvas' path, going beyond the conventional truth and realizing the ultimate truth (T30N1564, P39b15).

Striving to challenge the view of reality in non-Mahāyāna Buddhism that is currently referred to as metaphysical realism, Mādhyamikas championed by Nāgārjuna are also confronted with several issues.[3] From the Yogācāra perspective, the major problem as pinpointed by Kuiji has to do with the ambivalent nature of illusory dharma and the impossibility of Buddhist practice (T45N1861, P249a22). The first issue can be elaborated in the following manner: if illusory dharmas are empty, are these dharmas empty the moment they arise? If they are empty, then they cannot arise. Yet, if they are not empty, then they are not illusory.[4] The second issue can be presented as such: if everything is empty, can sentient beings engage in Buddhist training? If they can, these sentient beings would have non-illusory existence and, therefore, would not be empty. Yet, if they cannot, Buddhism as a religious tradition should have no practitioners, as nothing would exist and there would be nothing to be trained.

In the narrative outlined by Kuiji, Yogācāra arises as a remedy for Madhyamaka. Given the limitation of the Madhyamaka refutation of essence, Kuiji ranks Madhyamaka as a school above early Buddhism and Abhidharma, but still lower than Yogācāra. In Kuiji's narrative, the Buddha taught a second time, secretively implying how all dharmas were empty by nature for the purpose of clearing up the misunderstandings of *svabhāva* (T45N1861, P249a20). Since Mādhyamikas articulate emptiness by indicating what it is *not*, Kuiji categorizes this approach to emptiness as that of "secretive saying (*yinmiyan* 隱密言)" (T45N1861, P249a21). From Kuiji's vantage point, Buddha employed the secretive saying of emptiness as a skillful means in order to encourage devotees to go beyond arhatship and turn to the Greater Vehicle of Mahāyāna. That is why Kuiji contends that Madhyamaka does not present the supreme truth but rather paves the way for the third stage of the Buddha's teaching—a view that equally demonstrates Kuiji's defense of the status of Yogācāra (T45N1861, P249a23).

Outlining the Buddha's teaching as that of three stages, Kuiji indicates the superiority of Yogācāra Buddhism over other Buddhist schools. Evidently, the three-stage doctrinal development envisaged by Kuiji is an idealization of history. Though Kuiji believed that the transmission of Yogācāra in East Asia would bring an end to doctrinal debates, history revealed otherwise. When Kuiji's master Xuanzang accomplished his study at Nālandā and brought more Buddhist texts back to the capital city of the Tang Empire, his effort did not end the doctrinal debate over *svabhāva*. Rather, it accelerated the split between early and later Yogācāra.

The Yogācāra Objections to Essence (*Svabhāva*)

Previously in Chapters 2 and 5, we were introduced to the difference between early and later Yogācāra. Early Yogācārins define the intentional structure of consciousness as either a one-place knowing or as a two-place knowing, in contrast to later Yogācārins who promote the threefold or fourfold intentional structure. Based on their dissimilar views of consciousness, early and later Yogācārins come to problematize the notion of *svabhāva* in their respective manners.[5] For early Yogācārins, everything is empty of *svabhāvic* existence because everything is an illusion derived from the movement of consciousness. As such, nothing truly exists but the original consciousness. Once the original consciousness ceases its movement and returns to the non-dual state, this consciousness becomes emptiness as such. On the other hand, from the standpoint of later Yogācārins, various things have no *svabhāvic* existence because they rely on the movement of consciousnesses to appear as phenomena in one's experience and therefore become interdependent with consciousnesses. In particular, later Yogācārins highlight how emptiness is the defining nature of consciousnesses devoid of illusion, which indicates that illusory dharma is not non-existent and emptiness is not the same as purified consciousness.

To examine the argumentation of the early Yogācārins especially that in the Chinese language context, we now turn to the treatises attributed to Paramārtha.[6] In his objection to *svabhāva*, Paramārtha expounds on how various things transformed by consciousness, as well as the consciousness itself, have no self-determined existence. That is to say, things external to consciousness have no *svabhāvic* existence because they are transformed from consciousness (T31N1616, P861b4) and even the transforming consciousness *per se* has no *svabhāvic* existence (T31N1616, P861b5). As such, emptiness results from the negation of the existence of objects on the outside and from the nullification of the existence of consciousness on the inside.

The early Yogācāra stance towards essence (*svabhāva*) and emptiness (*śūnyatā*) is grounded in their definition of consciousness. Formulating consciousness as one-place knowing or as two-place knowing, early Yogācārins contend that as long as consciousness is in function, it generates subject–object dualities that animate a wide range of illusory dharmas in the experience of sentient beings (T31N1587, P62c12). It is therefore a consensus among early Yogācārins that all illusions stem from the transformation of consciousness and as such nothing external to consciousness has *svabhāvic* existence (T31N1587, P62c13). Although early Yogācāra scriptures present the mind of a sentient being as that which consists of all eight types of consciousness, they underscore how the eighth consciousness serves as the origin from which the other seven are derived (T31N1587, P62b16). When the original consciousness transforms, it gives rise to subject–object duality in which the subjective side becomes the seventh consciousness, and the objective side turns into the first six consciousnesses (T31N1587, P62b17).

Considering how the original consciousness gives rise to other consciousnesses that further generate all illusion, early Yogācārins interpret awakening as a recuperation of the non-dual state of mind. As such, in their pronouncement that nothing exists but consciousness, early Yogācārins actually mean that nothing exists but the original consciousness devoid of duality (T31N1587, P62c14). Equally, to attain awakening, it requires a sentient being to negate duality and terminate the transformation of consciousness. Emptiness, therefore, entails the absence of *svabhāva* and is further equated with the non-dual state of mind.

More importantly, Paramārtha envisages this non-dual state of mind as the ninth consciousness called *amoluoshi* (阿摩羅識, *amalavijñāna*) (T31N1587, P62c19). As detailed in the texts attributed to Paramārtha, the immaculate state of mind is purified from the polluted eighth consciousness. Following this line of reasoning, Paramārtha suggests that for the original consciousness, if it is polluted by false duality and covered by ignorance, it exists as the illusory consciousness (*xuwangshi* 虛妄識) *qua* the eighth consciousness (T31N1616, P864a25-7). Yet, sentient beings can make an effort to purify the original consciousness into the mind of immaculate suchness *qua* the ninth consciousness (*amoluoqingjingxin* 阿摩羅清淨心) (T31N1616, P864a28). By then, the illusory consciousness transforms into the ninth *amalavijñāna* that is tantamount to emptiness and the pure dharma realm (T30N1584, P1022a16-17). Such a depiction of the original consciousness is syncretized with the view of *tathāgatagarbha* (*rulaizang* 如來藏) as the Buddha nature inherent in all sentient beings only temporally covered by ignorance (T30N1584, P1018c6). As noticed by Takasaki Jikidō, when Paramārtha translates Buddhist scriptures, he succeeds in fusing these translations with his comprehension of doctrinal ideas (Takasaki 1986: 262). As a result, Paramārtha develops an eclectic view of the mind that harmonizes the Yogācāra analysis of consciousness with the theory of *tathāgatagarbha*. It is for this reason that master Yinshun remarks that Paramārtha enriched and advanced early Yogācāra viewpoints transmitted from South Asia (Yinshun 1988: 212).

To elaborate on the conception of emptiness and the refutation of *svabhāva*, Paramārtha turns to the three natures theory. In it, the three natures are known as: the false imagined nature or simply the imagined nature (*bianjisuozhixing* 遍計所執性, *parikalpitasvabhāva*) of illusions perceived by ignorant sentient beings; other dependent nature or simply the dependent nature (*yitaqixing* 依他起性,

paratantrasvabhāva) of consciousness's transformation; and lastly, the absolute nature (*yuanchengshixing* 圓成實性, *pariniṣpannasvabhāva*) of things in the cosmos. Paramārtha refers to them as *fenbiexing* (分別性), *yitaxing* (依他性), and *zhenshixing* (真實性), respectively (T31N1587, P63a17–21). Since illusions have no *svabhāvic* existence but are only falsely imagined to be *svabhāvic*, the imagined nature of illusion is empty and not real (T31N1587, P63a19). What generate illusions are subject–object dualities stemming from the transformation of consciousness (T31N1587, P63a20). As such, duality characterizes the dependent nature, which marks this nature as equally non-existent (T31N1587, P63a26–b6). Removed and purified from illusion, the original consciousness evolves into the luminous mind as the mind of immaculate suchness, which unveils the last absolute nature (T31N1587, P63a21). Only the absolute nature has real existence.

Scrutinizing early Yogācāra's stance on emptiness (*śūnyatā*) and essence (*svabhāva*), Xuanzang and his disciples bring to light several limitations of the argumentation of early Yogācārins. Above all, early Yogācārins like Paramārtha assimilate all eight types of consciousness into one original consciousness. As such, early Yogācārins fail to acknowledge the unique epistemic function (*yong* 用) of each *vijñāna* (T31N1585, P1a16). Besides, early Yogācārins deem illusory dharmas to be non-existent, which makes their position similar to that of Mādhyamikas when it comes to the question of the ontological status of arising and perishing phenomena. That is why Mei Guangxi remarks that early Yogācārins do not fully distance themselves from the Mādhyamikas (Mei 1931: 345).

In proposing a resolution to these issues, later Yogācārins represented by Xuanzang and his disciples go beyond the polarity of existence (*you* 有) and non-existence (*wu* 無). Thereby, we can derive three types of existence from their writings: the seemingly real existence, the fictitious existence, and the real existence. Each of these can be further associated respectively with the dependent nature, the imagined nature, and the absolute nature. As such, Xuanzang and his disciples *ipso facto* shift the focus from whether things exist to how things exist in the experience of sentient beings.

The term "seemingly real" as either *xushi* (虛實) (T31N1585, P59a8), or *siyou* (似有) (T31N1585, P46c9) can be found in Xuanzang's characterization of the transformation of consciousness.[7] The use of such a term shows that this transformation, though being empty of any *svabhāvic* existence, maintains a distinct way of existing (*you* 有) (T31N1585, P39a3). If they were non-existent, the existential status of illusory dharmas at the moment they arise from consciousness would also become ambivalent. This comes to be how Xuanzang designates the existence of that which derives from the transformation of consciousness (T31N1585, P46c8–9). That is to say, since these later Yogācārins promote the fourfold intentional structure and perceive consciousness as that which gives rise to the seeing part *qua* the intending act and the image part *qua* the intended phenomenon, they characterize the seeing part and the image part as that which is as seemingly real as consciousness itself (T31N1585, P59a8–9). This seemingly real existence opens the door to a possibility. When consciousness transforms, it follows the fourfold intentional structure to generate the image part, the seeing part, the self-awareness, and the reflexive awareness of this self-awareness. All of these four parts have the seemingly real existence and this existence can further be cognized in two manners: sometimes sentient beings come to see these four parts as they really are and thus realize emptiness and interdependence; yet, at other times, sentient beings misperceive them—especially the seeing part and the image part—as *svabhāvic*, which further gives rise to a wide range of attachments.

We can locate the term "fictitious existence (*jiayou* 假有, *prajñaptisat*)" used by Xuanzang and his disciples to define that which is produced by misconception (T31N1585, P47c11). Indeed, Xuanzang speaks of those of the imagined nature as the fictitious names (*jiaming* 假名) (T31N1585, P47a10). In virtue of the innate attachments, we, the sentient beings, habitually internalize the misconceptions of the self and other beings in the cosmos as *svabhāvic*. To consolidate the self-other polarization in our discriminative attachments, we further produce categories and concepts to differentiate the self from the other. These categories and concepts are fictitious names insofar as our self-identity is not immutable but constituted through our constant interactions with the rest of the world. As such, Xuanzang implicitly associates fictitious existence with *svabhāva*, in that *svabhāva* is nothing but a fictitious name. In the opening paragraph of the *CWSL*, Xuanzang underscores the critical function of fictitious names (T31N1585, P1a20). To be more specific, these fictitious names perform a critical function when they are employed as the skillful means for Bodhisattvas to educate the ignorant ones. In these scenarios, Bodhisattvas use these fictitious names not to consolidate misperception, but to criticize ignorance, which explains why Xuanzang does not deem illusions to be non-existent but describes their existence as fictitious.

Contrariwise, we can discern the term "real existence (*shiyou* 實有, *dravyasat*)" used by Xuanzang to define how things actually are when we remove all misperceptions from our experience (T31N1585, P47c13). As is stated in the *CWSL*, the fictitious names are produced by misperception and can be purified once sentient beings like us see things as they really are, which further reveals the fluid transformability of the fictitious existence and the real existence (T31N1585, P47c12). To elucidate how false conceptualization obstructs us from perceiving this real existence, Yogācārins pinpoint two types of obstructions: the obstructions of defilement (*fannaozhang* 煩惱障, *kleśāvaraṇa*) that arise from self-attachments (T31N1585, P48c7), and the obstructions of knowledge (*suozhizhang* 所知障, *jñeyāvaraṇa*) that emerge from dharma-attachments (T31N1585, P48c9-11). These obstructions and attachments can be removed, as long as sentient beings like us come to engage in various types of Buddhist practices at the prescriptive level, which we will revisit in the final part of this book.

We can trace how Xuanzang connects these three types of existence—the fictitious existence, the seemingly real existence, and the real existence—with the aforementioned three natures in the *CWSL*. He first unpacks how the existence of the imagined nature is fictitious (T31N1585, P47a10). When consciousness transforms itself, the seemingly real seeing part and image part arise. Among all eight types of consciousness, only the sixth and seventh consciousnesses can falsely imagine these parts as *svabhāvic* (T31N1585, P45c26-7). False imaginations further pollute the transforming consciousnesses. As such, the imagined nature together with anything characterized by it has only fictitious existence and is not ultimately real (T31N1585, P47c9).

This transformation of consciousness, since it generates the seeing part and the image part that are seemingly real, opens up the possibility of either polluting consciousness with misperceptions or purifying consciousness by seeing things as they are. That is why this transformation has real existence (T31N1585, P47c11). In other words, the second dependent nature, as well as anything marked by it, is real (T31N1585, P59a8).

Eventually, when false conceptions are removed, the absolute nature of consciousness will be realized, the salient feature of which is the real existence (T31N1585, P46b7–8). Kuiji clarifies that the absolute nature is synonymous with the true nature of being empty, also known as suchness and emptiness (T43N1830, P546b3–5). These three natures that consecutively characterize the polluted state, the neutral state, and the pure state of the mind of a sentient being, hence become interdependent with consciousness (T31N1585, P46c13).

In facilitating our understanding of Xuanzang and his disciples' account of three natures, it is helpful to turn to the well-known Chan analogy of mountains as mountains. When our mindset is characterized by the first imagined nature, we see mountains as mountains and waters as waters that are *svabhāvic*, that is, invariant across time and space, independent of and irrelevant to ourselves. The second dependent nature enables us to recognize our false imagination and understand that the mountain and water in our perceptions are phenomena transformed from consciousness. Thus, we no longer see mountains as mountains, waters as waters. Eventually, when we realize the absolute nature of things as they actually are, we again see mountains as mountains, waters as waters—though not in a *svabhāvic* sense, but as interdependent with ourselves in our lived experiences.

Given the explication of the three natures account proposed by Xuanzang and his disciples, we can deepen our understanding of the early–later distinction among Chinese Yogācārins. As previously examined, early Yogācārins like Paramārtha argue that all consciousnesses can falsely imagine. They continue to negate the real existence of the second dependent nature. In their interpretation of the last nature, early Yogācārins equate it with the consciousness of suchness, further making emptiness tantamount to the non-dual state of mind. Later Yogācārins represented by Xuanzang and his disciples conceive of consciousness as well as its transformation in a different manner. They borrow philosophical binaries from the lexicon of their then-contemporary Chinese intellectuals to unpack the interplay between the fictitious (*jia* 假) existence of illusions in the imagined nature and the genuine (*zhen* 真) existence of suchness in the absolute nature. As such, upon acknowledging the existence of illusory dharmas, these later Yogācārins contend that only the seventh and sixth consciousnesses can misperceive and falsely imagine. They continue to acknowledge the real existence of the second dependent nature, which is specified as seemingly real. Regarding the last nature, Xuanzang and his disciples demarcate emptiness from consciousness, insofar as emptiness is not the non-dual state of mind *per se*, but the defining nature of purified consciousnesses (T45N1861, P259a14).

To elaborate on this conception of emptiness, Kuiji specifies the distinction between empty (*kong* 空, *śūnya*) and emptiness (*kongxing* 空性, *śūnyatā*) (T44N1835, P2b29). In the Sanskrit language, one can add the affix -*tā* to an adjective, from which there derives a noun of more abstract meaning. Therefore, *śūnyatā* entails a more abstract form of *śūnya*. That said, although relating the notion of emptiness to its Sanskrit origin, Kuiji does not perceive emptiness as the more abstract meaning of the empty. Rather, playing with the nuance of words in the Chinese language, Kuiji puts forward his innovative interpretation. He speaks of emptiness as the nature of being empty (T44N1835, P2b28), and defines empty as that which is absent of "grasping" (*qu* 取, *grāha*) (T43N1830, P546a2). Here, grasping is another way of describing false imagination and misperception (T43N1830, P546a1). As such, grasping appears when someone misperceives the seeing part of consciousness as the *svabhāvic* act of grasping, and misconceives of the image part as the *svabhāvic* image to be grasped. In this sense, to be empty amounts to a negation of *svabhāva*. Accordingly, grasping will be removed once this sentient being sees things as they really are (T43N1830, P546a28). Along with the absence of grasping, there comes the removal of attachments (T43N1830, P546a3). Subsequently, the true nature of things in the cosmos will be realized (T43N1830, P546a4). In other words, after negating *svabhāva*, the nature of being empty of *svabhāvic* qualities unveils itself as emptiness or suchness (T43N1830, P546a5). In this manner, Kuiji stresses that the concept of "empty" indicates a negation of misperception, grasping, and false imagination, whereas the concept of emptiness presents a positive articulation of the true nature of things in the cosmos. To be more specific, emptiness is not an abstract void. Quite to the contrary, emptiness (*kongxing* 空性) expresses the nature (*xing* 性) of being empty (*kong* 空) of *svabhāva* (T44N1835, P2b29).

Kuiji's interpretation of emptiness is notably indebted to his master Xuanzang who is particularly critical of the nihilistic view that equates emptiness with nothingness. Against this backdrop, Xuanzang continues to foreground how emptiness evinces the nature of how things actually are (T31N1585, P39b15–19). That is why those that are genuinely empty do not become the void but still also have their nature (*xing* 性) (T31N1585, P39a3). Consequently, for Xuanzang and his disciples, consciousness-only bespeaks how everything is "not independent of consciousness (*bulishi* 不離識)" (T31N1585, P39a3). It differs from the early Yogācāra viewpoint that nothing except for the non-dual state of mind exists. Since all the phenomena in one's experience arise from the movement of consciousness, these phenomena are only as seemingly real as consciousness. Once a sentient being removes any falsely imagined fictitious existence from these phenomena, the true nature of consciousness, as well as its transformation, is realized, which evinces the nature of being truly empty, otherwise known as emptiness. Articulated in this manner, emptiness is not the same as but comes to define the purified consciousness. Far from being a void, emptiness shows how things actually are and therefore yields the underlying principle that regulates the arising and perishing of dharmas. As such, later Yogācārins present a viewpoint different from that in early Yogācāra, which is illustrated in Table 1.

Now that we have clarified the later Yogācāra view of existence, essence, and emptiness, we can continue to explore whether Xuanzang and his disciples can resolve the issues in the Madhyamaka account of emptiness in a more plausible way. Kuiji has identified the two problems as: that of the existential status of illusory dharma; and that of the impossibility of Buddhist practice (T45N1861, P249a22). If illusory dharmas do have a distinct form of existence in our experience, they can rise and perish at any moment. Likewise, sentient beings like us can engage in various practices to become one with emptiness through removing misperceptions and purifying consciousness. In

Table 1 The contrast between early Yogācāra and later Yogācāra

	Viewpoints	Early Yogācāra	Later Yogācāra
Descriptive level	Intentional structure	The onefold or twofold structure	The threefold or fourfold structure
	Origin of illusion	As long as each consciousness transforms, there will be subject–object dualities from which illusions arise. All consciousnesses can produce illusions.	Illusions derive from misperceptions of the seventh and sixth consciousnesses. Only the seventh and the sixth can produce illusions.
	Relationship of consciousnesses	The first seven consciousnesses surface out of the original consciousness *qua* the eighth consciousness. "All consciousnesses have different *yong* (functions) but share the same underlying *ti* (諸識用別體同)" (T31N1585, P1a16).	The first seven consciousnesses depend on the eighth consciousness to arise, but they cannot be assimilated into the eighth consciousness. "Since the function of each consciousness is distinct from others, the nature [of its *ti*] shall be demarcated from others as well (以作用別性各不同)" (T43N1830, P241a17).
Explicative level	Definition of Consciousness-only	Consciousness-only means that nothing exists but the original consciousness. (metaphysical idealism)	Consciousness-only means that everything depends on the mind to appear as phenomena for someone. (transcendental idealism as correlative non-dualism)
	Elaboration of the three natures	The imagined nature and the dependent nature both allude to duality and are therefore illusory and have no existence.	The imagined nature indicates misperception and therefore, has only fictitious existence, rather than real existence. The dependent nature has (seemingly) real existence.
	Interpretation of emptiness	To awaken means to sweep the "dust" and uncover the non-dual state of mind. The non-dual state of mind is emptiness; it is also the ninth consciousness.	To awaken means to purify misperception and acquire the pure state of mind. Emptiness is the defining feature of pure consciousness, but not the same as consciousness.
Prescriptive level	Prescription of awakening	The mind is originally luminous, only temporarily covered by dust *qua* illusion and ignorance. All sentient beings have Buddha nature and can become awakened.	The mind is not originally luminous but can be purified through making an effort. Some sentient beings have no Buddha nature. There are also five different families of sentient beings.

the following chapters, when I use phrases along the lines of "becoming one with emptiness," I do not mean to equate consciousness to emptiness. This phrase will indicate, rather, the way in which our consciousness embraces the nature of its emptiness and how it embodies the underlying principle of arising and perishing. The Yogācāra stress on the wondrous existence of transformable dharmas likewise becomes foundational to their interpretation of Buddha nature and to their promotion of the *gotra* system.

Essence, Emptiness, and Existence

With respect to their views of essence, emptiness, and existence, Xuanzang and his disciples propose their own theories concerning these concepts. Differing from the early Yogācāra negation of the existence of illusory dharmas, these later Yogācārins introduce a more positive way of understanding the existence of illusions and consciousnesses. As previously analyzed, Xuanzang and his disciples introduced three types of existence—fictitious, seemingly real, and real—to capture the three modes of being for a phenomenon in a sentient being's experience when it is respectively perceived as *svabhāvic*, as transformed by consciousness, and as it actually is. Nagao Gadjin describes this positive view of existence as the later Yogācāra insight of "absolute emptiness and wondrous being" (Nagao 1991: 214). However, what does this "wondrous being" entail? Does this existence (*you* 有) allude to another *svabhāva* that endures throughout cyclical time? This question redirects us to the notion we have encountered earlier, namely, that of *ālambanapratyaya* (*suoyuanyuan* 所緣緣).

The concept of *ālambanapratyaya* has been used to describe a perceived phenomenon and differentiate such a phenomenon from an external object, which further allows Yogācārins to distance themselves from the early Buddhist and Abhidharma style of realism. As Xuanzang clarifies in the *CWSL*, to be qualified as *ālambanapratyaya* or *suoyuanyuan* in Chinese, a dharma needs first to meet the criteria of being a *suoyuan* (所緣, *ālambana*) as an object intended by consciousnesses (T31N1585, P40c15). Thus, *paramāṇu* (*jiwei* 極微)—which is the smallest basic component of things, similar to a particle—does not meet the criteria, insofar as they are too small to be discerned (T31N1624, P888b12). Second, this dharma should have real existence so that it can be qualified as a condition (*yuan*, 緣, *pratyaya*). For instance, when someone claims to have seen two moons in the sky, the second moon is a delusion and has no real existence (T31N1624, P888b19). Consequently, the so-called second moon is not qualified as a condition. Kuiji further clarifies the meaning of existing dharma (*youfa* 有法) in the following way: anything that is not contaminated by false imagination and not being grasped as *svabhāva*, can be considered to have a real existence, either as seemingly real dharmas or as the real consciousnesses (T43N1830, P500b21).

From Kuiji's delineation of existing dharma, we can derive the understanding of reality presented in the doctrine of later Yogācāra. On the one hand, consciousness is not exhaustive of reality. As we have seen in the example of two moons, if reality were merely a mental fabrication, we would not be able to differentiate the real moon from the delusional one. This view that nothing exists but consciousness is espoused by early Yogācārins, not by later Yogācārins like Xuanzang and his disciples. On the other hand, reality is not *svabhāvic*. As indicated above, the existence of *svabhāvic* objects is fictitious and cannot be qualified as a condition. While early Buddhists and the Abhidharma followers acknowledge the existence of *svabhāvic* reality through their articulation of knowledge, Xuanzang and his disciples divorce themselves from such realism.

For later Yogācārins like Xuanzang and his disciples, any *svabhāva* is characterized by the defining qualities of being immutable (*chang* 常) (T43N1830, P244c22), self-determined (*zhuzhai* 主宰) (T43N1830, P239c3), and persistent throughout time and space (*bian* 遍) (T43N1830, P244c23). In this regard, the existence of dharma is not *svabhāvic*, because dharmas arise and perish constantly in virtue of consciousness. Whenever these dharmas appear in the experience of sentient beings by virtue of consciousness, the existence of appeared phenomena becomes seemingly real. Likewise, the existence of consciousness is far from immutable, insofar as consciousness incessantly transforms itself moment by moment and becomes interdependent with its transformation. Through the transformation of consciousnesses, these real dharmas appear as images/phenomena. Subsequently, either sentient beings see these seemingly real dharmas as they actually are and realize emptiness, or sentient beings misconceive this seemingly real existence as something *svabhāvic* to form attachments.

Our discussion of the Yogācāra view of reality permits us to inquire into the metaphysical position endorsed by Xuanzang and his disciples through their articulation of emptiness (*śūnyatā*) and essence (*svabhāva*).[8] To demarcate their standpoint from that of early Yogācārins like Paramārtha, let us recall the early Yogācāra view of reality. As previously mentioned, early Yogācārins perceive the original consciousness as the ground for everything in the cosmos and it becomes tantamount to emptiness once it is purified of dualities. Considering how the original consciousness is exhaustive of all realities, we interpret the viewpoint of early Yogācāra as metaphysical idealism. Early Yogācārins, who lived in the time when terms such as metaphysics or realism were not incorporated into the popular discourse of Buddhism, had employed a different terminology to express their viewpoint: "all consciousnesses have different *yong* (functions) but share the same underlying *ti* (諸識用別體同)" (T31N1585, P1a16). With the help of the *ti–yong* binary, early Yogācārins like Paramārtha envisage the original consciousness as the origin of all consciousness and transformed illusions. Articulated as the underlying *ti*, the original consciousness is tantamount to an absolute idea. That is why nothing exists but this absolute idea.

Different from early Yogācārins, Xuanzang and his disciples do not speak of the original consciousness as the cosmic origin and an absolute idea. By acknowledging the existence of seemingly real dharmas, these later Yogācārins espouse realism in an empirical, conventional sense. That said, even though they affirm the momentary existence of seemingly real phenomena in sentient beings' experience, they do not go any further in depicting such existence as *svabhāvic*, therefore distancing themselves from the early Buddhist and the Abhidharma version of realism. Implying their support for what can be interpreted as empirical/conventional realism, Xuanzang and his disciples affirm the existence of an intersubjectively accessible world through their analysis of other minds. They further proclaim that the intersubjective world, the corporeal bodies of all beings, as well as consciousnesses, are neither similar nor dissimilar because these three factors are mutually interdependent (T31N1624, P889a9).

More importantly, through their conception of seemingly real existence, Xuanzang and his disciples express their view of subjectivity as the transcendental ideality, which can be inferred from the notion of the *ti* (體) of consciousness. As previously mentioned, early Yogācārins perceive the original consciousness as the origin and root—namely, as the *ti*—of all other types of consciousness. Later Yogācārins, however, argue otherwise. Promoting Dharmapāla's characterization of fourfold intentional structure, Xuanzang and his disciples highlight how the seeing part and the image part represent the function (*yong* 用) *qua vijñapti*, whereas the underlying self-awareness and the reflective awareness of this self-awareness epitomize the underlying *ti qua vijñāna* (T43N1830, P487a13–14). The *ti* of consciousness entails what has been coined by European philosophers, such as Husserl, as subjectivity. While these Yogācārins object to the existence of a *svabhāvic* self, they do not negate subjectivity but rather highlight its role in the lived experience of sentient beings.

To be more specific, subjectivity exists either passively in the seventh and eighth consciousnesses, or actively in the first six consciousnesses. Although this subjectivity is not equivalent to a *svabhāvic* ego nor exhaustive of all real objects, it characterizes the transformation of consciousness that serves as the necessary condition for the possibility of phenomena to appear in the mind. On the basis of this transformation, a subject further comes to determine how this possibility is realized in an intersubjective world—realized as seemingly real, fictitiously real, or absolutely real. Differing from early Yogācārins who envisage the original consciousness as an absolute idea, later Yogācārins perceive subjectivity as an ideality in the transcendental sense that is correlated with empirical reality. It is this correlation that secures the non-dual transformability of ignorance and awakening.

As such, we interpret the worldview embraced by Xuanzang and his disciples as transcendental idealism, parallel to that of Husserl, which yields a version of correlative non-dualism. To repeat, such a version of transcendental idealism suggests that the mind of a sentient being serves as the necessary condition for the possibility of phenomena in the experience and reaches out to other minds to constitute the intersubjectively accessible cosmic horizon. The correlation of transcendental ideality and empirical reality further undergirds the non-duality of binaries, especially the fluidity from ignorance to awakening. Therefore, the metaphysical position of later Yogācāra, likewise, can be demarcated from the early Yogācāra metaphysical idealism, and it is equally different from the early Buddhist and Abhidharma version of metaphysical realism.

Xuanzang illustrates this correlative non-dualism through the interplay between the mindset of an ignorant one (*yufu* 愚夫) (T31N1585, P46c9) and that of a wise one (*zhizhe* 智者) (T31N1585, P48b4). As demonstrated by the *CWSL*, sentient beings under the ignorant mindset enact their way of being a subject—namely, their subjectivity—in an incorrect manner (T31N1585, P48a7). That is why, in virtue of the function of the seventh and sixth consciousnesses, they falsely imagine various phenomena as *svabhāvic* entities (T31N1585, P48a7). False imagination continues to propel these ignorant ones to embrace an egocentric lifestyle, conduct non-altruistic actions, and cultivate egocentric worldviews (T31N1585, P48a8). Evil, subsequently, arises from egoism and Yogācārins refer to this cultivation as perfuming (*xunxi* 熏習) the seeds in the storehouse consciousness, analogous to the generation of more possibilities of future egoistic views or actions (T31N1585, P8b8).

Contrarily, the subjectivity of those with wisdom allows them to open their eyes to the real existence of things in the cosmos that arise and perish moment by moment. Prior to becoming one with emptiness, those with wisdom can make a consistent effort to purify previous misperceptions. Shortly after, they will realize their interdependence with the ignorant ones and revitalize their compassion. Navigating life in this intersubjectively accessible world, these wise ones follow the Bodhisattvas' path to help the ignorant ones. In this process, Bodhisattvas come to play with the fictitious existence of anything that stems from false imagination as the skillful means to waking up ignorant ones from their mistakes. That is to say, Bodhisattvas use concepts and categories as a critique of ignorant viewpoints and actions. Only when all sentient beings manage to purify their minds, will the ultimate awakening be achieved. Indeed, purification of consciousness entails a long process of de-habitualizing oneself from egoism and re-habitualizing through a collaborative effort.

As such, the interplay between the wise and the ignorant illustrates the way in which subjectivity serves as the transcendental ideality that correlates with empirical reality so as to secure the non-dual transformability of ignorance and awakening. Perceived in this way, transcendental idealism for Xuanzang and disciples is not only a worldview of correlative non-dualism, but also a norm for collaborative practice. It is both an explication of the nature of reality and a prescription of what to do in everyday life. In Kuiji's terms, the Buddha used his third lecture to teach the ultimate meaning of existence and emptiness for the purpose of encouraging everyone to embark on the Bodhisattvas' path (T45N1861, P249a23). Now that the definition of essence in Husserl and the meaning of *svabhāva* and emptiness in Yogācāra are clear, we can proceed to tackle the problem of essence in the upcoming chapter.

9

Essence in Comparative Philosophy

The problem of essence—as introduced in the Prologue—comes into existence when we accept a specific set of presuppositions about the meaning of essence. As such, this problem will be resolved once these presuppositions are removed. That is why before tackling the problem of essence, I would like to invite readers to take a step back and think about how the term "essence" has been used in a multicultural and multilingual context. In contemporary studies of philosophy, scholars speak of essence as the necessary attribute and property that cannot be lacked by an object.[1] For instance, we might say that a cat person has many characteristics, such as loving cats, being able to afford cat food, knowing how to contact a vet, etc. Among these, the essence of a cat person is the attribute of loving cats, rather than that of knowing how to contact a vet. In common vernacular, the concept of essence is usually used in contrast with the accidental, unnecessary, or contingent properties of an object.

Turning back to our discussion, the difficulty in understanding the notion of essence stems from the fact that neither Husserl nor Chinese Yogācārins have directly utilized the English word "essence" in their investigation of consciousness. As stated previously, Husserl employs the German term "*Wesen*," further borrowing "*eidos*" from Greek and "*essentia*" from Latin. When we shift our attention to the Chinese context, the situation becomes more complicated. In our previous analysis, we came across at least three Chinese characters that are often paraphrased as the English term essence, the three being *svabhāva* (*zixing* 自性), *ti* (體),[2] and *xing* (性).[3] Additionally, the concepts of *jing* (精, spirit), *qing* (情, disposition), and *qi* (氣, vital energy) are also rendered as "essence" in the English language scholarship of Chinese philosophy (Ivanhoe & Van Norden 2005).

When scholars of Chinese philosophy reserve the word "essence" to translate these many terms, they probably intend to highlight how these terms denote a sense of being the necessary, must-have, attribute of things. Furthermore, these terms, such as *ti* (體) and *xing* (性), are often paired with *yong* (用) and *xiang* (相), a correlation which might likewise strike translators as parallel to that of the essential and the accidental. Although scholars championed by A. C. Graham welcome this translation (Graham 1967), others represented by Irene Bloom (1997) and Roger Ames (2002) tend to be more critical. Kwong-loi Shun particularly questions whether the nuance of the Aristotelian distinction of the essential and the accidental can be transported into the writings of early Chinese philosophers (Shun 1997). Accordingly, a closer examination is required when we explore whether the widely adopted definition of essence—as used in common English vernacular—can be directly and easily imposed on Husserl and Chinese Yogācārins. As such, we hope to avoid overgeneralizing their positions and misrepresenting their thoughts, which constitutes a crucial step in overcoming Orientalism.

Through this examination, I maintain that, on the one hand, Husserl's understanding of essence marks his break from the Cartesian dualism at the heart of mainstream Enlightenment thinking, which results in his distinct contribution to the intellectual history of European philosophy. And on the other hand, Xuanzang and his disciples employ an innovative interpretation of emptiness (*śūnyatā*) and essence (*svabhāva*), which constitutes a crucial moment in Chinese intellectual history and develops Buddhist thought outside the South Asian context. Positioning these philosophers in their respective contexts, we obtain access to their lived realities that are embedded in language and culture throughout history. Towards the end of this chapter, we will resolve the problem of essence at the explicative level of our comparative project. Our intercultural discussions of essence *de facto* problematize the overgeneralized East-West dichotomy in the Orientalist discourse, through which we advance our comprehension of a meaningful life in a multicultural world.

Essence in Husserl's Phenomenology: A Reappraisal

Essence is one of only a few concepts fundamental to Euro-American philosophy, especially in the branch of metaphysics. Modern scholars often trace the distinction between the essential as that which is *in* an object and the accidental as that which is said *of* an object to the philosophical writings of Aristotle (Robertson & Atkins 2016; Cohen 2016). In truth, the intellectual history of the concept of essence predates Aristotle and can be found in Plato. Therefore, the following section will introduce the consecutive articulations of essence provided by Plato, Aristotle, and Thomas Aquinas, which constitutes the basic meaning of this term in early modern philosophy and sets the stage for Husserl's elaboration of essence. The purpose of this exposition is not to defend Husserl against others, nor to demonstrate how Husserl's theory is inherently distinct. Rather, we position Husserl in dialogue with previous thinkers throughout the process of modernization, as a means of highlighting the diversity of viewpoints in the tradition commonly known as Western philosophy. As such, this section is also dialogical and comparative by nature.

Writing in Greek, neither Plato nor Aristotle could employ the English term "essence." In the translation of Platonic concepts, essence has been utilized to paraphrase either the Greek term *ousia* (οὐσία) (Silverman 2002), or that of *eidos* (εἶδος) (Ricoeur 2013). As indicated in the *Parmenides*, the concept of *ousia*—the literal meaning of which is "being" or "entity"—is an integral part of Plato's account of *eidos*.[4] Plato formulates *eidos* as the universal, independent, *sui generis* ideas that he distinguishes from the particulars (*Parmenides* 129a). Indeed, *eidos* exists in itself, transcending the sensible world of particulars (Plato, *Parmenides* 129a). The sensible particulars can relate to *eidos* through partaking of it (Plato, *Parmenides* 129b). Considering how the particulars are constantly in change, they cannot be used to define an existing thing as such (Plato, *Parmenides* 130a). What defines an entity—or in other words, what defines *ousia*—is the *eidos* rather than the particulars of a thing. As such, *eidos* encompasses *ousia*, both of which allude to essence in the Platonic sense that is delineated as a nonsensible, transcendent quality.

In the English language scholarship of Aristotle, *ousia* is often translated as "substance" and *eidos* as "form" (Bostock 1994), and the Greek phrase "*to ti ên einai (τὸ τί ἦν εἶναι)*"—literally meaning what being is for or what-being-is—is paraphrased as *essence* (Cohen 2016). This translation *per se* bespeaks the distinction between the Aristotelian system and the Platonic one. For Plato, *eidos* entails that which is universal, transcendent, and separate from particulars, whereas Aristotle expresses his critique of this separation in his *Metaphysics* (7.7.1032b19–20).[5] For Aristotle, *eidos* is always instantiated in and therefore indivisible from things of its sort *qua* matters (*Metaphysics* 7.8.1033b11–16). That is to say, the universal *eidos* does not exist separately from the particular matters, but rather always appears in a compound with them (Aristotle, *Metaphysics* 7.8.1033b25–6). Considering how *eidos* informs matter and enables matter to actualize its final formation (Aristotle, *Metaphysics* 7.17.1041a6–9), *eidos* takes priority over the matter in the compound. For instance, a chunk of wood is the material that can be made into a table and indeed has the potential of becoming a dining table, yet the potential is not actualized until the form of a table is offered, that is, until the matter is informed. As such, *eidos* becomes the essence of the compound, further becoming the primary substance (Aristotle, *Metaphysics* 7.7.1032b1). In this regard, a substance is the first category that does not refer to anything, but others will refer to it (Aristotle, *Metaphysics* 7.1.1028a31–6). In contrast to other accidental attributes, a substance can become essential (Aristotle, *Metaphysics* 7.3.1029a12–16). From an Aristotelian point of view, the primary substance of an essence is *sui generis*, eternal, and immutable, though not transcending the particulars.

The translation of "what being is" to "essence" can be traced back to Medieval times when the scholastics evoked the term *essentia* to paraphrase "*to ti ên einai*" in Aristotle's writings. Considering how the term essence has been incorporated into the Latin lexicon, one will not be surprised at how the discussion of essence is closely associated with that of "existence" and "being" in scholastic philosophy. Take St. Thomas Aquinas,[6] for instance, who defines essence as that which is demarcated and signified by existence, in his essay *On Being and Essence (De Ente et Essentia)* (30).[7]

Given the distinction between substances and accidents, essence (*essentia*) can be further classified in two ways: either true and proper as in substances; or restricted as in accidents (Aquinas, *De Ente et Essentia* 32). In total, there are three types of substances: composites of matter and form, immaterial forms, and one with the purest or simplest form (Aquinas, *De Ente et Essentia* 60). In the first case, the essence of a composite embraces both its matter and form, insofar as its matter serves as the principle of individualization (Aquinas, *De Ente et Essentia* 36), whereas its form informs and actualizes the matter (Aquinas, *De Ente et Essentia* 35). As such, the essence of a composite unfolds as that which "abstracts from every being, but in such a way that prescinds from no one of them" (Aquinas, *De Ente et Essentia* 47). In the second case, the essence of immaterial forms, otherwise known as separate substances—*inter alia* soul and intelligence—is delineated by its existence as a potentiality (Aquinas,

De Ente et Essentia 55). What determines such potentiality is the first cause *qua* God, whose essence is the same as existence (Aquinas, *De Ente et Essentia* 60).

Articulated in an Aristotelian manner, the essence of God is the *sui generis*, self-determined, immutable, eternal, and absolutely perfect existence (Aquinas, *De Ente et Essentia* 60–1). As suggested by Aquinas (*De Ente et Essentia* 66), the essence is complete only for God. Caused and shaped by God, immaterial substances, such as intelligence or soul, take it as their essence to be the existence of the received and the partial (Aquinas, *De Ente et Essentia* 62–3). Considering how intelligence arises because of God, Aquinas remarks that anyone can know about a phoenix but still have no knowledge of its existence in reality (*De Ente et Essentia* 55). Actualized by form, the composite substance of both matter and form has its essence as the existence of the received, limited, divided, and designated (Aquinas, *De Ente et Essentia* 65). Further caused by substances, accidents are not composed of form and matter, but rather result from them (Aquinas, *De Ente et Essentia* 67–70). The essence of accidents, accordingly, unravels itself as the existence of being secondary, qualified, and restricted (Aquinas, *De Ente et Essentia* 68). Throughout his exposition of essence and existence, Aquinas *ipso facto* highlights how the essence of God is the purest form, in effect, as the *essence* of essence. Therefore, only in the third case of the purest form—namely, only in God— does essence (*essentia*) and existence (*ente*) become one.

The brief exposition above demonstrates how the term essence has been incorporated into the discourse of European philosophy. In the wake of modernization, the discussion of essence and existence becomes increasingly associated with experience and consciousness. The turn towards the subject was explicitly made by René Descartes who not only placed subjective experience at the center of his philosophical discussion but also derived moral values and motivations from it.[8] According to Descartes, what defines the essence of each person is not its way of existing but rather its capacity of thinking. As he details in *Discourse on the Method* (*Discours de la Méthode*), what defines the essence (*essentia*) of someone being the "I" is not existence but rather the capacity of thinking (DM 32). Essence as that which is defined by thinking prior to being is enclosed in his proclamation: "I think, therefore I am (*cogito, ergo sum*)" (DM 33). Following the demarcation of essence from existence, Descartes separates the thinking mind/soul from the unthinking body, which results in the disengagement of the self from the rest of the world (DM 33). This is how Descartes initiates his mind–body dualism that is characterized by what Charles Taylor refers to as the disengaged reason (Taylor 1989: 143). At this point, essence is not only *sui generis*, self-determined, and immutable, but rather, and more importantly, the essence of a person is characterized by interiority and becomes confined to the mind. While the mind is disembedded from bodily experience, the world likewise becomes disenchanted and reduced into a mechanic system undergirded by natural physical laws.

Against the background of the centuries-long discussion of essence, Husserl foregrounds how essence defines appearance in pure consciousness with its implicit allusion to existence. Following modern philosophers, Husserl contends that essence is not demarcated nor signified by existence but rather defines the existence of phenomena in one's experience. Nonetheless, Husserl refuses to join forces with Descartes insofar as he is critical of the ways in which Cartesian dualism characterizes the essence of a person in terms of interiority.

To trace his refutation of Cartesian dualism, we again turn to the four phases of Husserl's philosophical thinking process. In the first stage, Husserl articulates phenomenology as the critique of psychologism. Unlike psychology with its focus on contingent psychological facts, Husserl maintains that phenomenology is a science of essence (Hua 19/2). As such, essence (*Wesen*) becomes the ideal union of matter and form of intentional mental acts at all levels, further contributing to the law-governed conditions for knowledge of contingent, accidental, empirical realities (Hua 18/236). Essence (*Wesen*) can be further differentiated into the intentional, semantic, and epistemic essences (Hua 19/417). Essence (*Wesen*) is also distinct from *essentia* (*Essenz*): while *essentia* is ascribed to the matter of intuitive acts, essence is articulated to capture the unity of both the matter and form of all intentional mental acts. In this phase, Husserl does not prioritize forms over matters, nor does he perceive conceptuality as the cause of human knowledge. Quite to the contrary, form and matter mutually define one another. Without matter, a form would be empty and unfulfilled. That is why meaning-intentions, otherwise known as concepts, need intuitions to fulfill their content and acquire their epistemic essence. Considering how essence represents the ideal, Husserl also perceives an essence as an Idea (Hua 18/237).

After his transcendental turn, Husserl renews his terminology, through which he evokes the Greek term *eidos* to capture the pure essence devoid of factuality that appears in pure consciousness after *epoché* (Hua 3/6). As such, *eidos* in the Husserlian context is not synonymous with the Platonic idea and the Aristotelian form (Hua 3/11). Rather, juxtaposing existence (*Existenz*) and essence (*Essenz*), Husserl tries to demarcate factual reality from phenomenological ideality (Hua 3/12). However, as his argumentation unfolds, Husserl does not stick with this juxtaposition in that he implies both essence and existence can be perceived differently by naturalists and phenomenologists. Another layer of complexity, therefore, is added to these two terms.

When one embraces naturalism, the existence of material reality in the actual spatiotemporal order—either as the physical reality or the psychological one—becomes perceived as pre-given and mind-independent. Subsequently, essence becomes a mental construct, as an abstract entity that one generalizes and extracts from empirically real matters of fact (Hua 3/42). As a mental construct, the naturalistic essence becomes *sui generis* and immutable. Later detailed in *Crisis*, Husserl maintains that naturalists—be they the physicists or the psychologists—strive to discover what "it is in itself (*was sie an sich ist*)," which is pre-given unconditionally in the material world or in the psychological activities (Hua 6/70). Perceived through the scope of naturalism, both existence and essence are reduced to factuality.

Husserl proposes that one can enact *epoché* to suspend any assumption of existence and essence in the natural attitude and enter the realm of pure consciousness. Hereby, phenomenological existence is characterized by ideality, as the salient feature of "the multitude of possible worlds (*mannigfaltiger möglicher Welten*)" (Hua 3/88). What undergirds these phenomenologically existent worlds is the pure essence that embraces both *noesis* and *noema* (Hua 3/270–4). As such, pure essence or *eidos* is not an abstract mental construct in itself, but a perceivable new object that serves as the ground for naturalistic essence. Unlike Aquinas, who conceives of essence as being demarcated and signified by existence, Husserl articulates pure essence (*eidos*) as that which defines the appearance of phenomena in pure consciousness.

In the last two phases of his philosophical process, when Husserl expands his inquiries from the foundation of knowledge to the fulfillment of a meaningful life, he makes an explicit departure from the Cartesian tradition. He particularly engages with Descartes in his *Cartesian Meditations*, complimenting Descartes's method of systematic doubt on the one hand and criticizing the solipsism inherent in Cartesian dualism on the other. As such, Husserl extends the examination of essence from the epistemological realm to the existential one. He contends that naturalistic essence is never truly as self-sufficient as it proclaims to be but is rather groundless insofar as it must turn to a person's lived experience in the shared lifeworld to fulfill its content and acquire its meaning (Hua 17/356). Considering how natural sciences build their theories in the belief of the absolute self-sufficiency of the naturalistic essence of various objects, natural sciences likewise are not self-sufficient but find their footing in phenomenology (Hua 6/65). Pure phenomenology reveals that the eidetic phenomenological essence is self-sufficient because it emerges out of the mutual constitution of all three components of intentionality (the underlying I-subject, the intending act, the intended phenomenon) (Hua 6/346). In this sense, phenomenological essence is far from being an absolute idea. More specifically, the self-sufficient *eidos* of each I-subject consists in its "being-for-one-another and mutual interpenetration (*Ineinander- und füreinanderseins*)" (Hua 6/346), which can be distinguished from the disembodied Cartesian essence. The essence of an I-subject is defined through its engagement with others and its embedment in the lifeworld. This is how Husserl demarcates the phenomenological essence from that in Cartesian philosophy.

Due to this distinct understanding of the self-sufficient *eidos*, Husserl does not move towards a theological discussion of the existence of God after his break with Cartesian dualism. Rather, he shifts his focus instead towards communal life where a plurality of persons can collaborate and make efforts together to constitute a shared lifeworld that is intersubjectively accessible and empirically real. In the final stage of his thought, Husserl expands his genetic phenomenology in which intentionality, as well as essence, stems from the moment-by-moment mutual constitution of I-subjects, intentional acts, and the intended phenomena (Hua 1/106). As such, the essence of each person is a twofold *a priori* as the "consciousness of oneself as being in the world (*Bewusstsein seiner selbst als in der Welt Seiend*)" (Hua 6/255), and "self-consciousness and consciousness of others are inseparable (*Selbstbewusstsein und Fremdbewusstsein untrennbar ist*)" (Hua 6/256). In other words, the pure essence of a person is its ability to be in the world with others in such a way that no one is an isolated, self-determined entity.

Our reappraisal of Husserl's notion of essence in the context of the concept's history motivates us to reflect on the generalized distinction between the essential and the accidental. Upon treating the essences merely as properties different from the accidents, one might confuse the distinction between the transcendental and the empirical, further overlooking Husserl's effort to demarcate *eidos* from non-eidetic, naturalistic essence. More importantly, the generalized discussion does not do justice to Husserl's contribution to the development of European philosophy, particularly how he problematizes the modern sense of essence in the wake of Cartesian dualism. Therefore, a historical overview of the concept of essence furnishes us with access to the lived reality of Husserl.

From Plato to Descartes, the essence of a person has become increasingly more interior, which sets the rift between the mind and the world as well as between the self and the other. The rift further underpins the scientific reductionism at the heart of naturalism that Husserl identifies as the trigger of the crisis of meaning in modern Europe. Having lived through this existential crisis, Husserl criticizes naturalism and clarifies how essence is far from a self-determined entity. His problematization of interiority does not directly yield a return to the superior transcendent deity. Rather, Husserl directs his focus to community building, which becomes his proposal for a phenomenological renewal of a meaningful life. Our overview of the intellectual history of the concept of essence in European philosophy, therefore, fulfills several purposes. It positions Husserl in dialogues with previous thinkers to reveal how the definition of essence has constantly been renegotiated. Moreover, it problematizes the Orientalist portrayal of the West, since we cannot speak of European philosophy in the singular but shall rather acknowledge the diversity of viewpoints inside this tradition.

Essence in Later Chinese Yogācāra: A Reappraisal

As previously discussed, the meaning of essence in Husserl's phenomenology cannot be exhausted by the essential–accidental binary. Shifting to the Chinese context, the current section explores how and why scholars are prone to summon this binary to translate ideas preserved in the Chinese language. Subsequently, this section will attempt to depict how the development of Buddhism unfolded as an innovative process in the Chinese context. Hereby, two philosophical binaries, *ti-yong* (體用) and *xing-xiang* (性相), serve as exemplars in the following investigation of the development of Buddhist thought from a time when the Doctrine of Dark Learning (*xuanxue* 玄學) was prevalent.

We have been introduced to the *ti-yong* binary in Chapter 5 when we tried to explain how Kuiji utilized this binary to define consciousness. The notion of *ti* (體) is usually paired with *yong* (用) and has frequently been translated as essence or substance in English. Here, we will revisit this binary to detail its philosophical origin. Throughout Chinese intellectual history, this *ti-yong* binary was officially incorporated into the philosophical discourse during the 200s CE through the effort of Wang Bi (王弼 226-49), one of the founders of the Doctrine of Dark Learning.[9] Wang creatively employed this body–function pair to account for the conception of *Dao* presented in the *Dao De Jing* (道德經).

As early as the Spring–Autumn Period (770-476 BCE), Laozi (老子)—a half historical, half mystical figure at that time—deployed the concept of the Dao to expound on the origin of the cosmos and the ultimate principle of change. The literal meaning of Dao translates to "the way." In the opening chapter of the *Dao De Jing*, Laozi depicts Dao through negation by demarcating it from what it is *not* (DDJ 1.1). As he further specifies, the nameless serves as the beginning of the cosmos whilst the named becomes the mother of a myriad of creatures (DDJ 1.2). As such, there is an interplay between the non-existence of names and the existence of names, which becomes the salient feature of the depiction of Dao.

Drawing on and developing the concept of Dao articulated by Laozi, Wang Bi equates the Dao with nothingness (*wu* 無). In his elaboration of the nameless and the named, Wang makes more explicit the metaphysical analysis of being and nothingness, or existence and non-existence. He interprets nothingness as the origin of the cosmos and existence as the way in which things grow, nurture, reproduce, and complete (ZJZ 1.2). Consequently, the Dao is the absolute nothingness that can generate all living beings in the cosmos.

Upon construing the Dao as nothingness, Wang continues to systematize the metaphysical theory of being and nothingness. In particular, he deploys the *ti–yong* binary to elucidate how the shapeless nothingness gradually informs and animates existence (ZJZ 38.2). To unpack this interplay between being and nothingness, Wang turns to the motherliness analogy.[10] In the Daoist framework, motherliness symbolizes the origin of life (ZJZ 1.2). It is an analogy to describe how sentient beings are children of a cosmic motherly body that animates them, breeds them, cultivates them, and cares for them (ZJZ 35.1). Although each sentient being will eventually outgrow the motherly body, its influence remains through the ways in which this sentient being behaves and becomes (ZJZ 38.2). In everyday life, when we come to meet the children of this cosmic mother, the underlying motherliness is rarely present and is therefore invisible. Nevertheless, we can still recognize the invisible motherliness from the visible children. To be more precise, the invisible motherly body manifests itself through the outcome of its children. Therefore, the dialectical relationship surfaces through the interplay between the invisible body of motherliness and its visible function of cultivating and preserving children.

Similar to how we conceptualize the invisible motherly body through its role in nurturing and cultivating its children, so too do we understand the body *qua* shapeless nothingness/Dao through its function of producing and preserving lives. Articulated in this manner, Dao or nothingness becomes the invisible motherly body that can enact the function of creating and caring for various forms of life. For Wang Bi, this parallel between nothingness and motherliness explains why Laozi refers to the named as the mother of a myriad of things in the cosmos (DDJ 1.2). Nothingness, since it is shapeless and nameless, cannot be observed in everyday life. We can only infer nothingness from seeing how various things in the cosmos arise from the state of non-existing, continue to grow and flourish, and eventually perish into the state of non-existing, *ad infinitum*. Every phase in growth entails a negation of the previous state, therefore indicating how nothingness nourishes the progress of life. That is the principle of how things change. Once we understand this principle, we likewise comprehend the complementary nature between the invisible, shapeless nothingness and its visible, shapeshifting function—the motherly body breeds its function; in return, the function manifests the body.

For this reason, I recommend using either the transliteration of *ti* or the translation of the motherly body to encapsulate the motherliness analogy utilized by Dark

Learning philosophers. As presented by this analogy, the concept of *ti* connects the abstract metaphysical discussion with the concrete lived experience, which epitomizes the style of philosophizing at that time. The nuance of *ti* is different than that of substance and essence—two terms that are commonly used to translate *ti* in the English language scholarship. Indeed, this interplay between the motherly body and the function entails complementarity, fluidity, and transformability, or in short, non-duality. In other words, the shapeless *ti* preserves the ground for and nourishes the *yong*, whereas the function of creating various forms of life derives from and manifests the motherly body. If one can follow the correlative nature of *ti* and *yong*, one can easily master the cosmic principle and rule the world effortlessly. That is why Wang Bi highlights that "acknowledging how nothingness exercises its function, one retains the mother [of the Dao], therefore able to regulate things without self-fatiguing (以無為用，德其母，故能己不勞焉)" (ZJZ 38.2). Contrariwise, if one overlooks the underlying origin of nothingness, one misreads the principle and abandons the root, further becoming unable to maintain worldly achievements (ZJZ 38.2).

The articulation of nothingness proposed by Wang Bi marked the beginning of the golden era for the doctrine of Dark Learning, further setting the intellectual stage for the transmission of Buddhism.[11] The lexicon of Chinese philosophy, which was expanded and enriched by Dark Learning thinkers, continued to be shared by Buddhists in their interpretation and translation of Buddhist concepts. What epitomized this translation was the way in which emptiness (*śūnyatā*) became paraphrased as nothingness (*wu* 無). This method of paraphrasing is commonly known as *geyi* (格義).[12] However, towards the second half of the fourth century, when more Buddhist texts became available in the Chinese language—specially through the effort of Kumārajīva (鳩摩羅什 344–413)—Buddhist clergy began reflecting on this method of paraphrasing. They discerned one major issue: if one equated emptiness with nothingness, then one would place more weight upon non-existence than existence, further deviating from the Buddha's teaching of the middle way.[13] In this process of revising the interpretation of emptiness, another pair also became popularized, that is, the nature–image (*xingxiang* 性相) binary.

During the Warring States period (475–221 BCE), Mengzi (孟子, Mencius, c. 372–289 BCE) elaborated on nature (*xing* 性) as the salient feature which demarcated humans from other animals (MZ 6A3). For Mengzi, "human nature's being good is like water's trending downward (人性之善也，猶水之就下也)" (MZ 6A2). In the wake of the doctrine of Dark Learning, Chinese scholars such as Guo Xiang (郭象 c. 252–312), for instance, extended the use of "nature" from exclusively that of humans to that of all beings in the cosmos (Feng 2009: 407). Through constant dialogues and debates with intellectuals in the Dark Learning tradition, Buddhists too began employing the nature–image (*xingxiang* 性相) binary to refine their understanding of emptiness. One representative was Sengzhao (僧肇 384–414). At that time, Sengzhao rose to prominence as the "best cleric in interpreting emptiness (解空第一)" (T45N1858, P150c05).

Following the Madhyamaka approach of secretive sayings, Sengzhao too utilizes the image–nature binary to unpack the twofold truth and emptiness. On the conventional level, illusorily images (*xiang* 相) arise in virtue of dependent assembling (*yuanhui* 緣

會) (T45N1858, P150c16). These images are ultimately non-existent (*wuyou* 無有) (T45N1858, P150c17). As such, the real images (*shixiang* 實相) of dharmas manifest the nature of dharmas (*faxing* 法性) *qua* original nothingness (*benwu* 本無), also known as the nature of being empty (*xingkong* 性空), while the nature of being empty serves as the ground for dependent assembling and constitutes the ultimate reality (T45N1858, P150c17-25). From the complementarity of the image and the nature of dharmas, there arises Sengzhao's pronouncement that "original nothingness, real image, dharma nature, the nature of being empty, the dependent assembling, all these concepts mean only one thing (本無、實相、法性、性空、緣會，一義耳)," all alluding to the middle way (T45N1858, P150c15).

Though still describing emptiness as what it is *not*, Sengzhao is able to enrich the meaning of emptiness with the help of the image–nature binary.[14] In his commentary on the *Vimalakīrti Sūtra*, Sengzhao follows Daosheng (道生 c. 360-434) to elaborate on the interplay between the nature of dharma (*faxing*法性) and the image of dharma (*faxiang*法相). That is to say, things arise and perish, and such an appearance (*mao*貌) is tantamount to the image (*xiang*相) of these things (T38N1775, P346b7). As underscored by Sengzhao, these images can be easily comprehended, which prevents sentient beings from seeing things as they are (T38N1775, P346b8). The moment sentient beings postulate these images as those to be perceived by and thus different from their mind (*xin*心), these sentient beings are also perplexed (*huo*惑) and incarcerated in dualistic thinking (T38N1775, P346b9-10). Nevertheless, such ignorance (*wuming*無明) can be removed through contemplative practice (T38N1775, P346b16). In this process, sentient beings will be awake (*ming*明) to the truth of non-duality (*wufenbie*無分別), which reveals how the self and the dharma, as well as their distinction, do not actually exist (T38N1775, P346b24). This non-existence amounts to the original status (*benfen*本分) of dharmas *qua* the nature (*xing*性) of dharma (T38N1775, P346c15). As further contended by Sengzhao, various types of dharma are originally empty and have no image, but they manifest as a variety of images due to the ignorant mindset (T38N1775, P347b2-3). Once sentient beings become awake, they come to realize that image of dharma is the image of nothingness (T45N1858, P150c24), and, in principle, dharma is emptiness by nature (T38N1775, P346c16).

Philosophical binaries, especially the underlying complementarity and transformability, provide Chinese clerics with a means to expound on the Buddha's teaching in the local linguistic and philosophical context. Since these binaries refute mutual exclusivity and the invisible origins (*ti* in the *ti-yong* binary and *xing* in the *xing-xiang* pair) reject a self-determined static entity, these Buddhists can discuss the complementarity of the underlying origin (*ti* and *xing*) and their manifestations (*yong* and *xiang*) without worrying about violating the Mahāyāna refutation of *svabhāva*. As such, Buddhists collaborate with their fellow literati to incorporate these philosophical binaries into the standard lexicon of Chinese philosophy.

Adopting existing terminology into the Chinese context, Xuanzang and his disciples insert their own understanding of the Buddhist doctrine in the translated texts. By means of the *ti-yong* and *xing-xiang* binaries, they enrich the discussion of emptiness, which demarcates later Yogācāra from early Yogācāra. As previously mentioned, early Yogācārins equate the immaculate original consciousness with emptiness and suchness.

Such an understanding remains quite popular since Sengzhao also equates dharma with the nature of dharma *qua* emptiness.

Xuanzang and his disciples, on the other hand, demarcate the nature of dharma from dharma as such. Accordingly, consciousness as a type of dharma—be it polluted or purified—cannot be equated with emptiness. In his elucidation of the gist of consciousness-only, Kuiji expounds on four aspects of this teaching. Among them, the first three correspond to the three natures theory. That is to say, the first aspect reveals that the absolute nature (*xing* 性) of being empty is the nature of suchness (*zhenru* 真如) for all dharmas, although the nature manifests itself as illusory images (T45N1861, P252c10). The second aspect refers to the dependent nature, since all things in the experience are transformed from consciousness (T45N1861, P252c18). The third aspect is related to the imagined nature that highlights how fictitious (*jia* 假) names presuppose the real existence (T45N1861, P252c21). Subsequently, the last aspect explicates the way in which emptiness and consciousness cannot be fused into one (T45N1861, P252c25). That is to say, the nature (*xing* 性) of being empty and the function (*yong* 用) of consciousness need to be differentiated (T45N1861, P252c26).

To understand Kuiji's differentiation between emptiness and consciousness, I propose to borrow the wave analogy articulated by Kuiji (T45N1861, P252c16). In light of this analogy, we can compare the nature of being empty to the fluidity of water, the images manifesting such a nature to the waves that constantly arise and perish. In the meantime, the *ti* of consciousness resembles the body of water, and the *yong* symbolizes the function of generating waves given certain causes and conditions. Just as the fluidity of water is different from the water body, so is the nature of emptiness dissimilar to the *ti* of consciousness. Likewise, the images of waves are distinguished from the function of generating waves, which bespeaks the distinction between that which is transformed by consciousness (i.e., the seeing part and the image part) and the function of transforming. As suggested by the wave analogy, it is crucial to demarcate consciousness that constantly transforms, from the perceived object, the fictitious *svabhāva*, and, eventually, emptiness (T45N1861, P252c26). Employing the *ti-yong* (body–function) and the *xing-xiang* (nature–image) binaries, Kuiji designates dissimilar roles to the *ti* and the *xing*. Quite different from Sengzhao and many early Yogācārins, Kuiji draws a clear line between emptiness and consciousness. Emptiness cannot be fused into consciousness since the former defines the salient nature of dharmas whereas the latter is one type of dharmas. In short, dharma and dharma nature are not the same. As such, Xuanzang and his disciples expand the explicit articulation of emptiness and develop the teaching of consciousness-only, further laying the foundation for later Yogācāra in East Asia.

When introducing Buddhism to Europe and North America, scholars often paraphrase the concepts of *ti* and *xing* as essence in the English language, insofar as these concepts allude to an underlying origin of all changes. The complementarity of body and function, as well as that of nature and image, further strikes these translators as being rather close to that between the essential properties in an object and the accidental properties of an object. Upon observing such resemblances, scholars championed by A. C. Graham speculate that this dialectical logic is fundamental to all reasoning. As such, Chinese philosophy and Euro-American philosophy are construed as different manifestations of one same core *qua* correlative thinking. Graham's account epitomizes the synthetic approach detailed in Chapter 1. In obscuring the complexity for both sides, the synthetic approach tends to hold scholars back from delving deeper into the foundational frameworks that undergird these articulations of correlative thinking in intellectual traditions across time and space. That is why scholars of comparative studies need to be mindful of the distinctiveness of traditions and their potential conflicts.

Indeed, our discussion in the previous section has sketched how philosophers in the European philosophical tradition continue to redefine the concept of essence in such a way that this concept has never maintained a fixed meaning. Our analysis in the current section details the rich nuances of the concept of essence that has been used to translate several Chinese concepts, *ti* (體 motherly body) and *xing* (性 nature) in Chinese philosophy. In translating these concepts as the singular notion of essence, scholars can easily overlook the subtle distinctions between these Chinese concepts. We have exposed the issue of overgeneralization in this section through tracing the development of Chinese Buddhist interpretations of essence and emptiness, a development emerged as a fruit of intercultural exchanges between East Asia and South Asia. Therefore, just like Husserl whose interlocutors include the most eminent minds throughout European history, Xuanzang and his disciples are constantly dialoguing with masters who lived in various stages of the history of Asia. As such, our investigation demonstrates how the nuance of the term "essence" is constantly being reshaped throughout the long history of transliteration and translation in multilingual contexts. Keeping this in mind, we can arrive at the last section of this chapter to tackle the problem of essence.

The Problem of Essence: A Reappraisal

In the Prologue, I introduced the problem of essence, for the purpose of recognizing the perceived incompatibility of Husserl's phenomenology and Chinese Yogācāra Buddhism. *Prima facie*, they seem to demonstrate two different or even disparate attitudes towards essence. For Xuanzang and his disciples, everything in the cosmos, including consciousness, is empty of *svabhāva*. Husserl, however, affirms the existence of essence and articulates phenomenology as the science of essence. With the help of the analysis in the previous sections, it is now possible to fully tackle the problem of essence. As to be seen shortly, the problem of essence comes into existence if and only if we adopt the philosophical presuppositions that treat "essence" as an intrinsic, immutable nature and perpetuate the overgeneralized East–West dichotomy. Once we remove these presuppositions and renounce the way of oversimplifying things as being mutually exclusive to one another, the problem of essence as articulated in this book can be resolved. The resolution brings us to reflect on how we become incapable of recognizing and resolving this problem in the first place, which helps us advance our understanding of a shared stress of Husserl and Chinese Yogācārins on non-dualism.

Upon his transcendental turn, Husserl begins to differentiate essence in the phenomenological sense from that in the naturalistic sense. Indulging in the natural attitude, one comes to perceive things as pre-given, mind-independent, and actually existent matters of fact (Hua 3/88). As such, essence perceived through the naturalistic scope becomes an abstract entity that one generalizes and extracts from empirically/factually real psycho-physical facts (Hua 3/42). As a mental construct, naturalistic essence becomes an absolute in itself that is *sui generis*, immutable, and irrelevant to individual differences.

As Husserl has debunked, naturalistic essence is not truly self-sufficient, in that it always turns to eidetic experience to fulfill its meaning. Differing from naturalistic essence, eidetic essence or *eidos* is self-sufficient. In the wake of *epoché*, one suspends assumptions about essence and existence. As a result, eidetic essence unveils itself in pure consciousness. *Eidos* is not a mental construct, but a new object that can be perceived. It defines what it is like to appear as a phenomenon after *epoché* and is characterized by ideality (Hua 3/88). As such, *eidos* is self-sufficient, not because it is an immutable, self-determined absolute idea, but rather because it arises through the moment-by-moment mutual constitution of consciousness as the ideal union of the I-subjects, the intending act, and the intended object (Hua 1/106). For each person, its self-sufficient eidetic essence as an I-subject becomes its being in the world and being with others (Hua 6/255–6).

The clarification of Husserl's notion of essence sets the stage for us to explore a solution to the problem of essence. First of all, the depiction of the naturalistic essence as an absolute idea in itself shares many similarities with the *svabhāva* criticized by Mahāyāna Buddhists, especially the nature of being self-determinant and invariant across time and space. Indeed, naturalism arises through the joint force of two doctrines related to Cartesian Dualism *qua* physicalism and psychologism, the former of which assumes the immutable nature of materiality whereas the latter perceives the mind as the absolute reality. As detailed in *Crisis*, naturalists strive to discover what "it is in itself" that is pre-given unconditionally in the material world or in psychological activities (Hua 6/70). Perceived as a mental construct, the naturalistic essence also becomes a *sui generis* unconditional entity in itself (Hua 6/70). Husserl remarks on the absurdity of upholding such a view of the lifeworld and of the human self. In Husserl's terms, natural sciences cannot be self-sufficient (Hua 6/65). In this way, naturalism shares many traits in common with the heretical approaches criticized by Xuanzang and his disciples. What characterizes the heretical approaches is their perception of the world and the human self as *svabhāvic*, namely, as immutable (*chang* 常), self-determined (*zhuzhai* 主宰), and persistent throughout time and space (*bian* 遍). In this regard, Husserlian selfhood is compatible with the Yogācāra view of no-self, insofar as the transcendental I-subject in the Husserlian sense is not tantamount to a *svabhāvic* self but rather shares parallels to the subjectivity of an underlying flow of consciousness.

Second, *eidos*, which alludes to the mutual constitution of subjectivity and objectivity, of ideality and reality, is compatible with the Yogācāra refutation of *svabhāva*, insofar as both Husserl and Chinese Yogācārins come to acknowledge the underlying interdependence of opposites. The mutual constitutions of the subject and the object, of the mind and the world, and of self-mind and other minds, do not perpetuate Cartesian dualism. Rather, the irreducibility of various actors in the process of mutual constitution reveals the true essence of how things are. If Husserl's notion of pure essence differs from the notion of *svabhāva* defined by Xuanzang and his disciples, the problem of essence is no longer an obstacle for our comparative study.

More importantly, since Husserl is not an exponent of absolutism and Xuanzang is not an advocate of nihilism, we can discern their middle ground. To be more specific, both Husserl and these Chinese Yogācārins refute *svabhāvic* essence in their support of correlative non-dualism. For them, the subjective mind serves as the necessary condition for the possibility of phenomena in experience and reaches out to other minds to constitute an intersubjectively accessible and empirically real lifeworld. As such, transcendental ideality becomes correlated with empirical reality, a correlation that secures the non-duality of binaries. It is this non-duality of binaries that makes the Husserlian *epoché* possible and the Buddhist awakening feasible. Their shared endorsement of correlative non-dualism reveals a common ground for Husserl and Chinese Yogācārins to engage in dialogues. That said, although Husserl and Chinese Yogācārins inquire into similar questions—and in figurative terms, travel the same road—they have their own interlocutors. As previously analyzed, Husserl develops his critique of naturalistic essence in dialogue with scientists of his era and with philosophers in the European intellectual tradition, as a reflection on the flourishing naturalism in the wake of Cartesian dualism that triggered the crisis of meaning in modern Europe. In contrast, Xuanzang and his disciples keep elaborating on their refutation of *svabhāva* through debates with Buddhists from other schools as well as Daoists and Confucians. Given this fact, we eschew the synthetic approach, rejecting the proposal of viewing Husserlian phenomenology and Yogācāra philosophy as manifestations of a higher, a-cultural theory for consciousness.

Similarly, we distance ourselves from the juxtapositional approach insofar as we detail how Husserl and Chinese Yogācārins do not have mutually exclusive standpoints but share similar views on non-dualistic interdependence. Our investigation, therefore, problematizes the overgeneralized East–West dichotomy in the Orientalist discourse. As detailed in the previous two sections, both European and Chinese philosophy are traditions with a plurality and diversity of viewpoints throughout history. Therefore, it is problematic to proclaim that the Western-self possesses an essence, be it rationality or individuality, in contrast to the Eastern-self that is said to have no such essence at all in a collectivist culture. Such an overgeneralized pronouncement proves to be a misrepresentation in that it deliberately glosses over the diverse voices and different viewpoints on both ends for ideological purposes. As we delve deeper into intellectual history, we obtain access to the lived realities of scholars, which demonstrates how the Orientalist presentation of the East and the West is in fact a misrepresentation.

Nonetheless, Yogācāra Buddhism is more than a Buddhist version of Husserlian phenomenology. For Husserl, his critique of naturalism contributes to the reflection on the ways in which the sense of the self becomes increasingly inward and, thus, closed to the rest of the world. After problematizing the absolutist understanding of essence and reflecting on the internalization of selfhood, Husserl turns to the exterior world to deliberate on community building. On his journey, Husserl is confident that transcendental idealism—as a version of correlative non-dualism that secures the connection between the natural attitude and the phenomenological attitude—furnishes people with the *epoché* needed to change their attitude in life and, therefore, overcome the crisis of meaning. As such, *epoché per se* alludes to a transformative process in Husserl's phenomenological project. Nevertheless, *epoché* remains a philosophical speculation. It does not, at least not explicitly, point to a mechanics that can inform a person about how to regulate individual life or how to interact with others in the community. That is why we speak of the prescriptive level as rather nascent in Husserl's phenomenology. Later phenomenologists aspire to complement the prescriptive level of phenomenology in their respective manners. Those represented by Hannah Arendt elaborate on the mechanics of building a community as a plurality of the I.[15] Those like Edith Stein turn to develop their articulations of the philosophy of religion and theological philosophy by means of phenomenology as a superior pursuit of transcendence. Many of them also join Frantz Fanon's initiative of employing phenomenology as a method of engaging in critical theories related to race, gender, and disability, etc.

While the prescriptive level remains nascent in Husserl's phenomenology, a more elaborative and systematic form of being prescriptive has been presented by Xuanzang and his disciples. In their version of correlative non-dualism, these Yogācārins explain the non-dual fluid transformation of ignorance and awakening as a principle and prescribe the mechanics for realizing such non-duality known as the Bodhisattva's path. That is why and how Yogācāra can be a source of inspiration for Husserlians at the prescriptive level. For Xuanzang and his disciples, their study of consciousness marks the turn from the exterior world to the interior mind, a turn that serves as a salient feature of Mahāyāna philosophy. Nevertheless, these Yogācārins, in their rejection of solipsism, inquire into our knowledge of other minds and subsequently shift their focus back to the exterior life of mutual constitution. In the Yogācāra framework, such a return to exterior life *is* the superior mission of the Bodhisattvas who have made the vow to help others and not let anyone fall behind. In the now approaching final part of our journey, we will elaborate on how the return to exteriority is nascent in Husserl's phenomenology, while exteriority becomes the superior goal for Yogācārins like Xuanzang and his disciples.

Part Four

The Destination

During the first three stages of our journey, we have followed Husserl and Chinese Yogācārins like Xuanzang and his disciples to observe how they travel the same road, but their wheels leave different tracks. At this point, we are approaching the destination of our journey where we will explore the final level of our comparative study. As introduced in the prologue, the prescriptive level is where philosophical insights are translated into action. More specifically, it is about how the worldview outlined in terms of correlative non-dualism can point to the principle and the mechanics of collaborative actions that not only enable a person to rehabitualize but also allow a society to reform and transform. I use the term "prescriptive level" to capture the instructional dimension in which normative values are articulated in connection with moral actions.

The prescriptive level thus entails:

1. Accounts that establish a series of moral values regarding what is good and what is not.
2. Accounts that inform normative actions and indicate why one should adhere to moral values.
3. Accounts that regulate one's actions—either general, everyday behaviors, or specific performances—for the purpose of contributing to the higher good.
4. Accounts that allude to the realization of awakening, along with the mechanics for such a transformative process.

As I will argue, the systematic account of the prescriptive level in Chinese Yogācāra makes it much more than a Buddhist version of Husserlian phenomenology. Considering that this level remains nascent in Husserl's philosophy, it is worthwhile to explore how Chinese Yogācāra can be a source of inspiration for Husserlians to elaborate on moral philosophy and social ontology. Indeed, as remarked by Husserl's assistant Eugen Fink, "the various phases of Buddhistic self-discipline were essentially phases of phenomenological reduction" (Cairns 1976: 50). Instead of reading Fink's remark as a suggestion of assimilating Yogācāra into phenomenology, I consider it his speculation on the ways in which phenomenological reduction can be informed by— or even be systematized in parallel to—the contemplative practice preserved in Buddhism. Nevertheless, contemplation is only one aspect of the realization of awakening envisioned by Xuanzang and his disciples. They have also outlined how contemplation paves the way for moral action and social construction.

Indeed, Husserl does entertain the possibility of a phenomenological account of morality at the prescriptive level. He uses the notion of attitude (*Einstellung*) to convey his translation of insights into actions (Hua 6/326). For Husserl, attitude entails a habitually formed way of living. By nature, an attitude is descriptive and normative in that it prescribes how people *should* live. Again, he contrasts phenomenologists with naturalists. While naturalism nourishes the paradox of subjectivity and disconnects the mind from the world, phenomenology brings people to see things as they actually are, through which people can reconnect themselves with the world in a meaningful way. Husserl continues to use the concept of renewal (*Erneuerung*) to characterize the process of switching from the natural to the phenomenological attitude through *epoché* (Hua 27/3). As such, a renewal becomes a transformative process of becoming awake (*erwacht*) to genuine humanity (Hua 27/51). Through a renewal of life, individuals will rehabitualize themselves, *viz.* to change their habitual way of perceiving and living, in order to regain a meaningful life on the personal and communal levels (Hua 27/50–2). As "a universal call in our sorrowful present (*der allgemeine Ruf in unserer leidensvollen Gegenwart*)" (Hua 27/3), a renewal will wake up individuals and their communities from naturalism, eventually ending the pervasive crisis of meaning in Europe (Hua 6/259).

Husserl appears confident that a phenomenological renewal can spontaneously prescribe a purely ethical life (Hua 27/45). Indeed, once a person embraces the phenomenological attitude, this person will come to see human essence as the twofold *a priori* of its being in the world and its being with others, which would then motivate this person to pursue an ethical life (Hua 27/52). Likewise, Husserl has investigated transcendental intersubjectivity in the analysis of empathy. However, many questions remain unanswered in the project of a phenomenological renewal of life. For instance, how does such a renewal take place through *epoché* and how shall a person conduct *epoché*? How shall one perform moral actions in light of transcendental intersubjectivity? That is why many scholars have discerned Husserl's aspiration of rethinking ethics and moral philosophy from a phenomenological perspective while acknowledging that Husserl never fully developed such phenomenological ethics (De Warren 2006; Crowell 2016). Hence, Husserl advocates for the possibilities of rehabitualization in terms of a renewal of life, yet he does not present the mechanics that would enable individuals to follow the phenomenological path. Consequently, I consider the prescriptive level to be nascent in Husserl's phenomenology.

While Husserl does not specify whether the phenomenological renewal of life is a sudden acquisition, Xuanzang and his disciples understand awakening differently. To realize the unity of knowing and doing, they maintain that sentient beings must undergo a long process of training to follow the Bodhisattvas' path (T31N1585, P48b11–20). These Chinese Yogācārins thus establish an elaborative system of normative values and techniques, which constitutes the prescriptive level of their philosophy. It is the prescriptive level that makes Yogācāra Buddhism much more than a Buddhist version of Husserlian phenomenology.

Instead of assimilating Yogācāra philosophy into phenomenology, I find it more fruitful to explore how Yogācāra philosophy can be a source of inspiration for

Husserlians to elaborate on moral philosophy and social ontology. In the last part of this project, I will prioritize the writings of Xuanzang and his disciples to detail their answers to the following interrelated questions: Is it possible for sentient beings to exercise agency and become awake from ignorance if they are so deeply indulged in the current attitude? Why is it important to sort these sentient beings into different groups given their dissimilar intellectual capacity and agency? Through what process can sentient beings exercise agency for realizing awakening at the individual and societal levels?

As such, Chapter 10 explores how agency is possible and explains that Xuanzang and his disciples articulate dependent arising in a distinctive way to enable their affirmation of agency without negating causality. Chapter 11 continues to tackle the controversial theory of *gotra*. Chinese Yogācārins like Xuanzang and his disciples do not promote the *gotra* theory to debase or demean sentient beings with a lower level of agency. Rather, they intend to highlight the compassion of Bodhisattvas and present their critique of incorrect aspirations in the pursuit of awakening. The last chapter addresses the question regarding how sentient beings can attain awakening as a collaborative achievement, which further expounds as to why the reading of Yogācāra Buddhism as a Buddhist version of Husserlian phenomenology has its own limitation.

The following three chapters serve an additional purpose, insofar as they counter a popular reading that typecasts Yogācāra philosophy—especially the version developed by Xuanzang and his disciples—as a socially disengaged philosophy of mind. This popular reading is commonly adopted by numerous modern Confucians, including Liang Shuming (梁漱溟1893–1988) and Xiong Shili (熊十力1885–1968), who are particularly concerned about how Buddhists prioritize the other-worldly awakening over this-worldly life (Liang 2004; Xiong 2008). On this front, I want to caution readers that this popular reading misapprehends Xuanzang and his disciples' interpretation of awakening. Based on their resolution to the problem of other minds, these Yogācārins outline self–other interconnectedness to argue for correlative non-dualism that undergirds the collaborative effort of sentient beings on the Bodhisattvas' path towards a universal awakening. As I have detailed in another article on Liang Shuming, there is equally a correlative non-duality between this-worldly life and other-worldly awakening (Li 2022). In outlining the socio-ethical aspect of the writings of Xuanzang and his disciples, I will make a case for perceiving Chinese Yogācāra as a socially engaged doctrine of consciousness-only. Therefore, the final part of our journey explains why we are not holding a one-way conversation to assimilate Yogācāra philosophy into Husserlian phenomenology. Traveling is, after all, a reciprocal process in that traveling opens the eyes of travelers and changes the travelers together with the space traveled. Indeed, traveling is the process through which we come to embrace correlative non-duality as a way of living and appreciate the diversity of cultures. It is a replacement for the Orientalist bifurcation of the world. Employing the "both–and" approach, our journey enables Husserl and Chinese Yogācārins to share their insights and move into a broader horizon, beyond Orientalism.

10

The Gate of Practice

If people wish to wake up from ignorance or switch from the natural attitude to the phenomenological one, they should exercise their agency to attain such awakening. The current chapter examines the possibility of agency and elaborates on how knowledge translates into action. In contemporary philosophy, agency is defined as the capacity for an individual to conduct a purposeful action.[1] By definition, there is a causal component of agency considering how someone is qualified as an agent when this individual can act to produce an effect and fulfill a purpose. While the theme of agency remains implicit and nascent in Husserl's articulation of attitude, Xuanzang and his disciples structure a systematic articulation of causality and agency.[2]

Buddhism is known for its theory of *karmic* causality. In early Buddhist teaching, various *karmas* arise in a causal chain, conspiring to entrap sentient beings in "endless cycles of birth and death (*shengsi xiangxu* 生死相續)" (T43N1830, P518b13). To stop this endless cycle of *saṃsāra*, sentient beings shall follow the path of practice to attain *nirvāṇa*. Such a viewpoint is expanded, and in the meantime, complicated by Madhyamaka clerics. Nāgārjuna, for instance, does not perceive *nirvāṇa* as the breakaway from *saṃsāra*. Rather, he highlights their non-duality—*nirvāṇa* is *saṃsāra* (T30N1564, P35b9–10). However, this non-duality soon poses a problem for agency. If *nirvāṇa* is *saṃsāra*, and the net of causality extends its arm to all stages of existence in the cosmos, it follows that everything, everyone, and, of course, every action is determined by their precedents. If all actions are predetermined, how can sentient beings freely exercise their agency? Does this mean that all sentient beings are nothing but puppets in the hands of *karmic* destiny?

These are the main questions that will be addressed in the current chapter. I contend that, for Xuanzang and his disciples, individuals do have agency, although such agency does not distort the prevailing causality in the cosmos. To unpack my viewpoint, I will first investigate the Buddhist articulations of causality preserved in the texts of early Buddhism, Madhyamaka, and Yogācāra, which is followed by a re-examination of the Yogācāra theory of mental factors, and a clarification of the meaning of awakening in the framework proposed by Xuanzang and his disciples. By resolving the dilemma of agency, these Chinese Yogācārins also open the gate to the Bodhisattvas' path.

Causes and Conditions

Since the concept of agency is closely related to the idea of causality, the current section centers on the Buddhist articulation of causality, which is an integral part of the theory of dependent arising (*yuanqi* 緣起, *pratītyasamutpāda*). Buddhists—be they Mahāyāna or non-Mahāyāna followers—propose the theory of dependent arising to explain why there is *saṃsāra*, when there is no self (T31N1585, P43a9). That is to say, since rebirth and reincarnation presuppose an indestructible soul, why is it the case that every sentient being still lacks a *svabhāvic* self?

According to early Buddhists, *saṃsāra* persists because of the pervasive effect of *karmic* causality. In other words, various *karmas* arise in a causal chain, which conspires to entrap sentient beings in "endless cycles of birth and death" (T43N1830, P518b13). It follows that sentient beings must attain *nirvāṇa* so as "to break away from death and rebirth and to leave *saṃsāra* (生死已斷，不復轉於五道)" (T2N109, P503b10).³ The ways in which *karmas* arise in a causal chain are encapsulated in the doctrine of twelve links. Kuiji expounds on the early Buddhist view of the twelve links (T43N1830, P518b27–520a9), as illustrated in Table 2.

As Table 2 suggests, sentient beings are trapped in *saṃsāra* and go through countless rounds of death and rebirth owing to the causal relationship of the twelve links. Early

Table 2 The early Buddhist theory of twelve links

Name of the link	Its cause and effects
Ignorance (*wuming* 無明, *avidyā*)	*Ignorance* of the truth of no-self acts as the beginning of the causal chain.
Actions (*xing* 行, *saṃskāra*)	Caused by ignorance, sentient beings conduct various egocentric *actions* (*saṃskāra*).
Consciousness (*shi* 識, *vijñāna*)	Actions in the previous life shape the *consciousness* of the zygote in the current life.
Names and forms (*mingse* 名色, *nāmārūpa*)	Once the zygote grows into an embryo, *names and forms* gradually appear.
Six sense sources (*liuchu* 六處, *ṣaḍāyatana*)	By the time the embryo is fully grown, the *six sense sources* of this life form become mature.
Contact (*chu* 觸, *sparśa*)	Newborns use these senses to get in *contact* with other sentient beings and things in the cosmos.
Feeling (*shou* 受, *vedanā*)	As they grow, they gradually acquire clear *feelings*.
Craving (*ai* 愛, *tṛṣṇā*)	These feelings evoke great *craving* for various objects.
Grasp (*qu* 取, *upādāna*)	Craving propels sentient beings to *grasp* these objects and perform egocentric actions that further generate mental defilements.
Existence (*you* 有, *bhava*)	When these actions come into *existence*, they continue to condition and determine these sentient beings' future cravings.
Birth (*sheng* 生, *jāti*)	These existing karmas determine the *birth* of these sentient beings in their next life.
Death (*si* 死, *jarāmarana*)	Upon *death*, these sentient beings, who have accumulated various karmas in the wake of ignorance, enter another round of life that is shaped by the twelve links, *ad infinitum*.

Buddhists detail how ignorance propelled sentient beings to undertake various actions in their previous life, which continue to shape the course of their current life and condition their future lives. In this manner, causality extends its arms to three time periods: to the life of the past; to the present life; and to the life ahead. Considering the two layers of causality—how the past determines the present and how the present will determine the future—Kuiji characterizes the early Buddhist notion of causality as that of "three times and two layers (*sanshi erchong yinguo* 三世二重因果)" (T43N1830, P528c20). In the early Buddhist framework, if sentient beings wish to become awake, they must break free from the causal chain by eradicating ignorance and acquiring the wisdom of no-self (T43N1830, P528c21-2). Such a break-away is known as *nirvāṇa*, which enables sentient beings to ascend from *saṃsāra* to the realm devoid of causality. Once the break-away is achieved, sentient beings transform into arhats. Therefore, the theory of twelve links connects the view of metaphysical realism with the soteriological goal of arhatship in early Buddhism.

In their critique of the early Buddhist view of causality, Mādhyamikas problematize the polarization of *saṃsāra* and *nirvāṇa* (T30N1564, P21b15-19). From the Madhyamaka vantage point, all things in the cosmos are interdependent. And thus, so are *saṃsāra* and *nirvāṇa*. That is why "*nirvāṇa* is *saṃsāra*; *saṃsāra* is *nirvāṇa*, for such is how things actually are (涅槃即生死、生死即涅槃，如是諸法實相)" (T30N1564, P21b19). The conclusion that *nirvāṇa* is *saṃsāra* is in line with the Madhyamaka notion of emptiness. The Mādhyamikas first refute the early Buddhist view of metaphysical realism. They elucidate that non-sentient dharmas are not self-determined *svabhāva*, if they can interact with each other in the causal chain. Mādhyamikas then turn towards the subject to explain how causality is equally not self-determined. Therefore, they make a shift in focus from how things really exist to how these things are perceived. In one's experience, if the perceiver has no permanent existence, neither does the perceived, because an object relies on a subject to appear as a phenomenon. Given that everything, be it a sentient being or non-sentient dharma, dependently arises in experience, nothing has essence (*svabhāva*) (T30N1564, P2b18-19). This is how Mādhyamikas develop the theory of emptiness through expanding the early Buddhist idea of no-self. Accordingly, the goal of individual liberation as the break-away of *saṃsāra* is deemed to be selfish and egoistic. Mādhyamikas contend that the awakened ones will comprehend the interdependence of various things in the cosmos, which serves as a source of inspiration for them to return to the realm of *saṃsāra* to help other sentient beings. From this altruism, there arises the Bodhisattva ideal, which embodies the wisdom of emptiness and compassion. In the Mahāyāna pursuit of awakening, the Bodhisattva ideal soon replaces that of the arhat.

Although the Madhyamaka refutation of the polarity of *saṃsāra* and *nirvāṇa* leads to the rise of the Bodhisattva ideal, their refutation remains vulnerable to one issue: if *nirvāṇa* is *saṃsāra*, and the net of causality extends its arms to all stages of existence in the cosmos, it follows that everything, everyone, and every action is determined by their precedents. Thus, if actions are predetermined, how can sentient beings actively exercise their agency?

That is why for Chinese Yogācārins like Xuanzang and his disciples, the clarification of dependent arising is a two-pronged project. Above all, they continue to expand on why there is *saṃsāra* when there is no-self. More importantly, they attempt to explore the possibility of awakening in their affirmation of the non-duality of *nirvāṇa* and *saṃsāra*.[4] Rearticulating the theory of dependent arising, these Yogācārins position the doctrine of twelve links in the framework of consciousness-only. Instead of unpacking these links as a system of causality of three times and two layers, they argue for understanding them as a "causality within one layer (*yichong yinguo* 一重因果)" (T43N1830, P528c27).[5] In the *CWSL*, Xuanzang introduces how to regroup the twelve links to account for dependent arising (T31N1585, P43b27–c26), as shown in Table 3.

In his reformulation of the twelve links, Xuanzang foregrounds the function of consciousness. As such, causality is not the externally self-determined reality but relies on the mind to work. The theory of dependent arising is also underpinned by the interplay between *vijñāna* as the *ti* of consciousness and its function of *vijñapti*. As suggested by Table 3, a sentient being's eighth *consciousness* stores both pure seeds and impure ones. While the pure seeds give rise to true perceptions, the impure ones will grow into misperceptions. Whenever the eighth consciousness functions, it transforms into the seeing part as well as the image part, further facilitating the activity of the other seven consciousnesses. When the seeing part—or rather, the subjective act of perceiving—is aimed at its image part *qua* the perceived phenomenon, both the act and the phenomenon obtain their *names and forms* along with the *six sense sources* of experience. This perceptual process is accompanied by mental factors, such as *contact* and *feeling*. On the basis of the functionality of consciousness, a sentient being is prone to misperceive such functionality and endures the rise of *craving* and *grasping*, which precipitates *ignorance* and produces egocentric *actions*. These actions, in turn, consolidate ignorance by planting more impure seeds in the eighth consciousness.

Table 3 Xuanzang's reformulation of the twelve links

Category	The links	Death and rebirth
The links that can influence (*nengyingzhi* 能引支)	Ignorance, actions	*Ignorance* triggers *actions*, which can exert influence on the seeds inside the eighth consciousness.
The links that can be influenced (*suoyinzhi* 所引支)	Consciousness, names and forms, six sense sources, contact, feeling	Due to the influence of ignorance and actions, *consciousnesses* give rise to the seeing and image parts, on the basis of which *names and forms, six sense sources*, and the mental factors of *contact and feeling* will arise consecutively.
The links that can generate (*nengshengzhi* 能生支)	Craving, grasp, existence	When someone misperceives things as *svabhāvic*, such misconception becomes the ground for the mental factors of *craving* and *grasping*, which brings more egocentric actions into *existence*.
Those that can be generated (*suoshengzhi* 所生支)	Birth and death	Such egocentric actions cultivate the *life* of this sentient being until *death*.

While these impure seeds come into *existence*, this sentient being's mind becomes even more contaminated and breeds the birth of another misperception in *this life* and so on until *death*.

Formulated in this manner, causality is not mind-independent, not a higher-order reality that is in itself, because actions are shaped and conditioned by a series of mental events, such as perceiving, feeling, and craving (T43N1830, P528c27–8).[6] Since all causes and effects can be traced back to consciousness, Xuanzang contends that there is no need to differentiate causality between three times and into two layers (T31N1585, P44b4). Rather, the endless cycle of death and rebirth is not determined by external conditions but contingent on inner causes *qua* consciousness, which explains a deeper meaning of consciousness-only (T31N1585, P45a12). That is why Xuanzang and his disciples promote the concept of causality within *one* layer. Later clerics characterize this view as "dependent arising from the eighth consciousness (*laiye yuanqi*賴耶緣起)" (Lü 1979; Sheng-yen 1999; Xia 2003).

The way in which Xuanzang and his disciples foreground the role of consciousness against the backdrop of reformulating the theory of dependent arising is, in fact, in line with their view of consciousness-only—that is, everything depends on consciousness to arise as a phenomenon in one's experience. More importantly, as clarified in Chapter 5, the mind of each individual is interconnected with other minds in such a way that the Yogācāra interpretation of dependent arising suggests how each individual sentient being is always born and reborn on a horizon shared by a plurality of sentient beings in multiple realms. One round of life after another, sentient beings internalize the ignorant perspective as a natural way of living and consolidate such ignorance as a habit in the shared memory to which sentient beings belong. For sentient beings entrapped in *saṃsāra*, Xuanzang and his disciples likewise present the possibility for awakening—contingent on being guided on the right path by the Bodhisattvas. The rebirth of Bodhisattvas thus needs to be demarcated from that of ignorant sentient beings. Characterizing the death and rebirth of Bodhisattvas as wondrous (*busiyi*不思議), these Chinese Yogācārins disseminate a message that Bodhisattvas are not reborn in a particular realm due to misperception but rather that they volunteer to enter *saṃsāra* under the guise of being a normal sentient being in order to help others (T31N1585, P45a).

As such, Xuanzang and his disciples problematize the early Buddhist doctrine of twelve links and the related linear view of time as expressed in the notion of causality of three times and two layers. Positioning dependent arising in the framework of consciousness-only, these Yogācārins envisage time as non-linear, intersubjective, and circular. It is this non-linear intersubjective circularity that makes it possible for Bodhisattvas to re-enter *saṃsāra* and become reborn in wondrous ways. As to be seen towards the end of this chapter, these Chinese Yogācārins expand the meaning of awakening as well. For them, awakening consists of two correlative aspects as the liberation for each individual and the enlightenment for others. Thus, instead of being an individual accomplishment, awakening becomes a collaborative achievement.

To further our understanding of how the early Buddhist account of dependent arising is contrasted with that in Chinese Yogācāra, I borrow the terms "agent-oriented" and "event-oriented" from the contemporary philosophy of action. According to those who endorse an agent-oriented type of causality, the cause of one's actions is attributed to the agent *per se* (Ginet 1990; O'Connor 2000; Lowe 2008; Schlosser 2015). In contrast, those who support the event-oriented type of causality ascribe the cause of actions to a purpose constituted in the event of "want-and-belief" (Goldman 1970; Davidson 1980; Dretske 1988). Therefore, the two camps come to explain the cause of actions differently. For instance, take the action of drinking a glass of water. Those who understand actions as caused by agents would conclude that Cindy wants to drink a cup of water because she is a human who has the capacity of doing so. As such, the cause of the action resides in the fact that Cindy is human. If she wants to negate the desire of drinking, she then has to change her existential status away from being human. Contrariwise, those in favor of event-oriented causality would maintain that Cindy drinks a cup of water, not because she is a human, but because of her current state of being thirsty. Once the event dissolves and her state of being thirsty vanishes, Cindy ceases craving water.

In Xuanzang's account of dependent arising, there is a shift from an agent-oriented type of causality (in early Buddhism) to an event-oriented one (in Yogācāra). That is to say, in the early Buddhist doctrine of twelve links, sentient beings have various kinds of cravings, because and only because they are born as such (T43N1830, P528c21). Hence, it is their existence that shapes their actions, entraps them in the net of causality, and incarcerates them in *saṃsāra*. To disable the trap, sentient beings must change their existence into arhats by means of *nirvāṇa* (T43N1830, P528c22). Articulated in this manner, *nirvāṇa* becomes the negation of and the antidote to *saṃsāra*. Since these early Buddhists attribute actions to the agent, they likewise ascribe liberation to a change of one's existential status.

Against this view, Xuanzang and his disciples perceive causality as that which is oriented towards events. As detailed in their account of dependent arising, actions stem from various mental events, such as perception, which cultivates a sentient being's state of craving and grasping. Described in this manner, actions are determined not by existence *per se* but by how this existence is perceived in each mental event (T43N1830, P528c28). The previous example of drinking water could be evoked to illustrate this type of causality: sentient beings like Cindy conduct the action of drinking water, not because they are humans, but because of their perception of the current state of being thirsty. In parallel, sentient beings are trapped in the net of causality, not because they are born as such, but due to the misperception of their existence. Following this line of reasoning, if sentient beings want to free themselves from the trap of *saṃsāra*, they do not have to change their existence into arhats. Instead, they shall revise the composition of their mental events through changing their way of perceiving—in short, they shall change their state of mind.

Now that Yogācārins attribute actions to mental events and ascribe liberation to the revision of perception, they secure the central role of consciousness from the descriptive level (as in the acquisition of knowledge) to the prescriptive level (as in the motivation of actions). This is how Xuanzang and his disciples fulfill the twofold purpose: first, they refashion the theory of dependent arising in the framework of consciousness-only, arguing that there is no permanent self but there is still *saṃsāra*, because of the functionality of consciousness; second, this rearticulation of dependent arising suggests how sentient beings have agency even when *nirvāṇa* is *saṃsāra*. The *karmic* law of causality indeed extends through every stage of *saṃsāra* over the entirety of cosmic history. This fact, nonetheless, does not negate the existence of agency. A sentient being has agency insofar as causality does not stem from its existence as a sentient being *per se* (the agent-oriented type of causality in early Buddhism), but from the way in which this sentient being perceives the state of affairs and constitutes wants-and-beliefs (the event-oriented type of causality in Yogācāra).

The different ways of perceiving further explain how agency is exercised. As previously mentioned, the misperception of things as *svabhāva* will result in craving and suffering. Contrariwise, upon seeing things as they really are, sentient beings become one with dependent arising and realize *nirvāṇa* in every moment of this-worldly life. By then, *nirvāṇa* becomes *saṃsāra*. Liberation from ignorance does not indicate an existence that transcends *saṃsāra* by breaking through the cosmic net of causality. Instead, upon transforming *nirvāṇa* into *saṃsāra*, sentient beings navigate their worldly life in virtue of causality without being trapped. This Yogācāra conception of *nirvāṇa* will be further elaborated towards the end of this chapter.

Agents Between the Good and the Evil

Upon affirming the existence of agency, we continue to detail the ways in which agency stems from knowledge. In this regard, it is helpful to revisit the concept of mental factors (*xinsuo* 心所, *caitasika/caitta*). Borrowing Husserl's conception of founding, we have previously explained how mental factors function on the basis of the functionality of consciousnesses. As such, mental factors equally have the fourfold intentional structure and Xuanzang utilizes the painter metaphor to unpack the cooperation between consciousness and its mental factors—that is, each sentient being is the painter of their own worldview, in the process of which consciousness sketches the outline of a mental image and mental factors add this image with numerous colors (T31N1585, P26c15–18). The subject of knowing becomes one with the agent of acting in virtue of these mental factors, especially the five omnipresent mental factors (*wu bianxing xinsuo* 五遍行心所, *pañca sarvatraga caittas*) (T31N1585, P11b16). As suggested by this name, these mental factors accompany all consciousness throughout beginningless time (T43N1830, P328b2). These five *caittas* are: contacting (*chu* 觸, *sparśa*), attending (*zuoyi* 作意, *manaskāra*), feeling (*shou* 受, *vedanā*), thinking (*xiang* 想, *saṃjñā*), and purposing (*si* 思, *cetanā*) (T31N1585, P11b–c). Surfacing one after another, these *caittas* explain the emergence of agency.

As detailed by Xuanzang in the *CWSL*, when consciousness is in function, it is accompanied first and foremost by the mental factor of *contacting*, which facilitates the encounter and meeting of three elements: the consciousness, the corresponding sense organ, and the correlated object (T31N1585, P11b19). That is why consciousness is able to perceive things that do not actually appear in front of a sentient being, exemplified by the mental acts of hallucination and imagination. The mental factor of *contacting* thus serves as the support of the rest of omnipresent *caittas*. When consciousness, sense organs, and the perceived object coordinate with one another harmoniously, the mental factor of *attending* is able to guide consciousness in shifting the focus from one phenomenon to another (T31N1585, P11c8–10). That is why Xuanzang characterizes this mental factor by its capacity of alerting the mind (*jinxin* 警心) (T31N1585, P11c7). Once consciousness continues to perform its function with the assistance of *contacting* and *attending*, the mental factor of *feeling* arises, through which a sentient being will find the perceived phenomenon to be favorable, unfavorable, or neutral (T31N1585, P11c11). As such, these *feelings* serve as the source of suffering for sentient beings (T31N1585, P11c12). Afflicted with suffering, sentient beings strive to designate names and words to perceived phenomena, an action that is driven by the mental factor of *thinking* (T31N1585, P11c23). Once a phenomenon is defined by names and words, the mental factor of *purposing* propels sentient beings to conduct moral actions that can be either good, or evil, or neutral (T31N1585, P11c25).

Let's use the example of Cindy's recollection of her cat to elucidate the functionality of these five omnipresent mental factors. In her recollection,[7] Cindy relives the previous moment when earlier that morning, her cat was sitting by the window and observing a flock of pigeons perched on the balcony. The cat that appears as the phenomenon of her recollection pertains to her previous experience, whereas her eye-consciousness exists within her at the current moment. In virtue of the mental factor *contacting*, Cindy's eye-consciousness is able to perceive the phenomenon of her preceding experience. Indeed, whenever consciousness gives rise to the seeing part and the image part, the mental factor of *contacting* arises accordingly to sustain the harmonious co-existence of various parts derived from consciousness (T43N1830, P328b15). As such, even when Cindy begins hallucinating and sees two cats by the window, *contacting* manages to connect her act of perceiving with the fictitious second-cat. While *contacting* ensures harmony among various parts of her perception, the mental factor of *attending* allows for the shift of focus (T43N1830, P330b26). Upon recollecting, Cindy focusses on her cat with the help of *attending*, while leaving the fuzzy backdrop of the pigeons aside. Then, Cindy becomes curious about the reaction of these pigeons to her cat. By force of *attending*, she can redirect her focus to these pigeons and bring that which was once immersed in the background of her perceptual field to the forefront. Subsequently, based on Cindy's perception of her cat, *feelings* arise and indicate how Cindy finds this mental episode amusing. This mental factor of *feeling* can bring to Cindy both delight and disgust, and further nourish the mental factor of craving (T43N1830, P331a22). Craving serves as the ground for *thinking* and by virtue of the mental factor of *thinking*, Cindy can thus evoke names and words to articulate the amusing behavior of her cat (T43N1830, P332a26). *Thinking* gives rise to the mental factor of *purposing* that drives consciousness to conduct a wide range of verbal and non-verbal actions.

The examination of these five mental factors outlines the process by which the perception of consciousness animates other mental states and eventually motivates actions. Actions and perceptions reciprocate each other, which leads to different types of moral life. Earlier we introduced how consciousness and its mental factors can possess four types of morality: good (*shan* 善, *kuśala*), evil (*e* 惡, *akuśala*), neutral with pollution (*youfuwuji* 有覆無記, *nivṛtāvyākṛta*), and neutral without pollution (*wufuwuji* 無覆無記, *anivṛtāvyākṛta*) (T31N1585, P12a20). For instance, the eighth consciousness is morally neutral and so are its mental factors—namely, the five omnipresent ones. Nevertheless, for the other seven consciousnesses, the case becomes more complicated. Due to their distinct ways of knowing, these consciousnesses are accompanied by respective types of mental factors that continue to prompt the subject of knowing to conduct various actions, and these actions in turn cultivate the way in which this subject perceives. As such, both subjectivity and agency furnish each individual with an open possibility.

Mona, the seventh consciousness, is always inclined to misperceive the seeing part of the eighth storehouse consciousness as the manifestation of a *sui generis*, immutable self. Upon the rise of this misperception, sentient beings become conditioned to an egocentric view of life. As such, they internalize this unchanging self-identity as a habitual lifestyle (T31N1585, P2a10), and perpetuate innate attachments to this self (T31N1585, P6c27). To further the discussion of these innate attachments, it is helpful to examine the mental factors that accompany the seventh consciousness. Aside from the omnipresent *caittas*, the seventh consciousness is constantly accompanied by four types of defilements (*fannao* 煩惱, *kleśa*) (T31N1585, P22a24). They are the mental factors of self-ignorance (*wochi*我癡), self-misunderstanding (*wojian*我見), self-conceit (*woman*我慢), and self-love (*woai*我愛) (T31N1585, P22a27). In other words, the function of the seventh consciousness serves as the ground for the ignorance of the truth of no-self. Driven by such self-ignorance, each sentient being tends to misperceive the functionality of consciousness as an immutable, *sui generis* entity *qua* a *svabhāvic* ego (T31N1585, P22a28). This self-misunderstanding continues to propel the sentient being to place the self in the center of its life, further consolidating egocentrism and animating self-conceit (T31N1585, P22a29). Subsequently, self-conceit energizes self-love and fuels various types of innate attachments to the self (T31N1585, P22b1–2). Accordingly, other dharmas are pushed to the outskirts of this self-centered worldview, which becomes the root of innate dharma-attachments. As Xuanzang remarks, these defilements facilitate the activity of the first six consciousnesses that motivate sentient beings to conduct morally good as well as morally evil actions (T31N1585, P22b6).

Indeed, the first six consciousnesses can have all four types of moral qualities (T31N1585, P26b11). When the sixth consciousness misperceives things as *svabhāvic* entities, it energizes innate attachments (T31N1585, P2a21), and empowers discriminative attachments (T31N1585, P7a6). This process can explain how the basic mental defilements arise (T31N1585, P31b18). Driven by such a wide range of afflictions, the subject produces theories and performs actions to uphold the egocentric worldview. Analogically, this is how verbal and non-verbal actions perfume the seeds in the eighth storehouse consciousness and nourish more misperceptions. In this process, secondary defilements arise, which include the mental factors of belligerence, resentment, hypocrisy, spite, jealousy, miserliness, deceit, dissimulation, arrogance, and ruthlessness (T31N1585, P33b1). These secondary defilements render the sentient being apathetic towards shame and embarrassment (T31N1585, P33b2). Eventually, this sentient being indulges in the state of lethargy, relentlessness, lack of faith and persistence, and laziness (T31N1585, P33b3). This is how egocentric sentient beings become incapable of changing their mode from being oblivious, easily distracted, and constantly misunderstanding others (T31N1585, P33b3). Thereafter, all kinds of morally egocentric actions emerge and widen the perceived self-other rift. As such, this sentient being is trapped in the egocentric worldview and consumed with all sorts of craving and suffering from this round of life into the next, *ad infinitum*.

However, once this sentient being is exposed to the wisdom of emptiness and altruistic compassion, the seeds of goodness begin to grow in the storehouse consciousness (T31N1585, P8c8). Most importantly, this allows for the reappearance of faith as a mental factor. On the basis of the perception of the sixth consciousness, faith arises and encourages sentient beings to uphold their trust in the wisdom of emptiness, in the *karmic* merit of altruistic deeds, and finally, in the possibility of awakening (T31N1585, P29b25-7). This conviction becomes deep enough that sentient beings will no longer be misled by incorrect opinions and will regain their sense of shame and embarrassment (T31N1585, P29c17). Using these emotions, sentient beings can reject attachments, anger, and desire. Gradually, sentient beings can demonstrate perseverance, despite all the obstacles and hardships in their path (T31N1585, P30a3-24). As a devotee, a sentient being will always remain at ease without being relentless (T31N1585, P30b5-7). Eventually, the devotee will achieve equanimity and is never willing to conduct actions to harm others (T31N1585, P30b23-9).

From the exposition of the mental factors of the six consciousnesses, it can be inferred that misperceptions give rise to an egocentric worldview and empower egoistic actions. On the contrary, correct perceptions encourage sentient beings to purify their consciousness and perform altruistic actions. Both egoistic and altruistic actions cultivate seeds in the storehouse consciousness, which conditions how sentient beings perceive and act. Borrowing the flame-wick analogy from the *Mahāyānasaṃgraha*, Xuanzang portrays the interplay between the actualized ones, *viz.* views and deeds, and the unactualized seeds. The flame burns the wick while the wick produces the flame and such is the reciprocity between the two, just as how the actualized views and deeds correlate with the unactualized seeds (T31N1585, P8c9).

To summarize, sentient beings not only have agency but can also exercise agency in different, or even opposite, manners. Either they follow misperceptions and conduct egocentric actions, or they see things as they really are and become motivated to perform altruistic deeds to awaken compassion. Now, considering the mutual advancement of knowing and doing, the line between subjectivity (in the epistemic sense) and agency (in the practical sense) gradually disappears. Agency becomes the embodied and habitualized subjectivity in every moment of daily life. This articulation of agency leads us to the upcoming question regarding the notion of *nirvāṇa* in the Yogācāra framework. As *saṃsāra* is not a break-away from *nirvāṇa*, liberation does not yield the transcendence of the worldly life. That being the case, how do Xuanzang and his disciples delineate the notion of *nirvāṇa*?

Awakening between *Saṃsāra* and *Nirvāṇa*

Upon refashioning the account of dependent arising to confirm the place of agency in his doctrine of consciousness-only, Xuanzang likewise rearticulates the idea of *saṃsāra*. He along with his disciples no longer envisions *saṃsāra* as separate from *nirvāṇa*.

In unpacking the Yogācāra notion of *nirvāṇa*, it will be of help to revisit the concepts of attachments and elaborate on how attachments are related to the obstruction of awakening.

Attachments stem from the functionality of the seventh and sixth consciousnesses. In virtue of these two consciousnesses, each sentient being is prone to embrace *svabhāvic* views of the self and of dharmas. While the former animates innate self-attachments, the latter empowers innate dharma-attachments. Internalized in this manner, these attachments penetrate a sentient being's natural way of living and perpetuate egocentrism at the habitual level. Based on these innate attachments, the sixth consciousness continues to create various criteria to differentiate others from oneself, which consolidates discriminative self-attachments and discriminative dharma-attachments. The self–other polarization conspires to push others to the fringes of the egocentric worldview at the conceptual level. From the self-attachments, there arise the obstructions of defilement (*fannaozhang* 煩惱障, *kleśāvaraṇa*) (T31N1585, P48c7). As the name suggests, this defilement obstructs the arrival of *nirvāṇa* and the achievement of no-self (T31N1585, P48c7). Further from the dharma-attachments, there stem the obstructions of knowledge (*suozhizhang* 所知障, *jñeyāvaraṇa*), which obstructs the emergence of *bodhi* and the elimination of *svabhāva* (T31N1585, P48c9–11).

As such, misperceptions serve as the root for attachments and obstructions. Together, they push sentient beings away from awakening. Compounding this, sentient beings are inclined to initiate various egoistic actions, which in turn consolidates their egocentric worldview. A causal chain, therefore, begins and entraps sentient beings in *saṃsāra*, and so on *ad infinitum*. Following this line of reasoning, if sentient beings wish to remove attachments and obstructions for the dawn of their awakening, they need to make a twofold effort. First, they must reshape their scope of perceiving things, so as to liberate themselves from discriminative attachments (T31N1585, P48c27). This is the first step towards awakening (T31N1585, P48c28). Upon removing discriminative attachments at the conceptual level, they must then proceed to purify all types of innate attachments at the habitual level. This process can be compared to that of rehabitualizing. That is to say, sentient beings must restructure their habitual ways of living and reform their lifestyle through a wide range of training and cultivation.

To expound on the Yogācāra view of rehabitualization, I propose to borrow the framework outlined by Victor Hori in his elaboration on awakening. According to Hori, awakening is realized upon attaining insight on two levels: the horizontal level where practitioners understand the conceptual meaning of Buddhist teaching preserved in scriptures; and the vertical level where practitioners go beyond language and conceptual thinking to become one with the teaching (Hori 2006: 206). In Hori's terms, the former demonstrates an insight within languages and conceptual thinking that concerns linguistic expression and cognitive comprehension, whereas the latter alludes to an insight that goes beyond the conceptual realm and guides sentient beings back to everyday experience (Hori 2006: 206). Here, I draw parallels of the Yogācāra two-step process of removing attachments and rehabitualizing one's lifestyle with Hori's description of the two-level insight. Indeed, it is not enough to understand emptiness and compassion as conceptual knowledge. Upon attaining these two insights, sentient beings must act to become one with them. To be more precise, it requires effort to make actions effortless. Only then as such can sentient beings eradicate the obstructions of defilement and the obstructions of knowledge.

When sentient beings realize the vertical and horizontal insights, they will be able to remove discriminative attachments and innate attachment, which further gives rise to the dependent-evolution (*zhuanyi*轉依, *āśraya-parivṛtti/āśraya-parāvṛtti*) (T31N1585, P51a3).[8] In the *CWSL*, Xuanzang specifies that dependent-evolution consists of two correlated aspects of *nirvāṇa* and *bodhi* (T31N1585, P51a8). That is to say, upon removing innate and discriminative attachments, a sentient being likewise eradicates obstructions of defilement and of knowledge. This sentient being can then realize *nirvāṇa*/liberation of its own mind and attain the great *bodhi*/enlightenment for helping others. Subsequently, compassion arises, which encourages this sentient being to guide others on the right path. Thus, I use the English term "awakening" to accentuate both the liberation of one's own mind and the enlightenment for other minds, in allusion to how awakening is a collaborative achievement. Table 4 demonstrates the aforementioned notion of dependent-evolution expressed by later Yogācārins.

As such, the concept of dependent-evolution becomes used by Xuanzang and his disciples to prescribe the way in which sentient beings collaborate with one another to transform the minds from the state of ignorance to the state of awakening. Articulated in this manner, *nirvāṇa* is not simply the liberation for each individual, nor a gateway for a sentient being to ascend to a realm devoid of causality. Quite to the contrary, Xuanzang perceives *nirvāṇa* as a liberation of one's mind within *saṃsāra* from egocentric views and lifestyle, a liberation that leads to and becomes correlated with the enlightenment for others. Liberation and enlightenment—or *nirvāṇa* and *bodhi*—constitute two correlated sides of awakening. Upon awakening, sentient beings act to embody emptiness in every movement of life in walking, talking, sitting, and sleeping. By then, sentient beings reshape the scope of perceiving and rehabitualize themselves in everyday actions. In this sense, sentient beings transcend *saṃsāra* by becoming one with it. Borrowing the river analogy that Xuanzang articulates in his description of consciousness, I propose to describe awakening in the following manner. After the

Table 4 The Yogācāra view of dependent-evolution

Viewpoints	The conceptual level	The habitual level	Obstructions	Awakening
Svabhāvic views of the self	Discriminative self-attachments (Originating from conceptualization)	Innate self-attachments (Originating habitually)	Obstructions of defilement	Great *nirvāṇa* (liberation of one's own mind)
Svabhāvic views of the dharmas	Discriminative dharma-attachments (Originating from conceptualization)	Innate dharma-attachments (Originating habitually)	Obstructions of knowledge	Great *bodhi* (enlightenment for other minds)
Purification of viewpoints	Horizontal insight (The conceptual level)	Vertical insight (The habitual level)	Prior to dependent-evolution	Upon realizing dependent-evolution

realization of awakening, sentient beings neither leave the river for good, nor continue to struggle to float. They resonate with the flow and become one with the river. *Saṃsāra* is the river of flowing water and therefore, so is *nirvāṇa*.

Nevertheless, Xuanzang and his disciples maintain that not all sentient beings can realize *nirvāṇa* and *bodhi* to the same extent (T31N1585, P55b20). Indeed, they sort sentient beings into five groups in their five-*gotra* account, in accordance with their respective subjectivity and agency. During the lifetimes of these Chinese Yogācārins, the *gotra* system undoubtedly provoked fierce controversies. So then, why would they promote the *gotra* system at all? This is a question that will be answered in the following chapter.

11

The Path Towards Awakening

In the preceding chapter, we examined the place of agency in the Yogācāra framework. Xuanzang and his disciples refashion the interpretation of dependent arising to affirm the existence of agency, which allows them to detail how sentient beings can enact their agency in different manners to conduct morally good or evil actions. These actions, in turn, condition and cultivate the ways in which sentient beings perceive the world. Understanding agency in this manner, these Yogācārins conceive of *nirvāṇa* not as a break-free from *saṃsāra*, but rather that *nirvāṇa* is an integral part of awakening, through which sentient beings become one with *saṃsāra*. However, Xuanzang and his disciples advocate for sorting sentient beings into five groups known as the five families (*gotra*) in accordance with their different levels of agency. Do they reject the consensus that all sentient beings have equal potential for realizing emptiness and compassion?

In this chapter, we embark on the task of analyzing the controversial implementation of *gotra* by these later Yogācārins. Hereby, we address three questions consecutively: first, does the *gotra* system predetermine a sentient being's life? Second, if the *gotra* system does not, what makes it possible for a sentient being to change its current membership in the *gotra* system? And third, when a sentient being is able to change its membership, what is the new path that it should follow? The answers to these questions allow me to argue that Chinese Yogācārins like Xuanzang and his disciples promote the *gotra* system to highlight the power of the Bodhisattvas' compassion in changing one's family membership in the *gotra* system and, effectively, the possibility for their awakening. Thus, the *gotra* system preserves the empirical/conventional differences of sentient beings—some who are able to realize Buddha nature on their own and others who are incapable of doing so—and promotes the possibility of universal awakening. Sentient beings can change family membership through the collaborative effort of self-power and other-power. In particular, empirical/conventional difference serves as a critique of various types of ignorance—a critique that entails the Yogācārins' awareness of incorrect aspirations in the pursuit of awakening. As such, what looks like a negation of universal awakening is in fact the first step to enriching the understanding of the Bodhisattvas' path.

Gotra and Buddha Nature

In answering the first question regarding whether the *gotra* system predetermines the life of a sentient being, we will position our discussion into the larger debate on Buddha nature that took place at the beginning of the Tang dynasty between these later Yogācārins and their interlocutors. For our purpose, we also need to clarify the meaning of the key concept of Buddha nature here. Also translated as Buddhahood, the concept of Buddha nature has been formulated by Buddhist clerics to describe the nature of the Buddha as the one who awakens the wisdom of emptiness and compassion (Chen 1964: 117; King 1991: 2; Gethin 1998: 252). For Buddhists in the Tang dynasty, since the Buddha embodies wisdom and compassion, the nature of the Buddha (*foxing*佛性) likewise entails emptiness (*kongxing*空性) and suchness (*zhenru*真如).[1] In general, the realization of Buddha nature is the ultimate goal that devotees must pursue through religious training.[2] After centuries of transmission and development in East Asia, the notion of Buddha nature or Buddhahood consistently captured the attention of major Buddhist philosophers.[3]

Towards the end of the Northern and Southern dynasties period (c. 386–589), Buddhists have reached the consensus that all sentient beings have Buddha nature and can become awakened.[4] Kenneth Chen characterizes this consensus as that of the universal salvation of Mahāyāna (Chen 1964: 125). Borrowing the maxim in the *Lotus Sūtra* and the *Mahāparinirvāṇasūtra*, Buddhists express their consensus by declaring that "all sentient beings, all have Buddha nature (一切眾生，悉有佛性)" (T43N1831, P610a25). One of the proponents of this Mahāyāna conception of universal salvation is Zhiyi (智顗 538-97), the founder of the Tiantai school of Buddhism. Drawing on and developing the Madhyamaka conception of the twofold truth, Zhiyi evokes the philosophical binary of *quan* (權, conventional) and *shi* (實, ultimate) to expound on emptiness (T33N1716, P693a20–3). By virtue of this philosophical binary, Zhiyi portrays the fluidity and transformability of the conventional and the ultimate—the ultimate truth of emptiness undergirds and gives rise to the conventionally true illusions, whilst conventional illusions reveal and manifest the underlying emptiness (T46N1911, P34a19–21). The complementarity of the conventional illusions and the ultimate emptiness amounts to the truth of the middle way.[5] Further applying the conventional–ultimate binary to the interpretation of Buddha nature, Zhiyi explains how and why all sentient beings have Buddha nature. He categorizes individual differences as parts of the conventional reality, Buddha nature as the ultimate emptiness (T33N1716, P693c19–27). Since the individual mind derives from and discloses the ultimate reality of Buddha nature, every sentient being can make an effort to realize their inherent Buddha nature, regardless of their dissimilar capacity at the conventional level (T33N1716, P693c28–694a10).[6] In other words, awakening is possible as long as sentient beings resolve to make an effort. Subsequently, Zhiyi designates Tiantai contemplative practice as the means to attaining the wisdom of seeing things as they are and realizing their innate Buddha nature.[7] Through reformulating the non-duality of the conventional and the ultimate, Zhiyi follows the middle way to reinforce the widely accepted consensus on all having Buddha nature (T33N1716, P741b17–21).[8]

Up until the seventh century, early Yogācārins in East Asia likewise espoused and promoted the view that all sentient beings have Buddha nature (T43N1830, P307a16). Their position, in part, alludes to the integration of the theory of *tathāgatagarbha* in their doctrine of consciousness-only. In light of the *tathāgatagarbha* theory, they contend that the mind—though originally luminous—is concealed by various types of defilements for the time being that arise from dualistic views in virtue of the activity of consciousness. Characterized by such a polluted mindset, ignorant sentient beings should engage in training to terminate the activity of consciousness, recuperate the originally immaculate luminous mind, remove mental defilements, and realize their innate Buddha nature (T31N1617, P872c).[9] The immaculate non-dual state of mind is therefore equated with emptiness and suchness. Douglas Berger speaks of this model of awakening as the recovery model, to be contrasted with the discovery model in later Yogācāra (Berger 2015: 129).

Growing up in this monastic culture, Xuanzang was familiar with the early Yogācāra understanding of Buddha nature. It is said that his teacher Śīlabhadra, however, was not sympathetic to the viewpoint documented in the *Lotus Sūtra*. Instead, this Nālandā master defended the five-*gotra* (*wuzhongxing* 五種性, *pañca gotrāḥ*) account in which sentient beings were arranged into five dissimilar families (*gotra*) (T43N1831, P610b29). The story continues that for obeying the will of his mentor Śīlabhadra, Xuanzang became an exponent of the *gotra* system. Although we can no longer attest to the authenticity of this story, historically, Xuanzang and his disciples indeed advocated the *gotra* system in East Asia during the seventh century.

Contrary to the view that all have Buddha nature, Xuanzang and his disciples contend that there are some sentient beings *without* Buddha nature. In his interpretation of the five-*gotra* account, Xuanzang's disciple Kuiji traces the origin of this account to the *Laṅkāvatārasūtra* in the following manner:

1. The *tathāgata* family (*rulaicheng zhongxing* 如來乘種性, *tathāgatayānābhisamayagotraḥ*), whose members can realize the wisdom of emptiness and compassion, become the awakened ones *qua* Buddhas, and attain the great *nirvāṇa* and great *bodhi* (T16N672, P597b20).
2. The indefinite family (*buding zhongxing* 不定種性, *aniyatagotraḥ*), whose members have the possibility of becoming an arhat, a *pratyekabuddha*, or a Buddha. The outcome of their training is undetermined and, thus, indefinite (T16N672, P597b24-8).
3. The hearer family (*shengwencheng zhongxing* 聲聞乘種性, *śrāvakayānābhisamayagotraḥ*), whose members hear about the Buddha's teaching of no-self and engage in Buddhist practices. Although they realize that there is no *svabhāvic* self and then become arhats, they are still ignorant of the empty nature of all dharmas (T16N672, P597b8-12).
4. The solitary family (*pizhifocheng zhongxing* 辟支佛乘種性, *pratyekabuddhayānābhisamayagotraḥ*), whose members realize the wisdom of emptiness and become *pratyekabuddha*. Yet, they prefer to practice in solitude, not willing to help others or to be helped, thus remaining ignorant of the Bodhisattvas' compassion (T16N672, P597b15).
5. The family without *gotra* (*wuzhongxing* 無種性, *agotrakaḥ*), whose members have no Buddha nature and cannot become a Buddha (T16N672, P597c9-11).

According to the *Laṅkāvatārasūtra*, members of the hearer family and the solitary family lack the ability to fully realize Buddha nature and therefore cannot themselves become a Buddha. Members of the last family without *gotra* are also known as the *icchantikas*. The *gotra* system appears to imply that the life of a sentient being is predetermined by its membership in these families. If this is the case, how is it possible for sentient beings to exercise agency? The *gotra* system seems to overthrow our conclusion from the previous chapter that all sentient beings can exercise agency in order to realize awakening.

To explore whether Xuanzang and his disciples espouse such determinism, it is helpful to revisit the notion of *gotra* itself. Although this Sanskrit term originally means the lineage of family and clan, Xuanzang reserves two Chinese concepts for *gotra*. In his translation, *gotra* is paraphrased as both *zhongxing* (種姓) and *zhongxing* (種性). The literal meaning of *zhongxing* (種姓) is the family-name (*xing*姓) of one's origin (*zhong*種), which is used interchangeably with *zhongxing* (種性) as the nature (*xing*性) of one's seeds (*zhong*種).[10] Connecting *gotra* with the theory of seeds, Xuanzang and his disciples implicitly insert their own understanding of Buddha nature to support their view of dependent-evolution (*zhuanyi* 轉依, *āśraya-parivṛtti*/*āśraya-parāvṛtti*).

As introduced earlier in Chapter 5, seeds symbolize the tendencies for consciousnesses to form *svabhāvic* or non-*svabhāvic* views, which further gives rise to a wide range of actions. Just like a seed, a tendency requires the proper conditions to realize itself (T31N1585, P9b23). Without such conditions, a seed may very well remain as nascent as a tendency, never coming into actual existence. Only under proper conditions, will a seed generate fruit and the tendency will come to fruition. Since each consciousness has its distinct way of perceiving, the realized viewpoint varies from one consciousness to the next (T31N1585, P9b26). Every viewpoint endures only for an instant in the experience and continues to nourish actions (T31N1585, P9b8–11). It, then, becomes the function of the seeds to serve as the direct cause of a wide range of actions. Some seeds are polluted by ignorance and can bring about misconceptions and misdeeds, whilst others are pure and lay the ground for awakening. As such, actions are always associated with the moral qualities of being good, evil, or neutral (T31N1585, P9b21). In turn, actions cultivate the seeds in the storehouse consciousness, planting possibilities for a viewpoint and then an action to arise, and so on *ad infinitum* (T31N1585, P9b18).

Afterward, Xuanzang explains how these seeds come into existence. He maintains that some seeds exist innately (*benyou* 本有) throughout beginningless time whereas others can be newly perfumed (*xinxun* 新熏) by recent actions (T31N1585, P8b23–c3). As seeds can be freshly cultivated, sentient beings who have no pure seeds retain the chance of acquiring such seeds later on. Xuanzang also reserves the possibility that the seeds in one's consciousness may be perfumed indirectly, not as a result of the direct causes (*yinyuan* 因緣, *hetupratyaya*) but as that of the upheaving condition (*zengshangyuan* 增上緣, *adhipatipratyaya*) *qua* the mind and actions of others—a viewpoint that alludes to the importance of community and collectivity in the Yogācāra architectonic of consciousness (T31N1585, P9c2–5).

Having rearticulated this understanding of seeds, let us return to the question concerning *gotra*. We have learned from the *CWSL* that a sentient being's family membership is determined by the nature of the seeds in the storehouse consciousness (T31N1585, P9a22). Those who have pure seeds, such as the Buddhas, belong to either the *Tathāgata* family or the indefinite one. Yet, those who have pure seeds as *arhats* and *pratyekabuddha* are classified as members of the hearer family and the solitary one. For those who have only impure seeds, they are considered the *icchantikas* of no Buddha nature. In their clarification of how the pure or impure quality of seeds shapes a sentient being's membership in the *gotra* system, Xuanzang and his disciples justify the interchangeability of *zhongxing* (種姓) as the family-name (姓) of one's origin (種) and *zhongxing* (種性) as the nature (性) of one's seeds (種).

Positioning the discussion of Buddha nature in this framework of seeds, Kuiji's disciple Huizhao scrutinizes the belief that all have Buddha nature (T45N1863, P409c16–18). Provided that all sentient beings have Buddha nature as an inherent quality, Huizhao questions whether they do in fact have Buddha nature in the current, specific moment. If they do have Buddha nature, all the seeds in their storehouse consciousness should be pure. Moreover, since pure seeds can only produce immaculate actions and perfume more pure seeds, there should not be any ignorance at the conventional level, which contradicts the fact that some sentient beings are ignorant and unawakened. However, if sentient beings do not have Buddha nature, there should be no pure seeds in their minds, which would render it impossible for them to achieve awakening—a result that refutes the premise that all sentient beings ultimately have Buddha nature. Now that Huizhao deems the Madhyamaka distinction of the conventional and the ultimate insufficient to make a case for awakening, he implicitly turns to the Yogācāra notion of the three natures in building his account of Buddha nature.[11]

Huizhao's diagnosis of the Madhyamaka view of Buddha nature is in line with the Yogācāra development of the Madhyamaka twofold truth. Similarly, his elaboration on Buddha nature parallels the Yogācāra theory of three natures. To be more specific, Huizhao elucidates three aspects of Buddha nature: the Buddha nature in principle (*lixing* 理性); the Buddha nature in practice (*xingxing* 行性); and the Buddha nature in secretiveness (*yinmixing* 隱密性) (T45N1863, P439a16). Connecting the analysis of Buddha nature with the Yogācāra account of three natures, Huizhao perceives Buddha nature as that which describes, in principle, the absolute nature of how things are in the cosmos (T45N1863, P439a18). That is why the Buddha nature in principle amounts to suchness devoid of any ignorance, misperceptions, and misdeeds (T45N1863, P439a19). Conversely, the Buddha nature in secretiveness entails how the mind is secreted and concealed through ignorance, a state that reflects the imagined nature (T45N1863, P439b10). Nevertheless, as stressed by Huizhao, "from the cessation of ignorance, there arises the principle of immaculateness. Such is the immaculate non-duality, which is why we say ignorance is awakening (即由斷無明，故得理清淨。清淨不二，故說無明，名為菩提)" (T45N1863, P439b24–5). Indeed, just as the dependent nature that encapsulates the open possibility between the imagined nature and the absolute nature, the Buddha nature in practice encloses the fluidity between awakening as that of the Buddha nature in principle and ignorance as that of the Buddha nature in secretiveness. That is why Huizhao portrays the Buddha nature in practice as that which penetrates the pure and the impure, which allows for the fluid change from one state to the other (T45N1863, P439a25).

As the development of Madhyamaka philosophy, Yogācāra enriches the twofold truth with the theory of three natures in the interpretation of emptiness. Such development in the understanding of emptiness yields their respective viewpoints on Buddha nature. Following the Madhyamaka doctrine of the twofold truth, Zhiyi interprets Buddha nature in terms of the conventional–ultimate binary, which allows for the elaboration on Buddha nature as the inherent quality of the ultimate truth provisionally covered by ignorance at the conventional level. In contrast, Yogācārins like Xuanzang and his disciples unpack Buddha nature in accordance with the three natures of the imagined, the dependent, and the absolute. They further underscore how Buddha nature is not innate but to be acquired through practice. Indeed, focusing on the Buddha nature in practice, these Yogācārins outline the ways in which sentient beings can make an effort in practice to enable the fluid change between Buddha nature in principle and Buddha nature in secretiveness—that is, between being awake as a Buddha and remaining ignorant without Buddha nature.

Such a fluid change entails how and why transcendental idealism—as a version of correlative non-dualism—is both explicative and prescriptive. It is through this fluid change that the *gotra* system is not pre-determinate but rather reserves the possibility of changing one's family membership. Due to the fluid change between Buddha nature in principle and Buddha nature in secretiveness, even the most ignorant ones retain the chance of growing pure seeds and changing their family membership. Yogācārins speak of this change in terms of dependent-evolution. Now, since membership in the *gotra* system results from the pure or impure quality of seeds, the change of family membership is realized through the appearance of new seeds. Reversely, even the most intelligent ones can lose the possibility of awakening when not making a proper effort. As such, the *gotra* system is not only prescriptive but also critical in that it alerts all sentient beings to the danger of improper and incorrect aspiration. How the Yogācāra framework argues that new seeds—either pure or impure—can be cultivated will be discussed further in the next section of this chapter.

During early Tang, Xuanzang openly supported the five-*gotra* account. His proposal of sentient beings without Buddha nature was severely criticized and defied by the majority of the Buddhist community (Chen 1964; Lü 1979). Upon Xuanzang's death, the debate between his disciples and his critics became even more intense (Xia 2003: 113). When Xuanzang's patron Emperor Taizong passed away, the new Emperor Gaozong (628–83) succeeded to the throne. Gaozong later entrusted the empire to his wife, Empress Wu Zetian (武則天 624–705). Empress Wu paid respect to early Yogācāra master Woncheuk and invited him back to the capital city to teach Buddhism (Xia 2003: 113). In this political climate, Kuiji left the capital city to stay on the outskirts of the center of power. Eventually, Xuanzang's disciples lost the upper hand in the debate over Buddha nature when they were no longer favored by the ruling class.

Self-power and Other-power

Over the years, Buddhist scholars have remarked how the *gotra* system, especially the conception of *icchantikas*, led to the downfall of Yogācāra Buddhism in East Asia (Chen 1964: 325; Lü 1979: 191; Xia 2003: 87). From their vantage point, the existence of *icchantikas* broke the consensus of all sentient beings having Buddha nature, which rendered the doctrine of consciousness-only unattractive to the East Asian laity. They further conjectured that Xuanzang knew very well the incompatibility of the five-*gotra* with the indigenous culture of Tang, but out of his deep respect for Śīlabhadra, Xuanzang continued to preach that some sentient beings, like the ignorant *icchantikas*, had no Buddha nature.

While filial piety towards patriarchs could be one factor for Xuanzang's promotion of the *gotra* system, it may not tell the whole story. This popular assessment overlooks how the relationship between religion and the state accelerated the decline of Yogācāra during the Tang dynasty (Yoshimura 1995; Liu 2009). More importantly, it obscures the philosophical justification of the *gotra* theory provided by Xuanzang and his disciples in the seventh century. As to be seen shortly, what first appears to be a negation of the *icchantikas*' capacity of attaining awakening is, in fact, an affirmation of the compassion of the Bodhisattvas and a critique of incorrect aspirations in the pursuit of awakening. The power of this compassion makes it possible for pure seeds to appear in the storehouse consciousness of the incurable *icchantikas*, further facilitating these *icchantikas*' endeavor to change their membership in the *gotra* system. The way in which *icchantikas* can retain the chance of awakening epitomizes how all sentient beings can transform their family membership through the joint effort of what we currently refer to as the self-power (*zili*自力) and the other-power (*tali*他力).[12]

To understand the standpoint of Xuanzang and his disciples, we need to examine their definition of *icchantika*. As Kuiji specifies, there is not merely one type of *icchantika*, but two (T45N1831, P610c2–8). The Sanskrit term *icchantika* is used to describe those who maintain their desires. Kuiji details that there are two kinds of desire-maintainers: those who are truly incapable of purifying their seeds due to their indulgence in desires and pleasures; and those who have made the great vow and hence desire to guide all sentient beings back on the right path. Among the two, the first type of *icchantika* consists of those who are genuinely incapable of awakening the wisdom of emptiness and thus are unable to conduct any compassionate deeds. In Yogācāra terms, they are sentient beings whose root of goodness has been burnt off (T43N1831, P610c2). That said, however, the Bodhisattvas are the second type of sentient beings without Buddha nature insofar as they have made the great vow to help others prior to becoming fully awakened (T43N1831, P610c4). By the force of the Bodhisattvas' vow, if ignorant sentient beings do not realize their Buddha nature, neither will the Bodhisattvas. To fulfill their vows, the Bodhisattvas will come to the most incurable ones to help them. Kuiji exalts this vow for it is the expression of the great compassion (*dabei* 大悲) of Bodhisattvas (T43N1831, P6111a28).

Reminding his readers that Bodhisattvas also pertain to the family of the *icchantikas*, Kuiji accentuates how the power of Bodhisattvas' great compassion assists the ignorant ones in cultivating pure seeds in their storehouse consciousness. For the most ignorant ones, their storehouse consciousnesses are occupied by impure seeds. As such, they have no Buddha nature and cannot become a Buddha in this cycle of life. Since it is impossible for the most ignorant ones to realize their Buddha nature through their own power, they must temporarily rely on the power of the Bodhisattvas' compassion. Through becoming acquainted with the Bodhisattvas and taking these Bodhisattvas as their good friends (*shanyou* 善友) (T45N1863, P442a5–9), these ignorant *icchantikas* will regain the possibility of cultivating pure seeds and growing the root of goodness (T45N1862, P375c5–11). This is how *icchantikas* have the possibility of changing their family membership in the *gotra* system. This manner in which Bodhisattvas assist ignorant ones in regaining pure seeds is described by Huizhao's disciple Zhizhou (智周, 668–723) as the transfer of merit (*huixiang* 迴向, *pariṇāmanā*)(T45N1864, P450b21–3).

As such, the power of the Bodhisattvas' compassion has been categorized as one of the upheaving conditions (*zengshanyuan* 增上緣, *adhipatipratyaya*) for the ignorant *icchantikas*' awakening (T45N1863, P447c8). Positioning the discussion in the context of the seeds, Huizhao elaborates on how others' teachings of emptiness and compassion as the upheaving condition can indirectly cultivate newly perfumed pure seeds in the minds of ignorant ones and facilitate their awakening of correct insights (T45N1863, P447c9–10). Assistance from others such as Buddhas and Bodhisattvas shall be distinguished from the direct cause (*yinyuan* 因緣) of newly perfumed pure seeds, insofar as the ignorant *icchantikas* have only impure seeds in their current minds and are thereby unable to grow any pure seeds themselves (T45N1863, P447c23–448a16).

The distinction between upheaving condition *qua* help from others and direct cause *qua* actions of oneself indicates how Xuanzang and his disciples strive to locate a middle way between making an effort on one's own and relying on the help of others. Indeed, others could assist a sentient being in awakening when one is temporarily unable to do so. Yet, this assistance does not constitute the direct cause of the appearance of pure seeds. Eventually, this sentient being will be able to make an effort to regrow the root of goodness and realize awakening. That is to say, the ignorant *icchantikas* can rely on the compassion of the Bodhisattvas as a skillful means, but the power of compassion can never replace the effort of oneself in the gradual process of changing one's membership in the *gotra* system.

In order to highlight the power of the Bodhisattvas' vow (菩薩願力), Jōkei (貞慶 1155–1213),[13] a Yogācārin in the late Heian and early Kamakura Japan, followed Kuiji and Huizhao to describe Bodhisattvas as the *icchantikas* of great compassion (*daihi sendai*大悲闡提) in contrast to the *icchantikas* without the root of goodness (*danzen sendai*斷善闡提) (T66N2263, P28a1–30b16). At that time, Japanese Buddhists more directly debated the idea of other-power, due to the ideological competition between Hossō and the newly arisen Pure Land schools.[14] Other-power is synonymous with the power of the Bodhisattvas' compassionate vow, contrasted with self-power that characterizes how sentient beings can make an effort on their own. Thus far, it becomes clear that the change of a sentient being's membership in the *gotra* system can happen through the collaborative effort of self-power and other-power. When sentient beings are incurably ignorant, they need to temporarily rely on the Bodhisattvas' compassion until they can exercise self-power to attain awakening.

To understand why others can perform assistive roles for individuals and cannot replace self-effort and self-power, it is necessary to revisit the Yogācāra view of other minds. Earlier in Chapter 5, we remarked that although our own minds cannot transform into that of others or *vice versa*, we nevertheless experience other minds through the second-person perspective. That is to say, we perceive others as our partners and friends with whom we co-exist and collaborate in cosmic history. This experience further demonstrates the self–other interdependence at the explicative level. When the Bodhisattvas attain initial awakening, realize the wisdom of non-duality, and comprehend such self–other interdependence, they voluntarily return to the realm of *saṃsāra* to help others, especially the most ignorant *icchantikas*. They do not perceive the *icchantikas* as their rivals but as their friends. Through interacting with the Bodhisattvas, the most ignorant ones are able to experience the minds of others *qua* the Bodhisattvas from the second-person perspective. This is how the *icchantikas* have access to wisdom and compassion, not through self-power but rather through the compassion of the Bodhisattvas. In light of the lamp analogy, the ignorant ones have no awakened mind or Buddha nature, but they can still experience the awakened minds of the Bodhisattvas through the second-person perspective, which can be compared to how one lamp that has not been ignited can enjoy the light and warmth from other lamps in the dark.

From the vantage point of the Bodhisattvas, it is through their compassion that the awakened pure mind can be manifested to the ignorant ones. Xuanzang and his disciples refer to this manifestation as the other-enjoyment body (*tashouyongshen* 他受用身, *parasaṃbhogakāya*) of Buddhas and Bodhisattvas. Kuiji further states that once sentient beings are exposed to this other-enjoyment body, their current membership in the *gotra* family will no longer obstruct their realization of Buddha nature (T45N1861, P373b15). It is through their experience of and interaction with the Bodhisattvas that the newly cultivated pure seeds begin to grow in the storehouse consciousness of the most ignorant ones. To be more specific, since these ignorant *icchantikas* do not perceive the other minds of Bodhisattvas from the first-person perspective, pure seeds do not appear in *icchantikas*' minds by the force of direct causes. Pure seeds are planted indirectly in the form of shared seeds by virtue of upheaving conditions. From then on, the seeds of Buddha nature will appear in the minds of the ignorant ones. And so, after several rounds of rebirth, even the most incurable *icchantikas* can change their *gotra* membership and realize their Buddha nature through self-power. This transition, in turn, explains why the *gotra* system is not predeterminate but malleable and able to accommodate the possibility of change.

Moreover, Xuanzang and his disciples highlight the Bodhisattvas' compassion for the additional purpose of criticizing incorrect aspirations in the pursuit of awakening. Comparing and contrasting Xuanzang's translation of the *Vimalakīrtisūtra* with that of Kumārajīva, it can be discerned that in Devi's answer to Śāriputra's question on the existence of *arhat*, *pratyekabuddha*, and *buddha*, Xuanzang does not follow Kumārajīva in portraying their difference as illusory and non-existent (T14N475, P548a22–4). On the contrary, Xuanzang specifies how this difference serves a critical function. Indeed, fictitious names exist as the skillful means to criticize ignorance. Xuanzang perceives these names as integral parts of the language of secretive saying, which corresponds to Kuiji's delineation of Madhyamaka in his *sūtra* classification system and Huizhao's depiction of the last nature in his threefold concept of Buddha nature (T14N476, P574a3). This secretive saying has two aspects. First, those who make a compromise and do not aspire to achieve the highest goal of awakening do end up as an *arhat* or a *pratyekabuddha* in their religious pursuit. Nevertheless, they are not left behind by the Bodhisattvas. That is why the second aspect of this secretive saying confirms the all-inclusive compassion of Bodhisattvas. A compassionate Bodhisattva temporarily manifests as an *arhat* or a *pratyekabuddha* in order to use this manifestation as a critique of incorrect aspirations for guiding those in the hearer and solitary families back to the right path (T14N476, P574a4–9). To put it differently, Xuanzang affirms the existence of the hearer and solitary families so that his fellow Yogācārins can have a language at their disposal to criticize incorrect aspirations. Those who have deviated from the Bodhisattvas' path due to these incorrect aspirations, can also return to the right path once they stay close with their good spiritual friends *qua* the Bodhisattvas.

As such, it can be explained why Xuanzang and his disciples spare no effort to promote the five-*gotra* account. Their purpose is not to demean those with lower capacity, but rather to highlight the Bodhisattvas' compassion, through the power of whom even the most ignorant ones have the chance of being awakened. Therefore, what looks like a negation of *icchantikas* to attain awakening is in fact an affirmation of the compassion of the Bodhisattvas and a critique of incorrect aspirations in pursuing the Buddhist path. As remarked by modern Yogācāra scholar Lü Cheng, the existence of the sentient beings without Buddha nature reveals the great virtue of Buddhas and Bodhisattvas (Lü 1986: 433).

This profound care for *icchantikas* prompts Xuanzang and his disciples to criticize early Yogācāra's support of the viewpoint that all sentient beings have Buddha nature. As previously mentioned, the underlying conviction of this early view is expressed in the following way: Buddha nature is the luminous mind innate to all sentient beings, yet such luminosity can be cloaked provisionally, a metaphorical way of describing various kinds of mental defilements in everyday life. Thus, there arises the maxim, "the nature of the [luminous] mind is originally pure, only being polluted by guest dust *qua* mental defilements (心性本淨，客塵煩惱所染)" (T31N1585, P8c20). As scrutinized in the *CWSL*, this maxim poses a paradox. If the original mind is temporarily covered by the dust—namely, by misperceptions and mental defilements—is the mind in this covered state pure or impure? If it is pure, then the dust should also be pure, misperception should also be an insight, and defilement should also be awakening (T31N1585, P8c24). If it is not, no pure seeds would remain in consciousness, which makes awakening equally impossible (T31N1585, P8c26). Given this paradox intrinsic to the view of the originally pure mind, Xuanzang contends that Buddha nature is not an intrinsic quality inherent to all sentient beings but rather an ideality to be realized through a collaborative effort of these sentient beings. Such a realization yields the universal appearance of pure consciousness, with emptiness as the defining nature of the non-dual state of mind(s) (T31N1585, P9a6).

In their critique of the concept of the originally pure mind, Xuanzang and his disciples raise a more practical concern. As documented in the *CWSL*, it is important to keep the line between the awakened ones and the unawakened commoners (T31N1585, P9a1). Early Yogācārins remove this line but are unable to adequately explain why, if human nature (unawakened) is already Buddha nature (awake), sentient beings must engage in monastic training and Buddhist practice. The *gotra* system provides a plausible answer to this question, in that it preserves the empirical differences of sentient beings—some able to realize Buddha nature on their own and others incapable of doing so—and simultaneously promotes the possibility of changing their family membership through the collaborative effort of self-power and other-power. To realize these possibilities, sentient beings must undergo rigorous training to improve themselves. This training unravels through the five stages of consciousness-only (*weishi wuwei*唯識五位), which together points to the correct way of pursuing the Bodhisattvas' path.

Five Stages of Realizing Consciousness-only[15]

To realize Buddha nature and transform from the state of ignorance to the state of awakening, sentient beings need to engage in the right practice. For Yogācārins, sentient beings need to go through five stages to dependently evolve their consciousness into wisdom. They refer to such intensive training at the prescriptive level as the five stages (*wuwei* 五位, *pañca vasthā*) of realizing consciousness-only (T31N1585, P48b11). Wisdom is realized when sentient beings acquire two types of insight: first, they shall obtain the horizontal insight that removes all discriminative attachments to the self and to the dharmas, at the conceptual level; then, they will realize the vertical insight that dissolves all innate attachments and enables sentient beings to become one with emptiness at the habitual level. Positioning the investigation of the five stages of consciousness-only in the framework of these two insights, I propose that we understand the realization of awakening as a process that takes place both horizontally and vertically. The introduction in the current section sets the stage for an in-depth analysis of why Husserl provides a rather nascent account of the prescriptive level. I will further elaborate as to why Yogācāra Buddhism is much more than a Buddhist version of Husserlian phenomenology in the following chapter.

For Xuanzang, it is a gradual process of entering the gate of consciousness-only and realizing awakening. This process is the Yogācāra articulation of the Bodhisattvas' path that begins with the stage of accumulation (*ziliangwei* 資糧位, *saṃbhāravasthā*) (T31N1585, P48b11). As the name suggests, it is when practitioners accumulate good *karmic* merits by staying close to good causes, good friends, and good intentions (T31N1585, P48c2). Although these practitioners have resolved to pursue the Bodhisattvas' path, they are not ready for purifying their consciousness yet. Because of this, they need to accumulate positive conditions for further practice. That is why Xuanzang compares practitioners at this stage as the ones who reside outside of the gate of consciousness-only (T31N1585, P48c3).

By virtue of their faith and perseverance, these practitioners will be able to enter the gate of consciousness-only (T31N1585, P49a3). As such, they continue their practice at the second stage of preparation (*jiaxingwei* 加行位, *prayogāvasthā*) (T31N1585, P48b12). At this point, these sentient beings attain the capacity of conducting contemplative practices to remove misperceptions and attachments (T31N1585, P49a26). Advancing their training, they come to eradicate conceptual misperceptions, eliminate discriminative attachments, and attain horizontal insight (T31N1585, P49c4–7). Therefore, this stage is named after how it prepares practitioners for the initial awakening.

An initial awakening entails the eradication of both innate and discriminative attachments, as well as the habitual and conceptual misperceptions, which is the goal of the third stage of seeing (*tongdawei* 通達位, *prativedhāvasthā*) (T31N1585, P49c5). That is also the moment when practitioners acquire the vertical insight and become one with emptiness. By then, emptiness becomes the way of life for these sentient beings, which is described as the realization of non-dual wisdom (T31N1585, P49c19). Upon accomplishing their training at the first three stages, these practitioners have acquired the two insights through purifying their sixth and seventh consciousnesses. That is to say, they have also removed the obstructions of defilement and knowledge at both the conceptual and habitual levels. By then, the evolution of consciousness/*vijñāna* into wisdom/*jñāna*, as encapsulated in the concept of dependent-evolution, subsequently begins. The sixth consciousness evolves into the wisdom of wondrous observation (*miaoguanchazhi* 妙觀察智, *pratyavekṣanājñāna*), through which sentient beings perceive things as they actually are (T31N1585, P56b16). The seventh consciousness turns into the wisdom of equality (*pingdengxingzhi* 平等性智, *samatājñāna*), inspiring sentient beings to treat others as their interdependent equals (T31N1585, P56b20).

In light of the interconnectedness of the minds of all sentient beings, these practitioners come to realize that the universal awakening is impossible, if ignorance still exists in the cosmos. Such a realization furnishes these practitioners with the motivation to return to *saṃsāra* and guide ignorant ones on the right path. Thereupon, those who have attained the horizontal and vertical insights become Bodhisattvas who enter the fourth stage of refinement (*xiuxiwei* 修習位, *bhāvanāvasthā*) (T31N1585, P48b13). At the fourth stage, Bodhisattvas are resolved to conduct the ten perfect actions for helping the ignorant ones and, in turn, refining their own realization of emptiness (T31N1585, P51b8–18). They will ameliorate their collaboration with others, through ten grounds (*shidi* 十地, *daśa bhūmayaḥ*) consecutively (T31N1585, P50c21-3). As a result, these Bodhisattvas will realize dependent-evolution and achieve universal awakening, which consists of both the *nirvāṇa*/liberation of their own minds and the *bodhi*/enlightenment for other minds (T31N1585, P54c21).

Once the universal awakening is achieved, these awakened ones transform the cosmos into a pure dharma realm, which announces the arrival of the ultimate stage (*jiujingwei* 究竟位, *niṣṭhāvasthā*) (T31N1585, P57a14–19). Now that all the minds are purified and nothing can cultivate impure seeds, the eighth storehouse consciousness becomes the mirroring wisdom of great perfection (*dayuanjingzhi* 大圓鏡智, *ādarśajñāna*) that enables the practitioner to become aware of all beings that have existed throughout the entire cosmic history without grasping them as *svabhāva* (T31N1585, P56a16–b13). Likewise, the first five consciousnesses transform into the wisdom of accomplishment (*chengsuozuozhi* 成所作智, *kṛtyānuṣṭhānajñāna*), which facilitates the Bodhisattvas' vow of helping others (T31N1585, P56b26).

These four kinds of wisdom fulfill their functions respectively (T31N158, P57a1): the mirroring wisdom of great perfection lays the ground for practitioners to acquire a holistic perception of all things in the cosmos, including other minds, which in turn allows for the liberation of one's own mind from various pollutions (T31N1585, P57a2); the wisdom of equality enables practitioners to purify the image of others' bodies and of the realm where others reside, which consequently facilitates the awakening of other minds (T31N1585, P57a3); the wisdom of wondrous observation inspires practitioners to observe their actions, to reflect on their mistakes and merits (T31N1585, P57a5); and eventually, the wisdom of accomplishment allows practitioners to use their corporeal bodies in their specific spatiotemporal locale to guide others on the right path (T31N1585, P57a4). The cosmos then becomes a pure dharma realm, and the universal awakening is realized through the collaborative effort of all sentient beings. Therefore, differing from Husserl who does not specify whether the renewal of life is a sudden acquisition, Xuanzang and his disciples depict awakening as a significantly gradual process.

12

Revisiting the Process of Awakening

Thus far, we have examined how agency is possible and how sentient beings can exercise their agency to realize universal awakening. In our analysis of agency, we have clarified how Husserl understands agency as a crucial aspect of the *attitude* embraced by a person, whereas Xuanzang and his disciples situate the existence of agency in their theories of dependent arising and mental factors. Furthermore, these Chinese Yogācārins highlight the role of Bodhisattvas in the realization of universal awakening, which does not explicitly appear in Husserl's writings. Now, to elaborate on the ways in which Husserl provides a nascent account of the prescriptive level of consciousness, the current chapter explores three aspects of such a realization: meditation for each individual; moral actions in a community; and social construction. As I will argue, it is the elaborative system of awakening that makes Yogācāra Buddhism much more than a Buddhist version of Husserlian phenomenology.

Epoché and Yogācāra Contemplation

Contemplative practice, also known as meditative practice, is a foundational practice in Buddhism for acquiring insight into seeing things as they actually are (Hopkins 1983; Williams 2009). The function of contemplation, in this case, might strike us as rather close to the Husserlian notion of *epoché*, a notion that entails a two-step practice through which we suspend all our presumptions of factual reality and return to pure consciousness in order to have an insight of essence. Indeed, scholars have proposed interpreting the contemplative practice in the Yogācāra system as a Buddhist version of *epoché* (Cairns 1976; Lau 2007a; Xiao 2009; Mei 2014). Nevertheless, this interpretation has its own limitation. As to be explained in this section, the Yogācāra contemplation is much more systemic than a Buddhist version of *epoché*. That is to say, although the function of *epoché* is compatible with Yogācāra contemplative practice, the content of the two is far from being identical. This is the case for two main reasons: first, *epoché* is a two-step process—suspending assumptions and observing essence—of one practice, whereas Chinese Yogācārins like Xuanzang and his disciples perceive these two steps as two separate practices that are different by nature; and second, the contemplative practice outlined by Kuiji consists of five steps, which is broader than the philosophical speculation offered by Husserl.

To begin, let us recapitulate Husserl's articulation of *epoché*. Husserl evokes the concept of *epoché* to describe a two-step process of suspending previous assumptions in the natural attitude and observing mental acts in pure consciousness. The former is known as phenomenological reduction *qua* bracketing, whereas the latter becomes referred to as transcendental reduction *qua* seeing the essence (Hua 3/60). While enacting *epoché*, a person first suspends all assumptions about factually existent actuality, subsequently returning to the domain of pure consciousness in order to grasp the essential conditions for the possibility of phenomena that manifest themselves through intentionality (Hua 3/57–60). Those that can appear as phenomena in pure consciousness are not limited to factually real objects but are also inclusive of ideal ones. Seeing the essence does not entail seeing in its literal sense as seeing with the eyes, but rather implies figuratively how a person grasps in one stroke any state of affairs, universal idealized object, or *a priori* self-evident laws of knowledge. As expected by Husserl, by embracing the phenomenological attitude in virtue of *epoché*, people can liberate themselves from the natural attitude and return to an authentic way of thinking and living (Hua 6/259). Husserl later refers to the awakening from naturalism by virtue of *epoché* as the "renewal" (Hua 27/4). In the wake of the renewal, each individual will be able to remedy the crisis of meaning and regain a meaningful life.

There are clear parallels between *epoché* and the meditative practice of calming and contemplating (*zhiguan* 止觀, *śamathavipaśyanā*).[1] After all, *śamathavipaśyanā*, known as *zhiguan* in the Chinese language, also consists of two consecutive steps of calming (*zhi* 止, *śamatha*) and contemplating (*guan* 觀, *vipaśyanā*), which allows the practitioner to sweep misperceptions from the luminous mind (T45N1861, P259b2). As a popular practice for realizing Buddha nature, *zhiguan* is enacted by devotees in many Buddhist schools, including Tiantai and early Yogācāra.

Differing from early Yogācārins, Xuanzang and his disciples do not perceive calming and contemplating as two steps of one meditative practice. As specified by Kuiji, calming and contemplating are two separate practices that are dissimilar by nature. Moreover, he maintains that insight is immediately acquired through clear contemplation (T45N1861, P259a28). And so, instead of following the early Yogācāra practice of *zhiguan*, Kuiji envisions contemplative practice in the later Yogācāra framework to be *xianguan* (現觀, *abhisamaya*)—the literal meaning of which is immediate insight in Chinese and clear contemplation in Sanskrit (T45N1861, P259b4).

In understanding why Kuiji insists on demarcating the Yogācāra contemplative practice of *xianguan* (immediate insight) from the popular *zhiguan* (calming and concentrating), it is helpful to turn to his articulation of the immediate insight (T45N1861, 259a28–b7). Kuiji positions his analysis in the Yogācāra framework of consciousness-only whereby all mental factors, just like consciousnesses, have their distinct functions and arise in accordance with the fourfold intentional structure. In clarifying the intentional structure of contemplation, Kuiji first distinguishes the act of contemplating from the phenomenon to be contemplated (T45N1861, P258b19–20). For Kuiji, all dharmas can appear as phenomena for contemplation, insofar as emptiness is the salient feature of how things actually are (T45N1861, P258b20). That which can perform the act of contemplating amounts to one of the many mental factors. Among them, the mental factor of concentration (*ding* 定, *samādhi*) guides the mind to calm down, whereas the mental factor of reasoning (*hui* 慧, *prajñā*) enables contemplation (T45N1861, P259a28). Moreover, after acquiring the insight in contemplation, the sentient being is able to remove misperceptions produced by the seventh and sixth consciousnesses. In this process, only the mental factor of reasoning arises and accompanies both consciousnesses. The mental factor of concentration, whose function is calming, is not affiliated with the seventh consciousness. That is to say, the mental factor of concentration cannot enact contemplation to acquire insights and it is not always present together with the mental factor of reasoning either. Such a mental factor, therefore, retains the function of preparing the mental factor of reasoning to contemplate (T45N1861, P259b3). As such, calming and contemplation are demarcated as two separate practices by Xuanzang and his disciples because these two practices are enacted by dissimilar mental factors. Accordingly, these two practices cannot be merged into one, because reasoning is the only mental factor that can enact contemplation to acquire insight and remove misperception from consciousnesses.

Epoché, however, is distinct from the meditative practice elaborated by later Yogācārins. While Xuanzang and his disciples envisage calming and contemplating as two separate practices, Husserl depicts *epoché* as a unified practice with two steps. Moreover, these Chinese Yogācārins depict contemplation as a mental act that arises upon the sixth and seventh consciousnesses. In phenomenology, *epoché* is not articulated—at least not explicitly—by Husserl as an intentional mental act in the phenomenological attitude. That becomes the first reason why Yogācāra contemplation cannot be simplified as a Buddhist version of *epoché* in the Husserlian sense. Moreover, Husserl formulates *epoché* mainly as philosophical speculation, which can be contrasted with Kuiji's articulation of contemplation as a five-step religious practice known as the five ranks (*wuchong* 五重) of contemplating consciousness-only (*guan weishi* 觀唯識) (T45N1861, P258b20-1).

It goes to say that while engaging in contemplative practice, sentient beings first come to realize that everything in the experience arises from the functionality of consciousness and, therefore, is not *svabhāvic* (T45N1861, P258b23). The first rank of consciousness-only, thus, requires sentient beings to develop the insight of distinguishing the real existence of consciousness from the seemingly real transformation and the fictitiously real names in misperception (T45N1861, P258b21). Then, sentient beings come to understand how consciousness has an intentional structure since every consciousness and its mental factors give rise to the seeing part, the image part, the underlying self-awareness, and the awareness of the self-awareness (T45N1861, P258c16). As such, they realize the second rank of consciousness-only that determines how various objects in one's experience depend on consciousness to appear as image parts—namely, as perceivable phenomena (T45N1861, P258c18). Subsequently, sentient beings comprehend that, just like dharma, the self is also not *svabhāvic* but rather depends on consciousness to appear as the seeing parts (T45N1861, P258c29). That becomes the third rank of consciousness-only through which sentient beings acquire insight into how the mind serves as the necessary condition for all phenomena (T45N1861, P258c26). The fourth rank of consciousness-only is related to the relationship of consciousness and mental factors (T45N1861, P259a4). By then, sentient beings realize that mental factors transform themselves through the fourfold intentional structure the same way as consciousnesses (T45N1861, P259a5). Eventually, sentient beings become one with the impermanent nature of things in the cosmos (T45N1861, P259a12). In the last rank of consciousness-only, sentient beings realize the interdependence and irreducibility of the principle and the event, the nature and the image, and the *ti* and the *yong* (T45N1861, P259a13–14).

Upon accomplishing the five ranks of contemplation, sentient beings acquire the horizontal and vertical insights. While their consciousnesses continue to function, sentient beings no longer misperceive the seeing part and the image part as *svabhāva*, and instead realize the interdependence of things in the cosmos (T45N1861, P259a13). Kuiji refers to the entirety of consciousness in this state as the immaculate mind of suchness, which is not the same as emptiness but characterized by it (T45N1861, P259a14). In the five stages of realizing consciousness-only, sentient beings arrive at the third stage of seeing upon completing the five-rank contemplation.

Compared with Kuiji's articulation of contemplation, Husserl has yet to detail how such a change of attitude can happen through *epoché* or how one can attest to it. Furthermore, it is not clear whether Husserl perceives *epoché* as the beginning of a set of detailed practices that can inform one about how to regulate individual life or how to interact with others in a community. This is not the case for Xuanzang and his disciples.[2] As presented and preserved in the biographies of these Yogācārins, they engaged in intensive contemplation as part of their daily routine (T50N2053).[3] If we interpret Kuiji's articulation of the five ranks of contemplating consciousness-only as *epoché* in the Husserlian sense, then we overlook how Yogācārins like Kuiji systematize their theory of contemplation as a development of the concept of *xianguan* and in constant exchange with their interlocutors who favor the practice of *zhiguan*.

Empathy and Moral Actions[4]

As outlined by Xuanzang and his disciples, when sentient beings acquire vertical and horizontal insights of seeing things as they actually are, they come to realize the interconnectedness of various things in the cosmos. Such interconnectedness alludes to the larger collective consciousness and motivates sentient beings to conduct altruistic actions. Xuanzang and his disciples capture the collectivity of consciousness in their investigation of the knowledge of other minds. They contend that each sentient being does have direct knowledge of the minds of others through what is currently known as the second-person perspective. Considering how the second-person perspective reveals the interconnectedness of all I-subjects at the descriptive level, it can serve as the starting point for people to think about their moral responsibility towards their "fellow humans (*nebenmenschen*)" (Hua 27/21). While Husserl also unpacks how the second-person perspective is indispensable to people's experience at the descriptive level, he does not move any further in explaining how such a perspective justifies moral actions for others. As I will argue in this section, although Yogācārins express a view of the experience of other minds that shares a similar function with what Husserl refers to as empathy at the descriptive level, Chinese Yogācārins, like

Xuanzang and his disciples, explicitly link the second-person experience with moral actions and prescribe instructions for such actions.

In his later writings, such as *Cartesian Meditations*, Husserl begins to tackle the issue of solipsism. When exploring how each subject is not a closed system but interdependent with others, Husserl expands intentionality from that of the *I* to that of the *we*, further bringing to light the second-person perspective of experience. In this exploration, he depicts the ways in which the consciousness of each I-subject presupposes and is contextualized in the collective consciousness of the *we* as a plurality of I-subjects. As such, Husserl can make a case for intersubjectivity that maintains the irreducible individuality of each person in a community and highlights their collaborative effort in constituting the shared primordial lifeworld. In his own terms, "the constitution of the world essentially involves a harmony of the monads" (Hua 1/138), and "each of us has a lifeworld, meant as the world for all" (Hua 6/257). Now, since alterity is an indispensable part of each individual's experience, the consciousnesses of sentient beings are interconnected. In other words, the identity of each sentient being is correlated with—though not assimilable nor reducible to—the identities of others. As clarified later by Husserl, the essence of each I-subject consists in its being in the world and being with others.

All the I-subjects in a community collaborate primordially to constitute the shared lifeworld. Usually, they are not actively aware of such a primordial constitution, unless they are deprived of it. Prolonged solitary confinement epitomizes this type of deprivation. After observing how the experiential structure of prisoners has been impaired by prolonged solitary confinement, Lisa Guenther remarks that this punishment can distort the lifeworld of prisoners (Guenther 2011: 259). Drawing on Husserl's writings of the lifeworld, Guenther explains how prolonged solitary confinement cuts inmates off from concrete social engagement and forces them to leave the mutual constitution of lifeworld with others, which eventually becomes a form of violence against the transcendental structure of human experience (Guenther 2011: 270). She continues to question whether there is a legitimate justification for prolonged solitary confinement knowing how such punishments can damage an individual (Guenther 2011: 275). Although Husserl prepares a wealth of resources for justifying the moral responsibilities towards others, his view of ethics as such remains nascent.

Equally acknowledging the interconnectedness of sentient beings, Xuanzang and his disciples put forward a systematic theory of moral actions. In the wake of the immediate insight of seeing things as they actually are, Buddhist practitioners realize the self–other interdependence and willingly return to *saṃsāra* as Bodhisattvas to conduct altruistic actions for helping others. In return, these moral actions sustain and refine these Bodhisattvas' acquired insight. Keeping in mind the interplay between doing and knowing, Yogācāra Buddhists cultivate themselves incessantly in their daily practices so that altruism can become as habitual as second nature. This process of rehabituation consists in engaging the ten perfect actions (十勝行) (T31N1585, P51b8):

1. Giving (*bushi* 布施, *dāna*) through which the Bodhisattvas are willing to donate their material treasure to those in need, give support to others to alleviate their suffering, and transmit the Buddha's teaching to others (T31N1585, P51b8).

2. The precept (*jie* 戒, *śīla*) to which the Bodhisattvas are committed when adhering to the commandments, conducting good actions, and complying with altruistic values (T31N1585, P51b9).
3. Forbearance (*ren* 忍, *kṣānti*) through which the Bodhisattvas will learn to tolerate hatred from others, embrace suffering in practice, and uphold an unmoving mindset in observing things in the cosmos (T31N1585, P51b10).
4. Perseverance (*jingjin* 精進, *vīrya*) through which the Bodhisattvas will make an effort to muster up the courage to overcome hardship, ameliorate their own capacity of conducting good deeds, and persist in benefiting others (T31N1585, P51b11–12).
5. Quiet rumination (*jinglü* 静慮, *dhyāna*) through which the Bodhisattvas will calm down their minds through living, in meritorious actions, and in benefiting others (T31N1585, P51b13).
6. Cognition (*bore* 般若, *prajña*) through which the Bodhisattvas will acquire non-discriminative cognition of the emptiness of the self, non-discriminative cognition of the emptiness of dharma, and non-discriminative cognition of overall emptiness (T31N1585, P51b14).
7. The skillful means (*fangbian* 方便, *upāya*) by which the Bodhisattvas will teach the truth of emptiness in an accessible manner, further enabling the transfer of their *karmic* merits to other sentient beings, and the return to *saṃsāra* to guide others on the right path (T31N1585, P51b15–16).
8. The vows (*yuan* 願, *praṇidhāna*) that the Bodhisattvas will make to achieve universal awakening and not leave any sentient beings behind (T31N1585, P51b16).
9. Resolve (*li* 力, *bala*) that the Bodhisattvas will exercise in knowing and doing (T31N1585, P51b17).
10. Wisdom (*zhi* 智, *jñāna*) realized by these Bodhisattvas to be self-benefiting and other-benefiting, through which they can see things as they are and guide all sentient beings to end suffering (T31N1585, P51b18).

These perfect actions are enacted by practitioners in all five stages of the Bodhisattvas' path. Yet, it is only at the fourth stage of refinement that these actions play a crucial role (T31N1585, P52b3–4). Xuanzang explains why this is the case. In the first two stages, practitioners have only attained an initial understanding of emptiness, and therefore some of the seeds for these perfect actions in the storehouse consciousness remain polluted by previous actions (T31N1585, P52b5). Even until the third stage of seeing, when devotees finally manage to acquire insights and remove attachments, some impure seeds remain inside the storehouse consciousness of these practitioners (T31N1585, P52b5). It is only by performing the ten perfect actions during the fourth stage of refinement that the Bodhisattvas are able to purify all the seeds prior to entering the final, ultimate stage (T31N1585, P52b6–8). Thereby, at the stage of refinement, the Bodhisattvas spare no effort in conducting the ten perfect actions, further purifying the actualized perceptions and actions and the unactualized seeds. Towards the end of this stage, they will be able to eradicate every possibility of misperception, attachment, and obstruction, be it at the conceptual level or the habitual one. By then, they will be able to realize dependent-evolution, attaining liberation of one's own mind and enlightenment for other minds (T31N1585, P51a21). And so as can be seen, while the ethical aspect remains nascent in Husserl's phenomenology, Yogācārins have provided a more elaborate and explicit account of moral actions, which further indicates why Yogācāra Buddhism cannot be assimilated into Husserlian phenomenology.

Communal Renewal and Social Construction[5]

As previously discussed, Xuanzang and his disciples contend that it is not enough to purify the mind of simply one sentient being. Considering the interdependence and interconnectedness of all sentient beings in the collective consciousness, true awakening will be realized when all consciousnesses are purified from misperceptions and attachments. It is through the collaborative effort of all sentient beings that consciousness can transform into wisdom and the cosmos can become a pure dharma realm. The idea of constituting an ideal realm through collaborative effort is entertained by Husserl in his proposal of a communal renewal that liberates Europe from its crisis of meaning. That is why Husserl envisions that a phenomenological version of ethics shall consist of two correlated aspects as the individual ethics (*Individualethik*) and the social ethics (*Sozialethik*) (Hua 27/21). As I will argue in this section, although the function of such communal renewal is compatible with that in Yogācāra Buddhism—the function being the liberation of all sentient beings from suffering and ensuring the flourishing of life—the content of social construction is closely related to the conception of Pure Land in Yogācāra Buddhism, which remains distinct from Husserl's view of communal renewal (Hua 27/31). That said, a subtle issue of elitism becomes inherent in both Husserl's call for a phenomenological renewal of community and Yogācārins' commitment to social reformation. To be more specific, they are confident that a group of advanced sentient beings will take the lead in building the ideal society. The question remains as to whether these advanced sentient beings, who might still become corrupt, should possess more power and authority than others.

Husserl expresses his views on social construction in the *Kaizo* articles. Witnessing how naturalism results in a crisis of meaning in Europe, Husserl not only appeals to a rehabitualization of the individual life but also advocates for a renewal of communal culture (Hua 27/30). In this sense, the call for renewal alludes to Husserl's deliberation on the urgency of becoming awake (*erwacht*) to genuine humanity (Hua 27/51). Just as for each individual, a remedy to the crisis of meaning is contingent on awakening from the natural attitude and accepting the phenomenological attitude. The phenomenological renewal of communal life takes place through the collaborative effort of community members in reforming the current culture towards that of a more authentic life. As per Husserl, when a group of individuals liberate themselves through conducting *epoché*, they acquire insight of true essence as being more fully in the world and being with others, so they will naturally have the desire to make the community a better place for themselves and for other community members (Hua 27/46). Awakened from the natural attitude, these individuals undertake the responsibility of convincing others, through providing ethical instructions, to inspire and enlighten more members of the community (Hua 28/52–4). Here, Husserl offers insight into how the well-being of each individual human is interdependent with their fellow humans in a community and how a better community will appear through a collaborative effort. So, while he lays out the principles for community building, Husserl does not detail the mechanics of such a communal renewal (Buckley 2019: 18).

Xuanzang and his disciples have expressed a compatible view of Husserl's concept of renewal in the idea of dependent-evolution as their expression of a universal awakening that brings about *nirvāṇa*/liberation of one's own mind and *bodhi*/enlightenment for other minds. Once consciousness evolves into wisdom, all misperceptions together with attachments and obstructions will be removed from both the actualized ones—*viz.* perceptions and actions—and the unactualized seeds in the eighth consciousness of sentient beings. This eighth consciousness will turn into the mirroring wisdom of great perfection and those who realize this wisdom will be able to access the subtle transformation of the storehouse consciousness, becoming further aware of the minds of sentient beings throughout every phase of the cosmic history without grasping them as *svabhāva* (T31N1585, P56a12–16). The seventh consciousness evolves into the wisdom of equality through which sentient beings embrace otherness as an indispensable part of their experience (T31N1585, P56a17–19). Subsequently, they feel the innate compassion of treating other beings impartially throughout cosmic history (T31N1585, P56a20–1). The sixth consciousness purifies itself into the wisdom of wondrous observation that helps sentient beings perceive various dharmas in the cosmos without misconceiving them as *svabhāva* (T31N1585, P56a21–5). The first five consciousnesses evolve into the wisdom of accomplishment and enable sentient beings to perceive objects throughout cosmic history (T31N1585, P56a26–8). As such, the evolution of consciousness into wisdom brings about the universal awakening of all sentient beings in the cosmos.

While Husserl does not depict the mechanics of such an awakening, Chinese Yogācārins like Xuanzang and his disciples outline such mechanics in the theory of three bodies (*sanshen*三身, *trikāya*).[6] Throughout history, the notion of three bodies has been utilized by Buddhist clergy to explain why the Buddha extends the body beyond the physical material form (Williams 2009: 173–4). In the wake of Cartesian dualism, it is natural for scholars to distinguish the mind from the body and the space, as if they are three separate entities. To be more specific, while the mind has been perceived as an interior entity to be disconnected from the material body and physical space, the body has been reduced to the material form as the *corpus* which occupies a locus and can move in the extended space. Against such mind–body dualism, Yogācārins like Xuanzang and his disciples problematize the boundary of the interior mind, the exterior body, and the extended space, so that the body is an embodied space of the mind.[7]

There are three further types of embodied space known as the dharma body, the enjoyment body, and the emanation body. Concerning the second of these, the purified eighth consciousness as the mirroring wisdom of great perfection manifests as the self-enjoyment body (*zishouyongshen* 自受用身, *svasaṃbhogakāya*) (T31N1585, P58a25). That is to say, this mirroring wisdom enables the awakened ones to perceive the holistic image of all things in the cosmos (T45N1861, P360a3). In a figurative sense, it seems that the bodies of the Buddhas are able to purely reflect and manifest the entirety of cosmic history as it actually is (T31N1585, P58a26–7). Since this self-enjoyment body is pure, the reflection on the mirroring wisdom of great perfection is devoid of any *svabhāvic* views, which becomes a source of the endless enjoyment of attaining liberation (T31N1585, P58c1–3).

Given that each sentient being is interdependent on one another throughout beginningless time, the purified seventh consciousness, now known as the wisdom of equality, gives rise to the other-enjoyment body (*tashouyongshen* 他受用身, *parasaṃbhogakāya*) (T31N1585, P58a24). Through the power of this other-enjoyment body, the Buddhas and Bodhisattvas are able to manifest various Pure Lands for the purpose of benefiting other sentient beings, including even the most ignorant *icchantikas* (T45N1861, P369a22). These Lands of Bliss—*inter alia*, those of Amitābha, Bhaiṣajyaguru, or Maitreya—attest to the great compassion of the Buddhas and Bodhisattvas. From time to time, they manifest their emanation body (*bianhuashen* 變化身, *nirmāṇakāya*) and temporally take on an illusory material form in virtue of the wisdom of accomplishment, the purpose of which is to confront sentient beings with their ignorance and guide them on the right path towards awakening (T31N1585, P58c14).

To foreground how emptiness defines the nature of things in the cosmos and how the pure dharma realm serves as the principle of change, Xuanzang and his disciples compare emptiness to the dharma body (*fashen* 法身, *dharmakāya*) that penetrates the arising and perishing of illusory dharmas (T31N1585, P57a12). Such a dharma body is also the pure dharma realm (T31N1585, P57a18). The entire cosmos is, thus, the embodied space for the awakened ones.

Since Yogācārins aim to realize the universal awakening of all sentient beings, they contend that only the pure dharma realm—as the realm of the awakened ones—has real existence. In contrast, various types of other-enjoyment bodies, otherwise known as the Pure Lands, are not ultimately real but rather serve as skillful means. Buddhist scriptures usually depict these lands of bliss manifested by the Buddhas and Bodhisattvas as the heavenly realms where pious devotees can ascend upon death if they manage to collect enough *karmic* merits during the current life cycle. Kuiji comes to depict these lands of bliss differently—not as an ultimately real transcendent realm, but rather as a temporarily real perfect society (T45N1861, P369b16).

In understanding Kuiji's concept of the Pure Land, it is helpful to recall our discussion on self-power and other-power in Chapter 11. Although Kuiji highlights the wondrous power of the Bodhisattvas' compassion, he is adamant that other-power is only a skillful means to awakening, rather than the ultimate method of such. After being guided to the gate of Yogācāra practice by the Bodhisattvas, sentient beings need to complete the journey throughout the five levels of consciousness-only themselves. Related to this line of reasoning, when the Bodhisattvas return to *saṃsāra* to help others, they use their compassion to construct a Pure Land (T45N1861, P369b21). They do not create a heavenly realm but rather collaborate to build an ideal society in which sentient beings will be furnished with sufficient resources and conditions for pursuing the Bodhisattvas' Path (T45N1861, P371a20). After being born and reborn in this ideal society, these ignorant sentient beings begin to familiarize themselves with wisdom and compassion. Gradually, they regain pure seeds in their minds and are then motivated to pursue goodness. From there onward, they purify their own minds through self-power and realize their self-enjoyment body by following the five stages of realizing consciousness-only (T45N1861, P371c5). As such, their life in this ideal society becomes a preparatory step for these sentient beings to achieve full awakening.

This discussion of Kuiji's approach to the Pure Land gives practical meaning to the interpretation of the Yogācāra worldview, which is interpreted as transcendental idealism *qua* correlative non-dualism. To be more specific, it shows that as sentient beings, we cannot determine the existence of the dharma body nor that of the pure dharma realm. However, we can exercise our intersubjective agency in changing how this dharma body appears for us and how we live in it. If we misperceive things in the cosmos as *svabhāva*, the dharma body manifests to us as the polluted realm, the realm of suffering—or in Buddhist terms, as *sahālokadhātu* (娑婆世界). Yet, upon purifying and removing these misperceptions and subsequent attachments, we embrace and immerse ourselves with the dharma body. Therefore, the existence of the enjoyment body suggests the non-dual transformation of the *sahālokadhātu* and the *dharmadhātu*. Indeed, the enjoyment body as an ideal society prepares sentient beings to make a collaborative effort to transform the polluted realm *qua sahālokadhātu* into the pure dharma realm (T45N1861, P372b29). The ideal society, as Kuiji indicates, is not a heavenly realm of transcendent existence to which we ascend upon death (T45N1861, P372b24–5). That is to say, the Bodhisattvas return to *saṃsāra* and help ignorant sentient beings by together constituting a Pure Land as an ideal society in *saṃsāra*. In this ideal society, ignorant sentient beings can accelerate the process of purifying their minds, cultivating pure seeds, and realizing the universal awakening. As such, every one of us has the responsibility of committing to the ten perfect actions and contributing to the realization of the pure dharma realm.

Xuanzang and his disciples are known for their faith in Maitreya's Pure Land, a faith that conveys their determination in building a perfect society ideal for pursuing the Bodhisattvas' path with the help of Maitreya Bodhisattva. As detailed by Xuanzang's disciple Kuiji, when sentient beings have done their best to perfect their society, Maitreya Bodhisattva will descend to the human realm and be reborn as a human to guide sentient beings in constituting the Pure Land on earth (T38N1772, P295b3). By then, all sentient beings will be reborn in the home of Maitreya and live in the land of bliss.[8] Thereafter and together with Maitreya, they will finalize their journey on the Bodhisattvas' path and realize the universal awakening in the pure dharma realm. As such, stemming from self–other interconnectedness, there arises the gist of Yogācāra Buddhism, its examination of consciousness at the descriptive level, its elaboration on emptiness at the explicative level, and its aspiration of a universal awakening at the prescriptive level.

Although Husserl provides a nascent account of awakening to genuine humanity through outlining the basic principles of renewing the European culture, he does not detail the mechanics of such a phenomenological renewal. It is the theory of awakening at the prescriptive level that eventually makes Yogācāra much more elaborate in this regard than Husserlian phenomenology. Nevertheless, as examined in this section, both Husserl and Chinese Yogācārins underscore how a group of more advanced individuals, represented by the ones who enact the phenomenological attitude and the Bodhisattvas, shall take the lead in perfecting a society. Positioning this viewpoint in the current context, we can clearly discern the subtle elitism in their proposals. Considering that Xuanzang and his disciples have proposed the possibility for advanced individuals to become corrupt in social interaction, we might want to question how to regulate these elites, on whom power and authority are conferred. On this front, both Husserl and Chinese Yogācārins do not provide us with any clear answers, which becomes another limitation of their theory of social construction.

Epilogue

Over the previous chapters, we have traveled alongside Husserl and Chinese Yogācārins like Xuanzang and his disciples, examining the perceived incompatibility that arises when scholars try to read Yogācāra Buddhism as a Buddhist version of Husserlian phenomenology. Husserl affirms the existence of essence and defines phenomenology as the science of essence, whereas Xuanzang and his disciples negate the existence of *svabhāva*—a term that is often translated as essence in English. Through our analysis, we have explained how the problem of essence is no longer an obstacle for the current project, which opens the door for a comparative study of the two.

In depicting our study as a four-part "journey," we began by elaborating on what this journey would entail, as we expounded on our methodologies. After scrutinizing previous approaches to comparative philosophy, we clarified how the "both–and" approach can avoid assimilating various traditions into a third entity and refrain from treating these traditions as mutually exclusive. Employing this approach, we positioned Husserl's phenomenology and Chinese Yogācāra philosophy in their respective context and linguistic system. For intercultural dialogues, depicting the context is important in that ideas are cultivated—though not always produced—by the greater sociopolitical climate in which they came to be. Contextualizing phenomenology and Yogācāra, we managed to eschew the overgeneralization and misrepresentation of their viewpoints, which marked the first step in overcoming Orientalism. As such, we traveled into the plurality of lived realities in these traditions as an endeavor to secure a middle ground for our study. This middle ground transpired when we presented the framework for comparing phenomenology and Yogācāra, a framework that outlined three levels—namely, the descriptive, the explicative, and the prescriptive levels—of both philosophical systems.

At the descriptive level of both intellectual traditions, Husserl's notion of intentionality can be related to Xuanzang and his disciples' view of the intentional structure of consciousness, although the two are not completely identical. To unpack this viewpoint, we have examined four phases in Husserl's philosophical thinking process through which he continued to enrich the notion of intentionality. We have also explored how Husserl's formulation of intentionality can be related to the articulation of consciousness in the writings of Xuanzang and his disciples—especially to their translation of *vijñāna* and *vijñapti* as consciousness and to their definition of the fourfold structure of consciousness. Returning to Husserl, we investigated how Xuanzang and his disciples' depiction of the intentional feature of mental acts complicated and complemented the Husserlian notion of intentionality. Traveling on the same "road," Husserl and these Chinese Yogācārins utilized their conceptions of intentionality to depict the origin of knowledge and highlight the function of intuition. Their contributions to the discussion of non-conceptuality problematize the overgeneralized East–West dichotomy at the center of Orientalism.

As we have seen, the "tracks" diverged at the explicative level where Husserl and the Chinese Yogācārins explained the ultimate nature of reality based on their own studies of intentionality. In his critique of naturalism, Husserl defined essence in contrast with factuality and utilized essence to capture that which defines things as they actually are. He, therefore, envisaged phenomenology as a science of essence. Xuanzang and his disciples, in their investigation of what defines things as they are, stressed that everything in the cosmos had no essential core and was therefore not *svabhāva*. As such, a perceived incompatibility transpired. We have coined the term "problem of essence" to capture this divergence, which indicated how Husserl and these Yogācārins seemed to have incongruent attitudes towards essence. After clarifying that what Husserl meant by essence was not the same as what Xuanzang and his disciples meant by *svabhāva*, we resolved this potential conflict. This solution further allowed us to interpret the worldview expressed by Husserl and these Yogācārins as transcendental idealism, which entailed a version of correlative non-dualism of the mind and the world, of the organism and its surroundings, and of self-mind and other minds. Although the problem of essence did not undermine our comparative study, it was hardly irrelevant. Investigating the problem of essence brought to the forefront important implications for a comparative study of philosophical traditions in a multicultural, multilingual context, beyond Orientalism.

Husserl and the Chinese Yogācārins arrived at the "destination" of their investigation of consciousness, a place where their philosophical insights informed their respective articulations of achieving awakening at the prescriptive level. Husserl's view of becoming awake to genuine humanity was rather nascent, in that he outlined basic principles for agency, liberation, contemplation, moral action, and social construction, but he did not detail the mechanics of a phenomenological renewal of individual and communal life. In contrast, Xuanzang and his disciples put forward an elaborate system of moral actions and religious practice known as the Bodhisattvas' path.

Throughout our journey, we have experimented with the "both-and" approach in comparative philosophy. Our experiment explored what is involved when a comparison is made across a cultural, historical, and linguistic divide. The goal of this study, therefore, is to clarify how the recognition and resolution of these perceived incompatibilities can advance our understanding of philosophical traditions in a multicultural and multilingual world. On the one hand, we come to see how the prescriptive level of Yogācāra Buddhism makes it much more than a Buddhist version of Husserlian phenomenology, and on the other, we can discern the nascent version of awakening in Husserl's phenomenology. We also observe the subtle elitism in both systems of thought. Comparing traditions in this manner, we *both* position them in their own context for exploring the middle ground *and* enable them to move into a broader horizon for further conversations and collaborations on shared philosophical questions. That is why the resolution of the problem of essence becomes a refutation of the East–West dichotomy at the center of Orientalism and a realization of the correlative non-duality of philosophical thoughts in the world of multiculturalism.

Indeed, what underpins Orientalism is the style of thinking that overgeneralizes philosophical traditions in terms of the East–West dichotomy. In light of this dichotomy, the East and the West are (mis)presented as a-spatiotemporal, a-historical, monolingual entities that are polar opposite and mutually exclusive to one another. Once this overgeneralized bifurcation becomes internalized as an indisputable philosophical presupposition in our worldview, we are not only being confronted with a set of philosophical problems exemplified by the problem of essence, but also being rendered incapable of finding a plausible approach to recognize and resolve these problems. The specters of Orientalism continue to stay with us. Inevitably, we arrive at the synthetic approach in which one dominant culture propels other cultures to homogenize or the juxtapositional approach that uses a radical understanding of difference to perpetuate the superiority of a particular culture. Nonetheless, once we eschew such overgeneralization and explore possibilities beyond mutual exclusivity, we are able to fully tackle the problem of essence. It means that we open our eyes to the rich nuance of this term "essence" by taking into account how it has been used in different languages by thinkers from various intellectual traditions throughout history. Mindful of such nuance, we come to see the possibility of locating a middle ground between our protagonists. It is partly because Husserl problematizes the absolutist understanding of essence, and Xuanzang and his disciples distance themselves from nihilism in their refutation of *svabhāva*, partly also because both Husserl and these Chinese Yogācārins embrace correlative non-dualism in their treatment of essence.

That is why eventually, our attitude determines the recognition and the resolution of a philosophical problem. As elucidated by both Husserl and these Chinese Yogācārins, it is eventually up to us to decide whether we want to tackle these problems and live a life of mutual flourishing. The functionality of consciousness gives us an open possibility. The practical meaning of correlative non-dualism is that we can always make an effort to reform and transform ourselves. Even when we come from traditions that seem to present incompatible viewpoints, we can still find a way to reflect upon those unquestioned philosophical presuppositions in our worldview, try to meet with others in the middle, and expand the shared horizon. If this is the case, then we need new theoretical tools and hermeneutic apparatuses to redefine recognition, redistribute the discursive resources in the field of philosophy, and represent the diversity of philosophical traditions beyond the East–West overgeneralization. Comparative philosophy, as outlined in this book, promotes the "both–and" approach that encapsulates correlative non-dualism. As such, it furnishes us with the tools for traveling in a plurality of lived realities across a cultural, historical, and linguistic divide.

The journey of recognizing and resolving philosophical problems in comparative philosophy, represented by the problem of essence in this book, does not lead us back to the starting point to cancel these problems for good, but rather deepens our understanding of these systems of thought. That is why traveling is a transformative process that changes the travelers together with the space traveled. It is and will always be a challenge to step out of the lived reality in which we find ourselves comfortable. Nevertheless, once we muster up the courage to leave our respective cultural comfort zones, we can both embark upon and enjoy a journey towards a broader horizon where we can thrive together in a multicultural world. And so, we must end our journey, all the while remembering that every ending is itself a new beginning.

Notes

Prologue

1 For a detailed study of Husserl's notes on Buddhism, see Fred Hanna 1995. Although Husserl seemed to envision a possibility for intercultural philosophy, he expressed a rather ambivalent viewpoint on non-European philosophical traditions, as he acknowledged the value of non-European perspectives all the while perpetuating a Eurocentric point of view (Buckley 2019: 20). Such an ambivalence has animated much scholarly debate on Husserl's approach to intercultural philosophy (Welton 1991; Steinbock 1994; Yu 2012).

2 One of the earliest monographs was composed in 1934 by Kitayama Junyu in this book *Metaphysik des Buddhismus* (Metaphysics of Buddhism). Since Kitayama did not directly compare Yogācāra with phenomenology but remained proficient in both traditions, scholars represented by Shiba Haruhide (1998) and Liangkang Ni (2010) continue to debate the extent to which his book was a phenomenological reading of Yogācāra ideas. Among the next generation of Husserlian scholars, Iso Kern penned several articles to bring Xuanzang into dialogue with Husserl (Kern 1992). Inspired by Kern, Zhang Qingxiong published a book in the Chinese language to compare Husserl's phenomenology with Xiong Shili's "new doctrine of consciousness-only (*xin weishilun* 新唯識論)" (Zhang 1995). Presenting an overview of both philosophical systems, Zhang did not explore the shared ground of these thinkers. Outside the Chinese language scholarship, Tao Jiang investigated the deep structures of consciousness in Xuanzang's account of the eighth consciousness *ālaya*, Karl Jung's depiction of unconsciousness, and Husserl's notion of transcendental consciousness, in his dissertation (Jiang 2001). Although Jiang (2006) focused more on psychoanalysis in the later published book, his stress of the importance of contextuality in comparative philosophy remains a source of inspiration for my project. At almost the same time when Jiang defended his dissertation, Dan Lusthaus (2002) published a monograph that engaged with Xuanzang's philosophical system. Lusthaus described his project of Buddhist phenomenology as a translation of Yogācāra philosophy in phenomenological terms (Lusthaus 2002: viii). Although Lusthaus underscored that he did not intend to reveal the third entity above phenomenology and Yogācāra (Lusthaus 2002: vii), his study makes it clear how phenomenology can enrich Yogācāra studies, yet it remains unknown what phenomenology can learn from Yogācāra philosophy. Back to the East Asian scholarship, Ng Yu-Kwan (aka. Wu Rujun) outlined a project of Yogācāra phenomenology that used Husserl's phenomenology as a framework for interpreting Yogācāra ideas. In his book, Ng centered his research on Indian Yogācāra philosophy developed by Vasubandhu, subsequently distancing himself from Xuanzang's theory (Ng 2002). Vasubandhu remained a focal point for Shiba Haruhide's comparative study of phenomenology and Yogācāra (Shiba 2003). In general, Yogācāra philosophy developed by Vasubandhu and other masters in Indo-Tibetan Buddhism has attracted

a lot of scholarly attention (Arnold 2012; Coseru 2012; Garfield 2015). Drawing upon their findings, I think a comparative study between these two traditions can be substantially advanced if we propose a detailed account of the methodology to allow for the possibility of recognizing and resolving the problem of essence that has constantly been glossed over in the field.

3 Here I follow previous scholars represented by Dan Lusthaus (2003), Zhihua Yao (2005), Erik Hammerstrom (2014), John Jorgensen (2014), Chen-Kuo Lin (2014), in referring to the tradition as Chinese Yogācāra. It shall be noted that the term "Chinese" is mainly used to describe the ways in which classical Chinese was the canonical language shared by East Asian Yogācārins at that time. A more detailed account of the usage of this term can be found in Chapter 2.

4 While T.R.V. Murti (1955) and Iso Kern (1992) have interpreted the Yogācāra approach to consciousness as phenomenological, it is fair to state that the term "Buddhist Phenomenology" is popularized by Dan Lusthaus in his book *Buddhist Phenomenology* (Lusthaus 2002).

5 Although numerous scholars have related to the tension between Buddhism and the contemporary philosophy of mind, they tend to put it aside as they focus on epistemology. For instance, Dan Arnold notices that the Indian Yogācāra master Dharmakīrti has expressed ambivalent views by defining reality as existing on its own and defying the description of reality as self-determined (Arnold 2012: 47). Yet, Arnold refrains from further examination of the said incommensurability. Similarly, in his investigation of the intentional structure of consciousness, Christian Coseru categorizes Dharmakīrti's ambivalent stance toward *svabhāva* as one of the many inconsistencies in Buddhist philosophy, but he perceives these inconsistencies as the limitation of the human mind (Coseru 2012: 39–41). Dan Lusthaus also stays away from issues related to the concept of essence by proposing to read the Buddhist negation of *svabhāva* as an epistemic conditionality, not as an ontological commitment (Lusthaus 2002: 6). His approach has been criticized by Alexander Mayer (Mayer 2009: 192–4). In part, the ways in which scholars shun the problem of essence expose a limitation in their methodology, which we will explore in Chapter 1.

6 The critique cumulated in the critical Buddhism movement since Buddhist scholars Hakamaya Noriaki (1997) and Matsumoto Shirō (1997) scrutinized the doctrine of *tathāgatagarbha* and explored how this doctrine made East Asian Buddhism less committed to social transformation. Almost at the same time, Robert Sharf (1993) and Brian Victoria (1997) detailed how D. T. Suzuki read *satori*, namely, the experience of sudden awakening, as an essence of Zen and construed Zen as a phenomenology of religious experience. We will explain the philosophical and political issues in Suzuki's expression of Zen in Chapter 1.

7 Followers of the Greater Vehicle *qua* Mahāyāna belittle non-Mahāyāna Buddhism as the Lesser Vehicle (Hīnayāna), a demeaning term that contemporary scholars have chosen to eschew (Collins 1982: 21). It is equally inaccurate to equate "Hīnayāna" with "Theravāda" (Silk 2002: 356). Therefore, we will either replace the said derogatory term with "early Buddhist philosophy," "pre-Mahāyāna Buddhist thinking," or "non-Mahāyāna thoughts inside the Buddhist community," etc. based on the context, or use the names of specific schools directly, such as Sarvāstivāda and Sautrāntika.

8 I coined the term "problem of essence" in the 2016 article "Buddhist Phenomenology and the Problem of Essence" in *Comparative Philosophy* (Li 2016: 59–89). However, the articulation of this problem at the time was too general and overly concise as I was unable to explore the nuance of the concept of essence in Husserl's phenomenology

and Chinese Yogācāra in that article. This book, therefore, brings forward a more advanced understanding of this problem.
9. I briefly mentioned the three-level framework in the 2017 article "From Self-Attaching to Self-Emptying" in *Open Theology* (Li 2017: 185). However, I did not elucidate upon the meaning of these three levels, nor did I relate these three levels to the writings of Husserl and Chinese Yogācārins. These limitations, however, will be addressed and overcome in this book.
10. Charles Taylor has unpacked how the sense of the self becomes progressively more inward in the wake of modernization in his book *Sources of the Self* (Taylor 1989).

1 Overcoming Orientalism with Multiculturalism

1. Garfield & Van Norden's editorial has received numerous comments. See https://www.nytimes.com/2016/05/11/opinion/if-philosophy-wont-diversify-lets-call-it-what-it-really-is.html.
2. In his book, Van Norden details how the lack of non-Euro-American philosophies reinforces the stereotype that these traditions are in some way inferior and backward (Van Norden 2017: 16). To complement the story outlined by Van Norden, I trace the ways in which the misrepresentation of these traditions can take on not just one but actually two different forms of Orientalism.
3. In his discussion, Taylor (1992) differentiates three types of recognition that I reformulate as the politics of universalism, the politics of difference, and the politics of recognizing the equal, irreducible value and worth of cultures. Although Taylor does not detail the last type of recognition, he considers it as the "midway between the inauthentic and homogenizing demand for recognition of equal worth, on the one hand, and the self-immurement within ethnocentric standards, on the other" (Taylor 1992: 72). To avoid confusion, I decide to refer to the first two not-so-authentic types of recognition by their respective names and determine the third type as *the* version of recognition promoted by Taylor. Here I also want to stress that Max Müller's project of universal religion exemplifies an extreme form of the politics of universalism while D. T. Suzuki's model exhibits an extreme form of the politics of difference. I italicize the term "extreme" to highlight how the said two models are mutually exclusive, which is not necessarily the case for other versions of the politics of universalism and difference. In a different context, the politics of universalism and the politics of difference can have their own constructive roles. Moreover, the extreme form of difference shall be demarcated from what Audre Lorde refers to as the "non-dominant difference" that underscores the interdependence of mutual difference instead of promoting the subordination of one group over another (Lorde 1984: 111). Readers will be able to discern a sharp contrast between the extreme form of the politics of difference and that of non-dominant difference. While the former perpetuates dominance, the latter problematizes this entire dichotomy of domination–subordination (Lugones 2014). To this end, the concept of non-dominant difference bespeaks the need for recognition, which is in line with Taylor's politics of recognizing the equal value and worth of cultures.
4. In this sense, recognition and redistribution are interrelated in our methodology insofar as the recognition of the equal, irreducible value and worth of cultures will open the door to the redistribution of various types of resources—not limited to socio-economic ones but also discursive ones—in a multicultural society. Since I have

not expanded my scope to critical issues related to economic injustice in this book, I confine my discussion mainly to the politics of recognition. Nevertheless, it does not mean I downplay the importance of the politics of redistribution as articulated by Nancy Fraser (2003; 2007) in her ground-breaking work.

5 I mainly turn to Max Müller and D. T. Suzuki to explain these two approaches since there has been more or less a consensus in the fields of philosophy and religious studies on the contribution and limitation of these two thinkers. They are, of course, hardly the only two scholars to be identified as proponents of the extreme forms of the politics of universalism and the politics of difference. I hereby leave it to the readers to deliberate on who else could be included among the same positions as taken by Müller or Suzuki.

6 In comparing and contrasting Zen with European philosophy, Suzuki puts forward these viewpoints in *Essays in Zen Buddhism First Series* (Suzuki 1927) and *Shin Buddhism* (Suzuki 1970).

7 Here, I use the term "existential crisis" to describe a crisis of meaning in which people find it hard to relate themselves meaningfully to their everyday life. This crisis captured the attention of many thinkers in the early 1900s, including Suzuki and, as we will see shortly afterward, Edmund Husserl.

8 As diving further into the topic of imperialism in modern Japan is beyond the scope of this book, I will not delve any further into this topic. Nevertheless, Masao Maruyama has detailed what I refer to as the extreme form of the politics of difference that facilitated the rise of "Japanese Ultranationalism" (Maruyama 1963), as well as Japan's transformation into an imperial power after the shortly bloomed Taishō democracy in the 1930s (Maruyama 1975). For more discussion on how Japanese imperialism was justified under the guise of resisting white imperialism, see Maurice B. Jansen 1984; Mark R. Peattie 1984; Peter Duus 1984; William Gerald Beasley 1987; Louise Young 1998.

9 Lugones's analysis centers on the lived experiences of people of color—especially women of color—which she contrasts with that of white/Anglo feminists (Lugones 2003: 89–92). For a further analysis of Lugones's concept of world-traveling, see Andrea Pitts 2020.

2 Contextualizing Chinese Yogācāra

1 Here, I follow on the heels of previous scholars such as Dan Lusthaus (2003), Zhihua Yao (2005), Tao Jiang (2006), Ching Keng (2009), Erik Hammerstrom (2014), John Jorgensen (2014), and Chen-Kuo Lin (2014; 2016; 2018b), in referring to the tradition as Chinese Yogācāra. It shall be noted that the term "Chinese" is mainly used to describe the canonical language *qua* classical Chinese. As such, my purpose is to show how the translation of Buddhist ideas from the Sanskrit language to the Chinese language yields an innovative development of the tradition. In parallel, when Japanese Hossō monks began composing their treaties in the local Japanese language, they championed a new development of the Yogācāra tradition outside the Chinese language context. Furthermore, I find it inaccurate to use "East Asian Yogācāra" in this book because my investigation centers on the doctrine specifically established by Xuanzang and his disciples inside the Tang Empire and have not fully extended my study to the writings composed by those outside this context. As readers will see, I

only use East Asian Yogācāra or Yogācāra in East Asia when I talk about the larger tradition both inside and outside Chinese empires. Representation matters. Here again, we follow the politics of recognizing the equal, irreducible value and worth of cultures. That is to say, we avoid one extreme of assimilating all Buddhist writings in East Asia into a homogenous entity. Likewise, we eschew the other extreme of treating one Buddhist tradition as a national treasure of one specific country. Relevant to recognition, readers will also see that I use South Asia more frequently than India, insofar as many eminent clerics in the traditionally defined Indian Mahāyāna Buddhism were not born and raised in modern-day India.

2   Drawing on Indo-Tibetan resources, scholars have explored various aspects of the treatises composed by or attributed to Vasubandhu, Asaṅga, Dignāga, and Dharmakīrti. Several of these scholars work on logic and theories of knowledge (Davidson 1985; Hayes 1989; Garfield 2002; Arnold 2005; Yao 2005; Flanagan 2011; Coseru 2012; Ganeri 2012; Gold 2014; Tzohar 2017), while others discuss the metaphysical positions endorsed by Yogācārins (Chatterjee 1962; Willis 1979; Kochumuttom 1982; Griffiths 1986; Hopkins 2002; Schmithausen 2005).

3   For a detailed study on the Sarvāstivāda and Sautrāntikas stances towards reality, see Chen-Kuo Lin 2007.

4   For this reason, Erik Zürcher defines Chinese Buddhism as the Buddhist conquest of China, or to be more precise, the Buddhist conquest of the Chinese gentry class (Zürcher 2007). As detailed by Pan Guiming, in the history of Chinese Buddhism, the Tiantai school rose to prominence under the auspices of the emperors of the Sui dynasty (Pan 1996).

5   The exchange between early Yogācāra and *tathāgatagarbha* has been examined by several scholars (Takasaki 1986; Yinshun 1988; Lai 2006). Recently, Ching Keng drew upon the manuscripts found in Dunhuang to explain how Paramārtha's original position was not very different from that of Xuanzang (Keng 2009). According to Keng, it was through the effort of later followers as well as the scholar-monks of the Huayan School that Paramārtha was portrayed as taking a position opposite to that of Xuanzang.

6   These Yogācārins propose different answers as to whether consciousness functions to give rise to the act of knowing and the phenomenon to be known. The term "*ākāra*" is utilized to characterize their respective understandings of the intentional structure of consciousness. Here, *ākāra* means "image" or "phenomenon." The meaning of *ākāra* has been expanded in the Chinese language Yogācāra literature, which can mean both an image and the act of perceiving an image. Xuanzang's disciple Puguang has detailed these two senses of *ākāra*, also translated as *xingxiang* 行相 (T41N1821, P26c1-29). Birgit Kellner has discussed the development of the concept of *ākāra* encapsulated in three frames (*ākāra* as external object's form, as a mode of function of grasping an object, and as the content of a grasping act) in Abhidharma philosophy (Kellner 2014: 298). For a detailed discussion on the nuance of *xingxiang* in the Chinese translations and interpretations of *ākāra*, see Ujike Akio 1969; Miyashita Seiki 1978; Fukuda Takumi 1993; Chen I-biau 2007; Ito Yasuhiro 2013; Fei Zhao 2016.

7   Paramārtha arrived in the capital city of the South dynasty only in 548. As such, he should have had access to the writings produced by South Asian Yogācārins in the early 500s. Although Takemura Makio suggests that Paramārtha was influenced by Sthiramati (Takemura 1985: 384), Lü Cheng contends that Paramārtha's position is closer to that of Nanda (Lü 1979: 149).

8. Interestingly, as Tang Yongtong noted in his research on the history of Buddhism in Tang, Xuanzang did not visit many Madhyamaka clerics prior to his journey to India (Tang 2000: 149).
9. Since our focus in this section remains on the doctrinal idea, we use "*vijñaptimātra*" in the subtitle, although the Chinese term "*weishi* (唯識)" has been evoked to translate both the school name of *vijñānavāda* and the doctrinal idea of *vijñaptimātra*.
10. Today, most scholars follow master Yinshun (印順 1906–2005) to refer to the distinction between early and later Yogācāra as that between the "true mind (*zhenxin* 真心)" and the "deluded mind (*wangxin* 妄心)" (Yinshun 1978: 5–6). Back to the Tang dynasty, Kuiji spoke of the distinction between early and later Yogācāra as that between the "Ancient Teaching (*gushuo* 古說)" and "Current Text (*jinwen* 今文)" (T45N1861, P247a15–16). In early Republican China, Lü Cheng (呂澂 1896–1989), popularized the terms "Ancient Learning (*guxue* 古學)" and the "Current Learning (*jinxue* 今學)" (Lü 1986: 74). Prior to Lü Cheng, the difference between early and later Yogācāra was long considered to be due to a dissimilar way of translating Yogācāra texts, which has been detailed by Mei Guangxi (梅光羲 1880–1947) in his article "On the Distinctions between the Old and the New Translations of the Dharma-image School (*xiangzong xinjiu liangyi butong lun* 相宗新舊兩譯不同論)" (Mei 1931). Drawing upon previous findings, I position the early–later distinction in our three-level framework and summarize their dissimilarities in Table 1 in Chapter 8.
11. Ching Keng clarifies two ways of using the concept of *tathāgatagarbha* (Keng 2009). That is to say, *tathāgatagarbha* in a more specific sense entails an innate luminous mind of suchness whilst a more general meaning of this concept describes the mind devoid of ignorance and illusion. In our book, we use *tathāgatagarbha* as that in the specific sense, which is also related to the understanding of awakening in early Yogācāra. As for the more general meaning of this concept, we use the term "Buddha nature" instead. We will further this discussion in Chapter 11.
12. Usually, *faxiang* is translated as "dharma-characteristic" since scholars contend that this Chinese term corresponds to the Sanskrit compound of *dharmalakṣaṇa*. My reservation of this translation comes from the widely accepted definition of this term in the Chinese language context. Since the Tang dynasty, the concept of *faxiang* has been paired with *faxing*. As such, while *faxiang* suggests how emptiness manifests itself through various types of images perceived in the eyes of sentient beings, *faxing* reveals the nature of dharmas as being empty. Taixu defines *faxiang* as the "manifested image (*xiangmao* 相貌)" of all dharmas (Taixu 1932: 184–5), which further presents that which is transformed and manifested by consciousness (Taixu 1932: 191). According to Ouyang Jingwu, Yogācārins use the concept of *faxiang* to point to the equality of all dharmas in that the theory of three natures can be impartially applied to all dharmas (Ouyang 1938: 130). Similarly, modern Confucian Xiong Shili specifies that the *xiang* of a dharma captures how this dharma "appears (*xianxian* 顯現)" and, therefore, can be understood as a "phenomenon (*xianxiang* 現象)" (Xiong 1985: 11). Drawing upon these interpretations, we can infer a consensus from scholar-monks and Buddhist scholars that *faxiang* is the image, not the characteristic, of dharmas manifested through the functionality of consciousness in the experience of sentient beings. That is why I follow these scholars to translate *faxiang* as dharma-image. It shall also be noted that the nuance of the term "*faxiang*" has been re-examined by several scholars who question whether *faxiang* can fully encapsulate the diversity of later Yogācāra (Yoshimura 2004; Lee 2015). Bearing this discussion in mind, I utilize the term "*weishi*" to refer to the main doctrinal idea proposed by Xuanzang and his disciples.

13 The lineage is expanded from the one presented by Zhihua Yao in his book on self-cognition (Yao 2005: 122), and from the one I outlined in the 2016 article on Yogācāra (Li 2016: 69).
14 The early–later distinction has attracted much scholarly attention (Paul 1984; King 1991; Wang 2001; Lusthaus 2002; Lee 2015). More detailed studies on this divide have been proposed by scholars in East Asia since the early Republican period. To name a few: Taixu [1923] 2005; Mei Guangxi [1931]2014; Ouyang Jingwu [1938]1995; Yinshun 1978; Lü Cheng 1986; Ueda Yoshifumi 1964; Fok Tou-hui 1979; Cheng Gongrang 2000; Sheng-yen 2005; Fu Xinyi 2006; Yang Weizhong 2008; Zhou Guihua 2009; Yoshimura Makoto 2013.
15 James Ford has provided a thorough study of the socio-historical context that catalyzed the development of Hossō in the Kamakura period in his book on Jōkei (Ford 2006).
16 For the study of the intellectual history of Yogācāra philosophy in Japan, see Yamasaki Keiki 1985; Yokoyama Kōitsu 1986, 1996; Fukihara Shōshin 1989; Nagao Gadjin 1991; Takasaki Jikidō 1992; Sueki Fumihiko 1992; Suguro Shinjō 2009.
17 Recent studies have explored the profound influence of the resurgence of Yogācāra thinking in the late Ming dynasty (Chu 2010; Brewster 2018; Lin 2018a). More importantly, Chien Kai-Ting (2014, 2015, 2017a, 2017b) has penned several articles detailing the major debates at the center of this resurgence.
18 Luo Cheng (2010) has detailed the history and activities of the publishing house in her monograph.
19 Welch reviewed the revival of Yogācāra as an integral part of Buddhist modernization in early Republican China (Welch 1968). Recently, there has been an increasing number of books that detail the relationship between the Yogācāra revival and Buddhist modernism in early Republican China (Aviv 2013; Chen 2013; Lusthaus 2014; Hammerstrom 2015; Ritzinger 2017),
20 Eyal Aviv has detailed Ouyang Jingwu's system of thoughts as well as the effort to rejuvenate Yogācāra in early Republican China (Aviv 2020). Jessica Zu has investigated Lü Cheng's approach to Yogācāra in her dissertation, which she referred to as Lü's project of developing a socio-soteriology from Yogācāra philosophy (Zu 2020).
21 In her dissertation, Rongdao Lai has detailed Taixu's plan for reforming monastic education as part of the Buddhist modernization project in the early Republican period (Lai 2013). For a detailed study of Taixu's Buddhist modernism, see Don Alvin Pittman 2001; Erik Hammerstrom 2014; Justin Ritzinger 2017.
22 Recently, there is an increasing number of scholarly writings that explore the interactions between the Yogācāra revival and modern Confucianism (Makeham 2003, 2008; Meynard 2011; Lynch 2018). John Makeham (2014) has edited a volume of collected essays to explore the influence of the Yogācāra revival on the intelligentsia in early Republican China.
23 There is a wealth of philosophical studies on Chinese Yogācāra in the English language scholarship. To name a few: Chen-Kuo Lin 1991; Dan Lusthaus 2002; Tao Jiang 2006; Ching Keng 2009; Wei-Jen Teng 2011; Zhihua Yao 2005, 2014.
24 This misinterpretation has since been corrected in the English and French translations of the *CWSL*. See: Louis de la Vallée Poussin 1928; Wei Tat 1973; Francis Cook 1999. Most recently, Gelong Lodrö Sangpo, Gelongma Migme Chödrön, and Alexander Mayer (2017) have composed a translation of the *CWSL* based on Louis de la Vallée Poussin's French version.

25 In Buddhist studies, scholars represented by Fu Xinyi (2002) and Xia Jinhua (2002) have raised questions on whether we should interpret Buddhist thought as a Buddhist version of ontology or metaphysics. They stress how Euro-American philosophers impose a specific understanding of existence and reality in their studies of ontology and metaphysics that is not always commensurable with that in Buddhism (Xia 2002: 133–9; Fu 2002: 15–27). Moreover, Husserlian scholars are also debating the place of ontology and metaphysics in Husserl's phenomenology.

3 Contextualizing Husserl's Phenomenology

1 Kern first introduced these three ways in his article on transcendental phenomenology (Kern 1962), which he further expanded in his book *Husserl und Kant* (Kern 1964).
2 For more studies on Kant's transcendental idealism and Husserl's phenomenology, see Iso Kern 1964; Tom Rockmore 2011; Sophie Loidolt 2015; Julia Jansen 2015, 2016, 2017.
3 As detailed by Nicholas de Warren (2014: 723), Husserl, similar to his contemporary Henri Bergson (1859–1941), also mobilized his writings to support his country's participation in the war. It then can explain why Husserl thought he would not be affected the mounting antisemitism in the 1930s.
4 Peter Gordon has employed the term "Weimar Modernism" to describe how the intelligentsia in Weimar Germany espoused an expressive turn in their balance between archaism and modernism (Gordon 2003). According to Gordon, this modernism shaped and conditioned thinkers in Weimar Germany regardless of their religious affiliation or philosophical expertise.
5 I have borrowed the concepts of "principle" and "mechanics" from Philip Buckley's article on Husserl's nascent account of ethics and social ontology (Buckley 2019: 17–18).
6 For further discussion on the notion of phenomenological theology and how it has been developed from Husserl's transcendental phenomenology, see Herbert Spiegelberg 1982; James Hart 1986; Dominique Janicaud 2000; Dan Zahavi 2017.
7 Gail Weiss, Anne Murphy, and Gayle Salamon (2020) have edited a volume of collected essays that introduce major themes in critical phenomenology.

4 Intentionality in Husserl's Phenomenology

1 For further discussions on intentionality in the philosophy of mind and philosophy of action, see Elizabeth Anscombe 1965; Fred Dretske 1980; John Searle 1982; Daniel Dennett 1987; Dan Arnold 2012.
2 According to Dan Zahavi, Husserlian scholars interpret intentionality in different manners, which further results in debates between the East Coast school and the West Coast school (Zahavi 2003). The West Coast school speaks of intentionality as a three-place relation (between the subjective act, the content of the act, and the object) and interprets *noema* as the generalization of meaning (Dreyfus 1982; Smith 1982; McIntyre1982; Føllesdal 1982). In contrast, the East Coast school argues that the intended object does not represent itself via *noema* but discloses itself as *noema* and stresses how intentionality enables a person to break the "egocentric predicament"

(Drummond 1990; Sokolowski 2000). An additional purpose of this chapter, therefore, is to outline the development of Husserl's conception of intentionality for showing how and why the meaning of this concept is open to debate.

3   I first differentiated these four phases in Husserl's philosophy in another article on self-consciousness (Li 2017: 186–8). However, I did not elaborate on how Husserl used the concept of intentionality to outline his view of knowledge. Nor did I elucidate Husserl's investigation of the plurality of minds. These limitations have been overcome in the current chapter.

4   The notion of "correlate" has been more frequently used by Husserl in *Ideas I*. There, he refers to the relation of *noesis* and *noema* as either the "*noetic–noematic* structures (*noetisch–noemtischen Structuren*)" (Hua 3/193), or as "the correlation between *noesis* and *noema* (*Korrelation zwischen Noesis und Noema*)" (Hua 3/189–90).

5   Although it is beyond the scope of the current section, I want to draw readers' attention to the fact that Husserl further advances his theory of truth in his account of self-evidence (*Evidenz*) (Hua 19/632). Self-evidence entails how an intentional act has its content fulfilled, either fully or partially, by directly given perceptual matter (Hua 19/631). That is to say, in self-evidence, what is meant becomes coincided with what is presented/given. Therefore, Husserl refers to self-evidence as "the act of this most perfect synthesis of coincidence (*der Akt jener vollkommensten Deckungssynthesis*)" (Hua 19/630). To underscore how *Evidenz* is not mentally fabricated but directedly given as the presentation of an intended object as such, John Findley has translated it as "self-evidence" (1970) in the English version of Husserl's *Logical Investigations*, although it is also common for Husserlians such as Dorion Cairns (1960), Fred Kersten (1983), and John Brough (1991) to translate this concept directly as "evidence." According to David Carr, since the English term "evidence" has a unique nuance in the field of law, it is more accurate to translate "*Evidenz*" as self-evidence to avoid possible ambiguities (Carr 1970: 128). In light of this concept of self-evidence, Husserl further differentiates four meanings of the notion of truth (Hua 19/632–3). As such, Husserl is able to provide a more nuanced view of justification. For more discussion on Husserl's account of self-evidence, see Dagfinn Føllesdal 1988; Dan Zahavi 2003; Philipp Berghofer 2018, 2019.

6   It must be noted that Brentano defied the label of psychologism, insofar as he contended that Husserl misrepresented and misunderstood his view of consciousness (Brentano 1995: 238).

7   Here, I primarily draw on the "Prolegomena" of *Logical Investigations* and the "Appendix to the Sixth Investigation" insofar as Husserl suggests that if one wants to eschew misunderstanding of his philosophy and to truly understand his critique of psychologism, the Appendix right after the Prolegomena will make for a required reading (Hua 18/xvii). For a further analysis of the Sixth Investigation, see Ullrich Melle 2002; Nicolas de Warren 2003.

8   Husserl has provided his own diagrams of this two-dimensional series (Hua 1/28; Hua 1/365).

9   The conception of passivity has been further developed by Maurice Merleau-Ponty (1945). Since the dawn of modern philosophy, intellectuals have downplayed the importance of sensation. Nevertheless, through the effort of phenomenologists, the importance of sensation has been rediscovered in that sensation is where the mind and the world first come into contact with one other. The inorganic, unanimated bodies in the world, though they are not capable of using language, still play a profound role in our experience due to the ways in which they collaborate with us to

form sensation, which prompts us to rethink how we engage with the environment and animals. For a closer investigation of passivity and sensation, please see Don Beith, *The Birth of Sense: Generative Passivity in Merleau-Ponty's Philosophy* (Beith 2018).
10 As recent research demonstrates, some traumatic experiences have the power of breaking the coalescence of our entire experience and therefore damaging the structure of our experience. When this coalescence can no longer be sustained, patients will suffer from a wide range of mental illnesses, such as PTSD, depression, and hallucination (Guenther 2013; Ratcliffe et al. 2014).
11 Following Frantz Fanon (1952), Alia Al-Saji (2010; 2019) refers to such a process of internalization as the naturalization of a perspective, which allows her to explore how colonial misrepresentation of marginalized group members is sedimented in the shared memory of people and remains influential in contemporary society.
12 Husserl details his understanding of apperception in the Fifth Meditation. Nevertheless, as clarified by Dermot Moran (2005: 224), Husserl articulates apperception very differently in this text compared to his definition of the same notion in his early writings. For our purpose here, we primarily focus on the articulation of this concept in Husserl's later writings represented by *Cartesian Meditations*.
13 In recent studies, the concept of collective consciousness, as a concept that defines an intentional act as collective, has animated much scholarly debate. To be more specific, the question remains unanswered as to whether the collective characterizes the subject (as a plurality of individual minds), the mode (as a collective act/action), or the content (as a collective object) (Schmid & Schweikard 2013). Following Hans Bernard Schmid (2014), I contend that the sense of the *we* is located in the subject, not in the mode or the content. For this reason, I highlight how collective intentionality is the intentionality for the plurality of individual minds.
14 Brentano's discussion of other minds predates the linguistic and behaviorist approaches, which remains influential in modern philosophy of mind (Ryle 1949; Malcolm 1958; Ayer 1963; Goldman 2006).

5 Intentionality in Chinese Yogācāra

1 Here, I need to highlight that by one-place knowing, I mean how *vijñāna* unifies the act of knowing and the phenomena to be known as one. That is why the eye-consciousness is also intentional and capable of perceiving (Yokoyama 1985). In Suguro Shinjō's terms, *vijñāna* shows the way of knowing that encompasses both the subject, the function, and the content, whereas *vijñapti* cannot serve as the subject (Suguro 1985: 125). Inspired by his research, I delve deeper into the etymological meaning of *vijñāna* and *vijñapti* to explore why Xuanzang translated them both as consciousness, an exploration being touched upon but not yet detailed by Suguro.
2 Zhou Guihua penned two articles in 2004 and 2007 to highlight that Xuanzang inaccurately translated both terms as consciousness, in that *vijñāna* means "consciousness (*shi* 識)" while *vijñapti* should be translated as "representation (*biaobie* 表別)" (Zhou 2004; 2007). Zhou specified that these two terms are indeed translated differently in Tibetan Buddhist literature.
3 Prior to Zhou Guihua, other scholars represented by Fok Tou-hui (1979) and Han Jingqing (1998) also proposed to translate *vijñapti* as "representation." Yeh Ah-Yueh

delineates three corresponding Chinese terms for *vijñapti* in Xuanzang's translations, which are *piao-seh* (aka. *biaose* 表色), *piao-yeh* (aka. *biaoye* 表業), and *liao-pei* (aka. *liaobie* 了別) (Yeh 1979: 176).

4 The commonly adopted translation of *ti–yong* is "essence–function." Charles Muller initiated a study of the *ti–yong* binary (essence–function) in Korean and Chinese Buddhism (Muller 1995; 1999). In a recent paper, Muller noticed Kuiji's application of this binary in his writings on Yogācāra (Muller 2016). Nevertheless, Muller has not yet elaborated on ways in which the *ti–yong* binary facilitated Kuiji's articulation of the concept of consciousness. That is the lacuna the current section attempts to fill.

5 The way in which Xuanzang used *vijñapti* to explain *vijñāna* has also been discerned by most Yogācāra scholars (Nagasawa 1953; Yeh 1981; Suguro 1985). As Suguro Shinjō once remarked, Yogācārins place the stress on the way in which objects are represented to the subjects in the process of knowing, rather than that which can know (Suguro 1985: 127).

6 Unlike *yong*, which is usually translated as "function," *ti* has been paraphrased differently in English language Buddhist scholarship, sometimes as "substance" (Wagner 2000, 2003) or "structure" (Wang 2012), sometimes as "nature" (Grosnick 1989) or "essence" (Grosnick 1989; Muller 1995; 1999). Nonetheless, considering how essence is also used to translate *svabhāva*, I will transliterate these two notions rather than translate them. In Chapter 9, I will elaborate on how *ti* shall be translated as "body" which is related to the notion of a motherly-body as the cosmic origin of generating and cultivating various existent realities.

7 As readers have probably also noticed, I use the concept of "image" to translate the Chinese term *xiang* that corresponds to the Sanskrit terms of "*nimitta*" and "*ākāra*." As such, this concept is treated as the synonym of phenomenal appearance, manifestation, and manifested phenomenon.

8 In the *CWSL*, Xuanzang explains how early and later Yogācārins outline the structure of consciousness differently. I have detailed the four characterizations of the intentional structure of consciousness elsewhere (Li 2016; 2017). As I mentioned in these two articles, Kuiji describes early Yogācāra master Sthiramati's position as onefold-only since Sthiramati perceives consciousness as the unified *zizheng* (自證 *svasaṃvitti*), and Nanda's position as twofold-only since Nanda conceives of consciousness as the interplay between the perceiving act and the perceived phenomenon (T43N1831, P609b5–c21).

9 Zhihua Yao has discussed *svasaṃvitti* together with its Chinese and Tibetan counterparts in his book where he listed several possible translations of this concept such as "self-realization," "self-cognition," and "self-awareness" (Yao 2005). In the study of Yogācāra in the Chinese language context, Thierry Meynard also uses "self-authenticating" to paraphrase *zizheng* (Meynard 2014). I opt for self-awareness to underscore the epistemic function of *zizheng* as presented by Xuanzang and his disciples, especially how *zizheng* entails an intuitive type of knowledge, which will be the central topic of Chapter 6.

10 Most scholars contend that Dignāga reintroduces *zizheng* to the intentional structure because, without this underlying self-awareness, consciousness will not be able to recollect itself (Yao 2005: 144). They thus interpret Xuanzang's notion of *yi* (憶) as recollecting. Inspired by Yao's analysis, I find this interpretation unclear. That is to say, if we read this as the memory argument in the *CWSL* and given that all consciousness has this threefold intentional structure, then we can infer that all eight types of consciousness have the capacity of recollecting. However, such an inference

contradicts two facts. First, aside from *laiye* and *mona*, the first six consciousnesses are discontinuous and can be interrupted. As such, how can all eight types of consciousness recollect their previous functionalities? And second, the capacity of consciousness is to perceive and to know, not to recollect. It is the mental factor of mindfulness (*nian* 念, *smṛti*) that can enact the capacity of recollecting, which Xuanzang details later in his elucidation on five types of *viniyata* (*biejing* 別境, determining mental factors) (T31N1585, P28b18–25). As such, I propose to translate "憶" not as recollection but as the preservation of previous moments, which is very close to Husserl's concept of retention.

11 Kuiji specifies that only the Saṃmatīya school and the Mahāsāṃghika school inside the non-Mahāyāna Buddhist communities do not follow this delineation of consciousness (T43N1830, P318b13).

12 Early Yogācārins like Paramārtha often use *citta* and *vijñāna* interchangeably (T31N1587, P63c16–17). By fixing the title for these consciousnesses, Xuanzang and his disciples intend to renew the meaning of consciousness-only, which will be unpacked in Chapter 8.

13 For recent scholarship on the study of the Buddhist approaches to selfhood presented in Indo-Tibetan Yogācāra doctrines and texts, please see Dan Arnold 2012; Christian Coseru 2012; Zhihua Yao 2005; Evan Thompson 2014; Jay Garfield 2015. To expand their analysis, I link the epistemological inquiries of self-knowledge with the existential question of attachments and suffering addressed by Yogācārins. I have conducted a preliminary analysis of the Chinese Yogācāra approach to selfhood in an earlier article (Li 2017). However, the analysis in that article remains too concise and also contains several spelling errors. That is why the current section builds upon and advances the data presented in the previous article.

14 I have interpreted seeds as "possibilities" in another article (Li 2017: 190). However, I no longer find this interpretation as plausible as "tendency" because the concept of possibility does not fully capture the potency of the seed metaphor.

15 Many scholars have examined the discussion of other minds in Indo-Tibetan Yogācāra Buddhism (MacKenzie 2017; Perrett 2017; Tzohar 2017; Prueitt 2018; Kachru 2019). In his book, *Contexts and Dialogue: Yogācāra Buddhism and Modern Psychology on the Subliminal Mind*, Tao Jiang also examines the problem of other minds articulated by Xuanzang in the *CWSL* (Jiang 2006). He draws a parallel between remote *ālambanapratyaya* and collective consciousness. Drawing on and developing his findings, I plan to delve deeper into this problem of other minds in Chinese Yogācāra and fill the existing lacuna. I have done a more detailed analysis of the problem of other minds in Chinese Yogācāra (Li 2019). For the current section, I have used the elements, with permission granted by Springer Nature, from this article "Through the Mirror: The Account of Other Minds in Chinese Yogācāra Buddhism" published in *Dao: A Journal of Comparative Philosophy, 18(3)*. However, I think some statements in that article can be further improved and updated as they are in this book.

16 As I have detailed in the article "Through the Mirror: The Yogācāra Account of Other Minds" (Li 2019: 443), existing scholarship proposes two interpretations of the later Yogācāra proposal. Dan Lusthaus argues for understanding the experience of other minds as inference (Lusthaus 2002: 503), whilst Louis de la Vallée Poussin conceives of this experience as a reproduction of other minds in one's own mind (La Vallée Poussin 1928: 430). Both interpretations, however, confine their scope to the first-person perspective and have not acknowledged the importance of self–other collaboration. As

previously mentioned, Tao Jiang stresses how the remote type of *ālambana* reveals the collectivity of consciousness (Jiang 2006: 73). Drawing upon Jiang's work, I specify how this collectivity suggests the second-person perspective of experience.

17 In a different article, Chen-Kuo Lin translates *qin suoyuanyuan* as the direct object of cognition that is further equated with "noema *qua* image" in contrast to the indirect object of cognition *qua shu suoyuanyuan* tantamount to "noema *qua* original stuff" (Lin 2018b: 253). Lin continues to specify that the universal (*gongxiang* 共相, *sāmānyalakṣaṇa*) refers to the conceptual construct, which is "created and superimposed by the conceptual mind upon the original stuff" (Lin 2018b: 253). For Yogācārins, universals can only be cognized through inference, which distinguishes universals from particulars to be cognized through direct perception. Nevertheless, I think it is crucial to observe that Lin never equates the universal with a noema *qua* original stuff. He only remarks that the universal is superimposed upon the noema *qua* original stuff. Relevant to this line of reasoning, I want to revisit Lin's translation of these two types of *ālambana*. When we translate intimate *ālambana* as the direct object of cognition and remote *ālambana* as the indirect object of cognition, we can leave our readers with the impression that intimate *ālambana* is to be cognized by direct perception and remote *ālambana* is to be conceptualized by inference. This impression is incorrect if we come to think about several consciousnesses that are not capable of inferring but still have their remote *ālambana*, say, the first five consciousnesses. That is why I translate *qin-shu* as the "intimate" and the "remote" not as the "direct" and "indirect." If this argumentation is tenable, it can also explain why and how Lin suggests that universals are superimposed upon and therefore presuppose the *noema qua* original stuff. Minamoto Juko (2009, 2011, 2014) provides a preliminary discussion of the concept of remote *ālambana* and a reflection of Yogācāra solipsism, although he has reservations regarding whether Xuanzang really resolves solipsism.

18 Kuiji stresses that the sense organs of eyes and ears are neither the intimate nor remote *ālambana* for eye-consciousness, insofar as these sense organs are neither the image parts of the eye-consciousness nor archetypes for this very eye-consciousness (T43N1830, P501a17–18).

19 In the late Ming dynasty, scholar-monks have debated the proper reading of this quote, especially whether this quote could be considered as a refutation of solipsism (Chien 2017b). As Chien Kai-Ting unpacks in his article, the discussion over solipsism was animated by the possibility that the perceived material universe for one individual is also shared by all sentient beings and therefore transformed as a collaborative effort of their minds. That is to say, scholar-monks in late Ming were not concerned explicitly by the characterization of other minds as remote *ālambana*.

20 Recently, Dan Zahavi (2021) has detailed Husserl's changing stances towards selfhood. As such, readers might ask whether Xuanzang and his disciples would consider Husserl's phenomenology to be vulnerable to the critique of innate self-attachments. To this end, I think it depends on how we interpret the minimal sense of selfhood in Husserl's work and how we elaborate on the affirmation of agency in Chinese Yogācāra literature. It would be fair to conclude that Husserl does problematize what Xuanzang and his disciples refer to as innate self-attachment, though in a way that is not as thoroughly as that of these Chinese Yogācārins, specifically because Husserl has yet to outline the detailed process of rehabitualization.

6 Intentionality and Non-conceptualism

1 Ever since the 1980s, the researches on non-conceptual content in experience and its related role in the production of knowledge have flourished (Evans 1982; Peacocke 1983; Cussins 1991; Tye 2005). In this burgeoning field, scholars have rediscovered the writings of Kant (Hanna 2005; Ginsborg 2008), Brentano (Dennett 1969, 1987; Dewalque 2013; Crane 2017), Husserl (Barber 2008; Hopp 2011), and premodern Indian Buddhists (Coseru 2015; Kramer 2018; Sharf 2018) to reaffirm the existence and justificatory function of non-conceptual content.

2 The question of whether there exists non-conceptual content in one's experience has attracted the attention of several Kantian scholars, see Wilfred Sellars 1956, 1968; John McDowell 1994, 2006; Robert Hanna 2005; Hannah Ginsborg 2006, 2008.

3 Recently, Walter Hopp has managed to integrate Husserl's conception of intentionality into the heated discussion on non-conceptualism. In his writing, Hopp focuses on what we call in our book the descriptive level of Husserl's phenomenology. Upon utilizing Husserl's theory of intentionality to justify non-conceptualism, Hopp makes a plea for suspending the explicative level at which Husserl puts forward transcendental idealism (Hopp 2011: 3). Through this plea, Hopp depicts genuine phenomenology as that which should be separated from transcendental idealism (Hopp 2011: 3). Such an approach that separates phenomenology from transcendental idealism has been scrutinized by Dan Zahavi in his book, *Husserl's Legacy: Phenomenology, Metaphysics, and Transcendental Philosophy* (Zahavi 2017: 5). For Zahavi, if one can fully understand Husserl's transcendental idealism, this person will have a better comprehension of Husserl's analysis of intersubjectivity and embodiment (Zahavi 2017: 6). Our examination of Husserl's phenomenology in Chapter 4 supports Zahavi's viewpoint. Consider the concept of intentionality. As previously examined, intentionality indicates the mutual constitution of the subjective act of perceiving and the object to be perceived. A relation as such entails not only an epistemic account of perception but also a viewpoint regarding the metaphysical status of objects that appear as phenomena in our consciousness. As we will see in Part 3, Husserl's non-conceptualism lays the ground for, and thus cannot be detached from, his transcendental idealism.

4 We are likewise presented with a reading of Yogācāra philosophy as a version of non-conceptualist epistemology. Exponents of this reading highlight how phenomenal consciousness serves as the foundation of knowledge in the Yogācāra framework. In his appeal for naturalizing Buddhist epistemology, Christian Coseru considers the Buddhist theory of knowledge as that which disqualifies the religious accounts of Buddhism (Coseru 2012: 57). In a recent paper, Bernard Faure reflects on this movement of naturalizing Buddhism, be it Abhidharma, Madhyamaka, or Yogācāra, and downplaying the devotional aspect of Buddhist traditions (Faure 2017: 122). Indeed, in the current secular age, scholars must remain value-neutral. Consequently, the Buddhist discussion of faith, soteriology, or religious practice shall be eschewed. Nonetheless, if we remain mindful of the context of our comparative study, then we will also be critical of this unquestioned assumption of being value-neutral. In the case of Yogācāra, the investigation of consciousness paves the way for them to account for how each individual is furnished with an open possibility between awakening and suffering. As such, to become awake from ignorance, a person not only needs to grasp true knowledge but also has to engage in religious training to habitualize this knowledge. This is how the Yogācāra epistemic inquiries are subservient to the

religious goal of awakening wisdom and compassion. This goal has to be kept in mind in our comparative study.
5   According to Japanese Hossō scholar-monk Zenshu (善珠723‐97), Kuiji's *Commentary of the Treatise on the Entering the Correct Principles of Hetuvidyā* enumerates only four types of direct perception, namely, that of the five senses, the sixth consciousness when it arises on the basis of and together with the five senses, the self-awareness, as well as meditative yogic experience because Kuiji intends to initiate dialogues with Buddhists and non-Buddhists alike (T68N2270, P420). In particular, as highlighted by Zenshu, the functionality of the eighth consciousness is also characterized as direct perception (T68N2270, P421b1).
6   As clarified by Lü Cheng, Kuiji was not able to complete his *Commentary of the Treatise on the Entering the Correct Principles of Hetuvidyā* and therefore the rest of the treatise was finished by his disciple Huizhao (Lü 1986: 1503). According to the recent study of Zheng Weihong, Huizhao's writing remains consistent with that of Kuiji in this commentary, which defies the view that this commentary of Buddhist logic composed in the Chinese language does not merit investigation (Zheng 2010).

Part Three The Tracks

1   In his book *Husserl's Legacy*, Zahavi outlines five different definitions of the concept of metaphysics to describe a number of presumptions that have been imported into the study of metaphysics by philosophers across time and place (Zahavi 2017: 66).
2   I have coined the term "problem of essence" in another paper (Li 2016). However, in that article, I put forward a rather general analysis of the meaning of essence in Husserl's writing and in Chinese Yogācāra, which I now find underdeveloped and insufficient. That is why an additional purpose of this part is to strengthen the understanding of the meaning of essence.

7 Essence in Husserl's Phenomenology

1   As previously mentioned, in another article, I have conducted a concise analysis of Husserl's concept of essence in which I demarcated the phenomenological essence as an ideal sense from the natural essence as an abstract concept (Li 2016: 79). Currently, I find this earlier analysis limited because it did not pinpoint the different ways in which Husserl used the term essence and therefore did not fully capture the nuance of this Husserlian concept. The differentiation between a phenomenological essence and a natural essence did not demonstrate how a person's attitude would determine the formation of essence. More importantly, the previous article did not clarify how Husserl expanded the notion of essence in his later work. These limitations have been tackled and overcome in the current chapter.
2   In a previous article, I examined three readings of Husserl's transcendental idealism (Li 2016: 74–5). They are the epistemological reading (Carr 1999), the metaphysical reading (Smith 2003), and the critical reading (Zahavi 2010b). In that article, I proposed to read Husserl's position as a version of correlative dualism (Li 2016: 75). However, I think this characterization is inaccurate, particularly because the concept of dualism remains too strong for Husserl. That is why I suggest reading Husserl's

position as a version of correlative non-dualism in this chapter, which I shall presently elaborate upon.

8 Essence in Chinese Yogācāra

1 In an earlier article, I examined the Yogācāra critique of *svabhāva* (Li 2016). However, there are several erroneous details in that article, particularly in the discussion on the relationship between Madhyamaka and Yogācāra. The way in which the philosophical binary has been utilized by Xuanzang and his disciples has also not been mentioned. More importantly, the interpretation of the Yogācāra view of reality, especially that of early Yogācāra, would benefit from additional primary resources. In this chapter, I will tackle these limitations in my attempt to develop a more plausible reading of the Yogācāra critique of *svabhāva*.
2 I have elaborated on four interpretations of Nāgārjuna's view of emptiness in a previous article (Li 2016). As described by Antoine Panaïoti (2013), they are the absolutist reading (Murti 1955), the nihilist reading (Narain 1964), the anti-realist reading (Siderits 1988), and the skeptical reading (Ganeri 2001).
3 In contemporary studies, scholars have discerned more issues regarding the existential status of illusory phenomena and the problem of logical infinite regress (Hayes 1989; Burton 1999; Yao 2010).
4 The Yogācāra critique of Madhyamika's viewpoint of emptiness is in line with its critique of Madhyamika's articulation of Buddha nature in the Chinese context, which will be detailed in Chapter 11.
5 We have referred to the scholarship on the early–later distinction in Chapter 2. Drawing on and developing their findings, I intend to delve deeper into these differences. In the following analysis, I clarify how the different interpretations of the intentional structure of consciousness lead to their respective understandings of three natures and emptiness in early and later Yogācāra. This analysis further allows me to argue for perceiving Yogācāra in East Asia as a creative development of the doctrine from South Asia.
6 Here, we specify that these treatises are attributed to Paramārtha, rather than authored, as recent studies have investigated how early Yogācārins continued to modify these treatises even after Paramārtha passed away (Keng 2009).
7 To end the *CWSL*, Xuanzang expounds on whether the seeing and the image parts are real. He enumerates three accounts, of which, according to Kuiji, the second one represents the correct view (T43N1830, P606a8–9). In the second account, Xuanzang explains how the seeing part and the image part are both transformed by consciousness, which suggests that those transformed by consciousness are as "seemingly real as consciousness (*xushi rushi* 虛實如識)" (T31N1585, P59a8). The key concept here is *xushi* 虛實, which I translate as "seemingly real." Previous scholars represented by Louis de la Vallée Poussin (1928: 717) and Wei Tat (1973: 807) considered *xushi* as a disjunctive conjunction and translated it as "false or real (*faux ou vrai*)." Although they did not explain their choice of translation, I conjecture that it is probably because of Kuiji's elaboration on the first account. As detailed by Kuiji, the second account is correct whilst the first is not, insofar as the first one deems the transformation of consciousness such as the seeing part and the image part to be *xu* 虛 (false and unreal) in contrast to the real (*shi* 實) consciousness (T43N1830, P605c14–18). As we will see later, the first account expresses the understanding of

consciousness-only in early Yogācāra, which Kuiji attributes to Nanda (T43N1830, P605c11). Later Yogācārins like Xuanzang and his disciples do not consider the transformation of consciousness in the same manner, since they specify how such a transformation (characterized by the second dependent nature) preserves an open possibility that allows sentient beings to either see how things really are or misperceive things as falsely *svabhāvic*. Interestingly, Xuanzang and his disciples again make a shift in focus *from* whether the seeing and image parts are real to *how* they are real. In Kuiji's terms, those that are transformed from consciousness such as the seeing part and the image part "share the same type of real existence (*yizhong shishi* 一種是實)" as consciousness and are not fictitious (*jia* 假) (T43N1830, P606a7–8). In order to pinpoint the specific type of real existence that defines consciousness and its transformation, I propose to translate *xushi* as that which encapsulates such open possibility that supports and therefore cannot be reduced to a disjunction. Thus, I consider *xu* as a modifier of *shi*. Accordingly, the concept of *xushi* 虛實 should be translated as a compound, whose meaning is "emptily real" or "seemingly real," which describes how a reality seems to be as real as the transforming consciousness but is ultimately empty. Upon translating *xu* 虛 as seemingly, we preserve the neutrality of this term, further sustaining the open possibility for both false views and correct insights. Earlier when explicating the three natures in the account of three natures, Xuanzang uses another concept, *siyou* 似有, to capture the metaphysical status of those that are transformed from consciousness. As Xuanzang unpacks, these seeing and image parts, "although they exist, are not genuinely real (*you er feizhen* 有而非真)" (T31N1585, P46c06). He, thus, depicts the existence of illusory seeing and image parts as "not ultimately real but seemingly real (*feiyou siyou* 非有似有)" (T31N1585, P46c9). Both notions here, either *xushi* 虛實, or, *siyou* 似有, as I suggest, are harnessed by Xuanzang to facilitate his depicting of the neutral reality of the seeing and the image parts transformed from consciousness. As to be seen shortly, the expression with a more negative denotation (viz. falsely, fictitious real), which we can locate in the *CWSL* is either *xuwang* 虛妄 (in contrast to *xushi* 虛實), or *jiayou* 假有 (contrasted with *siyou* 似有). Nevertheless, such seemingly real existence of that which is transformed from consciousness, to be certain, is not mind-independent. I am confident that the current translation makes more sense, since it shows (1) how the transformation of consciousness is seemingly real, so suchness is not unreal, and (2) consciousness together with its transformation is not completely an illusory seeming to be deemed false, which conforms to the elaboration of the rest of the second account put forward by both Xuanzang (T31N1585, P59a9–11) and Kuiji (T43N1830, P606a13–19).

8   I have enumerated three readings of the Yogācāra metaphysical position elsewhere (Li 2016; 2017). To repeat, they are absolute idealism (Chatterjee 1962), realist pluralism (Kochumuttom 1982), metaphysical idealism (Schmithausen 1987; 2005).

9 Essence in Comparative Philosophy

1   This way of defining essence as necessary attributes or properties, in contrast to accidental properties—namely, unnecessary and contingent ones of an object—yields the modality account of essence. To challenge this modal characterization of essence, contemporary philosophers propose two alternatives: the definitional characterization and the explanatory characterization. Championed by Kit Fine, some philosophers put

forward the definitional characterization, according to which, essences are properties that define an object as such and allow us to know what an object is (Fine 1994). Fine pinpoints several counterexamples to the modal characterization of essential properties that eventually propel modalists such as Sam Cowling to modify and refine their characterization (Cowling 2013). Besides, other philosophers (Copi 1954; Gorman 2005) propose a third characterization that considers essential properties as those that can explain fundamentally the object's possession of its other properties. For more discussion on essence, see Edward Zalta 2006; Fabrice Correia 2007; Berit Brogaard & Joe Salerno 2013; Sam Cowling 2013; Nathan Wildman 2013; David Denby 2014; Philip Atkins & Teresa Robertson 2016.

2   In his study of Korean Buddhism, Charles Muller (1999; 2016) translates *ti* as essence, which is paired with *yong*, or function. In the English language scholarship of Confucianism and Daoism, *ti* is also frequently paraphrased as "essence" (Wittenborn 1991).

3   For the translation of *Xing* (性) as essence in Buddhist studies, please see Klaus-Dieter Mathes's German translation of *Unterscheidung der Gegebenheiten von Ihern Wesen* (辨法法性論, *Dharmadharmatāvibhāga*) (Mathes 1996). In Confucianism, *Xing* is also paraphrased as the essence of being human, commonly in the studies on Mencius (孟子 c. 372–289 BCE) (Ames 2002), Zhu Xi (朱熹 1130–1200) (Allen 2015), and on Wang Fuzhi (王夫之 1619–92) (Liu 2017). For a critical reflection of this translation, see Irene Bloom 1997; Roger Ames 2002; David Wong 2015.

4   As detailed by Samuel Rickless, the *Parmenides* turns out to be both a summary and a problematization of the theory of Forms, presented by Plato (Rickless 2016). While the summary reinforces the distinction between forms and particulars, the problematization accentuates the dialectical relationship between the two.

5   For more in-depth studies of the conception of essence in Aristotle's *Metaphysics*, see Frank Lewis 1984; Alan Code 1986; Charlotte Witt 1989; Norman Dahl 1997, 2007; David Charles 2002; Lucas Angioni 2014.

6   For more in-depth studies of the conception of existence or being in Aquinas's metaphysics, see Joseph Bobik 1988; Leo Elders 1992; John Wippel 1995, 2000; Anthony Kenny 2010; Lawrence Dewan 2006.

7   For Aquinas (*De Ente et Essentia*, 31), essence can also be understood as what previous thinkers referred to as the form due to its function of determination, or as nature since it can be grasped by the intellect.

8   For Descartes's contribution to the modern sense of the self, see Charles Taylor, *Sources of the Self* (Taylor 1989: 143–58).

9   In the later Eastern Jin dynasty (317–420), Yuan Hong (袁宏 328–76) summarized three phases of the development of the Doctrine of Dark Learning. As concluded by most modern scholars (Tang 2001; Ge 2008; Feng 2009), debates constantly occurred among members of the gentry class as to the relationship between existence (*you* 有) and nothingness (*wu* 無), as well as how one should understand the interplay between the Dao, existence, and nothingness. The representative of the first phase (*c.* 200–250) was Wang Bi who revered the notion of nothingness and equated nothingness with the Dao. In the second phase (*c.* 250–260), most literati began to reflect on how existence could arise from nothingness, gradually shifting their focus to naturalness (*ziran* 自然), namely, the ultimately harmonious unity of both existence and nothingness. Thinkers of the last phase (*c.* 260–290) further accentuated the dialectical relationship between existence and nothingness in their elaboration of reciprocal efficacy (*xiangyin* 相因) and individual transformation (*duhua* 独化). For the English language

scholarship on Dark Learning in the Six Dynasties (220–589), please see Livia Knaul 1985; Brook Ziporyn 2003; Feng Youlan (aka. Fung, Yu-Lan) 1948, 2016.

10 In the original text, Wang directly used the Chinese term "mother (*mu* 母)." The mother analogy proves to be crucial in Daoism, especially for various Daoist rituals, iconography, and cosmology (Despeux & Kohn 2003; Lee 2014; Nelson & Yang 2016; Wang 2017). However, considering that our book is taking shape in a modern context, I anticipate some level of push back from readers when they see the following articulation: that the role of a mother manifests itself in her function of giving birth to a son. One can misread this articulation as an indication that the role of women is *solely* defined by fertility and the ability to conceive offspring. In another paper, Robin Wang expounds how gender is a social construct and cannot be equated with biological sex; for instance, being feminine does not automatically entail being a woman biologically (Wang 2016). Since Daoists revere the transformative power of the Dao, there is a possibility that one could self-identify as a mother even though this person is not the biological mother of a child, such as is seen in many Daoist mystic stories and hagiographies. Indeed, one can understand the concept of mother as a figurative way of depicting the living energy that flows in the cosmos. This is why I paraphrase *mu* as motherliness, to highlight the fluidity of concepts of gender and sex in Daoism.

11 For a more detailed presentation of this part of the intellectual history, see Ge Zhaoguang (Ge 2008: 359–61).

12 Considering the adoption of *Geyi* in this period, many scholars remark that Buddhism has been influenced by dark learning (*xuanxuehua* 玄學化) (Feng 2009: 425). This remark, however, seems to overlook the agency of Chinese Buddhist clerics. Indeed, the development of Chinese Buddhism cannot be reduced to a passive reception of South Asian thought, either in the case of Xuanzang or in the case of previous scholar-monks like Paramārtha (Paul 1981, 1984; Funayama 2008). Nor shall it be simplified as an active sinicization. Rather, there is a mutual constitution and reciprocal engagement of ideas between these two systems of thought. For the literature on how to understand the concept of Chinese Buddhism, please see Kenneth Chen 1973; Robert Sharf 2002; Erik Zürcher 2007; Hu Shih 2013. For a more in-depth analysis of the relationship between Buddhism and Daoism, please see Stephen Bokenkamp 2007; Christine Mollier 2008; James Robson 2010.

13 In his "Treatise on the Non-Real and the Empty (*buzhenkong lun* 不真空論)," Sengzhao (僧肇 384–414) scrutinizes three readings on emptiness in his era. The first one is named by Sengzhao as the reading of "no-mind (*xinwu* 心無)" in which emptiness is tantamount to the non-existence of mind, although things in the world are not non-existent (T45N1858, P152a16). For Sengzhao, this reading acknowledges the quiescence of the spirit (*shen* 神) but fails to appreciate the illusory existence of worldly objects (T45N1858, P152a16). The second reading is branded "just-form (*jise* 即色)," which clarifies how "form is not its own form" (T45N1858, P152a17). Examining this viewpoint, Sengzhao explains how it acknowledges that various forms *qua* objects have no *sui generis*, self-determined existence, but it still fails to elucidate why they are empty (T45N1858, P152a19). The last reading is known as "original nothingness (*benwu* 本無)," for which all existent things are originally from nothingness (T45N1858, P152a20). For Sengzhao, all three readings do not follow the Buddha's teaching of the middle way and are therefore unable to expound how various objects are illusorily existent images at the conventional level but ultimately become empty at the ultimate level (T45N1858, P152a29–b3). Articulated as such, Sengzhao

puts forward his view of emptiness—that the non-real is the empty (*buzhenkong* 不真空) (T45N1858, P152c). Through his analysis, Sengzhao implicitly criticizes the trend of equating emptiness with nothingness, insofar as this equation, especially as seen in the last reading of original nothingness, prioritizes nothingness over existence, thereby lacking in conformity with the Buddha's teaching of the middle way.

14 Gradually, this binary sets up a paradigm for clerics to differentiate between a diversity of doctrinal viewpoints inside the Buddhist community. In particular, Huayan masters such as Fazang (法藏 *c*. 643-712) and Zongmi (宗密 780-841) promoted this paradigm in their *sūtra* classification systems in which they divide various Buddhist schools into two camps (T42N1826, T48N2015). Those that focus more on clarifying the nature of emptiness are known as the schools of dharma-nature (*faxingzong* 法性宗), which include the Sanlun School, the Tiantai School, the Huayan School, and the Chan School. Others represented by Xuanzang and his disciples that investigate how illusory images reveal the underlying nature of emptiness are members of the schools of dharma-image (*faxiangzong* 法相宗).

15 For more discussion on Hannah Arendt's view of the plurality of the "I," see Sophie Loidolt 2017.

10 The Gate of Practice

1 A more precise term would be "intention/intentional," rather than "purpose/purposeful." However, as the term "intentional" takes on distinct nuances in Husserl's phenomenology, readers may find it confusing to see the term appear in our discussion of agency, where intention involves not primarily a subject–object correlation in the epistemic sense but more that of an agent–patient connection in the performative sense. Thus, I eschew the standard terminology and opt for the synonym "purpose/purposeful." Elisabeth Anscombe, for instance, has explored the possibilities of connecting "intentionality" as the purpose of action with "intentionality" as the directedness of mental acts (Anscombe 1957). For more discussion of agency, see Alvin Goldman 1970; Elizabeth Anscombe 1981; Robert Audi 1986; Markus Schlosser 2015.

2 Recently scholars have discovered some of Husserl's discussions of action and agency in his unpublished manuscripts which have just been published in an edited volume under the title *Studien zur Struktur des Bewusstseins* (*Studies of the Structure of Consciousness*)" (Hua 43). These discussions have laid the foundation for a more in-depth phenomenological investigation of action and agency (Melle 2015; Uemura 2015; Marín-Ávila 2015).

3 The Buddha's first lecture is documented in the *Sūtra of the Buddha Turning the Dharma-Wheel* (佛說轉法輪經), and the Chinese version was translated by An Shigao (安世高) in the second century. This text details the four noble truths. First, life is endless suffering (T2N109, P503b20). Second, the five aggregates (*wuyin* 五陰) conspire to generate suffering (T2N109, P503b25). That is to say, sentient beings do not know they are comprised of five aggregates but rather misperceive these five elements as a permanent self. From such misperception, attachments arise, further causing endless suffering (T2N109, P503b26-7). Third, to end suffering, one must change its current state and detach from all attachments (T2N109, P503b27-8). Fourth, to do so, one needs to pursue the eightfold path (T2N109, P503b29). As a result, one will be able to attain *nirvāṇa*, "never being reborn after this round of life,

further leaving *saṃsāra* for good, and no longer being burdened by suffering (是生後不復有，長離世間，無復憂患)" (T2N109, P503c12–13).

4   There has been a wealth of scholarship on the notion of dependent arising in the English language studies of Yogācāra (Griffiths 1986; Nagao 1991; Garfield 2002; Lusthaus 2002; Waldron 2003; Gold 2015). These studies, in their focus on Indo-Tibetan recourses, prioritize the epistemic and ontological function of this notion. On the conception of dependent arising in Chinese Yogācāra, Yeh Ah-Yueh has been the pioneer of such research. She investigates the rearticulations of the theory of twelve links in early and later Yogācāra (Yeh 1981). Drawing on and developing their research, I will explore how Xuanzang and his disciples articulate the idea of dependent arising and how their articulation sets the stage for them to argue for the possibility of what is currently known as agency in contemporary philosophy.

5   One of the hidden themes here is the Buddhist conception of temporality. For sure, in their problematization of the early Buddhist view of causality, Mahāyāna clerics scrutinize the linear conception of time proposed by Abhidharma clerics. There are comparative studies of Husserl's view of inner time and that in Xuanzang's doctrine of consciousness-only (Kern 2012; Zhang 2015). Recently, Jianjun Li (2016) has investigated the view of temporality proposed by Xuanzang. While Li relates Xuanzang's notion of temporality to the eighth consciousness, he has yet to bring to light how time is non-linear, intersubjective, and circular as expressed in the Yogācāra concept of causality within one layer, which is equally distinctive from, for instance, Dōgen's view of the absolute now.

6   Consciousness, mental factors, and external objects play different roles in this articulation of dependent arising. The seeds in *laiye* and the actualized ones such as actualized views and deeds become the direct cause (*yinyuan* 因緣, *hetupratyaya*) of the entire chain (T31N1585, P40a22). The constantly acting *laiye* preserves all previous events of perception and thus serves as the immediate condition (*dengwujianyuan* 等無間緣, *samanantarapratyaya*) which sustains the entirety of experience (T31N1585, P40b7). Real objects external to consciousness, as long as they are not falsely imagined by sentient beings, become the previously mentioned *ālambanapratyaya* (*suoyuanyuan* 所緣緣). Other mental factors, such as craving, grasping, faith, and perseverance, can be either advantageous or disadvantageous to our authentic knowing. These factors are, therefore, categorized as the upheaving condition (*zengshangyuan* 增上緣, *adhipatipratyaya*) (T31N1585, P41a6).

7   As previously mentioned in Chapter 5, it is the mental factor of mindfulness (*nian* 念, *smṛti*) that can enact the capacity of recollecting, a mental factor that accompanies the sixth consciousness in the mind of an ignorant sentient being (T31N1585, P28b18–25).

8   For an in-depth study on the notion of *āśraya-parivrtti/āśraya-parāvṛtti* in the Indo-Tibetan literature of Yogācāra, see Yokoyama Kōitsu 1978; Ronald Davidson 1985. For studies on the notion of *zhuanyi* articulated by Chinese Yogacarins, see Takemura Makio 1976; Ng Yu-Kwan 1978; Alan Sponberg 1979; Lü Cheng 1986; Chao Tung-Ming 2011. Lusthaus also examined this notion in his *Buddhist Phenomenology* (Lusthaus 2002). All these scholars acknowledge that the Yogācāra theory of knowledge is subservient to the goal of realizing the wisdom of emptiness and compassion. The current English language scholarship of Yogācāra philosophy does not prioritize the analysis of the notion of *āśraya-parivrtti* in the wake of the epistemic reading of the doctrine of consciousness-only. Rather than provide another thorough analysis of the notion of *āśraya-parivrtti*, I will instead draw upon previous research

and focus on the soteriological aspect of this evolution and detail how *āśraya-parivrtti* is an integral part of the Bodhisattvas' path.

11 The Path Towards Awakening

1. For instance, Zhiyi (智顗 538–97) explains how the negation of ignorance reveals the insight of Buddha nature, which resembles the ways in which the jewels are disclosed and the suchness is unveiled (T46N1911, P10c12). Similarly, the master of Huayan Buddhism, Fazang (法藏 c. 643–712) equates Buddha nature with emptiness and suchness with the reference to *Mahāparinirvāṇasūtra* (T45N1866, P487c17–19).
2. As suggested by Ching Keng and Eyal Aviv, Buddha nature is the first, broad meaning of the Sanskrit term *tathāgatagarbha*, in contrast to the second, narrow meaning that entails an innate quality of being awakened (Keng 2009; Aviv 2020). To differentiate these two meanings, we reserve the concept of *tathāgatagarbha* for the second meaning and resolve to use the notion of Buddha nature in the general debate over awakening.
3. In her book, *Buddha Nature*, Sallie King investigates the *Treatise on Buddha Nature* where she sketches the debates between Xuanzang and followers of Paramārtha (King 1991). Drawing on her findings, I will position this debate in the early–later divide in Chinese Yogācāra, with reference to more Yogācāra texts in the Chinese language.
4. For a quick review of this part of the history, see Kenneth Chen (1964: 125).
5. Zhiyi widely utilizes Chinese philosophical terminologies, such as *quan-shi* (權實, conventional-ultimate) (T33N1716, P693a20–3), in his elaboration of emptiness, subsequently expanding the twofold truth into the threefold truth, and consequently putting forward his creative interpretation of the Buddha's teaching (T46N1911, P34a19–21). For studies on Zhiyi's threefold truth, see Paul Swanson 1990; Ng Yu-Kwan 1993.
6. For Chinese Buddhists at that time, the terminologies they employed to capture the conventional differences and ultimate identity are the three vehicles (三乘) and the one vehicle (一乘) (T33N1716, 700b17–21). Recently, Zijie Li has examined how Chinese clerics before Xuanzang innovatively translated and interpreted the concept of Buddha nature, suchness, and *tathāgatagarbha* to describe awakening as a recuperation of the originally pure mind (Li 2020). The notion of three vehicles—the vehicles of *śrāvaka*, *pratyeka*, and *buddha*—is formulated to capture three types of results of sentient beings' religious training, in contrast to the idea of one vehicle that entails how sentient beings ultimately have innate Buddha nature. As analyzed by Fujita Kōtatsu, the idea of one vehicle bespeaks the stance toward Buddha nature preserved in the *Lotus Sūtra* revered by the Tiantai School of Buddhism (Fujita 1975: 82). While Tiantai clergy follow the *Lotus Sūtra* to deem the three vehicles to be conventional, Yogācārins perceive these three vehicles as the ultimate (Lü 1986: 433). There are also many other ways of referring to this debate in doctrinal philosophy, such as "all having Buddha nature (悉有佛性)" versus "sentient beings without nature (有情無性)" (Xia 2003: 88) or "all natures to be realized (一性皆成)" versus "five natures being distinctly different (五姓各別)" (Yoshimura 2002: 35). To help readers access the core of the idea of all having Buddha nature, I express the teachings articulated by Chinese Buddhists without introducing too many doctrinal terms. In the greater East Asian context, clerics in Japan and Korea continued to develop their creative articulations of Buddha nature. For instance, Dōgen (1200–53), the prominent

Sōtō cleric, creatively interprets the verse "一切眾生，悉有佛性" by equating the three parts, 一切眾生=悉有=佛性, further suggesting that all sentient beings are, in fact, Buddha nature (T82N2582, P91c). By rejecting the polarity between the nature of sentient beings and that of the Buddha, Dōgen advocates that all sentient beings are Buddha nature, which not only revolutionizes the doctrine of *tathāgatagarbha* that underscores the entire debate over Buddha nature but also advances the conception of absolute non-duality in Japanese Buddhist philosophy.

7 Swanson refers to the real nature of things, the wisdom of seeing things as they are, and the wide range of religious practices, as the three aspects of Zhiyi's articulation of Buddha nature (Swanson 1989: 173).

8 Regarding Zhiyi's stress on the middle way between the ultimate and the conventional, Paul Swanson also argues for interpreting it as the expression of Buddha nature and the nature of reality in virtue of the threefold pattern (Swanson 1989: 174).

9 In his study of the debate over Buddha nature, Lü Cheng mainly explores the divide inside the Yogācāra School of consciousness-only (Lü 1986: 425). While Lü mainly focuses on the writings of Kuiji and Huizhao, recent studies in Japanese scholarship detail the arguments from both sides of the debate over Buddha nature (Fukihara 1973; Rhodes 1994; Yoshimura 2009). Outside the Yogācāra school, clerics, such as the third patriarch of Huayan Buddhism, Fazang (法藏 c. 643–712), and the ninth patriarch of Tiantai Buddhism, Jinxi Zhanran (荊溪湛然 711–82), have composed commentaries that challenge the *gotra* system endorsed by Xuanzang's followers (Wang 1942: 194). In Japan, Yogācārins debated the same issue concerning Buddha nature during the Nara Period, and later during the Kamakura period. At that time, their rivals were clerics not only from the long-established schools that were in favor of the "one-vehicle" but also from the newly founded schools of Zen and Pure Land (Yamasaki 1985).

10 In his etymological analysis of the Sanskrit term *gotra*, Lü Cheng suggests that *gotra* is comprised of two parts, *go-* and *-tara*, the literal meaning being "virtue" and "carrying beyond" and as such, *gotra* yields the sense of being saved by virtue, which alludes to the cause of goodness (Lü 1986: 426). Takasaki Jikidō expresses a similar viewpoint in his study of early Yogācāra and *tathāgatagarbha* that *gotra* is translated both as 種姓 and 種性 because *gotra* is connected with seeds and perceived as a transcendental capacity (Takasaki 1986: 23). Also, in his insightful dissertation *Yogācāra Buddhism Transmitted or Transformed*, Ching Keng examines how and why the two concepts—namely 佛性 (Buddha-nature) and 佛姓 (Buddha-*gotra*)—have been treated as synonyms in Chinese Buddhism (Keng 2009). As argued by Keng, the conflation of these two Chinese concepts represents another creative understanding of Buddhism in the local intellectual context. Keng further specifies in a separate paper that early Yogācārins who wrote in the Chinese language suggested how Buddha nature, as the unpolluted emptiness, is interconnected with the polluted illusory Buddha-*gotra* (Keng 2011: 69–98).

11 In his study of Huizhao's *The Treatise on the Revealing of the Middle and the Sun-like Wisdom* (能顯中邊慧日論), Fukihara Shōshin analyzes the three senses of Buddha nature penned by Huizhao, in which he also remarks how these three senses are related to the three natures in the Yogācāra framework (Fukihara 1966: 17–18). However, Fukihara has not explained yet how they are related. Drawing upon and developing Fukihara's insight, I elaborate on the parallel.

12 To clarify, the notion of self-power or other-power, as suggested by the Chinese characters, does not reaffirm the existence of a *svabhāvic* self (*wo* 我). Although both

zi (自) and *wo* (我) have been translated as "self" in English, the former is utilized to capture the agency of an individual. Indeed, in the discussion of agency, Buddhists in East Asia evoke the *zi–ta* (自他) binary in a creative way to articulate ideas regarding actions without violating the doctrine of no-self.

13 As many scholars have noted, Jōkei associates the theory of Buddha nature quite explicitly with the theory of three natures and that of three non-natures, insofar as he promotes the differentiation of five families with the help of the three natures, while reaffirming the account of all having Buddha nature through the conception of three non-natures (Kamata 1971: 534; Yamasaki 1985: 254).

14 For a critical English translation of this text, see Morrell, "Jōkei and the Kōfukuji petition" (1983: 6–38).

15 I have outlined these five stages in another article: "From Self-Attaching to Self-Emptying" (Li 2017: 194–6). However, my description back at the time misuses the term "*mārga*" for "*vasthā*." I also failed to connect these five stages with the two types of insights and did not include any discussion of other minds into the previous analysis. These are the limitations that this section will now tackle and overcome.

12 Revisiting the Process of Awakening

1 Scholars have used different English terms, including "concentration and insight" (Chen 1964), "calming and contemplation" (Donner & Stevenson 1993; Kantor 2009), and "clear serenity, quiet insight" (Swanson 2018) to translate the notion of *zhiguan*, in their study of the Tiantai contemplative practice. Regarding Yogācāra Buddhism, most studies are dedicated to resources in the Indo-Tibetan tradition. Paul Griffiths (1986), for instance, examines one particular meditative practice called *nirodhasamapatti*, literally translated as "attainment of cessation" in Buddhist traditions of Theravāda, Vaibhāṣika, and Yogācāra. In another paper, Nagao Gadjin (1978) inquires into the relationship between emptiness and meditation in early Yogācāra. Stefen Anacker (1978) investigates the notion of mindfulness in Vasubandhu's *Mahyāntavibhāgabhāṣya*. Regarding *abhisamaya*, "the immediate insight," Hayajima Kyosei (1956), Mano Ryūkai (1969), and Ronald Davidson (1993) have examined the etymology of this term, as well as the development of this practice in the Indo-Tibetan context. In his dissertation on Kuiji's interpretation of Yogācāra, Alan Sponberg (1979) sketched the notion of five-level contemplation, which is referred to as five-rank contemplation in this book. Though not detailing the early–later divide on the theory of meditative practice, Sponberg made a case for his argument that the notion of contemplation yields the most original contribution Kuiji has made to the development of Yogācāra thought (Sponberg 1979: 78). Drawing on the aforementioned research, I position Kuiji's elaboration on contemplation in the Yogācāra framework of consciousness, further examining the place of contemplation in Yogācāra practice. Differing from Sponberg, who interprets this contemplative practice for gradually realizing the insight of consciousness-only, I argue for perceiving this account of contemplation as the first step towards gradual realization, which is followed by moral actions and social constructions.

2 Prior to Xuanzang's return to the Tang Empire, the meditative practice of calming and contemplating had already become prevalent. This meditative practice, as detailed by Zhiyi in his manual of *The Great Calming and Contemplating* (*mohe zhiguan* 摩訶止

觀), entails a system detailing how to monitor one's breath, regulate one's dietary routine, and conduct various ritual acts of bathing and chanting (T46N1911).
3 For instance, even before Xuanzang entered *nirvāṇa*, he immersed himself in intense contemplation while the clergy in the Ci'en Temple performed the death bed ritual and were chanting *sūtras* for him (T50N2053, P277b1–11).
4 As stressed by Barbra Clayton, ethics is the key to understanding Buddhist teaching (Clayton 2006: 2). When it comes to Buddhist ethics, existing scholarship tends to categorize the Buddhist teaching of moral actions in four fields: normative ethics (thoughts on the bases and justifications of moral guidelines); meta-ethics (concerning the principles of moral truth), applied ethics (moral guidelines for specific cases), and descriptive ethics (how people actually behave) (Harvey 2000: 2).

There is a wealth of scholarship on normative ethics. According to Christopher Gowans (2014) and Charles Goodman (2017), the articulation of moral rules and precepts has been interpreted in four different ways. First, Buddhist ethics have been read as utilitarianism, given that Buddhist followers undertake religious training to overcome suffering through liberation and enlightenment (Kalupahana 1976; Barnhart 2012; Harris 2015). Second, Buddhist ethics are seen as virtue ethics, considering how Buddhist training serves as the method for cultivating various virtues and realizing a flourishing life (Keown 1992; Harvey 2000). Third, character consequentialism has been read as a utilitarian hybrid of virtue ethics that rejects the dichotomy between inner virtue and outer action for a teleological cultivation of morality (Clayton 2006; Goodman 2009). Fourth, aretaic consequentialism as another attempt to combine hedonism and virtue ethics that perceives Buddhist training as the development of virtuous characters for oneself through which one could attain happiness (Siderits 2007). Nevertheless, several scholars represented by Charles Hallisey (1996), refuse to impose the framework of normative ethics upon Buddhist theories, insofar as Buddhism encompasses a plurality of traditions and therefore does not present a universal viewpoint on ethics. This is probably also the case for later Yogācāra Buddhism. As previously mentioned, religious training and moral actions in Yogācāra are subservient to the realization of dependent-evolution, which entails a twofold awakening as the liberation of oneself and the enlightenment for others. Articulated in this manner, Buddhist moral actions not only fulfill the goals of self-cultivation and happiness for oneself but also go beyond them.

Meta-ethics, according to Michael Huemer, addresses the ultimate question of whether objective moral values exist (Huemer 2005: 4). Those who acknowledge this existence are known as moral realists in contrast to moral anti-realists who negate the existence of such objective moral values (Huemer 2005: 4). By objectivity, Huemer means a non-subjective feature, in contrast to a subjective one that always depends on our psychological attitude or response towards things—an attitude that has the tendency to elicit our actions (Huemer 2005: 2). Regarding the degree to which moral anti-realists deny the existence of objective moral values, their standpoints can be further categorized into three types: subjectivism (for which moral values are inherently subjective), non-cognitivism (moral evaluation does not yield any propositions about objective existence), and nihilism (there is no such thing as an objective value) (Huemer 2005: 4). Contrariwise, there are two varieties of moral realism: ethical naturalism (objective moral properties exist but such properties can be reduced to non-evaluative ones) and ethical intuitionism (objective moral properties exist and are irreducible, which we can know intuitively) (Huemer 2005: 6). From Huemer's outline, we can infer that the concern for meta-ethics in contemporary philosophy is the existence of objective moral value. This concern, however, differs enormously from that of Chinese Buddhists who lived in the 600s. Furthermore, the latter do not deliberately demarcate meta-ethics from applied ethics or normative ethics. Nevertheless, if we agree to follow Huemer's line of thinking, we might be able to classify ethics in the Yogācāra sense as a type of ethical intuitionism in terms of meta-ethics. That is to say, we have an intuitive and irreducible knowledge of right and wrong (in virtue of the function of consciousnesses and their mental factors), which urges us to conduct moral deeds.

Applied ethics center the discussions on moral actions in instantiated cases, such as the treatment of animals, environmental protection, etc. We have not seen many discussions on these subject matters in Xuanzang and Kuiji's writings. Nevertheless, in the liturgical texts composed by Kuiji's disciples, there are traces of such accounts that can be interpreted in terms of applied ethics.

5 The Yogācāra view of social construction is further detailed in *The Treatise on the Sūtra of Buddha Stage* (佛地經論) (T26N1530). While it is beyond the scope of the current section to explore the account of social ontology presented in this treatise, it deserves to be examined in a future research project.
6 Early Yogācārins likewise put forward their respective theory of three bodies: the purified eighth consciousness amounts to the dharma body, the immaculate seventh consciousness entails the enjoyment body, while the other six consciousnesses in their pure form give rise to the emanation body.
7 In a different article, Setha Low (2003) details the general understanding of an embodied space from an anthropological perspective.
8 When it comes to proselytization, this premodern version of a Pure Land on Earth was far less attractive than a wondrous heavenly realm where sentient beings arrive after death. Nevertheless, along with the revival of Yogācāra Buddhism in early Republican China, this conception of a pure land likewise was rediscovered by Buddhist reformers and scholars, among others, Ven. Taixu (太虛 1890–1947) who has been recognized as the founder of modern humanistic Buddhism. It is beyond our scope to investigate how the premodern conception of Maitreya's Pure Land on Earth inspired Taixu's humanistic Buddhism, which has elsewhere attracted scholarly attention (Ritzinger 2017).

Bibliography

Primary Sources

An, Shigao 安世高, trans. (1924), 佛說轉法輪經 [*Sūtra of the Buddha Turning the Dharma-Wheel*], T.2, No.109 (see Takakusu et al., 1924–32).

Aquinas, Thomas (1968), *On Being and Essence*, trans. Armand Maurer, Toronto: Pontifical Institute of Mediaeval Studies.

Aristotle (1952), *The Works of Aristotle*, trans. John Alexander Smith and William David Ross, Oxford: Clarendon.

Bandhuprabha 親光 (1924), 佛地經論 [*The Treatise on the Sūtra of Buddha Stage*], trans. Xuanzang, T.26, No.1530 (see Takakusu et al., 1924–32).

Brentano, Franz (1995), *Psychology from an Empirical Standpoint*, trans. Antos Rancurello, Burnham Terrell, and Linda McAlister, New York: Routledge.

Daoxuan 道宣 (1924), 續高僧傳 [*The Expanded Biographies of Great Masters*], T.50, No.2060 (see Takakusu et al., 1924–32).

Descartes, René (1996), *Discourse on the Method and Meditations on First Philosophy*, trans. Elizabeth Sanderson Haldane and George Robert Thompson Ross, New Haven: Yale University Press.

Dignāga 陳那 (1924), 觀所緣緣論 [*The Treatise on the Contemplation of the Condition of the Perceived Phenomena*], trans. Xuanzang, T.31, No.1624 (see Takakusu et al., 1924–32).

Dōgen 道元 (1924), 正法眼藏 [*Treasure of the True Dharma Eye*], T.82, No.2582 (see Takakusu et al., 1924–32).

Fazang 法藏 (1924a), 十二門論宗致義記 [*Commentary of the Viewpoints of Buddhist Schools through Twelve Gates*], T.42, No.1826 (see Takakusu et al., 1924–32).

Fazang 法藏 (1924b), 華嚴一乘教義分齊章 [*Chapters on the Doctrine of Difference and Identity of the One Vehicle of Huayan*], T.45, No.1866 (see Takakusu et al., 1924–32).

Gadamer, Hans-Georg (1989), *Truth and Method*, trans. Joel Weinsheimer and Donald Marshall, London: Sheed and Ward.

Hori, Victor Sōgen, trans. (2003), *Zen Sand: The Book of Capping Phrases for Kōan Practice*, Honolulu: University Press of Hawaii.

Huizhao 慧沼 (1924a), 勸發菩提心集 [*Advice on Awakening the Bodhicitta*], T.45, No.1862 (see Takakusu et al., 1924–32).

Huizhao 慧沼 (1924b), 能顯中邊慧日論 [*The Treatise on the Revealing of the Middle and the Sun-like Wisdom*], T.45, No.1863 (see Takakusu et al., 1924–32).

Husserl, Edmund (1950a), *Cartesianische Meditationen und Pariser Vorträge. Hua 1*, ed. Stephan Strasser, The Hague: Martinus Nijhoff Publishers.

Husserl, Edmund (1950b), *Ideen zu einer reinen Phänomenologie und Phänomenologischen Philosophie, Erstes Buch. Hua 3*, ed. Walter Biemel, The Hague: Martinus Nijhoff Publishers.

Husserl, Edmund (1952), *Ideen zu einer reinen Phänomenologie und Phänomenologischen Philosophie, Zweites Buch. Hua 4*, ed. Marly Biemel, The Hague: Martinus Nijhoff Publishers.

Husserl, Edmund (1954), *Die Krisis der Europäischen Wissenschaften und die Transzendentale Phänomenologie. Hua 6*, ed. Walter Biemel, The Hague: Martinus Nijhoff Publishers.
Husserl, Edmund (1956), *Erste Philosophie (1923/1924), Erster Teil. Hua 7*, ed. Rudolf Boehm, The Hague: Martinus Nijhoff Publishers.
Husserl, Edmund (1966), *Vorlesungen zur Phänomenologie der Inneren Zeitbewusstseins. Hua 10*, ed. Rudolf Boehm, The Hague: Martinus Nijhoff Publishers.
Husserl, Edmund (1970), *Philosophie der Arithmetik. Hua 12*, ed. Lothar Eley, The Hague: Martinus Nijhoff Publishers.
Husserl, Edmund (1973), *Zur Phänomenologie der Intersubjektivität, Zweiter Teil. Hua 14*, ed. Iso Kern, The Hague: Martinus Nijhoff Publishers.
Husserl, Edmund (1974), *Formale und Transzendentale Logik. Hua 17*, ed. Paul Janssen, The Hague: Martinus Nijhoff Publishers.
Husserl, Edmund (1975), *Logische Untersuchungen, Erster Bund. Hua 18*, ed. Elmar Holenstein, The Hague: Martinus Nijhoff Publishers.
Husserl, Edmund (1984), *Logische Untersuchungen, Zweiter Bund. Hua 19*, ed. Ursula Panzer, The Hague: Martinus Nijhoff Publishers.
Husserl, Edmund (1989), *Aufsätze und Vorträge. 1922-1937. Hua 27*, ed. Thomas Nenon and Hans Rainer Sepp, Dordrecht: Kluwer Academic Publishers.
Husserl, Edmund (2020), *Studien zur Struktur des Bewusstseins. Hua 43*, ed. Ullirch Melle and Thomas Vongehr, Dordrecht: Springer.
Jōkei 貞慶 (1924), 唯識論同學鈔 [*The Study of the Doctrine of Consciousness-only*], T.66, No.2263 (see Takakusu et al., 1924–32).
Kant, Immanuel (1998), *Critique of Pure Reason*, trans. Paul Guyer and Allen Wood, Cambridge: Cambridge University Press.
Kuiji 窺基 (1924a), 觀彌勒上生兜率天經贊 [*Complimenting Maitreya Ascending to the Tuṣita Heaven*], T.38, No.1772. (see Takakusu et al., 1924–32).
Kuiji 窺基 (1924b), 成唯識論述記 [*Commentary of the Perfection of Consciousness-only*], T.43, No.1830 (see Takakusu et al., 1924–32).
Kuiji 窺基 (1924c), 成唯識論掌中樞要 [*Handbook to the Treatise on the Perfection of Consciousness-only*], T.43, No.1831 (see Takakusu et al., 1924–32).
Kuiji 窺基 (1924d), 唯識二十論述記 [*Commentary of the Twenty Verses on Consciousness-only*], T.43, No.1834 (see Takakusu et al., 1924–132).
Kuiji 窺基 (1924e), 辯中邊論述記 [*Commentary of the Treatise on Distinguishing the Boundary of the Middle*], T.44, No.1835 (see Takakusu et al., 1924–32).
Kuiji 窺基 (1924f), 因明入正理論疏 [*Commentary of the Treatise on the Entering the Correct Principles of Hetuvidyā*], T.44, No.1840 (see Takakusu et al., 1924–32).
Kuiji 窺基 (1924g), 大乘法苑義林章 [*Chapters on the Mahāyāna Dharma Garden and the Forest of Meaning*], T.45, No.1861 (see Takakusu et al., 1924–32).
Kumārajīva 鳩摩羅什, trans. (1924), 維摩詰所說經 [*The Sūtra of Vimalakīrti*], T.14, No.475 (see Takakusu et al., 1924–32).
Laozi 老子 (2001), *Tao Te Ching: A Bilingual Edition*, trans. D. C. Lau, Hong Kong: Chinese University of Hong Kong Press.
Mengzi 孟子 (2003), *Mencius*, trans. Irene Bloom, New York: Columbia University Press.
Merleau-Ponty, Maurice (1945), *Phénoménologie de la Perception*, Paris: Gallimard.
Mingxiang 冥祥 (1924), 大唐故三藏玄奘法師行狀 [*The Chronicle of Xuanzang, the Tripiṭaka Dharma Master of the Great Tang*], T.50, No.2052 (see Takakusu et al., 1924–32).

Nāgārjuna 龍樹 (1924), 中論 [*The Treatise on the Middle*], trans. Kumārajīva, T.30, No.1564 (see Takakusu et al., 1924–32).
Paramārtha 真諦 (1924a), 決定藏論 [*The Treatise on the Matrix of Determination*], T.30, No.1584 (see Takakusu et al., 1924–32).
Paramārtha 真諦 (1924a), 轉識論 [*The Treatise on the Transforming Consciousness*], T.31, No.1587 (see Takakusu et al., 1924–32).
Paramārtha 真諦, trans. (1924c), 十八空論 [*Eighteen Verses on the Empty*], T.31, No.1616 (see Takakusu et al., 1924–32).
Paramārtha 真諦, trans. (1924d), 三無性論 [*The Treatise on Three Non-Natures*], T.31, No.1617 (see Takakusu et al., 1924–32).
Plato (1997), *Plato: Complete Works*, ed. John Cooper, Indianapolis: Hackett.
Puguang 普光 (1924), 俱舍論記 [*Commentary of Abhidharmakośakārikā*], T.41, No.1821 (see Takakusu et al., 1924–32).
Sengzhao 僧肇 (1924a), 注維摩詰經卷 [*Commentary of the Sūtra of Vimalakīrti*], T.38, No.1775 (see Takakusu et al., 1924–32).
Sengzhao 僧肇 (1924b), 肇論 [*Treatises Composed by Sengzhao*], T.45, No.1858 (see Takakusu et al., 1924–32).
Śikṣānanda 實叉難陀, trans. (1924), 入楞伽經 [*The Sūtra of Entering Laṅkā*], T.16, No.672 (see Takakusu et al., 1924–32).
Takakusu, Junjirō 高楠順次郎, Watanabe, Kaigyoku 渡辺海旭, and Ono, Genmyo 小野玄妙, ed. (1924–32), 大正新脩大藏經 [*The Taishō Tripiṭaka*], Tokyo: 東京: Taisho Shinshu Daizokyo Kanko Kai. The SAT Daizōkyō Text Database https://21dzk.l.u-tokyo.ac.jp/SAT/index_en.html (accessed 1 May 2021).
Vasubandhu 世親 (1924a), 十地經論 [*The Treatise on the Sūtra of Ten Stages*], trans. Bodhiruci, T.26, No.1522 (see Takakusu et al., 1924–32).
Vasubandhu 世親 (1924b), 阿毗達磨俱舍論 [*Abhidharmakośakārikā*], trans. Xuanzang, T.29, No.1558 (see Takakusu et al., 1924–32).
Wang, Bi 王弼 (2011), 老子道德真經注 [*The Commentary of the True Teaching of the Way and the Virtue*], Beijing: Zhonghua Shuju.
Xuanzang 玄奘, trans. (1924a), 說無垢稱經 [*The Sūtra on the Teaching of Non-Pollution*], T.14, No.476 (see Takakusu et al., 1924–32).
Xuanzang 玄奘 (1924b), 成唯識論 [*The Treatise on the Perfection of Consciousness-only*], T.31, No.1585 (see Takakusu et al., 1924–32).
Xuanzang 玄奘 (1924c), 大唐西域記 [*Records on the Western Regions of the Great Tang*], T.51, No.2087 (see Takakusu et al., 1924–32).
Yancong 彥悰 (1924), 大唐大慈恩寺三藏法師傳 [*The Biography of the Tripiṭaka Dharma Master of the Ci'en Temple of the Great Tang*], T.50, No.2053 (see Takakusu et al., 1924–32).
Zenshu 善珠 (1924), 因明論疏明燈鈔 [*Illumination of the Lamp on the Commentary of Hetuvidyā*], T.68, No.2270. (see Takakusu et al., 1924–32).
Zhizhou 智周 (1924), 大乘入道次第 [*Gradual Entering the Path of Mahāyāna*], T.45, No.1864 (see Takakusu et al., 1924–32).
Zhiyi 智顗 (1924a), 妙法蓮華經玄義 [*The Profound Meaning of the Lotus Sūtra*], T.33, No.1716 (see Takakusu et al., 1924–32).
Zhiyi 智顗 (1924b), 摩訶止觀 [*The Great Calming and Contemplating*], T.46, No.1911 (see Takakusu et al., 1924–32).
Zongmi 宗密 (1924), 禪源諸詮集都序 [*The Preface to the Interpretations of the Various Origins of Chan*], T.48, No.2015 (see Takakusu et al., 1924–32).

Secondary Resources in East Asian Languages

Cao, Yan 曹彥 (2014),"从梵语波你尼文法论论证玄奘"唯识"翻译和理解的正确性 [Justifying the Correctness of Xuanzang's Translation and Comprehension of 'Consciousness-only' in accordance with the Pāṇini Grammar Rules of the Sanskrit Language]," 武汉大学学报 [*Wuhan University Journal of Humanity and Social Science*], 6: 28–37.

Chao, Tung-Ming 趙東明 (2011),"轉依理論研究：以《《成唯識論》》及窺基《《成唯識論述記》》為中心 [A Study of Fundamental Transformation (āśraya-parivrtti/āśraya-parvāvrtti) in the *Cheng Weishi Lun* and Kuiji's *Commentary on the Cheng Weishi Lun*]," Ph.D. Diss., National Taiwan University, Taipei.

Chen, I-Biau 陳一標 (2007),"唯識學「行相」（ākāra）之研究 [A Study of the Concept of Ākāra in the Doctrine of Consciousness-only]," 正觀 [*Satyabhisamaya: A Buddhist Studies Quarterly*], 43: 5–21.

Cheng, Gongrang 程恭讓 (2000), 抉择于真伪之间：欧阳竟无佛学思想探微 [*A Discernment between the True and the Fake: On Ouyang Jingwu's Buddhist Thoughts*], Shanghai: East China Normal University Press.

Cheng, Jianhua 成建華 (2013),"关于'唯识'一词的再思考 [Rethinking the Notion of Consciousness-only]," 哲学研究 [*Philosophical Researches*], 12: 55–9.

Cheng, Jianhua 成建華 (2014),"关于'唯识'一词翻译问题的再思考 [Rethinking the Translation of Consciousness-only]," 法音 [*Dharma Voice*], 3: 12–18.

Chien, Kai-Ting 簡凱廷 (2014),"晚明義學僧一雨通潤及其稀見著作考述 [Investigation of the Rare Writings of Late Ming Scholar-monk Yiyu Tongrun]," 臺大佛學研究 [*Taiwan Journal of Buddhist Studies*], 28: 143–90.

Chien, Kai-Ting 簡凱廷 (2015),"晚明唯識學作品在江戶時代的流傳與接受初探 [Initial Study of The Transmission and Reception of Late Ming Yogācāra Writings in Edo Japan]," 中華佛學研究 [*Chung-Hwa Buddhist Studies*], 16: 43–72.

Chien, Kai-Ting 簡凱廷 (2017a),"被忘卻的傳統：明末清初《成唯識論》相關珍稀注釋書考論 [A Forgotten Tradition: The Lesser Known Late-Ming and Early-Qing Annotations of the *Cheng Weishi Lun*]," 漢學研究 [*Chinese Studies*], 35(1): 225–60.

Chien, Kai-Ting 簡凱廷 (2017b),"空印鎮澄對相宗學說之商榷 [Scrutinizing Kongyin Zhencheng's Interpretation of Faxiang Theories]," 中華佛學研究 [*Chung-Hwa Buddhist Studies*], 18: 1–39.

Feng, Qi 冯契 (2009), 中国古代哲学的逻辑发展 [*The Logical Development of Traditional Chinese Philosophy*], Shanghai: East China Normal University Press.

Fok, Tou-hui 霍韜晦 (1979), 安慧《三十唯識釋》原典譯注 [*An Annotated Translation of Sthiramati's Commentary on the Thirty Verses of Consciousness-only*], Hong Kong: Chinese University of Hong Kong Press.

Fu, Xinyi 傅新毅 (2002),"佛学是一种本体论吗 [Is the Buddha Dharma a Type of Ontology]?," 南京大学学报 [*Journal of Nanjing University*], 39: 15–24.

Fu, Xinyi 傅新毅 (2006), 玄奘评传 [*Biography of Xuanzang*], Nanjing: Nanjing University Press.

Fukihara, Shōshin 富貴原章信 (1966),"慧日論の仏性説 [The Notion of Buddha Nature in *On the Revealing of the Middle and the Sun-like Wisdom*]," 大谷学報 [*The Otani Gakuho*], 46(2): 1–21.

Fukihara, Shōshin 富貴原章信 (1973),"霊潤神泰の仏性論争について [The Debate on Buddha Nature Between Reijun and Shintai]," 同朋仏教 [*The Doho Bukkyo*], 5: 57–71.

Fukihara, Shōshin 富貴原章信 (1989), 日本唯識思想史 [*The Intellectual History of Consciousness-only in Japan*], Tokyo: Kokusho kankōkai.

Fukuda, Takumi 福田琢 (1993), "『俱舍論』における '行相' [Ākāra in the *Abhidharmakośabhāṣya* VII13]," 印度学仏教学研究 [*Journal of Indian and Buddhist Studies*], 41(2): 180–4.
Ge, Zhaoguang 葛兆光 (1986), 禅宗与中国文化 [*Chan Buddhism and Chinese Culture*], Shanghai: Shanghai People Press.
Ge, Zhaoguang 葛兆光 (2008), 中国思想史 [*Intellectual History of China*], Shanghai: Fudan University Press.
Han, Jingqing 韓鏡清 (1998), "唯識三十頌 [Thirty Verses of Consciousness-only]," 甘露 [*The Sweet Dew*], Vol3: 64.
Hayajima, Kyosei 早島鏡正 (1956), "Abhisamaya (現観) について [On Abhisamaya]," 印度学仏教学研究 [*Journal of Indian and Buddhist Studies*], 4(2): 546–9.
Ito, Yasuhiro 伊藤康裕 (2013), "対象のākāraについて [About Ākāra of Cognitive Objects]," 仏教学 [*Bukkyo Gaku, Journal of Buddhist Studies*], 54: 65–85.
Kamata, Shigeo 鎌田茂雄 (1971), "南都教学の思想史的意義 [The Significance of the Intellectual History of the Nara Teachings]," in Kamata Shigeo 鎌田茂雄 and Tanaka Hisao 田中久雄 (eds), 鎌倉舊佛教 [*The Old Buddhism of Kamakura*], 528–69, Tokyo: Iwanami Shoten.
Keng, Ching 耿晴 (2011), "「佛性」與「佛姓」概念的混淆：以《佛性論》與《大乘起信論》為中心 [The Conflation of Buddha-nature and Buddha-gotra: An Analysis Based on the *Treatises of Buddha Nature* and *The Awakening of Faith*]," 漢語哲學新視域．政治大學哲學系 [*New Perspectives of Philosophy in the Chinese Language. Department of Philosophy at National Chengchi University*], 69–98.
Kern, Iso 耿宁 (2012), 心的现象 [*The Phenomenon of Mind*], trans. Ni Liangkang 倪梁康, Zhang Qingxiong 张庆熊 and Wang Qingjie 王庆节, Beijing: Commercial Press.
Lai, Shen-Chon 賴賢宗 (2006), 如來藏說與唯識思想的交涉 [*The Exchange between Tathāgatagarbha and the Yogācāra Doctrine of Consciousness-only*], Taipei: Sinwenfeng Press.
Lai, Shen-Chon 賴賢宗 (2009), 佛教诠释学 [*Buddhist Hermeneutics*], Beijing: Beijing University Press.
Lau, Lawrence. Y. K. 劉宇光 (2007a), "從現象學還原法試探「五重唯識觀」的哲學意蘊 [The Investigation of the Philosophical Meaning of the 'Five Steps of Realizing the Insight on Consciousness-only' from the Leans of Phenomenological Reduction]," 現象學與人文科學 [*Phenomenology and Humanities*], 3: 111–67.
Lau, Lawrence. Y. K. 劉宇光 (2007b), "書評：悅家丹《佛教現象學：佛教瑜伽行派與《成唯識論》哲學研究》 [Book Review: Dan Lusthaus's *Buddhist Phenomenology*]," 現象學與人文科學 [*Phenomenology and Humanities*], 3: 247–61.
Li, Zijie 李子捷 (2020), 『究竟一乘宝性論』と東アジア仏教 —— 五―七世紀の如来蔵．真如．種姓説の研究 [*The Ratnagotravibhāga and East Asian Buddhism: A Study on the Tathāgatagarbha, Tathatā and Gotra between the 5th and 7th Centuries*], Tokyo: Kokusho Kankōkai.
Liang, Shumin 梁漱溟 (2004), 东西文化及其哲学 [*Eastern Western Cultures and Their Philosophy*], Beijing: Commercial Press.
Lin, Chen-Kuo 林鎮國 (2018a), "論證與釋義：江戶時期基辨與快道《觀所緣緣論》註疏的研究 [Syllogism and Exegesis in Kiben's and Kaidō's Commentaries on Dignāga's *Ālamabanaparīkṣa* Verses 1–3]," 佛光學報 [*Fo Guang Journal of Buddhist Studies*], 4(2): 373–420.
Liu, Shu-Fen 劉淑芬 (2009), "玄奘的最後十年 [The Last Ten Years of Xuanzang's Life]," 中華文史論叢 [*Journal of Chinese Literature and History*], 3: 1–97.

Luo, Cheng 羅琤 (2010), 金陵刻经处研究 [*A Study of the Jinling Sutra Publishing House*], Shanghai: Shanghai People Press.

Lü, Cheng 吕澄 (1979), 中国佛学源流略讲 [*A Brief Study of the Development of Chinese Buddhism*], Beijing: Beijing Shuju.

Lü, Cheng 吕澄 (1986), 吕澄佛学论著选集 [*Lü Cheng's Writings on Buddhism*], Jinan: Qilu Shuju.

Lü, Cheng 吕澄 (2007), 因明入正理论讲解 [*Commentary of Nyāyapraveśatākaśāstra*], Beijing: Zhonghua Shuju.

Mei, Guangxi 梅光羲 ([1931]2014), "相宗新旧两译不同论 [On the Distinctions between the Old and the New Translations of the Dharma-image School]," 梅光羲著述集 [*The Selected Writings of Mei Guangxi*], 339–45, Shanghai: Dongfang Chubanshe.

Mei, Wenhui 梅文辉 (2014), "从现象学看 '五重唯识观' [*Viewing the 'Five Ranks of Contemplating Consciousness-only' from the Perspective of Phenomenology*], M.A. diss., Huazhong University of Science and Technology, Wuhan.

Minamoto, Juko 源重浩 (2009), "初期唯識思想と独我論 [Early Yogācāra and Solipsism]," 印度学仏教学研究 [*Journal of Indian and Buddhist Studies*], 58(1): 117–21.

Minamoto, Juko 源重浩 (2011), "「本質」と「疎所縁縁」 [Essence and Secondary Object-support-condition]," 印度学仏教学研究 [*Journal of Indian and Buddhist Studies*], 60(1): 104–9.

Minamoto, Juko 源重浩 (2014), "新古唯識における相違点 [The Difference between Old and New Yogācāra]," 印度学仏教学研究 [*Journal of Indian and Buddhist Studies*], 63(1): 135–40.

Miyashita, Seiki 宮下晴輝 (1978), "心心所相応義におけるākāraについて [On Ākāra in the Light of Citta-caitta-samprayukta Theory]," 印度学仏教学研究 [*Journal of Indian and Buddhist Studies*], 26(2): 663–4.

Moro, Shigeki 師茂樹 (2017), "八世紀における唯識学派の対外交流：崇俊法清（詳）を中心に [International Relations of the Chinese Yogācāra School in the 8th Century: Focusing on Chongjun and Faqing (Faxiang)]," 印度学仏教学研究 [*Journal of Indian and Buddhist Studies*], 66(1): 1–9.

Nagasawa, Jitsudo 長沢実導 (1953), "Vijñaptiと Vijñāna [Vijñapti and Vijñāna]," 印度学仏教学研究 [*Journal of Indian and Buddhist Studies*], 1(2): 420–1.

Ng, Yu-Kwan 吳汝鈞 (1978), 唯識哲學 ：關於轉識成智理論問題之研究 [*The Philosophy of Consciousness-only: On the Theoretical Question of Perfecting the Transforming Consciousness into Wisdom*], Kaohsiung: Fo Guang Culture.

Ng, Yu-Kwan 吳汝鈞 (2002), 唯識現象學 [*The Phenomenology of Consciousness-only*], Taipei: Taiwan Student Book.

Ni, Liangkang 倪梁康 (2009), "赖耶缘起与意识发生——唯识学与现象学在纵-横意向性研究方面的比较与互补 [Dependent Arising from the Perspective of Ālaya and the Origin of Consciousness—Comparison and Complement of the Conception of Intentionality at the Horizontal and Vertical level of the Doctrine of Consciousness-only and Phenomenology]," 世界哲学 [*World Philosophy*], 4: 43–59.

Ouyang, Jingwu 欧阳竟无 ([1938]1995), "辨唯识法相 [Differentiating Consciousness-only and Dharma-image]," 欧阳竟无集 [*The Selected Writings of Ouyang Jingwu*], 130–3, Beijing: China Social Sciences Press.

Pan, Guiming 潘桂明 (1996), 智顗评传 [*A Critical Biography of Zhiyi*], Nanjing: Nanjing University Press.

Sheng-yen 聖嚴 (1999), 印度佛教史 [*History of Indian Buddhism*], Taipei: Dharma Drum Culture.

Sheng-yen 聖嚴 (2005), 探索識界：八識規矩頌講記 [*Exploring the Realm of Consciousness: Elaboration of Xuanzang's Verses on the Rules of Eight Consciousnesses*], Taipei: Dharma Drum Culture.

Shiba, Haruhide 司馬春英 (1998), "唯識思想と現象学―北山淳友『仏教の形而上学』を中心に― [Consciousness-only Thought and Phenomenology—Kitayama Junyu's *Metaphysics of Buddhism*]," 近代仏教 [*Kindai Bukkyō, Journal of the Modern Buddhism*], 5: 29–38.

Shiba, Haruhide 司馬春英 (2003), 唯識思想と現象学：思想構造の比較研究に向けて [*Consciousness-only Thought and Phenomenology: Comparative Studies of the Structure of Thought*], Tokyo: Taisho University Press.

Sueki, Fumihiko 末木文美士 (1992), "日本法相宗の形成 [The Establishment of Japanese Hossō School]," 仏教学 [*Bukkyo Gaku, Journal of Buddhist Studies*], 32: 21–39.

Suguro, Shinjō 勝呂信靜 (1985), "唯識說的理論體系之形成 [The Establishment of Yogācāra's Theoretical System]," in Takasaki Jikidō 高崎直道 (ed.) and Li Shijie 李世傑 (trans.), 唯識思想 [*The Theories of Consciousness-only*], 109–56, Taipei: Hua Yu Press.

Suguro, Shinjō 勝呂信靜 (2009), 唯識思想の形成と展開 [*The Formation and Development of the Conception of Consciousness-Only*], Tokyo: Sankibo Bushorin.

Taixu 太虛 ([1923]2005), "唯識讲要 [Lectures on Consciousness-only]," 太虛大师全书第九卷：法相唯识学（二）[*The Collected Writings of Master Taixu Vol9: The Dharma-Image School of Consciousness-only 2*], 264–93, Beijing: Zongjiao Wenhua Chubanshe.

Taixu 太虛 ([1932]2005), "法相唯识学概论 [On the Doctrine of Dharma-Image Consciousness-only]," 太虛大师全书第十卷：法相唯识学（三）[*The Collected Writings of Master Taixu Vol10: The Dharma-Image School of Consciousness-only 3*], 179–238, Beijing: Zongjiao Wenhua Chubanshe.

Takasaki, Jikidō 高崎直道, ed. (1985), 唯識思想 [*The Theories of Consciousness-only*], trans. Li Shijie 李世傑, Taipei: Hua Yu Press.

Takasaki, Jikidō 高崎直道, ed. (1986), 如來藏思想 [*Introduction to the Doctrine of Tathāgatagarbha*], trans. Li Shijie 李世傑, Taipei: Hua Yu Press.

Takasaki, Jikidō 高崎直道 (1992), 唯識入門 [*Entering the Gate of Consciousness-only*], Tokyo: Shunjusha Publishing.

Takemura, Makio 竹村牧男 (1976), "転依―二分依他 [*Asraya-parivrtti* and *ubhayabhagapatita-paratantrasvabhava*]," 印度学仏教学研究 [*Journal of Indian and Buddhist Studies*], 25(1): 201–4.

Takemura, Makio 竹村牧男 (1985), "地論宗、攝論宗、法相宗 [The Dilun School, The Shelun School, and the Faxiang School]," in Takasaki Jikidō 高崎直道 (ed.) and Li Shijie 李世傑 (trans.), 唯識思想 [*The Theories of Consciousness-only*], 373–430, Taipei: Hua Yu Press.

Tang, Yongtong 汤用彤 (2000), 隋唐佛教史稿 [*Historical Materials of Buddhism in Sui-Tang Dynasties*], Shijiazhuang: Hebei People Press.

Tang, Yijie 汤一介 (2001), 郭象与魏晋玄学 [*Guoxiang and the Dark Learning in Wei and Jin*], Beijing: Beijing University Press.

Ueda, Yoshifumi 上田義文 (1964), 唯識思想入門 [*An Introduction to the Doctrine of Consciousness-only*], Kyoto: Asoka Shorin.

Ujike, Akio 氏家昭夫 (1969), "唯識説におけるākāraの問題 [The Problem of Ākāra in Vijñānavāda]," 印度学仏教学研究 [*Journal of Indian and Buddhist Studies*], 17(2): 679–83.

Wang, Enyang 王恩洋 ([1942]2005), "佛教对于将来人类之任务、种性 [Buddhism's Tasks for Future Humans, Seed Nature]," in Taixu 太虛, 太虛大师全书30 [*Collected Writings of Master Taixu Vol. 30*], 185–98, Beijing: Zongjiao Wenhua Chubanshe.

Wu, Baihui 巫白慧 (2006), "梵本《唯识三十颂》汉译问题试解 [On the Chinese Translation of the Sanskrit Text *Thirty Verses of Consciousness-only*]," 法音 [*Dharma Voice*], 1: 15–18.

Xia, Jinhua 夏金华 (2002), "佛学理论中有本体论学说吗 [Is there an 'Ontology' in Buddhist Theories?]," 上海社科院学术季刊学报 [*Quarterly Journal of the Shanghai Academy of Social Sciences*], 3: 133–9.

Xia, Jinhua 夏金华 (2003), 缘起，佛性，成佛 [*Dependent Arising, Buddha Nature, and the Realization of the Buddhahood*], Beijing: Zongjiao Wenhua Chubanshe.

Xiao, Yongming 肖永明 (2009), "唯识观行的现象学开展 [A Phenomenological Deduction of the Realization of Insight on Consciousness-only]," 法音 [*Dharma Voice*], 1: 7–11.

Xiong, Shili 熊十力 (1985), 佛家名相通释 [*A Comprehensive Glossary of Buddhist Concepts*], Beijing: Zhongguo Dabaike Quanshu Chubanshe.

Xiong, Shili 熊十力 (2008), 新唯识论 [*The New Doctrine of Consciousness-Only*], Shanghai: Shanghai Shudian.

Yamasaki, Keiki 山崎慶輝 (1985), "日本唯識の展開 [The Development of Consciousness-only in Japan]," in Yamasaki Keiki 山崎慶輝 and Hiraoka Jōkai 平岡定海 (eds), 南都六宗 [*The Six Nara Schools*], 242–68, Tokyo: Yoshikawa Kōbunkan.

Yang, Weizhong 杨维中 (2008), 中国唯识宗通史 [*A Thorough History of Chinese School of Consciousness-only*], Nanjing: Fenghuang Press.

Yeh, Ah-yueh 葉阿月 (1981), "唯識思想的十二緣起說 [The Theory of Twelve Links in the Doctrine of Consciousness-only]," 國立臺灣大學哲學論評 [*National Taiwan University Philosophical Review*], Vol4: 61–75.

Yinshun 印順 (1978), 唯識學探源 [*An Investigation of the Origin of the Doctrine of Consciousness-only*], Taipei: The Great Vehicle Culture.

Yinshun 印順 (1988), 如來藏之研究 [*The Study of Tathāgatagarbha*], Taipei: Zhengwen Publishing House.

Yokoyama, Kōitsu 橫山紘一 (1978), "転依に関する若干の考察 [A Consideration of A Consideration of *Asraya-para (-pari-) vrtti*]," 印度学仏教学研究 [*Journal of Indian and Buddhist Studies*], 27(1): 230–3.

Yokoyama, Kōitsu 橫山紘一 (1985), "世親的識轉變 [The Vijñānapariṇāme in Vasubandhu]," in Takasaki Jikidō 高崎直道 (ed.) and Li Shijie 李世傑 (trans.), 唯識思想 [*The Theories of Consciousness-only*], 157–204, Taipei: Hua Yu Press.

Yokoyama, Kōitsu 橫山紘一 (1986), 唯識とは何か [*What is Consciousness-Only*], Tokyo: Shunjusha Publishing.

Yokoyama, Kōitsu 橫山紘一 (1996), わが心の構造：「唯識三十頌」に学ぶ [*The Structure of My Mind: Learning from the Thirty Verses of Consciousness-Only*], Tokyo: Shunjusha Publishing.

Yoshimura, Makoto 吉村誠 (1995), "大唐大慈恩寺三蔵法師伝の成立について [The Completion of the Biography of the Tripitaka Master of the Great Ci'en Temple of Tang]," 仏教学 [*Bukkyo Gaku, Journal of Buddhist Studies*], 37: 79–113.

Yoshimura, Makoto 吉村誠 (2002), "唯識学派の理行二仏性説について [On the Theory of Twofold Buddha-dhātu of Weishi School]," 東洋の思想と宗教 [*Thought and Religion of Asia*], 19: 21–47.

Yoshimura, Makoto 吉村誠 (2004), "中国唯識諸学派の称呼に ついて [On the Designations of the Chinese Consciousness-only Schools]," 東アジア仏教研究 [*The Journal of East Asian Buddhist Studies*], 2: 35–48.

Yoshimura, Makoto 吉村誠 (2009), "唐初期の唯識学派と仏性論争 [The Conflict of Theories of Buddha-nature and the Weishi (唯識) school in Early Tang Dynasty],"

駒沢大学仏教学部研究紀要 [*Journal of the Faculty of Buddhism of the Komazawa University*], 67: 35–49.

Yoshimura, Makoto 吉村誠 (2013), 中国唯識思想史研究：玄奘と唯識学派 [*A Study of the Intellectual History of Consciousness-only in China: Xuanzang and the School of Consciousness-only*], Tokyo: Daizō Shuppan.

Zhang, Qingxiong 张庆熊 (1995), 熊十力的新唯识论与胡塞尔的现象学 [*Xiong Shili's New Doctrine of Consciousness-only and Husserl's Phenomenology*], Shanghai: Shanghai People Press.

Zhang, Xianglong 张祥龙 (2015), "唯识宗的记忆观与时间观 [The Conception of Memory and Time in the Doctrine of Consciousness-only]," 现代哲学 [*Modern Philosophy*], 5: 55–61.

Zheng, Weihong 郑伟宏 (2010), 因明大疏校释、今译、研究 [*An Annotated Edition of the Greater Commentary of Hetuvidyā with Contemporary Translation and Scholarly Study*], Shanghai: Fudan University Press.

Zhou, Guihua 周贵华 (2004), "唯识与唯了别——"唯识学"的一个基本问题的再诠释 [Consciousness-only and Representation-only—Readdressing a Basic Question in the Doctrine of Consciousness-only]," 哲学研究 [*Philosophical Researches*], 3: 59–65.

Zhou, Guihua 周贵华 (2007), "再论唯识与唯了别 [On Consciousness-only and Representation-only]," 上海大学学报 [*Journal of Shanghai University*], 4: 77–82.

Zhou, Guihua 周贵华 (2009), 唯识通论 [*On Consciousness-only*], Beijing: China Social Sciences Press.

Secondary Resources in Euro-American Languages

Allen, Barry (2015), *Vanishing into Things: Knowledge in Chinese Tradition*, Cambridge: Harvard University Press.

Al-Saji, Alia (2010), "The Racialization of Muslim Veils: A Philosophical Analysis," *Philosophy and Social Criticism*, 36(8): 875–902.

Al-Saji, Alia (2019), "Glued to the Image: A Critical Phenomenology of Racialization through Works of Art," *The Journal of Aesthetics and Art Criticism*, 77(4): 475–88.

Ames, Roger (2002), "Mencius and a Process Notion of Human Nature," in Alan Kam-Leung Chan (ed.), *Mencius: Contexts and Interpretations*, 72–90, Honolulu: University Press of Hawaii.

Anacker, Stefan (1978), "The Meditational Therapy of the *Madhayāntavabhāgabhaṣya*," in Minoru Kiyota and Elvin Jones (eds), *Mahāyāna Buddhist Meditation: Theory and Practice*, 83–113, Honolulu: University Press of Hawaii.

Angioni, Lucas (2014), "Definition and Essence in Aristotle's 'Metaphysics' vii 4," *Ancient Philosophy*, Vol34: 75–100.

Anscombe, Elizabeth (1957), *Intention*, Oxford: Blackwell.

Anscombe, Elizabeth (1965), "The Intentionality of Sensation: A Grammatical Feature," in Ronald Butler (ed.), *Analytic Philosophy*, 158–80, Oxford: Blackwell.

Anscombe, Elizabeth (1981), *Ethics, Religion, and Politics*, Minneapolis: University of Minnesota Press.

Arnold, Dan (2005), *Buddhists, Brahmins, and Belief: Epistemology in South Asian Philosophy of Religion*, New York: Columbia University Press.

Arnold, Dan (2012), *Brains, Buddhas, and Believing: The Problem of Intentionality in Classical Buddhist and Cognitive-Scientific Philosophy of Mind*, New York: Columbia University Press.

Audi, Robert (1986), "Acting for Reasons," *Philosophical Review*, 95(4): 511–46.
Aviv, Eyal (2013), "The Root that Nourishes the Branches: The Yogācārabhūmi's Role in 20th Century Chinese Scholastic Buddhism," in Ulrich Timme Kragh (ed.), *The Foundation for Yoga Practitioners: The Buddhist Yogācārabhūmi Treatise and Its Adaptation in India, East Asia, and Tibet*, 1078–91, Cambridge: Harvard University Press.
Aviv, Eyal (2020), *Differentiating the Pearl from the Fish-Eye: Ouyang Jingwu and the Revival of Scholastic Buddhism*, Leiden: Brill.
Ayer, Alfred Jules (1963), *The Concept of a Person*, London: Macmillan.
Bambach, Charles (2013), "Weimar Philosophy and the Crisis of Historical Thinking," in Peter Gordon and John McCormick (eds), *Weimar Thought: A Contested Legacy*, 133–49, Princeton: Princeton University Press.
Barber, Michael (2008), "Holism and Horizon: Husserl and McDowell on Non-conceptual Content," *Husserl Studies*, 24(2): 79–97.
Barnhart, Michael (2012), "Theory and Comparison in the Discussion of Buddhist Ethics," *Philosophy East and West*, 62(1): 16–43.
Beasley, William Gerald (1987), *Japanese Imperialism, 1894–1945*, Oxford: Oxford University Press.
Beith, Don (2018), *The Birth of Sense: Generative Passivity in Merleau-Ponty's Philosophy*, Columbus: Ohio University Press.
Bennett, Max and Hacker, Peter (2008), *History of Cognitive Neuroscience*, Oxford: Wiley-Blackwell.
Berger, Douglas (2015), *Encounters of Mind: Luminosity and Personhood in Indian and Chinese Thought*, Albany: State University of New York Press.
Berghofer, Philipp (2018), "Husserl's Conception of Experiential Justification: What It Is and Why It Matters," *Husserl Studies*, 34(2): 145–70.
Berghofer, Philipp (2019), "On the Nature and Systematic Role of Evidence: Husserl as a Proponent of Mentalist Evidentialism?," *European Journal of Philosophy*, 27(1): 98–117.
Bermúdez, José Luis (2007), "What is at Stake in the Debate about Nonconceptual Content?," *Philosophical Perspectives*, 21(1): 55–72.
Beyer, Christian (2020), "Edmund Husserl," in Edward Zalta (ed.), *The Stanford Encyclopedia of Philosophy*. https://plato.stanford.edu/archives/win2020/entries/husserl/ (accessed 1 May 2021)
Binder, Thomas (2017), "Fran Brentano: Life and Work," in Uriah Kriegel (ed.), *The Routledge Handbook of Franz Brentano and the Brentano School*, 15–20, New York: Routledge.
Bloom, Irene (1997), "Human Nature and Biological Nature in Mencius," *Philosophy East and West*, 47(1): 21–32.
Bobik, John (1988), *Aquinas on Being and Essence*, Notre Dame: University of Notre Dame Press.
Bokenkamp, Stephen (2007), *Ancestor and Anxiety*, Berkeley: University of California Press.
Borup, Jørn (2004), "Zen and the Art of Inverting Orientalism," in Peter Antes, Armin Geertz, and Randi Warne (eds), *New Approaches to the Study of Religion, Volume 1: Regional, Critical, and Historical Approaches*, 451–87, Berlin: De Gruyter.
Bostock, David (1994), *Aristotle Metaphysics. Book Zeta and Eta*, Oxford: Clarendon.
Brewster, Ernest (2018), "What is Our Shared Sensory World? Ming Dynasty Debates on Yogācāra versus Huayan Doctrines," *Journal of Chinese Buddhist Studies*, 31: 117–70.

Brogaard, Berit and Salerno, Joe (2013), "Remarks on Counterpossibles," *Synthese*, 190 (4): 639–60.
Brough, John, trans. (1991), *On the Phenomenology of the Consciousness of Internal Time*, Dordrecht: Kluwer Academic Publishers.
Buckley, Philip (2019), "Phenomenology as Soteriology: Husserl and the Call for 'Erneuerung' in the 1920s," *Modern Theology*, 35(1): 5–22.
Burton, David (1999), *Emptiness Appraised: A Critical Study of Nāgārjuna's Philosophy*, New York: Routledge.
Cairns, Dorion, trans. (1960), *Cartesian Meditations*, The Hague: Martinus Nijhoff.
Cairns, Dorion (1976), *Conversations with Husserl and Fink*, The Hague: Martinus Nijhoff.
Carr, David, trans. (1970), *The Crisis of European Sciences and Transcendental Phenomenology*, Evanston: Northwestern University Press.
Carr, David (1999), *The Paradox of Subjectivity: The Self in the Transcendental Tradition*, Oxford: Oxford University Press.
Carruthers, Peter (2000), *Phenomenal Consciousness: A Naturalistic Theory*, New York: Cambridge University Press.
Carson, Cathryn (2013), "Method, Moment, and Crisis in Weimar Science," in Peter Gordon and John McCormick (eds), *Weimar Thought: A Contested Legacy*, 179–201, Princeton: Princeton University Press.
Charles, David (2002), *Aristotle on Meaning and Essence*, Oxford: Clarendon.
Chatterjee, Ashok Kumar (1962), *The Yogācāra Idealism*, Varanasi: Bhargava Bhushan Press.
Chen, Bing (2013), "Reflections on the Revival of Yogācāra in Modern Chinese Buddhism," in Ulrich Timme Kragh (ed.), *The Foundation for Yoga Practitioners: The Buddhist Yogācārabhūmi Treatise and Its Adaptation in India, East Asia, and Tibet*, 1054–77, Cambridge: Harvard University Press.
Chen, Kenneth (1964), *Buddhism in China: A Historical Survey*, Princeton: Princeton University Press.
Chen, Kenneth (1973), *Chinese Transformation of Buddhism*, Princeton: Princeton University Press.
Chu, William (2010), "The Timing of the Yogācāra Resurgence in the Ming Dynasty (1368– 1643)," *Journal of the International Association of Buddhist Studies*, 33(1–2): 5–25.
Clayton, Barbra (2006), *Moral Theory in Śāntideva's Śikṣasamuccaya: Cultivating the Fruits of Virtue*, New York: Routledge.
Code, Alan (1986), "Aristotle: Essence and Accident," in Richard Grandy and Richard Warner (eds), *Philosophical Grounds of Rationality: Intentions, Categories, Ends*, 411–39, Oxford: Clarendon.
Cohen, Marc (2016), "Aristotle's Metaphysics," in Edward Zalta (ed.), *The Stanford Encyclopedia of Philosophy*. https://plato.stanford.edu/archives/win2016/entries/aristotle-metaphysics (accessed 1 May 2021).
Collins, Steven (1982), *Selfless Persons: Imagery and Thought in Theravāda Buddhism*, Cambridge: Cambridge University Press.
Cook, Francis, trans. (1999), *Three Texts on Consciousness Only*, Berkeley: Numata Center for Buddhist Translation and Research.
Copi, Irving (1954), "Essence and Accident," *Journal of Philosophy*, 51(23): 706–19.
Coseru, Christian (2012), *Perceiving Reality: Consciousness, Intentionality, and Cognition in Buddhist Philosophy*, Oxford: Oxford University Press.

Coseru, Christian (2015), "Taking the Intentionality of Perception Seriously: Why Phenomenology is Inescapable," *Philosophy East and West*, 65(1): 227–48.
Correia, Fabrice (2007), "(Finean) Essence and (Priorean) Modality," *Dialectica*, 61(1): 63–84.
Cowling, Sam (2013), "The Modal View of Essence," *Canadian Journal of Philosophy*, 43(2): 248–66.
Crane, Tim (1992), "The Nonconceptual Content of Experience," in Tim Crane (ed.), *The Contents of Experience*, 136–57, Cambridge: Cambridge University Press.
Crane, Tim (2017), "Brentano on Intentionality," in Uriah Kriegel (ed.), *The Routledge Handbook of Franz Brentano and the Brentano School*, 41–8, New York: Routledge.
Crowell, Steven (2016), "Second-Person Phenomenology," in Thomas Szanto and Dermot Moran (eds), *Phenomenology of Sociality: Discovering the 'We'*, 70–92, New York: Routledge.
Cussins, Adrian ([1991] 2003), "Content, Conceptual Content, and Nonconceptual Content," in York Gunther (ed.), *Essays on Non-conceptual Content*, 133–64, Cambridge: MIT Press.
Dahl, Norman (1997), "Two Kinds of Essence in Aristotle: A Pale Man Is Not the Same as His Essence," *Philosophical Review*, 106(2): 233–65.
Dahl, Norman (2007), "Substance, Sameness, and Essence in 'Metaphysics' VII 6," *Ancient Philosophy*, 27(1): 107–26.
Davidson, David (1980), *Essays on Actions and Events*, Oxford: Clarendon.
Davidson, Ronald (1985), "Buddhist Systems of Transformation: Āśraya-parivṛtti among the Yogācāra," Ph.D. Diss., University of California, Berkeley, Berkeley.
Davidson, Ronald (1993), "Preliminary Studies on Hevajra's Abhisamaya and the Lam-'bras Tshogs-bshad," in Steven Goodman and Ronald Davison (eds), *Tibetan Buddhism: Reason and Revelation*, 107–32, Albany: State University of New York Press.
De La Valleé Poussin, Louis, trans. (1928), *Vijñaptimātratāsiddhi: La Siddhi de Hiuan-Tsang*, Paris: P. Geuthner.
Denby, David (2014), "Essence and Intrinsicality," in Robert Francescotti (ed.), *Companion to Intrinsic Properties*, 87–110, Berlin: De Gruyter.
Dennett, Daniel (1969), *Content and Consciousness*, London: Routledge & Kegan Paul.
Dennett, Daniel (1987), *The Intentional Stance*, Cambridge: MIT Press.
Despeux, Catherine and Kohn, Livia (2003), *Women in Daoism*, Cambridge: Three Pines.
Dewalque, Arnaud (2013), "Brentano and the Parts of the Mental: A Mereological Approach to Phenomenal Intentionality," *Phenomenology and the Cognitive Sciences*, 12(3): 447–64.
Dewalque, Arnaud (2017), "The Rise of the Brentano School," in Uriah Kriegel (ed.), *The Routledge Handbook of Franz Brentano and the Brentano School*, 225–50, New York: Routledge.
Dewan, Lawrence (2006), *Forms and Being: Studies in Thomistic Metaphysics*, Washington: Catholic University of America Press.
De Warren, Nicolas (2003), "The Rediscovery of Immanence: Remarks on the Appendix to the Logical Investigations," in Daniel Dahlstrom (ed.), *Husserl's Logical Investigations*, 147–66, Dordrecht: Kluwer Academic Publishers.
De Warren, Nicolas (2006), "On Husserl's Essentialism: Critical Notice," *International Journal of Philosophical Studies*, 14(2): 255–70.
De Warren, Nicolas (2014), "The First World War, Philosophy, and Europe," *Tijdschrift voor Filosofie*, 76(4): 715–37.
De Warren, Nicolas and Vongehr, Thomas, eds (2018), *Philosophers at the Front: Phenomenology and the First World War*, Leuven: Leuven University Press.

Donner, Neal and Stevenson, Daniel (1993), *The Great Calming and Contemplation: A Study and Annotated Translation of the First Chapter of Chih-I's Mo-ho Chih-kuan*, Honolulu: University of Hawaii Press.

Dretske, Fred (1980), "The Intentionality of Cognitive States," *Midwest Studies in Philosophy*, 5(1): 281–94.

Dretske, Fred (1988), *Explaining Behavior: Reasons in a World of Causes*, Cambridge: MIT Press.

Dreyfus, Hubert (1982), "Husserl's Perceptual Noema," in Hubert Dreyfus and Harrison Hall (eds), *Husserl Intentionality and Cognitive Science*, 97–124, Cambridge: The MIT Press.

Drummond, John (1990), *Husserlian Intentionality and Non-Foundational Realism: Noema and Object*, Dordrecht: Kluwer Academic Publishers.

Dummett, Michael (1993), *Seas of Language*, Oxford: Oxford University Press.

Duus, Peter (1984), "Economic Dimensions of Meiji Imperialism," in Ramon Myers and Mark Peattie (eds), *The Japanese Colonial Empire, 1895–1945*, 128–71, Princeton: Princeton University.

Elders, Leo (1992), *The Metaphysics of Being of St. Thomas Aquinas in a Historical Perspective*, Leiden: Brill.

Evans, Gareth (1982), *The Varieties of Reference*, Oxford: Clarendon.

Fanon, Frantz (1952), *Peau Noire, Masques Blancs*, Paris: Éditions du Seuil.

Faure, Bernard (1993), *Chan Insights and Oversights: An Epistemological Critique of the Chan Tradition*, Princeton: Princeton University Press.

Faure, Bernard (2017), "Can (and Should) Neuroscience Naturalize Buddhism?," *International Journal of Buddhist Thought and Culture*, 27(1): 113–33.

Feng, Youlan (aka. Fung, Yu-Lan) (1948), *A Short History of Chinese Philosophy*, New York: Free Press.

Feng, Youlan (aka. Fung, Yu-Lan) (2016), *Chuang-Tzu: A New Selected Translation with an Exposition of the Philosophy of Kuo Hsiang*, Dordrecht: Springer.

Findley, John Niemeyer, trans. (1970), *Logical Investigations*, New York: Routledge.

Fine, Kit (1994), "Essence and Modality: The Second Philosophical Perspectives Lecture," *Philosophical Perspectives*, 8: 1–16.

Flanagan, Owen (2011), *The Bodhisattva's Brain: Buddhism Naturalized*, Cambridge: MIT Press.

Fodor, Jerry (2003), *Hume Variations*, Oxford: Oxford University Press.

Ford, James (2006), *Jōkei and Buddhist Devotion in Early Medieval Japan*, Oxford: Oxford University Press.

Forman, Robert (1990), "Introduction: Mysticism, Constructivism, and Forgetting," in Robert Forman (ed.), *The Problem of Pure Consciousness: Mysticism and Philosophy*, 3–52, Oxford: Oxford University Press.

Føllesdal, Dagfinn (1982), "Husserl's Notion of Noema," in Hubert Dreyfus and Harrison Hall (eds), *Husserl Intentionality and Cognitive Science*, 73–80, Cambridge: The MIT Press.

Føllesdal, Dagfinn (1988), "Husserl on Evidence and Justification," in Robert Sokolowski (ed.), *Edmund Husserl and the Phenomenological Tradition*, 107–30, Washington: Catholic University of America Press.

Fraser, Nancy and Honneth Axel (2003), *Redistribution or Recognition? A Political-Philosophical Exchange*, trans. Joel Golb, James Ingram, and Christiane Wilke, London: Verso.

Fraser, Nancy (2007), "Reorienting the Feminist Imagination: From Redistribution to Recognition to Representation," in Jude Browne (ed.), *The Future of Gender*, 17–34. Cambridge: Cambridge University Press.

Fujita, Kōtatsu (1975), "One Vehicle or Three," trans. Leon Hurvitz, *Journal of Indian Philosophy*, 3(2): 79–166.
Funayama, Toru (2008), "The Work of Paramārtha: An Example of Sino-Indian Cross-Cultural Exchange," *Journal of the International Association of Buddhist Studies*, 31(1-2): 141–85.
Gallagher, Shaun (2001), "The Practice of Mind: Theory, Simulation or Primary Interaction?," *Journal of Consciousness Studies*, 8(5-7): 83–108.
Ganeri, Jonardon (2001), *Philosophy in Classical India*, New York: Routledge.
Ganeri, Jonardon (2012), *The Self: Naturalism, Consciousness, and the First-Person Stance*, Oxford: Oxford University Press.
Garfield, Jay (2002), *Empty Words: Buddhist Philosophy and Cross-Cultural Interpretation*, Oxford: Oxford University Press.
Garfield, Jay (2015), *Engaging Buddhism: Why it Matters to Philosophy*, Oxford: Oxford University Press.
Garfield, Jay and van Norden, Bryan (2016), "If Philosophy Won't Diversify, Let's Call It What It Really Is." *New York Times*, 11 May https://www.nytimes.com/2016/05/11/opinion/if-philosophy-wont-diversify-lets-call-it-what-it-really-is.html (accessed 1 May 2021).
Gethin, Rupert (1998), *The Foundations of Buddhism*, Oxford: Oxford University Press.
Ginet, Carl (1990), *On Action*, Cambridge: Cambridge University Press.
Ginsborg, Hannah (2006), "Kant and the Problem of Experience," *Philosophical Topics*, 34(1): 59–106.
Ginsborg, Hannah (2008), "Was Kant a Nonconceptualist?," *Philosophical Studies*, 137(1): 65–77.
Gold, Jonathan (2014), *Paving the Great Way: Vasubandhu's Unifying Buddhist Philosophy*, New York: Columbia University Press.
Gold, Jonathan (2015), "Without Karma and Nirvāṇa, Buddhism Is Nihilism," in Jay Garfield and Jan Westerhoff (eds), *Madhyamaka and Yogācāra: Allies or Rivals?* 214–41, Oxford: Oxford University Press.
Goldman, Alvin (1970), *A Theory of Human Action*, Englewood Cliffs: Prentice-Hall.
Goldman, Alvin (2006), *Simulating Minds: The Philosophy, Psychology, and Neuroscience of Mindreading*, Oxford: Oxford University Press.
Gomez, Juan Carlos (1996), "Second Person Intentional Relation and the Evolution of Social Understanding," *Behavioral and Brain Studies*, 19(1): 129–30.
Goodman, Charles (2009), *Consequences of Compassion*, Oxford: Oxford University Press.
Goodman, Charles (2017), "Ethics in Indian and Tibetan Buddhism," in Edward Zalta (ed.), *The Stanford Encyclopedia of Philosophy*. https://plato.stanford.edu/archives/spr2017/entries/ethics-indian-buddhism (accessed 1 May 2021).
Gordon, Peter (2003), *Rosenzweig and Heidegger: Between Judaism and German Philosophy*, Berkeley: University of California Press.
Gordon, Peter and McCormick, John (2013), "Introduction: Weimar Thought: Continuity and Crisis," in Peter Gordon and John McCormick (eds), *Weimar Thought: A Contested Legacy*, 1–14, Princeton: Princeton University Press.
Gorman, Michael (2005), "The Essential and the Accidental," *Ratio*, 18(3): 276–89.
Gowans, Christopher (2014), *Buddhist Moral Philosophy*, New York: Routledge.
Graham, Angus Charles (1967), "The Background of the Mencian Theory of Human Nature," *Tsing Hua Journal of Chinese Studies*, 6: 215–71.
Griffiths, Paul (1986), *On Being Mindless: Buddhist Meditation and the Mind-body Problem*, La Salle: Open Court.

Griffiths, Paul (1990), "Pure Consciousness and Indian Buddhism," in Robert Forman (ed.), *The Problem of Pure Consciousness: Mysticism and Philosophy*, 71–97, Oxford: Oxford University Press.
Grosnick, William (1989), "The Categories of T'i, Hsiang, and Yung: Evidence that Paramārtha Composed the Awakening of Faith," *Journal of the International Association of Buddhist Studies*, 12(1): 65–92.
Guenther, Lisa (2011), "Subjects Without a World? An Husserlian Analysis of Solitary Confinement," *Human Studies*, 34(3): 257–76.
Guenther, Lisa (2013), *Solitary Confinement: Social Death and Its Afterlives*, Minneapolis: University of Minnesota Press.
Gunther, York (2003), "Preliminaries," in York Gunther (ed.), *Essays on Non-conceptual Content*, 1–21, Cambridge: MIT Press.
Hakamaya, Noriaki (1997), "Thoughts on the Ideological Background of Social Discrimination," in Jamie Hubbard and Paul Swanson (eds), *Pruning the Bodhi Tree: The Storm over Critical Buddhism*, 339–55, Honolulu: University of Hawai'i Press.
Hallisey, Charles (1996), "Ethical Particularism in Theravāda Buddhism," *Journal of Buddhist Ethics*, 3: 32–43.
Hammerstrom, Erik (2014), "Yogācāra and Science in the 1920s: The Wuchang School's Approach to Modern Mind Science," in John Makeham (ed.), *Transforming Consciousness: Yogācāra Thought in Modern China*, 170–200, Oxford: Oxford University Press.
Hammerstrom, Erik (2015), *The Science of Chinese Buddhism: Early Twentieth-century Engagements*, New York: Columbia University Press.
Hanna, Fred (1995), "Husserl on the Teachings of the Buddha," *The Humanistic Psychologist*, 23(3): 365–72.
Hanna, Robert (2005), "Kant and Nonconceptual Content," *European Journal of Philosophy*, 13(2): 247–90.
Harman, Gilbert (1987), "(Nonsolipsistic) Conceptual Role Semantics," in Ernest LePore (ed.), *New Directions in Semantics*, 55–81, London: Academic Press.
Harris, Stephen (2015), "On the Classification of Śāntideva's Ethics in the *Bodhicaryāvatāra*," *Philosophy East and West*, 65(1): 249–75.
Hart, James (1986), "A Precis of a Husserlian Phenomenological Theology," in James Hart and Steven William Laycock (eds), *Essays in Phenomenological Theology*, 89–168, Albany: State University of New York Press.
Harvey, Peter (2000), *An Introduction to Buddhist Ethics*, Cambridge: Cambridge University Press.
Hayes, Richard (1989), *Dignāga on the Interpretation of Signs*, Dordrecht: Kluwer Academic Publishers.
Hopkins, Jeffrey (1983), *Meditation on Emptiness*, London: Wisdom.
Hopkins, Jeffrey (2002), *Reflections on Reality: The Three Natures and Non-natures in the Mind-only School*, Berkeley: University of California Press.
Hopp, Walter (2011), *Perception and Knowledge: A Phenomenological Account*, Cambridge: Cambridge University Press.
Hori, Victor Sōgen (2000), "Kōan and Kenshō in the Rinzai Zen Curriculum," in Steven Heine and Dale Wright (eds), *The Kōan: Texts and Contexts in Zen Buddhism*, 280–315, Oxford: Oxford University Press.
Hori, Victor Sōgen (2006), "Zen Kōan Capping Phrase Books: Literary Study and the Insight 'Not Founded on Words or Letters,'" in Steven Heine and Dale Wright (eds), *Zen Classics: Formative Texts in the History of Zen Buddhism*, 171–214, Oxford: Oxford University Press.

Hori, Victor Sōgen (2016), "D. T. Suzuki and the Invention of Tradition," *The Eastern Buddhist*, 47(2): 41–81.
Hu, Shih (2013), "The Indianization of China: A Case Study in Cultural Borrowing," in Chou Chih-P'ing (ed.), *English Writings of Hu Shih, Vol. 2*, 147–63, Dordrecht: Springer.
Huemer, Michael (2005), *Ethical Intuitionism*, New York: Palgrave Macmillan.
Huemer, Wolfgang (2019), "Franz Brentano," in Edward Zalta (ed.), *The Stanford Encyclopedia of Philosophy*. https://plato.stanford.edu/archives/spr2019/entries/brentano (accessed 1 May 2021).
Ivanhoe, Philip and van Norden, Bryan (2005), *Readings in Classical Chinese Philosophy*, Indianapolis: Hackett.
Jacobs, Hanne (2013), "Phenomenology as a Way of Life? Husserl on Phenomenological Reflection of Self-Transformation," *Continental Philosophy Review*, 46(3): 349–69.
Janicaud, Dominique (2000), *Phenomenology and the Theological Turn*, New York: Fordham University Press.
Jansen, Julia (2015), "Transcendental Philosophy and the Problem of Necessity in a Contingent World," *Metodo. International Studies in Phenomenology and Philosophy*, 1(1): 47–80.
Jansen, Julia (2016), "Kant's and Husserl's Agentive and Proprietary Accounts of Cognitive Phenomenology," *Philosophical Explorations*, 19(2): 161–72.
Jansen, Julia (2017), "On Transcendental and Non-Transcendental Idealism in Husserl: A Response to De Palma and Loidolt," *Metodo. International Studies in Phenomenology and Philosophy*, 1(1): 27–39.
Jansen, Maurice (1984), "Japanese Imperialism: Late Meiji Perspectives," in Ramon Myers and Mark Peattie (eds), *The Japanese Colonial Empire, 1895-1945*, 61–79, Princeton: Princeton University.
Jiang, Tao (2001), "The Storehouse Consciousness (Ālayavijñāna) of Wei-Shi (Yogācāra) Buddhism: The Buddhist Phenomenology of the Unconscious," Ph.D. Diss., Temple University, Philadelphia.
Jiang, Tao (2006), *Contexts and Dialogue: Yogācāra Buddhism and Modern Psychology on the Subliminal Mind*, Honolulu: University of Hawai'i Press.
Jorgensen, John (2014), "Indra's Network: Zhang Taiyan's Sino-japanese Personal Networks and the Rise of Yogācāra in Modern China," in John Makeham (ed.), *Transforming Consciousness: Yogācāra Thought in Modern China*, 64–103, Oxford: Oxford University Press.
Kachru, Sonam (2019), "Ratnakīrti and the Extent of Inner Space: An Essay on Yogācāra and the Threat of Genuine of Solipsism," *Sophia*, 58(1): 61–83.
Kalupahana, David (1976), *Buddhist Philosophy: A Historical Analysis*, Honolulu, HI: University of Hawai'i Press.
Kantor, Hans-Rudolf (2009), "Zhiyi's Great Calming and Contemplation," in William Edelglass and Jay Garfield (eds), *Buddhist Philosophy: Essential Readings*, 334–47, Oxford: Oxford University Press.
Katz, Steven (1978), "Language, Epistemology, and Mysticism," in Steven Katz (ed.), *Mysticism and Philosophical Analysis*, 22–74, Oxford: Oxford University Press.
Kellner, Birgit (2014), "Changing Frames in Buddhist Thought: The Concept of Ākāra in Abhidharma and in Buddhist Epistemological Analysis," *Journal of Indian Philosophy*, 42(23): 275–95.
Keng, Ching (2009), "Yogācāra Buddhism Transmitted or Transformed? Paramārtha (499-569 CE) and His Chinese Interpreters," Ph.D. Diss., Harvard University, Cambridge.

Kenny, Anthony (2010), "Concepts, Brains, and Behaviour," *Grazer Philosophische Studien*, 81(1): 105-13.
Keown, Damien (1992), *The Nature of Buddhist Ethics*, New York: Palgrave.
Kern, Iso (1962), "Die Drei Wege zur Transzendental-Phänomenologischen Reduktion in der Philosophie Edmund Husserls," *Tijdschrift voor Filosofie*, 24(2): 303-49.
Kern, Iso (1964), *Kant und Husserl*, The Hague: Martinus Nijhoff.
Kern, Iso (1992), "Object, Objective Phenomenon and Objectivating Act According to the 'Vijñaptimātratāsiddhi' of Xuanzang (600-664)," in Debi Prasad Chattopadhyaya, Lester Embree, and Jitendra Nath Mohanty (eds), *Phenomenology and Indian Philosophy*, 262-9, Albany: State University of New York Press.
Kersten, Fred, trans. (1983), *Ideas Pertaining to a Pure Phenomenology and to a Phenomenological Philosophy*, The Hague: Martinus Nijhoff.
King, Sallie (1991), *Buddha Nature*, Albany: State University of New York Press.
Kitayama, Junyu (1934), *Metaphysik des Buddhismus: Versuch einer philosophischen Interpretation der Lehre Vasubandhus und seiner Schule*, Stuttgart: Verlag von W. Kohlhamer.
Knaul, Livia (1985), "Kuo Hsiang and the Chuang Tzu," *Journal of Chinese Philosophy*, 12(4): 429-47.
Kochumuttom, Thomas (1982), *A Buddhist Doctrine of Experience*, Delhi: Motilal Banarsidass Publishers.
Komarovski, Yaroslav (2012), "Buddhist Contribution to the Question of (Un)mediated Mystical Experience," *Sophia*, 51(1): 87-115.
Kramer, Jowita (2018), "Conceptuality and Non-conceptuality in Yogācāra Sources," *Journal of Indian Philosophy*, 46(2): 321-38.
Kriegel, Uriah (2017), "Introduction," in Uriah Kriegel (ed.), *The Routledge Handbook of Franz Brentano and the Brentano School*, 1-12, New York: Routledge.
Lai, Rongdao (2013), "Praying for the Republic: Buddhist Education, Student-monks, and Citizenship in Modern China (1911-1949)," Ph.D. Diss., McGill University, Montreal.
Lee, Kyoo (2014), "On the Transformative Potential of the 'Dark Female Animal' in *Daodejing*," in Ashby Butnor and Jennifer McWeeny (eds), *Asian and Feminist Philosophies in Dialogue*, 57-77, New York: Columbia University Press.
Lee, Sumi (2015), "Redefining the 'Dharma Characteristics School' in East Asian Yogācāra Buddhism," *The Eastern Buddhist*, 46(2): 41-60.
Levine, Michael (2016), "Does Comparative Philosophy Have a Fusion Future," *Confluence: Online Journal of World Philosophies*, 4: 208-37.
Lewis, Frank (1984), "What is Aristotle's Theory of Essence?," *Canadian Journal of Philosophy*, 14(Sup.1): 89-131.
Li, Jianjun (2016), "What is Time? Yogācāra-Buddhist Meditation on the Problem of the External World in the *Cheng Weishi Lun*," *Azijske študije*, 4(1): 35-57.
Li, Jingjing (2016), "Buddhist Phenomenology and the Problem of Essence," *Comparative Philosophy*, 7(1): 59-89.
Li, Jingjing (2017), "From Self-Attaching to Self-Emptying: An Investigation of Xuanzang's Account of Self-Consciousness," *Open Theology*, 1: 184-97.
Li, Jingjing (2019), "Through the Mirror: The Yogācāra Account of Other Minds," *Dao: Journal of Comparative Philosophy*, 18(3): 435-51.
Li, Jingjing (2020), "D. T. Suzuki and the Chinese Search for Buddhist Modernism," in John Harding, Victor Sōgen Hori and Alexander Soucy (eds), *Buddhism in a Global Eye*, 83-102, London: Bloomsbury.

Li, Jingjing (2022), "Liang, the Buddhist," in Philippe Major and Thierry Meynard (eds), *Dao Companion to Liang Shuming*, forthcoming, Dordrecht: Springer.
Lin, Chen-Kuo (1991), "The Saṃdhinirmocana Sūtra: A Liberating Hermeneutics," PhD Diss., Temple University, Philadelphia.
Lin, Chen-Kuo (2007), "Object of Cognition in Dignāga's *Ālambanaparīkṣāvṛtti*: On the Controversial Passages in Paramārtha's and Xuanzang's Translation," *Journal of the International Association of Buddhist Studies*, 30(1): 117–38.
Lin, Chen-Kuo (2014), "The Uncompromising Quest for Genuine Buddhism," John Makeham (ed.), *Transforming Consciousness: Yogācāra Thought in Modern China*, 343–76, Oxford: Oxford University Press.
Lin, Chen-Kuo (2016), "*Svalakṣaṇa* (Particular) and *Sāmānyalakṣaṇa* (Universal) in Abhidharma and Chinese Yogācāra Buddhism," in Bart Dessein and Wei-Jen Teng (eds), *Text, History, and Philosophy*, 375–95, Leiden: Brill.
Lin, Chen-Kuo (2018b), "How to Attain Enlightenment Through Cognition of Particulars and Universals," in Sandra Wawrytko and Youru Wang (eds), *Dao Companion to Chinese Buddhist Philosophy*, 245–62, Dordrecht: Springer.
Liu, JeeLoo (2017), *Neo-Confucianism: Metaphysics, Mind, and Morality*, New York: John Wiley.
Lodrö Sangpo, Gelong, Migme Chödrön, Gelongma, and Mayer, Alexander, trans. (2017), *Vijñapti-mātratā-siddhi: A Commentary (Cheng Weishi Lun) on Vasubandhu's Triṃśikā by Xuanzang. The Collected Works of Louis de La Vallée Poussin*, New Delhi: Motilal Banarsidass Publishing House.
Loidolt, Sophie (2015), "Transzendentale Philosophie und Idealismus in der Phänomenologie," *Metodo. International Studies in Phenomenology and Philosophy*, 1(1),103–35.
Loidolt, Sophie (2017), *Phenomenology of Plurality: Hannah Arendt on Political Intersubjectivity*, New York: Routledge.
Lorde, Audre (1984), *Sister Outsider*, Trumansburg: Crossing Press.
Low, Setha (2003), "Embodied Space(s): Anthropological Theories of Body, Space, and Culture," *Space and Culture*, 6(1): 9–18.
Lowe, Edward Jonathan (2008), *Personal Agency: The Metaphysics of Mind and Action*, Oxford: Oxford University Press.
Lugones, María (2003), *Pilgrimages/Peregrinajes: Theorizing Coalition Against Multiple Oppressions*, Lanham: Rowman and Littlefield Publishers.
Lugones, María (2014), "Radical Multiculturalism and Women of Color Feminisms," *Journal for Cultural and Religious Theory*, 13(1): 68–80.
Lusthaus, Dan (2002), *Buddhist Phenomenology: A Philosophical Investigation of Yogācāra Buddhism and the Ch'eng Wei-shih Lun*, New York: Routledge.
Lusthaus, Dan (2003), "The *Heart Sūtra* in Chinese Yogācāra," *International Journal of Buddhist Thought and Culture*, 3: 59–103.
Lusthaus, Dan (2014), "Lü Cheng, Epistemology, and Genuine Buddhism," in John Makeham (ed.), *Transforming Consciousness: Yogācāra Thought in Modern China*, 318–43, Oxford: Oxford University Press.
Lynch, Catherine (2018), *Liang Shuming and the Populist Alternative in China*, Leiden: Brill.
MacKenzie, Matthew (2017), "Luminous Mind: Self-Luminosity versus Other-Luminosity in Indian Philosophy of Mind," in Joerg Tuske (ed.), *Indian Epistemology and Metaphysics*, 335–54, London: Bloomsbury.
Makeham, John (2003), *New Confucianism: A Critical Examination*, New York: Palgrave Macmillan.

Makeham, John (2008), *Lost Soul: "Confucianism" in Contemporary Chinese Academic Discourse*, Cambridge: Harvard University Press.
Makeham, John, ed. (2014), *Transforming Consciousness: Yogācāra Thought in Modern China*, Oxford: Oxford University Press.
Malcolm, Norman (1958), "Knowledge of Other Minds," *The Journal of Philosophy*, 55(23): 969–78.
Mano, Ryūkai (1969), "On Abhisamaya," *Journal of Indian and Buddhist Studies*, 17(2): 911–17.
Margolis, Eric and Laurence, Stephen (2014), "Concepts," in Edward Zalta (ed.), *The Stanford Encyclopedia of Philosophy*. https://plato.stanford.edu/archives/spr2014/entries/concepts (accessed 1 May 2021).
Marín-Ávila, Esteban (2015), "Social Acts as Intersubjective Willing Actions," in Marta Ubiali and Maren Wehrle (eds), *Feeling and Value, Willing and Action. Essays in the Context of a Phenomenological Psychology*, 245–61, Dordrecht: Springer.
Maruyama, Masao (1963), *Thought and Behaviour in Modern Japanese Politics*, trans. Ivan Morris, London: Oxford University Press.
Maruyama, Masao (1975), *Studies in Intellectual History of Tokugawa Japan*, trans. Hane Mikiso, Princeton: Princeton University Press.
Mathes, Klaus-Dieter, trans. (1996), *Unterscheidung der Gegebenheiten von Ihren Wesen*, Swisttal-Odendorf: Indica et Tibetica Verlag.
Matsumoto, Shinrō (1997), "The Doctrine of *Tathāgata-garbha* is not Buddhist," in Jamie Hubbard and Paul Swanson (eds), *Pruning the Bodhi Tree: The Storm over Critical Buddhism*, 165–73, Honolulu: University of Hawai'i Press.
Mayer, Alexander (2009), "A Review of Buddhist Phenomenology: A Philosophical Investigation of Yogācāra Buddhism and the Ch'eng Wei-shih Lun," *Journal of Buddhist Ethics*, 16: 191–216.
McDowell, John (1994), *Mind and World*, Cambridge: Harvard University Press.
McDowell, John (2006), "Sensory Consciousness in Kant and Sellars," *Philosophical Topics*, 34(1): 311–26.
McIntyre, Ronald (1982), "Intending and Referring," in Hubert Dreyfus and Harrison Hall (eds), *Husserl Intentionality and Cognitive Science*, 215–32, Cambridge: The MIT Press.
Melle, Ullrich (2002), "Husserl's Revision of the Sixth Logical Investigation," in Dan Zahavi and Frederik Stjernfelt (eds), *One Hundred Years of Phenomenology*, 111–23, Dordrecht: Springer.
Melle, Ullrich (2015), "Studien zur Struktur des Bewusstseins: Husserls Beitrag zu einer phänomenologischen Psychologie," in Marta Ubiali and Maren Wehrle (eds), *Feeling and Value, Willing and Action. Essays in the Context of a Phenomenological Psychology*, 3–11, Dordrecht: Springer.
Meynard, Thierry (2011), *The Religious Philosophy of Liang Shuming: The Hidden Buddhist*, Leiden: Brill.
Meynard, Thierry (2014), "Liang Shuming and His Confucianized Version of Yogācāra," in John Makeham (ed.), *Transforming Consciousness: Yogācāra Thought in Modern China*, 201–41, Oxford: Oxford University Press.
Millikan, Ruth (2000), *On Clear and Confused Ideas*, Cambridge: Cambridge University Press.
Mollier, Christine (2008), *Buddhism and Taoism Face to Face*, Honolulu: University of Hawaii Press.
Moran, Dermot (2005), *Edmund Husserl: Founder of Phenomenology*, Malden: Polity.
Moran, Dermot (2012), *Husserl's Crisis of the European Sciences and Transcendental Phenomenology: An Introduction*, Cambridge: Cambridge University Press.

Morrell, Robert (1983), "Jōkei and the Kōfukuji Petition," *Japanese Journal of Religious Studies*, 10(1): 6–38.
Mou, Bo (2003), "Editor's Introduction," in Bo Mou (ed.), *Comparative Approaches to Chinese Philosophy*, xv–xxii, New York: Routledge.
Mou, Bo (2010), "On Constructive-Engagement Strategy of Comparative Philosophy: A Journal Theme Introduction," *Comparative Philosophy*, 1(1): 1–32.
Muller, Charles (1995), "The Key Operative Concepts in Korean Buddhist Syncretic Philosophy: Interpenetration (通達) and Essence-Function (體用) in Wŏnhyo, Chinul and Kihwa." *Bulletin of Toyo Gakuen University*, 3: 33–48.
Muller, Charles (1999), "Essence-Function and Interpenetration: Early Chinese Origins and Manifestations," *Bulletin of Toyo Gakuen University*, 7: 93–106.
Muller, Charles (2016), "The Emergence of Essence-Function (ti-yong) 體用 Hermeneutics in the Sinification of Indic Buddhism: An Overview," *Critical Review of Buddhist Studies*, 19: 111–52.
Müller, Max ([1870]2002), "On False Analogies in Comparative Theology," in Jon Stone (ed.), *The Essential Max Müller: on Language, Mythology, and Religion*, 91–108, New York: Palgrave Macmillan.
Müller, Max (1872), *Lectures on the Science of Religion*, New York: Charles Scribner and Company.
Müller, Max ([1893]2002), "The Parliament of Religions in Chicago," in Jon Stone (ed.), *The Essential Max Müller: on Language, Mythology, and Religion*, 343–52, New York: Palgrave Macmillan.
Murti, Tirupattur Ramaseshayyer Venkatachala (1955), *The Central Philosophy of Buddhism: A Study of the Madhyamaka System*, London: George Allen and Unwin.
Nagao, Gadjin (1978), "What Remains in Śūnyatā," in Minoru Kiyota and Elvin Jones (eds), *Mahāyāna Buddhist Meditation: Theory and Practice*, 66–82, Honolulu: University Press of Hawaii.
Nagao, Gadjin (1991), *Madhyamaka and Yogācāra*, trans. Leslie Kawamura, Albany: State University of New York Press.
Narain, Harsh (1964), "Śūnyavāda: A Reinterpretation," *Philosophy East and West*, 13(4): 311–88.
Nelson, Eric and Yang, Liu (2016), "The Yijing, Gender, and the Ethics of Nature," in Ann Pang-White (ed.), *The Bloomsbury Research Handbook of Chinese Philosophy and Gender*, 267–89, London: Bloomsbury.
Ng, Yu-Kwan (1993), *T'ien-T'ai Buddhism and Early Mādhyamika*, Honolulu: University of Hawaii Press.
Ni, Liangkang (2010), "The Ultimate Consciousness and Ālaya-vijñāna: A Comparative Study on Deep-structure of Consciousness between Yogācāra Buddhism and Phenomenology," in Chung-Chi Yu (ed.), *Phenomenology 2010, Vol. 1: Selected Essays from Asia and Pacific: Phenomenology in Dialogue with East Asian Tradition*, 81–112, Bucharest: Zeta Books.
O'Connor, Timothy (2000), *Persons and Causes: The Metaphysics of Free Will*, Oxford: Oxford University Press.
Panaïoti, Antoine (2013), *Nietzsche and Buddhist Philosophy*, Cambridge: Cambridge University Press.
Paul, Diana (1981), "The Structure of Consciousness in Paramārtha's Purported Trilogy," *Philosophy East and West*, 31(3): 297–319.
Paul, Diana (1984), *Philosophy of Mind in Sixth-Century China: Paramārtha's Evolution of Consciousness*, Palo Alto: Stanford University Press.

Peacocke, Christopher (1983), *Sense and Content: Experience, Thought, and Their Relations*, Oxford: Oxford University Press.

Peattie, Mark (1984), "Japanese Attitude Towards Colonialism, 1895–1945," in Ramon Myers and Mark Peattie (eds), *The Japanese Colonial Empire, 1895–1945*, 80–127, Princeton: Princeton University.

Perrett, Roy (2017), "Buddhist Idealism and the Problem of Other Minds," *Asian Philosophy*, 27(1): 59–68.

Pittman, Don Alvin (2001), *Toward a Modern Chinese Buddhism: Taixu's Reforms*, Honolulu: University of Hawaii Press.

Pitts, Andrea (2020), "World-Travelling," in Gail Weiss, Ann Murphy, Gayle Salamon (eds), *50 Concepts for a Critical Phenomenology*, 343–50, Evanston: Northwestern University Press.

Prueitt, Catherine (2018), "Karmic Imprints, Exclusion, and the Creation of the Worlds of Conventional Experience in Dharmakīrti's Thought," *Sophia*, 57(2): 313–35.

Ratcliffe, Matthew; Ruddell, Mark; and Smith, Benedict (2014), "What is a Sense of Foreshortened Future? A Phenomenological Study of Trauma, Trust and Time," *Frontiers in Psychology*. 5: 1–11.

Reddy, Vasudevi (1996), "Omitting the Second Person in Social Understanding," *Behavioral and Brain Sciences*, 19(1): 140–1.

Rhodes, Robert (1994), "A Controversy over the Buddha-nature in T'ang China," *Ōtani Gakubō* 大谷学報, 73(4): 1–24.

Rickless, Samuel (2016), "Plato's *Parmenides*," in Edward Zalta (ed.), *The Stanford Encyclopedia of Philosophy*. https://plato.stanford.edu/archives/spr2016/entries/plato-parmenides (accessed 1 May 2021).

Ricoeur, Paul (1967), *Husserl: An Analysis of his Phenomenology*, trans. Edward Ballard and Lester Embree, Evanston: Northwestern University Press.

Ricoeur, Paul (2013), *Being, Essence, and Substance in Plato and Aristotle*, trans. David Pellauer and John Starkey. Cambridge: Polity.

Ritzinger, Justin (2017), *Anarchy in the Pure Land: Reinventing the Cult of Maitreya in Modern Chinese Buddhism*, Oxford: Oxford University Press.

Robertson, Teresa and Atkins, Philip (2016), "Essential vs. Accidental Properties," in Edward Zalta (ed.), *The Stanford Encyclopedia of Philosophy*. https://plato.stanford.edu/archives/sum2016/entries/essential-accidental (accessed 1 May 2021).

Robson, James (2010), "Among Mountains and Between Rivers: A Preliminary Appraisal of the Arrival, Spread, and Development of Daoism and Buddhism in the Central Hunan [Xiangzhong] Region," *Cahiers d'Extrême-Asia*, 19: 9–45.

Rockmore, Tom (2011), *Kant and Phenomenology*, Chicago: University of Chicago Press.

Rothberg, Donald (1990), "Contemporary Epistemology and the Study of Mysticism," in Robert Forman (ed.), *The Problem of Pure Consciousness: Mysticism and Philosophy*, 163–210, Oxford: Oxford University Press.

Ryle, Gilbert (1949), *The Concept of Mind*, London: Hutchinson's University Library.

Said, Edward (1978), *Orientalism*, New York: Pantheon Books.

Schlosser, Markus (2015), "Agency," in Edward Zalta (ed.), *The Stanford Encyclopedia of Philosophy*. https://plato.stanford.edu/archives/fall2015/entries/agency (accessed 1 May 2021).

Schmid, Hans Bernard and Schweikard, David (2013), "Collective Intentionality," in Edward Zalta (ed.), *The Stanford Encyclopedia of Philosophy*. https://plato.stanford.edu/archives/sum2013/entries/collective-intentionality (accessed 1 May 2021).

Schmid, Hans Bernard (2014), "Plural Self-Awareness," *Phenomenology and the Cognitive Sciences*, 13(1): 7–24.
Schmithausen, Lambert (1987), *Ālayavijñana: On the Origin and the Early Development of a Central Concept of Yogācāra Philosophy. Part 1: Text and Part2: Notes, Bibliography and Indices*, Tokyo: The International Institute for Buddhist Studies.
Schmithausen, Lambert (2005), *On the Problem of the External World in the Ch'eng Wei Shih Lun*, Tokyo: The International Institute for Buddhist Studies.
Searle, John (1982), "What is an Intentional State," in Hubert Dreyfus and Harrison Hall (eds), *Husserl Intentionality and Cognitive Science*, 259–76, Cambridge: The MIT Press.
Sellars, Wilfred (1956), *Empiricism and the Philosophy of Mind*, Cambridge: Harvard University Press.
Sellars, Wilfred (1968), *Science and Metaphysics: Variations on Kantian Themes*, New York: Routledge.
Sharf, Robert (1993), "The Zen of Japanese Nationalism," *History of Religions*, 33: 1–43.
Sharf, Robert (2002), *Coming to Terms with Chinese Buddhism: A Reading of the Treasure Store Treatise*, Honolulu: University of Hawai'i Press.
Sharf, Robert (2018), "Knowing Blue: Early Buddhist Accounts of Non-Conceptual Sense Perception," *Philosophy East and West*, 68(3): 826–70.
Shun, Kwong-loi (1997), *Mencius and Early Chinese Thought*, Stanford: Stanford University Press.
Siderits, Mark (1988), "Nāgārjuna as Anti-Realist," *Journal of Indian Philosophy*, 16(4): 311–325.
Siderits, Mark (2003), *Personal Identity and Buddhist philosophy: Empty Persons*, Burlington: Ashgate.
Siderits, Mark (2007), "Buddhist Reductionism and the Structure of Buddhist Ethics," in Purusottama Bilimoria, Joseph Prabhu, and Renuka Sharma (eds), *Indian Ethics: Classical Traditions and Contemporary Challenges*, 283–306, Burlington: Ashgate.
Siderits, Mark and Katsura, Shōryū, trans. (2013), *Nāgārjuna's Middle Way: Mūlamadhyamakakārikās*, Boston: Wisdom Publications.
Siderits, Mark (2014), "Comparison or Confluence in Philosophy?," in Jonardon Ganeri (ed.), *The Oxford Handbook of Indian Philosophy*, 76–86, Oxford: Oxford University Press.
Siderits, Mark (2016), "Response to Levine," *Confluence: Online Journal of World Philosophies*, 1(1): 128–30.
Silk, Jonathan (2002), "What, if anything, is Mahāyāna Buddhism?," *Numen*, 49(4): 355–405.
Silverman, Allan (2002), *The Dialectic of Essence*, Princeton: Princeton University Press.
Smith, Arthur David (2003), *Routledge Philosophy Guidebook to Husserl and the Cartesian Meditations*, New York: Routledge.
Smith, David Woodruff (1982), "Husserl on Demonstrative Reference and Perception," in Hubert Dreyfus and Harrison Hall (eds), *Husserl Intentionality and Cognitive Science*, 193–214, Cambridge: The MIT Press.
Smith, David Woodruff (2007), *Husserl*, New York: Routledge.
Sokolowski, Robert (2000), *Introduction to Phenomenology*, Cambridge: Cambridge University Press.
Spiegelberg, Herbert (1982), *The Phenomenological Movement: A Historical Introduction*, Dordrecht: Springer.
Sponberg, Alan (1979), "The Vijñaptimātratā Buddhism of the Chinese Monk K'uei-chi," Ph.D. Diss., University of British Columbia, Vancouver.

Steinbock, Anthony (1994), "The Project of Ethical Renewal and Critique: Edmund Husserl's Early Phenomenology of Culture," *Southern Journal of Philosophy*, 32(4): 449–64.
Steinbock, Anthony (1995), *Home and Beyond: Generative Phenomenology after Husserl*, Evanston: Northwestern University Press.
Suzuki, Daisetsu Teitaro (1927), *Essays in Zen Buddhism First Series*, London: Luzac Press.
Suzuki, Daisetsu Teitaro (1934), *Essays in Zen Buddhism Third Serie*s, London: Luzac Press.
Suzuki, Daisetsu Teitaro (1938), *Zen Buddhism and Its Influence on Japanese Culture*, Kyoto: Eastern Buddhist Society.
Suzuki, Daisetsu Teitaro (1970), *Shin Buddhism*, New York: Harper and Row Publisher.
Swanson, Paul (1989), *Foundations of T'ien-T'ai philosophy: The Flowering of the Two Truths Theory in Chinese Buddhism*, Berkeley: Asian Humanities Press.
Swanson, Paul (1990), "T'ien-t'ai Chih-I's Concept of Threefold Buddha Nature: A Synergy of Reality, Wisdom, and Practice," in Paul Griffiths and John Keenan (eds), *Buddha Nature: A Festschrift in Honor of Minoru Kiyota*, 171–80, Reno: Buddhist Books International.
Swanson, Paul (2018), *Clear Serenity, Quiet Insight: T'ien-t'ai Chih-I's Mo-ho Chih-kuan*, Honolulu: University of Hawaii Press.
Taylor, Charles (1989), *Sources of the Self*, Cambridge: Harvard University Press.
Taylor, Charles (1992), "The Politics of Recognition," in Amy Gutmann (ed.), *Multiculturalism: Examining the Politics of Recognition*, 23–75, Princeton: Princeton University Press.
Taylor, Charles (2007), *A Secular Age*, Cambridge: Harvard University Press.
Taylor, Charles (2012), "Interculturalism or Multiculturalism," *Philosophy and Social Criticism*, 38(4–5): 413–23.
Teng, Wei-Jen (2011), "Recontextualization, Exegesis, and Logic: Kuiji's (632–682) Methodological Restructuring of Chinese Buddhism," Ph.D. Diss., Harvard University, Cambridge.
Thompson, Evan (2014), *Waking, Dreaming, Being: New Light on the Self and Consciousness from Neuroscience, Meditation, and Philosophy*, New York: Columbia University Press.
Tye, Michael (2000), *Consciousness, Color, and Content*, Cambridge: MIT Press.
Tye, Michael (2005), "On the Nonconceptual Content of Experience," in Maria Reicher and Johann Marek (eds), *Experience and Analysis*, 221–39, Vienna: Öbv and hpt.
Tzohar, Roy (2017), "Imagine Being a Preta: Early Indian Yogācāra Approaches to Intersubjectivity," *Sophia*, 56(2): 337–54.
Uemura, Genki (2015), "Husserl's Conception of Cognition as an Action: An Inquiry into Its Prehistory," in Marta Ubiali and Maren Wehrle (eds), *Feeling and Value, Willing and Action. Essays in the Context of a Phenomenological Psychology*, 119–37, Dordrecht: Springer.
Van Norden, Bryan (2017), *Taking Back Philosophy: A Multicultural Manifesto*, New York: Columbia University Press.
Victoria, Brian (1997), *Zen at War*, New York: Weatherhill.
Wagner, Rudolf (2000), *The Craft of a Chinese Commentator: Wang Bi on the Laozi*, Albany: State University of New York Press.
Wagner, Rudolf (2003), *A Chinese Reading of the Daodejing: Wang Bi's Commentary on the Laozi with Critical Text and Translation*, Albany: State University of New York Press.
Waldron, William (2003), *The Buddhist Unconscious*, New York: Routledge.
Wang, Robin (2012), *Yinyang: The Way of Heaven and Earth in Chinese Thought and Culture*, Cambridge: Cambridge University Press.

Wang, Robin (2016), "Yinyang Gender Dynamics: Lived Bodies, Rhythmical Changes, and Cultural Performances," in Ann Pang-White (ed.), *The Bloomsbury Research Handbook of Chinese Philosophy and Gender*, 205–28, London: Bloomsbury.

Wang, Robin (2017), "Dao becomes Female: The Gendered Reality, Knowledge, and Strategy for Living," in Ann Garry, Serene Khader, and Alison Stone (eds), *The Routledge Companion to Feminist Philosophy*, 35–48, New York: Routledge.

Wang, Youxuan (2001), *Buddhism and Deconstruction: Towards a Comparative Semiotics*, New York: Routledge.

Wei, Tat, trans. (1973), *Ch'eng Wei-Shih Lun: Doctrine of Mere-Consciousness by Tripitaka-Master Hsüan Tsang*. Hong Kong: The Ch'eng Wei-Shih Lun Publication Committee.

Weiss, Gail, Murphy, Ann, and Salamon, Gayle, ed. (2020), *50 Concepts for a Critical Phenomenology*, Evanston: Northwestern University Press.

Welch, Holmes (1968), *The Buddhist Revival in China*, Cambridge: Harvard University Press.

Welton, Donn (1991), "Husserl and the Japanese," *The Review of Metaphysics*, 44(3): 575–606.

Welton, Donn, ed. (2003), *The New Husserl*, Bloomington: Indiana University Press.

Wildman, Nathan (2013), "Modality, Sparsity, and Essence," *Philosophical Quarterly*, 63(253): 760–82.

Williams, Paul (2009), *Mahāyāna Buddhism: The Doctrinal Foundations*, 2nd ed., New York: Routledge.

Willis, Janice (1979), *On Knowing Reality: The Tattvārtha Chapter of Asaṅga's Bodhisattvabhūmi*, New York: Columbia University Press.

Wippel, John (1995), *Metaphysical Themes in Thomas Aquinas*, Washington: Catholic University of America Press.

Wippel, John (2000), *Metaphysical Thought of Thomas Aquinas*, Washington: Catholic University of America Press.

Witt, Charlotte (1989), *Substance and Essence in Aristotle: An Interpretation of Metaphysics VII-IX*, Ithaca: Cornell University Press.

Wittenborn, Allen (1991), *Further Reflections on Things at Hand: A Reader*, Lanham: University Press of America.

Wong, David (2004), "Relational and Autonomous Selves," *Journal of Chinese Philosophy*. 31(4): 419–32.

Wong, David (2015), "Early Confucian Philosophy and the Development of Compassion," *Dao: A Journal of Comparative Philosophy*, 14(2): 157–94.

Yao, Zhihua (2005), *The Buddhist Theory of Self-cognition*, New York: Routledge.

Yao, Zhihua (2010), "Typology of Nothing: Heidegger, Daoism, and Buddhism," *Comparative Philosophy*, 1(1): 78–89.

Yao, Zhihua (2014), "Yogācāra Critiques of the Two Truths," in Chen-Kuo Lin and Michael Radich (eds), *A Distant Mirror: Articulating Indic Ideas in Sixth and Seventh Century Chinese Buddhism*, 313–34, Hamburg: Hamburg University Press.

Yeh, Ah-Yueh (1979), "The Characteristics of 'Vijñāna' and 'Vijñapti' on the Basis of Vasubandhu's Pañcaskanda-Prakaraṇa," *Annals of the Bhandarkar Oriental Research Institute*, 60(4): 175–98.

Young, Iris (1988), "Five Faces of Oppression," *The Philosophical Forum*, 19(4): 270–90.

Young, Louise (1998), *Japan's Total Empire: Manchuria and the Culture of Wartime Imperialism*, Berkeley: University of California Press.

Yu, Chung-Chi (2012), "Husserl on Ethical Renewal and Philosophical Rationality," *Investigaciones Fenomenológicas*, 9: 145–56.

Zahavi, Dan (2003), *Husserl's Phenomenology*, Stanford: Stanford University Press.

Zahavi, Dan (2005), *Subjectivity and Selfhood: Investigating the First-Person Perspective*, Cambridge: MIT Press.
Zahavi, Dan (2010a), "Empathy, Embodiment and Interpersonal Understanding: From Lipps to Schutz," *Inquiry*, 53(3): 285–306.
Zahavi, Dan (2010b), "Husserl and the Absolute," in Carlo Ierna, Hanne Jacobs and Filip Mattens (eds), *Philosophy, Phenomenology, Sciences*, 71–92, Dordrecht: Springer.
Zahavi, Dan (2017), *Husserl's Legacy: Phenomenology, Metaphysics, and Transcendental Philosophy*, Oxford: Oxford University Press.
Zahavi, Dan (2021), "From the Ego to Pure Ego to Personal Ego," in Hanne Jacobs (ed.), *The Husserlian Mind*, 269–280, New York: Routledge.
Zalta, Edward (2006), "Essence and Modality," *Mind*, 115(459): 659–93.
Ziporyn, Brook (2003), *The Penumbra Unbound: The Neo-Taoist Philosophy of Guo Xiang*, Albany: State University of New York Press.
Zhao, Fei (2016), "A Study of the Usages and Meanings of Ākāra in Abhidharma," M.A. Diss., University of Washington, Washington.
Zu, Jessica (2020), "Theorizing Social Consciousness: Lü Cheng (1896–1989) and the Rise of A New Buddhist Idealism in Modern China," Ph.D. Diss., Princeton University, Princeton.
Zürcher, Erik (2007), *The Buddhist Conquest of China*, Leiden: Brill.

Index

Notes are given as [page number] n.

Abhidharma clerics 24, 119, 131
absolute nature
    of consciousness 127
    of essence 4
abstract thought 53–4, 85, 88, 90–1, 110
accidents 137–8, 140, 215n
accumulation 179
actions 159–60, 162, 172
active genesis 40, 60, 73, 92, 114
activity 60–1, 63, 73
agency
    awakening 153, 183
    causality and 155–6, 161
    good–evil 161–4
    nirvāṇa 161, 169
    possibility of 8, 153, 155
    sentient beings 164, 172
agent-oriented causality 159–60
akāra 203n
Al-Saji, Alia 44
alaiyeshi 72
ālambana 78–9, 211n
ālambanapratyaya 130
alterity 65
altruism 164, 187
Ames, Roger 135
Anscombe, Elizabeth 51
anticipation 59, 61
apperception 61–4, 74–5, 94, 208n
applied ethics 223n
appresentation 64
Aquinas, Thomas 136, 137–8, 140
Arendt, Hannah 65, 149
arhatship 120
Aristotle 36, 136–7, 139
Asaṅga 24
assimilation 16
attachments 165
    see also dharma-attachments;
        self-attachments

attending 162
attitudes 55, 152
authentic thought 106–8
awakening 8, 33, 43–4, 80, 169–81, 183–93
    agency and 153, 183
    dependent arising 158, 159
    emptiness and 124
    levels of 152, 165–6, 179, 192, 196
    in phenomenology 196
    prescriptive level 152, 179, 192, 196
    saṃsāra/nirvāṇa 164–7

Berger, Douglas 171
beschreibende 42
Binder, Thomas 36
Bloom, Irene 135
bodhi 166–7
Bodhisattvas 8, 77, 126
    awakening 159, 175, 177, 180
    compassion 176, 178, 191
    perfect actions 187–8
    refinement 188–9
Bodhisattva's path 6, 32, 44, 83, 119, 133, 149, 196
body–function binary *see ti–yong* binary
"both-and" approach 6, 9–11, 19–21, 44, 83, 101, 196–7
Brentano, Franz 2, 35–7, 39, 54, 56, 62–3, 87, 105
    Psychology from an Empirical Standpoint 36
Buddha nature 169–74, 175, 177–9, 220n, 222n
Buddhism 119, 141, 206n, 217n, 224n
    causality 155, 157
    compassion 77
    consciousness, structure of 72
    contemplation 151–2, 183
    dependent arising 156
    direct perception 94

epistemology 212n
epoché 183
essentialism fusion 2
ethics 223n
karmic causality 155
non-rationality 13–14, 15
perfect actions 187–8
phenomenology and 1, 8, 20, 43
philosophical binaries 144–5
philosophies of religion 12–13
Pure Lands 191
sentient beings 6
svabhāva concept 119–20, 123–4, 131, 133
as transcendental 44
transmission of 143
Xuanzang's role 23, 28
see also Chinese Buddhism; Japanese Buddhism
Buddhist phenomenology 2

caittas 161, 163
calming 184–5, 222n
Carr, David 42
Carson, Cathryn 40
Cartesian dualism 115–16, 138, 140, 190
Cartesian method of doubt 38
categorial forming 107
categorial intuition 53, 60–1, 94, 107–8
see also perception
causality 155–7, 158, 159–60, 161
Chen, Kenneth 119, 170
Chinese Buddhism
  definition 203n
  development of 217n
  ethics 224n
  philosophies of religion 12–13
  Xuanzang 23
Chinese-Sanskrit language differences 69, 202n
Chinese Yogācāra
  awakening meaning 159, 183
  "both-and" approach 20
  contextualizing 10, 23–33
  descriptive investigations 48, 186–7
  essence in 119–33, 135–6, 141–6, 148
  gotra system 169
  intentionality in 49, 67–83, 99
  non-conceptualism 93–8

paradigm for 6
prescriptive level 151
two-level reading 43
use of term 1
Christianity 12–15
collective consciousness 64, 186–7, 189, 208n
colonialism 14, 19
communal life 64
communal renewal 189–93
community building 141
comparative philosophy 196–7
  Buddhism/essentialism 2
  contextualization 17–18
  correlative non-dualism 5
  cultural exchange 18
  essence in 135–49
  juxtapositional approach 11–16, 19–20
  methodology 9
  non-conceptualism 86
  Orientalism 6, 8
  synthetic approach 11–16, 19–20
comparativism, use of term 17
compassion 77, 166, 176, 178, 191
concentration 185
concepts
  definition 86–8, 90
  as mental representations 88–9
conceptual content 90
conceptualism 39, 49, 53, 86
confluence philosophy 17
Confucianism 30–1, 153
consciousness
  absolute nature of 127
  constituents of 71
  definition 7
  dependent arising theory 159
  description of 97
  dualism and 25–6
  eight-types system 24–5, 32–3, 72, 74–6, 79, 81–2, 96, 124, 126, 158, 163–4, 180, 190, 209n
  emptiness and 123–4, 130, 145
  essence and 20, 21, 43, 138
  experience association 138
  fourfold structure 71, 90, 93–5, 195
  functionality of 47–8, 72, 74, 76, 82, 158, 160–2, 197
  as intentionality 1–3, 5–6, 55, 67–83, 85, 209n

mental factors relationship 185–6
psychological approach 37
purification of 133, 138
seeds concept 172
temporality 59–60
threefold structure 72
transformation of 75, 124–7, 131–2, 214n
translation of term 70–1
consciousness-only doctrine 1–2, 6, 20, 25–8, 67, 120–1, 159
   as epistemic inquiry 31–2
   five stages of realization 179–81, 191–2
   mental factors 184
   other minds 77
   sentient beings 185–6
   see also weishi
contacting 161–2
contemplation 151–2, 183–6, 222n
content
   definition 88
   non-conceptual 86–7, 90, 97
contextuality 10, 17–18, 195
conventional–ultimate binary 170, 173–4
corporeal body 75–6
correlation concept 57, 207n
correlative non-dualism 5, 8, 104, 113, 117, 132, 148, 151, 174, 197, 213n
Crane, Tim 36
craving 158, 160
crisis of meaning 39–41, 189
critical phenomenology 41, 44
Crowell, Steven 65
cultural imperialism 9, 11, 14–15, 16
cultures, equal value of 18
CWSL *see The Treatise on the Perfection of Consciousness-only*

Dao concept 141–2, 216n
Daoist philosophy 70, 217n
Daosheng 144
Dark Learning doctrine 141, 142–3
defilements 163, 165
dependent arising 156, 157–61, 219n
dependent-evolution 166, 166, 174, 180, 190
Descartes, René 80, 82, 138, 141
   Cartesian Meditations 140
   Discourse on the Method 138

descriptive, use of term 97
descriptive ethics 223n
descriptive–explicative–prescriptive framework 6–7, 10, 32–3
descriptive level
   consciousness 160
   empathy at 186–7
   intentionality 195
descriptive phenomenology 37, 42, 43, 47–8
desire-maintainers 175
dharma-attachments 76–80, 126, 165
dharma body 190–2
Dharma-Image School of Consciousness-only 28
Dharmapāla 26, 71
dharmas
   consciousness as 145
   image–nature binary 144
   mind-independent existence 24
   reality and 130–1
   svabhāva and 121–2
dialectical logic 70
differentiation 94
Dignāga 26, 27, 71
Dilun group 25–8
direct perception 93–6, 213n
directedness 52–5
discriminative self-attachments 76, 165
dualism 13, 25–6, 77, 115, 124–5
   see also Cartesian dualism; correlative non-dualism

East–West dichotomy 4, 13
   Orientalism 5, 7, 14, 16, 44–5, 86, 148, 195–7
ego, elevation of 40, 61, 75
egoistic actions 164
ego–cogito–cogitatum 58–62, 64, 114
eidetic, use of term 110
eidetic essence 110–11, 147
eidetic intuition 109
eidos 38, 104
   definition 109
   essence and 116–17, 140, 147
   mutual constitution 147
   noesis–noema 110–11
   Plato's account of 136–7, 139
elitism 189, 193

emanation body 190–1
empathy 64, 65, 186–9
empirical approach 37, 115
empirical existence 112
emptiness 3–4, 21, 25–6, 130–3, 180
   consciousness differentiation 145
   conventional–ultimate binary 170
   dharma body 191
   essence connection 119–20, 121–8, 143–5
   non-existence and 217n
   saṃsāra and 157
   three natures theory 173–4
empty/emptiness distinction 127–8, 133
enjoyment body 190–2
enlightenment *see bodhi*
epistemic essence 104, 106
epistemic inquiry 31–2
epistemology 48, 212n
epoché 38, 54, 56–7, 148–9
   contemplation 183–6
   eidetic essence 110–11, 147
   naturalistic essence 139
   phenomenological renewal 152
   two-step process 183
equality, wisdom of 180–1, 190–1
erklärende 42
erroneous knowledge 94
essence 130–3
   in Chinese Yogācāra 119–33, 135–6, 141–6, 148
   in comparative philosophy 135–49
   consciousness and 20, 21, 43
   definition 135–6, 215n
   in Husserl's phenomenology 103–17, 135–6, 146, 148, 213n
   naturalism 40–1, 103, 108–9, 114–16, 139, 141, 147–8, 196
   phenomenology link 2, 7
   "problem of" 4, 146–9, 196, 197, 200n, 213n
   quality/matter union 2–3
   refutation of 119, 121–3, 195
   transcendental idealism 5
   translation of term 100–1
   Yogācāra objections to 123–30
   see also svabhāva
essence–function *see ti-yong* binary
essentialism–Buddhism fusion 2

ethics 5–6, 65, 83, 189–90, 223n
Euro-American culture 14–15, 19
European culture, renewal of 8
European philosophy
   rationality 13–14
   translations 21
European science, crisis of 39–41
Evans, Gareth 88–9
event-oriented causality 159–60
evil–good, agency between 161–4
existence 110–13, 125–6, 130–3, 137–8, 216n
existential crisis 13, 202n
experience 85–6, 138
"explicative" concept 99–100
explicative level
   consciousness 32, 43
   intentionality 196
explicative phenomenology 38, 42
expressive acts 105–6
exteriority 44, 149
eye-consciousness 211n

factual existence 56, 100, 110
faith 164
fallacy 92, 96
false imaginations 126–8, 132–3
Fanon, Frantz 65, 149
faxiang 204n
feelings 81, 162
fictitious existence 126
Fink, Eugen 151
first-person standpoint 65, 78
form–matter dependence 139
form–particulars distinction 216n
forming 107
founding 52–4, 57, 61, 90–2, 161
friendship 65
fulfillment 53–4, 91–2, 106–7

Gadamer, Hans-Georg 10, 19
Galileo Galilei 115
Gaozong, Emperor 29, 174
Garfield, Jay 11
genesis 40, 60–1, 73, 92, 114
genetic phenomenology 104, 115, 116, 140
German culture 39–40
good–evil, agency between 161–4
Gordon, Peter 41

gotra system 153, 167, 169–75, 176–9, 221n
Graham, Angus Charles 135, 145–6
grasping 128, 158, 160
Greek philosophy 21, 35–6, 38
Guenther, Lisa 44, 187
Guo Xiang 143

hanchuan weishi 1, 23
Heian Japan 30
historical contextuality 18
homogenous culture 18
Hori, Victor 13, 15, 89, 165
Hossō school 29–30
Huizhao 94, 173, 176, 213n
Husserl, Edmund
　Buddhist encounters 1
　Cartesian Meditations 187
　Crisis 82, 114, 139, 147
　Greek philosophy 21
　Ideas 37–9, 108, 110, 114
　Kaizo articles 64, 65
　Logical Investigations 37, 55, 105, 107, 109, 207n
　Meditations 61, 82, 114
　non-conceptualism 90–3
　Philosophy of Arithmetic 37
　transcendental turn 6–7, 37–9, 42, 108–13
Husserl's phenomenology
　awakening 181, 183
　"both-and" approach 20, 83
　consciousness, constituents of 71
　contextualizing 10, 35–49
　epoché 184–6
　essence in 103–17, 135–6, 146, 148, 213n
　intentionality in 48–9, 51–65, 70, 87, 99, 212n, 218n
　paradigm for 6
　prescriptive level 149
　self-awareness 81
　two levels in 41–5

I-You relationships 65, 78
icchantikas 172–3, 174–6, 178
idealism *see* speculative idealism; transcendental idealism
identification concept 54, 92
ignorance
　awakening from 132–3, 144, 149, 153
　Buddha nature in 124, 173
　as moral quality 82
　negation of 220n
　self-attachment 73, 79, 163
　subjectivity 132–3
illusions 26, 72, 122–5, 127–8, 130
image concept 71–3, 78, 93–4, 97, 125–6, 128, 158, 209n, 214n
image–nature binary 143–5
immaterial forms 137–8
impression 59
inauthentic thought 107, 115
inference 94–6
innate attachments 76, 79, 163, 165
inner perception 36
intentional essence 80–3, 104–9
intentionality 48, 68–74, 206n
　in Chinese Yogācāra 49, 67–83, 99
　consciousness as 1–3, 5–6, 55, 67–83, 85, 209n
　definition 2, 6, 38
　descriptive level 195
　as directedness 52–5
　ego elevation 40
　explicative level 196
　in Husserl's phenomenology 48–9, 51–65, 70, 87, 99, 212n, 218n
　of mental factors 80–3
　as mutual constitution 89–90
　as *noesis–noema* 3, 38, 51, 104, 109–10
　non-conceptualism and 85–101
　phenomenology and 42
　psychology and 37
　twofoldness of 36
　of the *we* 62–5
intuition 38–9, 53–4, 90–1
　ego-cogito-cogitatum 60–1
　essence 105–9
　founding 53
　fulfillment 54
　non-conceptual 85, 89
　reason in 41

Japanese Buddhism 15, 176
Japanese imperialism 202n
Japanese *weishi* 29–30
Jiang, Tao 17, 18–19

Jōkei 30
"journey–road–track–destination" analogy 5–7
judgment 57
justification 92, 93, 96
juxtaposition 11–16, 19–20, 148

Kant, Immanuel 38–9
  Critique of Pure Reason 38, 86–7
karmic causality 121, 155–6
Kern, Iso 20, 38
Kitayama Junyu 199n
knowledge
  direct perception 95
  measuring production of 93–4
  non-conceptualism 85–6, 90
  objects as cause of 72
  possibility of 54
  principles of 52
  as source of justification 93
Kuiji
  calming/contemplation 184
  causality 157
  compassion 176
  consciousness 28, 96, 127, 145, 186, 214n
  contribution of 222n
  desire-maintainers 175
  empty/emptiness distinction 127–8, 133
  essence 119, 120, 122–3
  inference 95
  mental factors 80
  other minds 77–8, 177
  Pure Land concept 191–2
  translations 69–70
  weishi 31

la Valleé Poussin, Louis de 78
Lai Shen-Chon 31
laiye 74–6, 79, 83, 94–5
Laozi 141–2
Lau, Lawrence Y.K. 31
Levine, Michael 17
Liang Shuming 153
liberation *see nirvāṇa*
lifeworld concept 64, 92, 116, 187
"lifting-out" method 17
lived realities
  plurality of 5, 10, 16–18, 19
  traveling 20
Lü Cheng 94, 95, 178
Lugones, María 19
Lusthaus, Dan 31

McCormick, John 41
Madhyamaka school 119–20, 122–3, 157, 173–4
Mahāyāna schools 1–3, 24, 119, 121–3, 170
Maitreya's Pure Land 192, 224n
material essence 109
matter
  definition 54
  as essence 137
  form dependence 139
  quality/matter union 2–3, 52, 105
Mayer, Alexander 31
meaning-intention *see* abstract thought
meanings, non-conceptualism 91–2
measuring doctrine 93–4
meditative practice *see* calming; contemplation
Mei Guangxi 125
melody 58–60
Mengzi 143
mental acts
  characterization of 37
  constituents of 51
  content/concepts 86–7, 89
  descriptive phenomenology 47–8
  intentionality 105
  perception 36
  phenomenology 41, 43
  quality/matter 52, 105
mental factors 72, 219n
  consciousness and 93–5, 158, 161–4, 185–6
  contemplation 184–5
  intentionality of 80–3
mental representations 88–9
meta-ethics 223n
metaphysical realism 122, 132
metaphysics 99–100, 103, 206n, 213n
methodology metaphors 9
mind–body dualism 138, 190
mind-independent existence 24, 77
mind-only doctrine 1, 67

misperception
  attachments and 79–80, 165
  awakening from 96
  Bodhisattvas 159
  consciousness 25, 75–6
  egoistic actions 164
  false imagination 128
  fictitious names 126
modernity 14
mona 72–3, 75, 79, 83, 95, 163
moral actions 186–9, 223n
moral qualities 82–3, 163
morality, types of 162–3
Moran, Dermot 41, 42, 116
motherliness analogy 142–3, 217n
Mou, Bo 19
Müller, Max 12–16
multiculturalism
  comparative philosophy 9
  essence problem 4
  Orientalism and 11–22
mutual constitution 89–90, 147
mysticism 89

Nagao Gadjin 130
Nāgārjuna 9, 121–2, 155
Nanda 26
"natural", concept of 111
natural existence 112–13
naturalism 39, 41, 55–6
  crisis of meaning 189
  essence and 40–1, 103, 108–9, 114–16, 139, 141, 147–8, 196
  phenomenology differences 42, 152
naturalistic essence 110, 139–40, 146–7, 148
"naturalistic", use of term 110–11
nature–image binary 143–5
natures, three accounts of 25, 101, 124, 127, 145, 173–4, 222n
Neumann, Karl Eugen 2
  The Sayings of Gautama Buddha 1
Ni, Liangkang 20
nihilism 223n
nirvāṇa 155, 157–8, 160–1, 164–7, 169
no-self 74–6, 121
noble truths depictions 120
noesis–noema 55–8, 60
  fallacy 92

intentionality as 3, 38, 51, 104, 109–10
  recollection 91
non-cognitivism 223n
non-conceptualism 85–101
non-dual wisdom 97–8
non-duality 148, 149
non-existence 217n
non-natures 222n
non-rationality 13–15, 45, 49, 97–8
non-self-sufficient essence 109
normative ethics 223n
nothingness 142–4, 216n

objectivity 57–8, 108, 111, 115–16, 223n
one-place knowing *see vijñāna*
ontology 5, 6, 206n
Orientalism
  comparative philosophy 6, 8, 9
  East–West dichotomy 5, 7, 14, 16, 44–5, 86, 148, 195–7
  multiculturalism and 11–22
  rationality/non-rationality 49, 97–8
  "reflecting" discourse 15
other-enjoyment body 191
other minds 62–3, 76–80, 176–7, 180–1, 186, 210n
other-power 174–9, 191, 221n
ousia concept 136–7

Paramārtha 123–5, 127, 203n
particulars–form distinction 216n
passive genesis 40, 61, 73, 92, 114
passivity 61, 63, 73–5, 207n
Peacocke, Christopher 87
perception
  actions and 162
  consciousness structure 95–6
  intuition and 91
  measuring knowledge 93–4
  psychological approach 36–7
  see also categorial intuition
perfect actions 187–8
perfuming 133, 172
phenomenological essence 140, 146, 213n
phenomenological existence 112–13, 139
phenomenological reduction 184
phenomenological renewal 152, 189–93
phenomenology

Buddhism and 1, 8, 20, 43
  contextualizing 10, 195
  definitions 47, 100
  epoché 185
  essence link 2, 7, 103, 114, 139, 196
  mental acts 41
  natural science contrast 42
  prescriptive level 7–8, 149, 151–2
  purity 54
  transcendental idealism separation 212n
  as transcendental philosophy 37–9, 55
  see also Husserl's phenomenology
philosophical binaries, Buddhism 144–5
physicalism 147
Plato 80, 136–7, 139, 141
plurality, lived realities 5, 10, 16–18, 19
politics of recognition 15–18
prescriptive level
  awakening 179, 192, 196
  consciousness 32–3, 160
  phenomenology 7–8, 149, 151–2
"problem of essence" 4, 146–9, 196, 197, 200n, 213n
problems in philosophy 2
protention 58–9
psychologism 39, 42, 54, 56, 105, 108, 115, 147
psychology
  intentionality and 37, 62–3
  as science 36
pure consciousness 42, 56–7, 110–12, 133, 138
pure essence *see eidos*
Pure Land concept 189, 191, 192, 224n
purposing 162, 218n

qin suoyuanyuan 211n
quality 2–3, 52, 82, 105

rationality
  cultural imperialism 15
  European philosophy 13–14
  limits of 13
  non-conceptualism and 97–8
  Orientalism 45, 49
real existence 126
realism, direct/indirect contrast 24
reality and existence 130–1

reason
  inference 95
  in intuition 41
reasoning as mental factor 185
recognition 11, 15–18, 201n
recollection 61, 91, 96
recollection–perception–anticipation 59–60
redistribution 201n
refinement 188–9
"reflecting" discourse 15
reflexive awareness 71, 81, 90, 93–4
regret 80–1
rehabiltualization 165, 187–8
religion, philosophies of 12–15
renewal 152, 184, 189–93
retention 58–9, 61
retention–impression–protention 59–60
reverse Orientalism 15
Ricoeur, Paul 41–2, 60
rope–snake analogy 96–7

Śīlabhadra 27, 171, 175
śūnyatā 121
Said, Edward 14
saṃsāra 155–8, 159–61, 164–7, 169
Sanskrit concepts/terms, translation 21, 67–8
Sanskrit–Chinese language differences 69, 202n
Sanskrit texts, translation 23, 24
Sanskrit *vijñaptimātra* 27–9
Sarvāstivādas 24
Sautrāntikas 24
science
  Brentano's turn to 36
  crisis of 39–41
scientific rationalism 40
scientific reductionism 115
second-person perspective 65, 78–9, 176–7, 186–7
secretiveness 173–4
seeds concept 74–5, 158–9, 164, 172–4, 176–7, 188, 210n
seeing concept 71–2, 79, 90, 93–5, 125–6, 158, 214n
seemingly real existence 125, 126, 132, 214n
self-attachments 74–6, 79, 126, 163, 165

self-awareness 71, 72, 81, 90, 93–5
self-enjoyment body 190–2
self-evidence 207n
self-power 174–9, 191–2, 221n
self-sufficient essence 109, 140, 147
selfhood 210n, 211n
semantic essence 104–6, 107, 108–9
Sengzhao 143–5
sensation 207n
senses 87–8, 94
sensory intuition 108
sentient beings
    agency 164, 172
    becoming 6
    consciousness-only doctrine 25, 179, 185–6, 191–2
    as devotees 164
    dharmas and 24
    five families of 169, 171–2
    gotra system 167
    svabhāva 3
Sharf, Robert 15
Shelun group 25–8
Shun, Kwong-loi 135
Siderits, Mark 17, 19
social construction 189–93
solipsism 21, 40, 60, 62, 211n
solitary confinement 187
speculative idealism 113
Sponberg, Alan 69
static phenomenology 104
Stein, Edith 44, 65, 149
Sthiramati 26
subconsciousness 89
subject–object duality 25–6, 124
subjectivism 54, 223n
subjectivity 113, 115, 116, 132–3
subliminal consciousness 74
substance as essence 137–8
suchness 127, 186
suffering 81–2, 120, 162
sui generis 75–6, 79, 83, 121, 138
śūnyatā 121, 127
    see also emptiness
sūtra classification system 119–20
Suzuki, D.T. 13–16, 86
svabhāva 3–4, 7, 76–7
    classification system 120
    critique of 20, 214n

    defining features of 119
    dharma body 192
    existence and 131–3
    natures 25
    refutation of 119, 121–3, 147
    rejection of 80, 195
    self-attachments 75
    see also essence
symbolic thinking 107–8
synthetic approach 146
synthetization 11–16

Taixu 205n, 224n
Taizong, Emperor 27–9, 174
Takasaki Jikidō 124
tathāgatagarbha 124, 170–1, 204n, 220n
Taylor, Charles 11, 16, 18, 44, 138
temporality 58–60, 219n
that-clause 87
thinking as mental factor 162
third-person standpoint 65, 78–9
three bodies theory 190, 224n
three vehicles 220n
ti concept 143, 145, 209n
ti-yong binary 69–71, 131–2, 141–5, 209n
Tiantai contemplative practice 170
transcendental *I* 63, 64, 147
transcendental idealism 5, 7, 38, 41, 43, 101, 104
    as correlative non-dualism 117, 148, 174, 213n
    phenomenology separation 212n
    subjectivity 113, 132
transcendental phenomenology 42, 51, 55, 108–13
transcendental philosophy 1, 2–3, 6–7, 37–9, 44, 55
transcendental reduction 184
transcendental *we* 63
transformation concept 73–5, 96–7
transformation of consciousness 75, 124–7, 131–2, 214n
translation
    by Kuiji 69–70
    consciousness term 70–1
    essence term 100–1
    Sanskrit concepts/terms/texts 21, 23–4, 67–8
    in Yogācāra 20, 67

traveling 20, 153
The Treatise on the Perfection of Consciousness-only (*CWSL*) 23, 31–2, 71–2, 77, 79–80, 82, 126, 130, 132, 158, 161, 166, 172, 178, 214n
Trendelenburg, Friedrich 36
twelve links doctrine 156–9, 156, 158
two-place knowing *see vijñapti*
Tye, Michael 88

unconsciousness *see* subliminal consciousness
universal intuition 53, 60–1
universal religion project 12–15
universals 211n

van Norden, Bryan, *Taking Back Philosophy* 11
Vasubandhu 24–6
Victoria, Brian 15
vijñāna 67–72, 208n
vijñapti 67–72, 208n
vijñaptimātra 27–9
virtue ethics 223n

Wang Bi 141–3
we
    intentionality of 62–5
    as plurality of I-subjects 187
Weierstrass, Karl 35
Weimar Germany 40–1
weishi 27–33
    see also consciousness-only doctrine
Welton, Don 42
Wen, Emperor 23–4, 26
Westernization 14–15
wisdom
    of equality 180–1, 190–1
    four kinds of 180–1
    ignorance interplay 133
    mirroring 190–1
    realizing 179, 188
Woncheuk 174
Woodruff, David 42
Wu Zetian, Empress 174

xiang 209n
xianguan 186

xing–xiang binary 144–5
Xiong Shili 153
Xuanzang
    agency 153, 169
    awakening 152, 179, 181
    Buddha nature 171, 174, 175, 177–8
    Buddhist doctrine 144
    consciousness 1–2, 6–7, 20, 67–8, 70–4, 83, 159, 195, 214n
    contemplation 184, 186, 223n
    dependent arising 158, 160
    emptiness concept 3–4, 125, 127, 128, 191
    essence concept 2, 5, 7, 101, 121, 123, 146, 148, 196
    existence 126, 130–1
    gotra system 172
    mental factors 80, 82, 162, 164
    misperception 96
    nirvāṇa 166
    non-conceptualism 85
    non-dual wisdom 97
    other minds 77–9
    phenomenology 7–8, 44
    prescriptive approach 149
    Pure Land concept 192
    renewal concept 190
    subjectivity 132
    Yogācāra before 23–7
xushi 214n

Yogācāra
    boundaries of 23
    consciousness, structure of 71–2
    consciousness-only, realizing 179
    contemplation 183–6
    contextualizing 10
    development of 119–21, 123
    early/later distinction 120, 129, 131–2, 144, 204n
    essence, objections to 123–30
    gotra system 169
    intentionality 1–2
    other minds 77
    prescriptive level 196
    translations 20, 67
    two-level reading 43
    before Xuanzang 23–7
    see also Chinese Yogācāra

yong concept 143, 209n
   see also *ti–yong* binary
Young, Iris 14

Zahavi, Dan 65, 99–100, 103
Zen Buddhism 13–15

zhiguan 184, 186, 222n
Zhiyi 170, 174
Zhizhou 176
Zhou Guihua 69
zizheng 209n

www.ingramcontent.com/pod-product-compliance
Lightning Source LLC
Chambersburg PA
CBHW062126300426
44115CB00012BA/1827